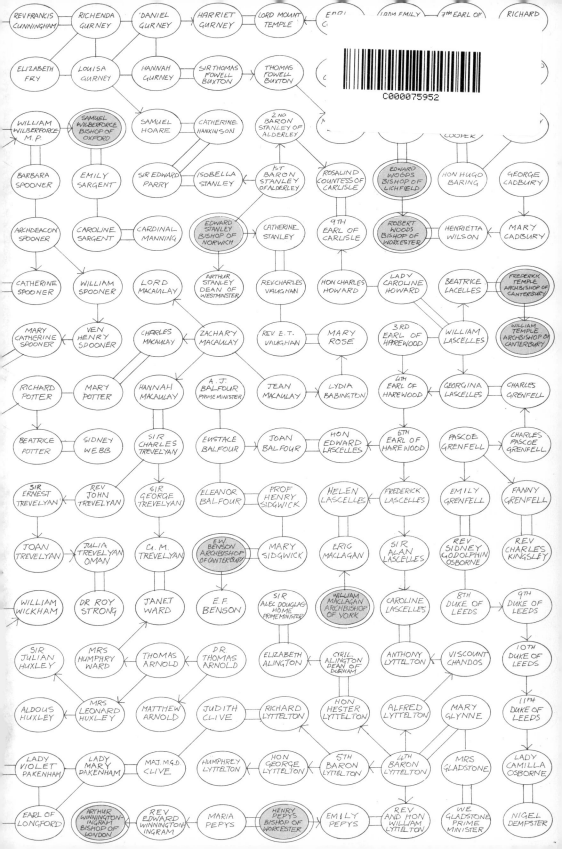

C000075952

The Flesh is Weak

By the same author

Gossip: A History of High Society
from 1920 to 1970

The Flesh is Weak

An Intimate History of
The Church of England

by

Andrew Barrow

HAMISH HAMILTON
LONDON

First published in Great Britain 1980
by Hamish Hamilton Ltd
Garden House, 57–59 Long Acre, London WC2E 9JZ
Copyright © 1980 by Andrew Barrow

British Library Cataloguing in Publication Data
Barrow, Andrew
    The flesh is weak.
    1.   Church of England – History
    I.   Title
    283'.42   BX5055.2

    ISBN 0-241-10234-0

Printed and bound in Great Britain at
The Camelot Press Ltd, Southampton

CONTENTS

Introduction	vii
The Reformation 1533–1553	1
The Marian Reaction 1553–1558	14
The Elizabethan Age 1558–1603	20
The Early Stuarts 1603–1642	33
The Civil War 1642–1649	51
The Commonwealth 1649–1660	59
The Restoration 1660–1688	64
The Revolution Settlement 1688–1714	77
The Eighteenth Century 1714–1793	87
The Napoleonic Wars 1793–1815	121
Agitation and Reform 1815–1833	130
The Victorian Era 1833–1890	141
The Edwardian Era 1891–1914	171
The First World War 1914–1918	184
Between the Wars 1918–1939	190
The Second World War 1939–1945	203
Modern Times 1945–1980	210
Selected Bibliography	235
Sources of Illustrations	237
Index	239

INTRODUCTION

'The Church of England is a lovable and infuriating body', said Dr. Robert Runcie on the day that it was announced that he was to become the 102nd Archbishop of Canterbury.

In this book, which tells the story of the Church of England from its inception at the time of the Reformation right through to the present day, I have focused on both aspects of this formidable institution.

The pages which follow feature saints and sinners, model parish priests and worldly bishops, brilliant orators, famous bores, lunatics, drug addicts, archbishops *manqués*, fighting parsons, pacifists, self-denying ascetics, notorious gourmets and other remarkable 'gentlemen of the gown'.

As the title suggests, I have paid a lot of attention to the human and vulnerable side of the clergy: their domestic life and illnesses, their leisure and sporting activities, and their eating, drinking and sexual habits. On the other hand, I have not ignored their sermons, hymns, good works and great achievements and the narrative that follows contains many examples of the Spirit being Willing as well as the Flesh being Weak.

I have extended the net to include organists, choir-masters, bell-ringers, grave-diggers, reverend school-masters and army and naval chaplains, and have also included the occasional doings of the parson's wife. To set the activities of these people in context, I have also noted the building of new churches, the installation of unusual organs, pulpits, bells, stained glass, and manorial pews and other church furniture and have closely followed the alteration, improvement or destruction of the parsonages and palaces where the servants of the Church have lived.

In the pages that follow, great state occasions and examples of devotion to duty will be found interspliced with scandalous events, defrockings, inter-episcopal quarrels and trivial domestic incidents. The reader must be prepared to jump from a great event such as the memorial service in St. Paul's Cathedral for the victims of the *Titanic* disaster to the death of an obscure Yorkshire parson in the hunting-field. Some readers may be distressed to find major ecclesiastical events omitted while extremely trivial ones are included. For example, I have omitted the disestablishment of the Irish church in 1869 but included the Dean of St. Paul's having his pocket picked on an Underground station in 1929.

I make no apology for borrowing a few items relating to recent years from my book *Gossip* and also adopting the same sternly chronological approach. In the story that follows, I have worked my way through, year by year and month by month from the enthronement of Thomas Cranmer in 1533 to that of Archbishop Runcie in 1980. Though many readers may prefer to dip into the book at random I hope that some will feel inspired to read through from start to finish.

Those that do will find many aspects of the church followed through. In the course of the 447 years covered, thirty-four different Archbishops of Canterbury are featured and their official London residence, Lambeth palace, is seen in a variety of different lights. Under Archbishop Cornwallis at the end of the eighteenth century, it is a place of revelry and dissipation. During the Civil War, it is a prison for Royalist clergy. Under Queen Victoria's Archbishop Benson it was the setting for a celebrated ecclesiastical trial. During the recent primacy of Dr. Coggan, it was the launching pad for a call to the Nation to renew its sense of moral purpose and, the following year, the setting for a tea party to launch a biography of Mrs. Coggan.

Similarly, I have tried to follow the great bishoprics across the centuries and note the changes that have occurred. For example, eighteen different bishops of Durham are mentioned, from Bishop Tunstall, who lived through the vicissitudes of the Reformation, to the present incumbent, Bishop Habgood, who in December 1976 urged the government to exercise caution in the development of its nuclear energy programme. Both these prelates have enjoyed the amenities of the historic Auckland Castle, their official residence in County Durham, but Dr. Habgood does not, alas, have the use of his predecessor's splendid London residence, Durham House off the Strand, which was pulled down in the eighteenth century to make way for the Adam brothers' Adelphi building, close to the site of the present Shell-Mex Complex. When he visits London today, the Bishop of Durham must presumably stay in an hotel, club, friend's house or perhaps in one of the new guest rooms at Lambeth Palace.

As the genealogical end-papers show, the Church of England is something of a family business. Many bishops are sons of bishops. Several archbishops are the sons or sons-in-law of other archbishops, and in the course of this narrative several great ecclesiastical dynasties emerge, flourish, disappear and then reappear.

Throughout the narrative, I have selected items to show the growth and development of English life and others to show how much clerical grandeur still lingers on. In this context, it is interesting to note that in 1980 many bishops still live in their historic homes, or at least in part of them, the Archbishop of Canterbury still takes precedence over all in the realm after the royal family and anyone attending a great ceremony in a cathedral today might conclude that the medieval form and structure of the church has in fact survived the centuries intact. Though the church's importance may be now greatly reduced much of the fabric of contemporary life has ecclesiastical origins, as the names of streets and buildings often bear witness.

One aspect of English life often reflected in these pages is the power of the mob. Englishmen's passions have often run high on matters of religion and the Church of England has never won the undivided loyalty of the nation. Much of the action in this book takes place in violent times. From the clergy-baiting days of the Reformation right through to the burning of Archbishop Lang's effigy by angry tithe-payers in 1935, the mob has been ready with a seemingly endless supply of dead cats and rotten eggs to hurl at church dignatories. At various stages of this story, bishops have been pulled out of their coaches, chased across the roof-tops, their houses set on fire and their robes ripped off. Lambeth Palace has been physically attacked on a number of occasions. At the time of the Gordon riots in 1780, 300 soldiers were installed to protect the Archbishop's home against a mob armed with drums and fifes.

There has been no shortage of material on which to draw. Library shelves groan with books on ecclesiastical matters, huge biographies of once-famous bishops and deans, the diaries of country parsons, treatises on the Antichrist, histories of the Lambeth Conferences, records of church courts and many other related subjects. I have only been able to pick at this vast carcass and, as the bibliography shows, my reading has been eccentric rather than comprehensive. Some books have been disappointing. For example, in his life of Bishop Bell of Chichester, F. A. Iremonger refers to the menu cards found among the Bishop's possessions when he died but does not once, in the course of this 400 page biography describe a single meal, or snack, this great Bishop consumed.

I regret that, for reasons of space, it has not been possible to explore many interesting-sounding avenues. For example, though a number of cricketing parsons will be found in the pages that follow, I have not investigated the history of inter-diocesan cricket matches. Among many learned papers which I am sorry to have left unread is Dr. U. P. Burke's psychoanalytic interpretation of Archbishop Laud through the thirty dreams recorded in his journal. Another area I would have liked to have probed more deeply is the close relationship between the Victorian parson and the railways. The indexes of *The Times* for this period contain references to an astonishing number of railway accidents involving clergymen and I have only been able to include a tiny percentage of these.

I would like to thank Hugh Montgomery-Massingberd and Hugo Vickers for reading the typescript and making various helpful suggestions, Andrew Edmunds for providing the cover and a lot of the eighteenth-century illustrations; Tino Zervudachi for his photograph of 37 Dover Street, Simon Barrow for photographing Archbishop Laud's tortoise at Lambeth Palace; also Caroline Tonson Rye, Gillon Aitken, Isobel Strachey and Elisa Segrave for helping in other ways and finally, my aunt Jean MacInnes for telling me the nickname of a recent Bishop of Carlisle.

THE REFORMATION

1533–1553

In medieval times, the church was rich, powerful and conservative. Its wealth was reflected in the great religious houses and cathedrals that had sprung up across the country, many of them adorned with superb stained glass and possessing valuable plate and other treasures. Management of the church was in the hands of a few leading bishops, feudal figures who not so long ago had commanded armies in the field – the Bishop of Durham had fought in the Battle of Crécy – and who now functioned as statesmen and ambassadors and were answerable only to papal authority. Many of them had stately official residences, both in their dioceses and in, or near, London. Some years before this narrative begins, this old-fashioned system had begun to come under attack. For several years there had been murmurs of dissatisfaction about the abuses and superstitions creeping into the church and, especially, its exploitation by Rome. New protestant ideas from the universities were beginning to catch on and a campaign had recently been launched to deprive the monasteries of their wealth. By 1533, England was in a state of turmoil and a momentous anti-clerical revolution was under way, of which the greedy King Henry VIII was to take full advantage. Supported by Archbishop Cranmer, who had no personal ambitions but was dedicated to the rooting out of the old religion and replacing it with a personal religion based on a close inter-pretation of the scriptures, Henry was to begin a mighty programme of church reform which was to be continued with even greater enthusiasm in the next reign. In the years that follow, Roman jurisdiction was cut off, the religious houses were dissolved and stripped of their fabric, the new Bible in English was circulated, the Book of Common Prayer came into use and the clergy were at last permitted to take wives. Those who went along with these reforms were handsomely rewarded: many ejected monks were given generous pensions, a few were made bishops and many laymen gained rich prizes in the scramble for church property. Those who held out and refused to repudiate the papal authority faced terrible penalties. As monastic masonry crashed, stained glass smashed and devout Catholics died horrible deaths at the stake, leading reformers commented on these events in lengthy, two-hour sermons from the open air pulpit at Paul's Cross, beside the old St. Paul's Cathedral in London.

1533 On December 3, 1533, Thomas Cranmer was enthroned as Archbishop of Canterbury. He walked barefoot through the streets of Canterbury and a magnificent banquet was served. It was said that the Prior of Christ Church contributed so many swans and partridges to the feast that he could only afford to give the King's secretary, Thomas Cromwell, a Christmas present of apples.

The new Archbishop, who had spent most of his life in academic seclusion as a little-noticed fellow of Jesus College, Cambridge, had been lent £1,000 by the King towards the expenses of entering his office and was to remain in debt throughout his life.

1534   Early the following year, the Bishop of Durham, Cuthbert Tunstall, who had written to the King protesting about his innovations and begging him to return to 'the paths of righteousness' was summoned to London. As he made his way south, royal agents headed north and ransacked his palaces. The bishop soon succumbed to the King's threats and avoided incarceration in the Tower of London.

A symbol of the ancient feudal power of the spiritual lords: the medieval gate-house to the palace of the Bishops of Bath and Wells

On March 30, 1534, the Succession Act came into force requiring all subjects to swear to accept the young princesses Mary and Elizabeth as Henry's successors in the event of there being no male heir. John Fisher, seventy-five-year-old Bishop of Rochester, and Sir Thomas More both refused to take this oath and were summoned before the Council, sitting in Lambeth Palace. Fisher was at once sent to the Tower, but Sir Thomas was permitted to wander about the spacious gardens of the palace and think the matter over.

Three weeks later, on April 20, the execution took place at Tyburn of Elizabeth Barton, popularly known as 'the Holy Maid of Kent'. This mysterious person, who suffered from a form of religious mania and had dared to announce that God found Henry's recent divorce from Catharine of Aragon abhorrent, has been exposed as a partial fraud. Several priests and friars who had tried to exploit her powers died with her.

At the end of 1534, the links with Rome were finally broken when the Act of Supremacy was passed declaring that Henry was 'the only supreme head of the Church of England' and giving him power to 'visit, repress, redress, reform, order, correct, restrain and amend all errors, heresies and abuses'.

Meanwhile, Archbishop Cranmer had sent over to Germany for his wife, Joan, whom he had secretly married two years earlier and who was to bear him two children. Clerical marriage was still strictly forbidden and Mrs. Cranmer remained very much in the background, meekly travelling in a tub or trunk and only protesting when it was put the wrong side up.

1535 In January, 1535, Thomas Cromwell was appointed Vicar-General, to exercise the Royal Supremacy in ecclesiastical matters. In the alarming events that were to follow, Archbishop Cranmer was to play a passive role, devoting much of his time to his work on the liturgy in English and his correspondence with Swiss and German scholars.

Five months later, on June 22, the elderly Bishop of Rochester, John Fisher, who had been in custody since refusing to swear to the Succession Act, was beheaded on Tower Hill. He had bravely referred to his approaching execution as his 'wedding day'. His head was later displayed on London Bridge and his body was stripped and left naked on the spot where he had died till evening, when it was taken to All Hallows Church, Barking.

The same month, the execution took place at Tyburn of Father Richard Reynolds, supposedly the most learned monk in England, the Rev. John Hailes, Vicar of Thistleworth, and three Carthusian priors, all of whom had refused to accept Henry as head of the church. They were treated with savage barbarity, being hanged in their religious dress, cut down alive, disembowelled and dismembered.

On July 6, the saintly Sir Thomas More met his death on Tower Hill, bravely telling his executioner, 'Pluck up thy spirits man and do not be afraid to do thine office.'

Meanwhile, the King and his Vicar-General Thomas Cromwell had begun to cast avaricious eyes on the wealth of the monasteries, abbeys and other religious houses, many of which had now grown excessively corrupt and which, as head of the church, Henry now claimed as his own property. On August 1, two leading clergymen, Dr. Richard Layton and Dr. Thomas Legh, were despatched on a rapid visitation of the religious houses. They were a haughty pair: Dr. Layton was said to have a 'satrapic countenance' and Dr. Legh was described as an insolent man who insisted on being received accompanied by a procession of fourteen men in livery.

These two officials soon turned in colourful reports of scandals and 'disgusting foulness' in the religious houses which shocked the public. At the convent at Littlemore near Oxford* it was found that the prioress's illegitimate daughter was being brought up on the premises and most of the nuns had broken out. At the monasteries inspected, dozens of monks admitted they had broken their vows of chastity and, at Bury St. Edmunds, the Abbot, John Melford, was found to be leading the life of a dissolute courtier, delighting in the company of women and in sumptuous banquets.

---

* Now the site of a famous lunatic asylum.

By the end of the year, several religious houses had voluntarily surrendered to the King.

Meanwhile, Henry had begun making alterations to the Chapel Royal at Hampton Court, where the music was said to be the envy of Europe. A fine vaulted ceiling with huge pendants was added to the building.

1536 On February 6 the following year the Archbishop of Canterbury, Thomas Cranmer, preached for two hours from the open air pulpit at Paul's Cross in the heart of London, defending the Royal Supremacy and adding a proof that the Pope was Antichrist.

The following month, the King visited the House of Commons in person to deliver a bill for the suppression of the smaller monasteries. It was estimated that this measure would increase the annual income of the Crown by £32,000 and bring in £100,000 worth of money, plate and jewels.

On May 17, an ecclesiastical court at Lambeth Palace presided over by Archbishop Cranmer came to the strange decision that the King's marriage to Anne Boleyn had been void from the start on the grounds of Henry's adultery with Anne's sister.

Two days later, Anne Boleyn was beheaded on Tower Green and her body was quickly buried in St. Peter's church in the precincts of the Tower. The King was now free to marry Jane Seymour.

On June 11, William Rugg, last abbot of the religious house of St. Benet's Hulme, who had signed a statement that the Bishop of Rome had no authority in England, was consecrated Bishop of Norwich.

The same summer, the death occurred of the Dean of St. Paul's, Dr. Pace, who had been *non compos mentis* for the last ten years, spending much of his time under restraint.

On October 6, the Rev. William Tyndale, whose celebrated translation of the New Testament had recently been published in Worms and smuggled into England, was executed at a castle near Brussels for heresy. Before being strangled and then burnt at the stake, he had prayed 'O Lord, open the King of England's eyes.'

Meanwhile, the King and his Council were facing a widespread insurrection against the religious changes. A rising of Lincolnshire gentlemen had been quickly suppressed but, in the middle of October, a large gathering of clergy and others mustered on Skipwith Moor in Yorkshire calling themselves 'The Pilgrimage of Grace' and swearing that their only objects were to restore Christ's church in its purity and put down heretical opinions. Within a few days, these rebels had seized the town of York, causing the Archbishop of York, Dr. Lee, to retreat to Pomfret Castle. The Bishop of Durham, Dr. Tunstall, was later besieged at Auckland Castle, where he added a handsome dining-room with a magnificent half-hexagon bay window.*

By the end of the year, this rebellion had been crushed. Most of the participants were pardoned but a number of leaders were tried for high treason and were to face savage executions. In Lancashire, the Abbots of Sawley and Whalley were hanged from their own steeples and another participant, the

---

* In 1979, the present Bishop of Durham declared that this window 'fits so badly that sitting in front of it is almost like sitting out of doors'.

The Pilgrimage of Grace: protestors against the religious changes take arms against the King and cause the Archbishop of York and Bishop of Durham to flee their palaces. Leaders of this rebellion later faced savage executions

Abbot of Fountains, who was also accused of stealing jewels and conveying them to a 'receiver' in London, was sent to the Tower.

1537 At the end of March, 1537, the dispossessed Abbot of Barlings, who had sold off his abbey plate, a monk named William Moreland and three secular clergy were found guilty of levying war against the King and were sentenced to be hung, cut down alive, disembowelled, their entrails burned while they were still alive, and beheaded. 'I have ordered the heads of these prisoners to be set up over London Bridge and at every gate', the Lord Chancellor later wrote to the Vicar-General.

A few weeks later, on May 25, the Abbots of Sedbergh and Thirsk were drawn through the streets of London on hurdles and executed at Tyburn. Several other priors, friars and monks perished at the same spot on the same day.

In July, the Archbishop of York, Dr. Lee, was able to report at Paul's Cross on 'the just execution of the Northern rebels'.

Meanwhile, the monasteries were being rapidly dismantled. In July, the Abbots of Bisham and Chertsey surrendered their houses to the King. Stones from the latter building were used to build Nonsuch Palace, the King's new house near Hampton Court which was intended to rival the French emperor's Château de Chambord.

A few days later, the Prior of Lewes was intimidated into yielding up his house, which the King had promised to give to Cromwell and the Duke of Norfolk. An Italian engineer skilled in the use of gun-powder was employed to pull down the priory, a magnificent old Cluniac foundation dating from the days of William the Conqueror.

On October 12, Jane Seymour gave birth to the son the King had long been waiting for. This joyful event was celebrated with bells being rung, *Te Deums* being sung in every parish church in London and a special service in St. Paul's Cathedral presided over by the Bishop of London, Dr. Stokesley, and the Bishop of Chichester, Dr. Sampson.

Twelve days later, the Queen died. A thousand masses were said for her soul and a service was held in St. George's Chapel, Windsor, conducted by Archbishop Cranmer, in his pontifical robes, six bishops and numerous abbots.

1538   On January 29, 1538, Boxley Abbey in Kent surrendered and the celebrated 'Rood of Grace', an effigy which nodded its head and rolled its eyes, was detached from the abbey's wall and found to be a piece of trickery worked by wires.

A few weeks later, on February 24, the former Dominican friar, John Hilsey, now Bishop of Rochester, denounced the use of relics and images in a sermon at Paul's Cross. 'The Rood of Grace' was broken up and its pieces thrown among the crowd. On the same occasion, the Bishop denounced as a fraud the famous 'Blood of Hailes', the supposed blood of Christ contained in a phial in a West Country monastery, which had turned out to be a mixture of clarified honey and saffron. This sermon was intended to prepare people for the general destruction of such relics.

On April 20, Robert Hobbes, head of the Cistercian abbey at Woburn in Bedfordshire, was hung on an oak tree beside the gate of his house. The abbey itself had already surrendered and its lease was soon to be acquired by the one-eyed Earl of Bedford, Great Steward of England.

Meanwhile, the houses of the friars had also been dissolved and many of them were to become martyrs. One of the first to perish was Friar Forrest, who was burned at Smithfield on May 20 after refusing to do penance for denying the King's supremacy. With the full agreement of Archbishop Cranmer, he met his death in a cradle of chains hung over the fire.

Six months later, on November 30, the Rev. John Lambart was put to death after being tried in the banqueting hall at Whitehall before the King. His offence had been to deny the Real Presence, a doctrine in which the King, who officiated at the trial dressed in white satin, firmly believed.

On December 17, the Pope at last prepared to promulgate a Bull of Excommunication deposing Henry VIII and absolving his subjects from obedience.

This pronouncement was reinforced by the publication in Rome of an open letter to the King by the English cardinal, Reginald Pole. 'Thou hast cast thy kingdom into miserable commotions and made it the spectacle of the world,' he wrote. 'Thy butcheries and horrible executions have made England the slaughterhouse of innocence. The holiest and most spotless men have been slaughtered in the most ghastly and unspeakable manner.'

1539   In April 1539, the Reformation was advanced by the publication of the first complete bible in English. Its printing, which had taken place in the recently ransacked house of the Grey Friars in London, had been financed by two city merchants, Edward Whitchurch and Richard Grafton, displaying, it

Title page of the Great Bible, showing the tyrannical Henry VIII giving out the first bible printed in English to Archbishop Cranmer and the Vicar-General Thomas Cromwell, who in their turn pass on the book to the bishops and gentry

has been said 'a curious picture of piety and business acumen'. It was to become known as the Great Bible. It was issued by Royal Authority and it was ordered that a copy should be placed in public view in every parish church in England. At St. Paul's Cathedral, no fewer than six copies were set up on desks.

The following month, the King made a further attempt to stamp out non-conformity in his realm by issuing a set of Six Articles, laying down savage penalties for priests who broke their vows of celibacy. There was a large crop of prosecutions when the act became law two months later and Archbishop Cranmer sent his wife and children back to Germany in a hurry and was now obliged to live alone at Lambeth Palace.

On November 15, the Abbot of Glastonbury was hung on Tor Hill outside his monastery. The same month, the Abbot of Reading was hung and, on December 1, the Abbot of Colchester was executed after making rash utterances about the King's avarice.

At Christmas, Anne of Cleves arrived in the country, escorted across the channel by a fleet of fifty ships. On December 29, she was magnificently entertained by Archbishop Cranmer at his palace at Canterbury and, eight **1540** days later, on January 6, 1540, she became Henry VIII's wife in a ceremony at Greenwich, conducted by Cranmer.

Ten days later, on January 16, the Benedictine monks of Westminster Abbey assembled in their chapter house to sign away their monastery church, cloisters, precincts and all their possessions to the 'Lord King'.

Two days later, Worcester Priory surrendered and the compliant ousted prior, Henry Holbeach, was appointed first Dean of Worcester.

On February 14, Stephen Gardiner, Bishop of Winchester, preached a sermon at Paul's Cross in which he attacked Lutheranism and also gloated over the ejection of the friars. 'Now they be gone with all their trumpery', he said, 'but the devil is not yet gone.'

A fortnight later, former Austin Friar Robert Barnes replied to this sermon, viciously attacking Bishop Gardiner. Barnes refused to recant and after a spell in the Tower of London was burnt at Smithfield as a heretic, begging in a speech at the stake that the King should punish adultery, fornication and swearing and 'set forth Christ's true religion'.

On March 23, the surrender of the great Augustinian abbey of Waltham in Essex marked the end of the dissolution process. Among those ejected was the abbey's master of choristers, Thomas Tallis, who was to find work as a lay clerk in Canterbury Cathedral and later become a Gentleman of the Chapel Royal at Greenwich.

Meanwhile the King's marriage to the good-natured Anne of Cleves had foundered and the royal eye had been caught by the pretty nineteen-year-old niece of the Duke of Norfolk, Catharine Howard. On July 28 they were married by the Bishop of Winchester, Stephen Gardiner, who had now emerged as the bishop most keen on the old Catholic tradition.

The same day saw the execution of Thomas Cromwell, once the King's right hand man. Archbishop Cranmer survived this dramatic turn of events by lying low and interfering as little as possible in public affairs. Among those who felt it prudent to flee the country altogether was former Carmelite monk John Bale who had renounced his vows and taken a wife.

8

Two days later, on July 30, the former chaplain to Catharine of Aragon, the Rev. Thomas Abell, who had been lingering in the Tower for the past five years and 'almost eaten up by vermin' was dragged to Smithfield on hurdles and executed.

1541 On March 14, the following year, the Rev. Nicholas Udall, headmaster of Eton, appeared before the Privy Council charged with 'unnatural crime' and the theft of the college plate. He was dismissed from his post and committed to Marshalsea prison but later re-emerged to become a prebend at Windsor, rector of Calborne on the Isle of Wight and, finally, obtained another headmastership, that of Westminster School.

Eight months later, on November 2, the King was worshipping in his fine new chapel at Hampton Court, when Archbishop Cranmer made a sudden appearance and, whispering, handed him a note revealing that the young Queen Catharine Howard had committed adultery a hundred times with a page in the royal household. At first the King refused to believe these allegations but after an all-night discussion in the Bishop of Winchester's palace at Southwark he became convinced and the Queen was put into the custody of armed guards to await her execution.

1542 The following year, Abbot Austen of Rewley near Oxford was found installed as Vicar of Whatcote, Warwickshire, which he was to hold until his death thirty years later, supplementing his handsome monastic pension of £22 a year with £12 a year from his living.

1543 In May, 1543, a plot by the prebendaries of Canterbury to seize Archbishop Cranmer at the Council table, charge him with heresy and send him to the Tower of London was foiled by the King, who summoned the Primate to Whitehall and presented him with a ring, the production of which would give him immunity from arrest.

Two months later, on July 12, the Bishop of Winchester, Stephen Gardiner, officiated at the King's marriage to Catharine Parr, which took place in the Queen's Closet at Hampton Court Palace. The new Queen made no secret of her protestant sympathies, her house having become a resort for leading reformers.

Meanwhile, Dr. John London, who had taken part in the Visitation of the monasteries, had unleashed a major purge on the Chapel Royal of St. George's, Windsor, and on July 26 John Merbecke, organist and minor composer in his own right, and two colleagues were found guilty of heresy and sentenced to death. The subsequent intervention of Bishop Gardiner caused Merbecke to be reprieved and re-instated.

On December 22 this year, Nicholas Heath, who was secretly in communication with Cardinal Pole and the Princess Mary about bringing back Romish influences, was elected Bishop of Worcester.

1544 The following June, the Dean of York, Dr. Richard Layton, who had exposed many scandals in the religious houses nine years earlier, died of dropsy. Following his death, it was discovered that this arrogant man had himself pawned plate belonging to York Minster.

1545 Seven months later, on January 10, 1545, Robert Holgate, Bishop of Llandaff, was translated to the see of York in a ceremony in the chapel at Lambeth Palace. Holgate was to make himself into the richest bishop in England by selling the King some sixty-seven manors belonging to the see.

9

Later this year, the King ordered Cranmer and two other bishops to 'peruse certain books of service' and push ahead with further liturgical changes.

1546   On May 29, 1546, the Archbishop of St. Andrews, Cardinal Beaton, was murdered in his bedroom.

Meanwhile, twenty-five-year-old Anne Askew, daughter of a Lincolnshire knight, had been charged with heresy concerning the blessed sacrament and had refused to recant. Suspected of receiving support from people in high places, she was placed on the rack in the Tower of London, but even after being severely tortured she refused to divulge any names. On July 16, she was burnt at Smithfield with three others. She had been so crippled by her experiences on the rack that she had to be carried to the stake in a chair.

The same summer, Dr Edward Crone, *enfant terrible* of the London clergy, was arrested on heresy charges but he was willing to betray the names of his friends at court and in the church and city and renounce his belief in the sacrificial character of the Mass in a sermon at Paul's Cross.

On September 26, the Bishop of London, Dr. Bonner, ordered the burning of *Ghoostly Psalms and Spiritual Songs* by Miles Coverdale, one of the translators of the Bible.

1547   Four months later, on the night of January 27, 1547, Archbishop Cranmer was summoned from his palace at Croydon, originally given to his predecessor Lanfranc by William the Conqueror, to attend the dying King. The Primate mounted his horse and rode hard for the royal palace at Whitehall where the King lay in a massive four-poster bed overlooking the Thames. The monarch was sinking fast and had lost the power of speech but on being asked to give some sign that he put his trust in God, 'did wring his hand as hard as he could'.

The following day, the King was dead. In the national mourning that followed, every parish church in England held a solemn dirge and tolled its bells, and requiem masses were offered for the dead king's soul.

On February 16, the funeral and burial service took place at St. George's Chapel, Windsor, with the black-vested Bishop of Winchester, Stephen Gardiner, celebrating the final requiem mass and burial office. Gardiner also preached a sermon, taking the text 'Blessed are the dead who die in the Lord'.

On February 20, nine-year-old Edward VI was crowned in Westminster Abbey. There was much pomp and ceremony but, out of consideration for the new King's age, the service was reduced to only two hours in length. Chief among the mitred figures was Archbishop Cranmer, who sang the High Mass from the altar steps and then loudly proclaimed the unfamiliar new doctrine of the Divine Right of Kings, declaring that the little boy king was 'God's vice-regent upon earth' and 'Christ's Vicar'. Many of those present hoped that Edward would continue his father's 'noble work in suppressing heathen rites and detestable idolatry'.

Control of the Privy Council quickly fell into the hands of the King's uncle, the Earl of Hertford, who was to acquire the titles of Duke of Somerset and Lord Protector of England and obtain from the puppet King extensive grants of church lands. Within weeks of his assumption of power, he was to begin building 'a large and goodly house' in the Strand, clearing the ground for its site by pulling down two churches on the spot, carting away the remains of the dead by whole cartloads and throwing them into a pit in Bloomsbury. To obtain his building materials, he pulled down part of the church of St. John of Jerusalem at Smithfield, the Clerkenwell Priory and part of the cloister of St. Paul's Cathedral. He also tried to lay hands on St. Margaret's, Westminster, but his men were driven away by furious parishioners.

On August 9, ex-monk Henry Holbeach was elected Bishop of Lincoln, in which he was to increase his personal wealth by conveying to the Crown two or three dozen manors belonging to the see.

On September 25, Stephen Gardiner, Bishop of Winchester, famous for his Romish sympathies, was committed to the Fleet prison.

At the end of the year, Parliament met and repealed the Act of Six Articles and a bill legalizing the marriage of the clergy was brought before the House of Commons. Many priests and nuns were to seize the opportunity to marry and, in the words of Hilaire Belloc, 'old lecherous priests and bishops went a-caterwauling'.

1548 Meanwhile, leading reformer Hugh Latimer had been released from the Tower of London, where he had spent most of the last few years. On January 18, 1548, he delivered his famous 'Sermon of the Ploughers' at Paul's Cross in which he inveighed against non-resident priests and held up the Devil as an example. 'He is the most diligent preacher of all others. He is never out of his diocese. He is ever at his plough.'

The following September, a number of bishops and divines met in secret at Chertsey to consider the new prayer book, drafted in exquisite English, though not fully appreciated at the time, by Archbishop Cranmer, and replacing the old monastic routine of hourly services with Morning and Evening Prayer. By the end of the year, it was ready to be printed and was debated in the parliament.

1549 On January 21, 1549, the Act of Uniformity was passed ordering that this new Book of Common Prayer and no other should be used from Whit Sunday onwards.

A few weeks later, Hugh Latimer began a series of Lenten addresses before the young King, in which he denounced all aspects of the old religion. The twelve-year-old King listened rapt in attention.

On June 15, the wealthy Archbishop of York, Robert Holgate, was publicly married to a certain Miss Barbara Wentworth.

The same month, the introduction of the new English Prayer Book was greeted with uprisings across the country and demands for the return of the old Mass, the restoration of the saints and statues and pictures of Jesus and Mary. The men of Cornwall and Devon gathered an army of 10,000 and attempted to take the town of Exeter, while in Norfolk a group of 20,000 mustered under a gentleman named Ket, overawing the city of Norwich. Force was used to suppress the rebellions and Ket and nine others were subsequently hung on a tree near Norwich known as 'The Oak of Reformation'.

On July 3, former Cistercian monk, John Hooper, who had recently returned from exile, was nominated Bishop of Gloucester. A leader of the advanced section of reformers, he had hesitated to accept this appointment wondering whether he should wear 'the idolatrous vesture of a bishop'.

11

Thomas Cranmer, who was raised to the Primacy from the humble post of Archdeacon. A master of English prose and principal author of the Book of Common Prayer, he was said to have 'an exquisite ear for the language of devotion'. His enemies made him out to be a 'monster of lust' on account of his having taken a wife

In October the Bishop of London, Edmund Bonner, was thrown into prison for not complying with the requirements of the court in matters of **1550** religion and on February 7, 1550, he was formally deprived of his see.

He was followed as Bishop of London by leading reformer, Nicholas Ridley, who was to behave very leniently to his predecessor's family, permitting Bonner's mother and sister to continue to reside at Fulham Palace and share his dinner table.

Three months later, on May 2, Archbishop Cranmer ordered the burning of a woman named Joan Bocher whose ideas of the incarnation – she had denied that Christ took the flesh of the outward man – were considered heretical. The young King had tried to delay the execution, hoping that she would be converted, and eventually signed the death warrant in tears.

In November this year, two of Princess Mary's chaplains were summoned before the Council and accused of saying the old Mass.

1551 Twelve months later, on November 12, 1551, three commissioners were appointed to look into claims by a certain Anthony Norman that the Archbishop of York's wife was really married to himself. The commissioners reported in favour of the wealthy Archbishop.

Meanwhile, the Protector Somerset had fallen foul of the new regime and **1552** been arrested and charged with high treason. On January 22, 1552, he was executed on Tower Hill and his place as head of the Council was taken by the new Duke of Northumberland, who was said to regard the church as 'no more than an object to be despoiled'.

Three months later, on April 6, a new Act of Uniformity ordered the use of the new revised prayer book and strict attendance at church on Sundays and Holy Days.

On August 15, Archbishop Holgate of York issued a set of injunctions to the clergymen of his see. They included instructions that 'vergers do attend divine service for the expulsion of beggars, other light persons and dogs forth of the church'.

The same month, former Carmelite monk John Bale, who had fled abroad during the last reign and taken a wife, returned to London and was presented with the see of Ossory in Ireland. Here, he was to infuriate his priests by advising them to marry and viciously attack his episcopal colleagues, describing them as 'the prelates of Antichrist's church, two horned monsters, great bellied bishops'.

1553 On December 11, Hugh Latimer preached at Paul's Cross drawing attention to the insanitary condition of the churchyard.

The following May, the Archbishop of York arrived at Hampton Court with a seventy-horse procession.

Meanwhile the young King was dying of tuberculosis. His death on July 6 threw protestants into confusion. In a sermon at Paul's Cross, divinity lecturer John Rogers warned the people to beware of 'pestilent popery, idolatry and superstition' and Archbishop Cranmer and the Bishop of London, Nicholas Ridley, were active participants in a plot to get the staunchly anti-Catholic Lady Jane Grey onto the throne.

Three days after the King's death, Bishop Ridley preached at Paul's Cross in favour of this candidate and branded Princess Mary and Princess Elizabeth as illegitimate. The following day, July 10, nineteen-year-old Lady Jane sailed from Sion House to the Tower, only to face a massive uprising against her and in favour of the devoutly Catholic Princess Mary.

On July 19, Mary was proclaimed Queen. Catholics went wild with excitement and Archbishop Cranmer fled to his house at Croydon, where he hoped to enjoy a few days' peace.

THE MARIAN REACTION

1553–1558

There now followed an alarming interlude. Shocked by the gaunt ruins of the religious houses now scattered across the country and horrified by the abolition of the Latin Mass, the devout young Queen was to attempt to put the clock back and restore the breach with Rome. Vehement persecution of the reformed clergy was placed in the willing hands of Bishops Bonner and Gardiner. Clergy who had taken the opportunity to marry during the previous reign were dispossessed, among them the Archbishop of York. Extreme protestants, who saw Mary as the Antichrist come to life, fled abroad. Of those who remained, no less than 276 were to die horrible deaths. Weavers, linen drapers, bricklayers and butchers perished alongside the clergy.

1553   Following the accession of Queen Mary on July 19, 1553, the Bishop of Winchester, Stephen Gardiner, was released from the Tower of London and appointed Lord High Chancellor. Archbishop Cranmer was bidden to keep within his palace at Lambeth.

On August 13, there was a violent scene at Paul's Cross when a dagger was thrown at the preacher, Dr. Gilbert Bourne, chaplain to the newly re-instated Bishop Bonner. The weapon lodged in the sidepost of the pulpit and Dr. Bourne was saved from worse injury by the intervention of prebendary John Bradford and others.

A week later, on August 20, Dr. Thomas Watson preached at the same spot protected by 200 soldiers. He urged his listeners to 'keep the old faith and edify the old temple again'.

On September 11, the Bishop of Gloucester, John Hooper, who had expressed his determination 'to tarry and live and die with my sheep', was committed to the Fleet prison where he was placed in 'a vile and stinking chamber' with 'a pad of straw' to lie on. While in this grim place, he was to write an exposition on the comfort of the Twenty Third Psalm.

On September 18, a notoriously loose Catholic scholar Hugh Weston was appointed Dean of Westminster. While here, he was to discover a plot to exhume and burn the remains of Henry VIII, but on account of his scandalous reputation, nobody believed him.

The same month, Archbishop Cranmer was summoned before the Council and sent to the Tower, along with his colleagues Latimer and Ridley.

On October 1, Mary was crowned Queen in Westminster Abbey. The ceremony was performed by Bishop Gardiner assisted by ten other bishops, all in mitres. The Bishop of Chichester, John Scory, who had quickly shed his wife on the Queen's accession, preached a sermon. At the banquet afterwards in Westminster Hall, the seventy-nine-year-old Bishop of Durham, Cuthbert Tunstall, who had recently been restored to Durham House in the Strand, sat on the Queen's left.

On October 4, Archbishop Holgate of York was accused of treason and committed to the Tower, and his five houses were seized. Among his confiscated possessions were a fine gold mitre, set with diamonds, sapphires and pearls, six or seven gold rings, five or six tons of wine, four or five score of horses, over 2,000 sheep and a bed of down with a red damask covering, lined with fustian and curtains of red sarsanet.

The following day, the Queen opened her first parliament. Both peers and commoners were ordered to attend her Majesty in a solemn Mass. Dr. Taylor, Bishop of Lincoln, and Harley, Bishop of Hereford, both refused to fall on their knees at the elevation of the host and were subsequently deprived of their sees.

One of the first actions of this parliament was to repeal the two Acts of Uniformity and reintroduce the forms of worship used in the reign of Henry VIII.

On November 13, Archbishop Cranmer was brought from the Tower of London to appear with Lady Jane Grey and her husband at the Guildhall charged with treason. The Archbishop was returned to fester in the Tower and Lady Jane and her husband were executed early the following year.

1554   On March 16, 1554, John Bird, one-eyed Bishop of Chester and former Carmelite friar was deprived of his see because he had taken a wife in the previous reign. 'The woman beguiled me,' he declared.

A few weeks later, on April 8, a dead cat with its head shaven in the manner of a priest and a wafer-like object in its mouth was found hung in Cheapside and exhibited at Paul's Cross by Dr. Henry Pendleton, chaplain to Bishop Bonner. A reward of twenty nobles was offered for the apprehension of those reponsible for this anti-Catholic prank.

Shortly afterwards, a pellet was fired at Dr. Pendleton when he was preaching at the same spot. It hit the wall of the cathedral near where the Lord Mayor was sitting and fell onto the shoulder of a man in the congregation.

Meanwhile, Cranmer, Latimer and Ridley had been taken from the Tower to Oxford, where, on April 14, they were examined at the University Church of St. Mary's and asked to justify their heresies. Standing between armed guards and leaning on a staff, the white-bearded Archbishop declared his disbelief in the doctrine of the Real Presence and the Mass being a sacrifice for the sins of the living and the dead. All three were found guilty of heresy.

Three months later, the devout Catholic Prince Philip of Spain arrived at Southampton and made his way to Winchester where a meeting with Queen Mary took place in Bishop Gardiner's palace beside the Cathedral. The couple were married a few days later on July 25. The ceremony was followed by a wedding feast at the Bishop's Palace, at which the Queen ate from gold plate and her husband from silver.

On November 11, Mary's third parliament met. The pious Queen was anxious to return lands seized from the church but was opposed by most of her Council. In a dramatic gesture, the Earl of Bedford tore his rosary from

The Bishops who Suffer'd
MARTYRDOM,
For the Protestant Faith
under the Persecution of
Q.MARY.
51.

BISHOP HOOPER.

BISHOP RIDLEY.

ARCHB^P CRANMER.

BISHOP FARRER.

BISHOP LATIMER.

No less than five bishops were executed during the turbulent reign of Bloody Mary

his girdle and threw it into the fire saying he valued Woburn Abbey far more than the guidance of the Church of Rome.

Meanwhile, the Queen's cousin, Cardinal Pole, who had spent much of his life abroad wearing disguise to escape the hired assassins of Henry VIII, was on his way to England to effect the reconciliation with Rome. On November 20, he sailed from Calais in the royal yacht and was met at Dover by crowds of nobility and clergy. During his triumphant journey to London, he paused at Rochester where he adopted the ancient pomp and insignia of a papal legate: the cross, two silver pillars and two silver pole-axes were now borne in front of him. He was received in London by Queen Mary and her consort on Saturday, November 24, having reached Whitehall by river.

The following Tuesday, in a subdued, almost inaudible voice, this skull-faced cardinal spoke to the Houses of Parliament, demanding the revocation of all anti-papal legislation.

On November 30, the Queen and many of her counsellors wept aloud as they proceeded from the Palace of Westminster, where they had knelt to receive absolution from the guilt of schism, into the palace chapel where the *Te Deum* was sung and Cardinal Pole pronounced a benediction.

The following Sunday, Bishop Gardiner preached for two hours to a record-breaking crowd of 15,000 at Paul's Cross, taking the text, 'It is time to wake out of sleep'.

On January 18, 1555, the wealthy Archbishop of York, Robert Holgate, who had been held in the Tower for the last fifteen months, was released from custody on payment of £1,000.

The same month, the Bishop of London, Edmund Bonner, along with eight other bishops and 160 priests made a grand procession through the streets of his diocese and held public services of thanksgiving for the return of Catholicism.

A reign of terror, fire and bloodshed now began, designed to root out heresy. The first martyr was protestant divine John Rogers, who was burnt at Smithfield on February 4. He is said to have met his wife and eleven children on his way to the stake.

On February 9, Dr. Rowland Taylor, Vicar of Hadleigh in Essex and a former chaplain to Archbishop Cranmer, was put to death in his parish.

The same day, John Hooper, Bishop of Gloucester, who had been held in disgusting conditions in the Fleet prison for the last seventeen months was burnt over a slow fire in his diocese. It took three-quarters of an hour for him to die and at one moment he cried out, 'For God's love, good people, let me have more fire!'

On February 19, Nicholas Heath was elected Archbishop of York. He was to use his influence with the Queen to procure considerable benefactions for his see and during his reign was to acquire the former residence of the bishops of Lincoln in the Strand and re-name it York House, though he was said to be the only Archbishop of York to ever live there.

On March 30, the Bishop of St. David's, Robert Farrer, was burnt at Carmarthen.

On Easter Day, there was a dramatic demonstration against this first crop of burnings when former protestant priest, Thomas Flower, rushed to the altar of St. Margaret's, Westminster, and lurched at the officiating priest with a wood-knife, striking him on the head and hand, causing blood to gush into the chalice itself and throwing the congregation into an uproar.

On May 30, the Rev. John Cardmaker, Prebendary of Wells, who had come up to London disguised as a merchant, was burnt at Smithfield.

On August 29, Prince Philip of Spain departed the shores of England and the Queen found solace with Cardinal Pole, who moved into lodgings in the royal palace at Greenwich.

On October 16, Archbishop Cranmer watched the burning of his colleagues Latimer and Ridley from the roof of his prison at Oxford. In his courageous dying words Latimer said, 'Be of good comfort, Master Ridley, and play the man. We shall this day light such a candle by God's grace in England as I trust shall never be put out.'

Two months later, on December 18, John Philpot, former Archdeacon of Winchester, also met his death with brave words. Kissing the stake at Smithfield, he declared, 'Shall I disdain to suffer at this stake seeing my Redeemer did not refuse to suffer a most vile death on the Cross for me?'

Meanwhile, Bishop Gardiner, said by his enemies to have horse's nostrils, a sparrow's mouth and a buzzard's nose, had died of gout. His body was carried to Winchester where it was buried with great solemnity in the cathedral. In his will, he left all his property, household furniture, silver vessels and coin to the Queen.

STEPHEN GARDINER,
Bishop of Winchester.

Stephen Gardiner, Bishop of Winchester. A leading persecutor of the reforming clergy, he was said to have a horse's nostrils, a sparrow's mouth and a buzzard's nose. He died of gout in 1555

1556   On February 14, the following year, the formal degradation of Archbishop Cranmer took place before the altar of Christ Church Cathedral at Oxford. The primate's head was shaven and he was dressed in grotesque canvas vestments, which were stripped off him one by one by Edmund Bonner, hot-tempered Bishop of London, and Thirlby, Bishop of Ely. His crozier had to be dragged from him by force. After this ceremony, Cranmer was put into the custody of the Dean of Christ Church, who provided him with ample quarters, good food and a garden to stroll in.

During the next few weeks, the former Archbishop, now under sentence of death, made a number of dramatic recantations and submissions, renouncing all his long-held beliefs and begging in vain for forgiveness.

On March 21, a solemn procession formed to lead Cranmer to St. Mary's Church where a sermon was preached by Dr. Cole, Provost of Eton, which reduced the condemned man to tears. After this discourse, Cranmer fell to his knees, read the Lord's Prayer and, then, to the confusion of all present, suddenly withdrew all his recent recantations and once again declared the Pope to be the Antichrist.

Then, in spite of his age, he ran to the stake, extending the hand that had signed the recantations into the flames, declaring, 'This hand hath offended'. He died without a cry of complaint.

Following her husband's death, Mrs. Cranmer went on to marry city merchant Edward Whitchurch, who had helped finance the printing of the Great Bible seventeen years earlier. She later contracted a third marriage to a certain Richard Croft.

On the day after Cranmer's death, the skull-faced Cardinal Pole was consecrated the new Archbishop of Canterbury. Though he was to secure a patent to have a hundred servants at his palace at Canterbury, his primacy was not a comfortable one, as he suffered from fever and bad dreams.

In July, the Queen ordered daily processions of clergy in London to beg for rain.

On September 7, a special licence was issued to re-establish the Benedictine monastery at Westminster Abbey. The Dean of St. Paul's, John Feckenham, was entrusted with the position of abbot and was to restore the building to its former glory and repair the shrine of Edward the Confessor, which had been desecrated in the interim.

1557 The following March, church bells were rung to celebrate the return to England, after a nineteen month absence, of Prince Philip of Spain.

Five months later, on August 15, the Dean of Windsor, Dr. Owen Oglethorpe, who was said to be torn between the old and new religions, was consecrated Bishop of Carlisle.

The same month, the Dean of Westminster, Hugh Weston, was deprived of his deanery after being found guilty of gross immorality. He was also deprived of the archdeaconry of Chichester – but permitted to keep his other livings.

1558 Fifteen months later, on November 17, 1558, Queen Mary died at St. James's Palace and, a few hours later, her faithful cousin Reginald Pole died at Lambeth Palace. It has been said that from his deathbed Pole heard the shouts greeting the new Queen.

When news of the end of this uncompromising regime reached Shropshire protestant Edward Burton he was so overcome with joy that he died of excitement.

THE ELIZABETHAN AGE

1558–1603

Elizabeth quickly reversed the settlement of her predecessor. Those in prison for their religious beliefs were released, refugees hurried home, Cranmer's liturgy again replaced the Latin Mass and, though the Queen hankered for a celibate priesthood and the parson's wife did not acquire her honoured position in society for several generations, the clergy were again permitted to marry. Resistance to these changes was only feeble. Within a few years, Anglicanism had taken root and a new social order based on the Bible – the most popular book in the country by the end of the reign – and the new Prayer Book, had come into existence. In the years ahead, the Queen, who liked to be known as the Supreme Governor of the Church of England and detested excessive religious zeal, was to use punitive methods to keep religious feuds in check and there were several martyrdoms. Meanwhile, in spite of the so-called Reformation, old evils flourished. There were several self-seeking courtiers among the bishops, as puritans were to point out with increasing pressure, and religious life in the parishes often seems to have been at a low ebb. Pluralism and absenteeism were rife and many parsons were ill-educated men who preferred their hunting, sex and booze to the care of their flocks. Many parishioners also behaved badly, bringing dogs into church, quarrelling over pews and abusing the churchyard. Nevertheless, thanks to the restraint exercised by the Supreme Governor and her success in imposing one religion on the nation, this was to some extent a Golden Age.

1558 One of the new Queen's first actions was to appoint the Rev. William Bill as preacher at Paul's Cross. In his sermon there on November 20, this noted protestant attempted to calm down people's vengeful reactions to the Catholics.

On December 12, the funeral of Queen Mary took place in Westminster Abbey. In a sermon on this occasion, John White, Bishop of Winchester, praised the former monarch and was promptly imprisoned in his palace at Southwark.

On Christmas Day, Queen Elizabeth ordered Bishop Oglethorpe of Carlisle, who was celebrating Mass, to omit the elevation of the host. He refused to comply and the Queen stormed out of the Chapel Royal as soon as the gospel was finished.

1559 On January 15, 1559, Elizabeth was crowned in Westminster Abbey with full ceremony. Organs, fifes, and trumpets were played, bells were rung but Bishop Oglethorpe again annoyed the Queen by elevating the host at Mass.

Ten days later, at the State Opening of Parliament, the Queen rudely ordered the abbot and monks of Westminster to extinguish their ceremonial tapers. 'Away with those torches', she snapped, 'we can see well enough.'

On February 9, the new government introduced a bill 'to restore the Supremacy of the Church of England to the Crown of the Realm'. An oath of supremacy was subsequently imposed on all ecclesiastical persons with loss of benefice the penalty for anyone who refused it.

On April 18, the Act of Uniformity was passed ordering the exclusive use of the 1552 Prayer Book and recognizing clerical marriages, though insisting that clergy wishing to marry must obtain the permission of their bishop, two justices of the peace and their bride's parents.

On May 30, the corpulent Bishop Bonner, whose cheeks were said by his enemies to be 'glutted with the flesh of martyrs', was thrown into the Marshalsea prison in Southwark, where he was to die ten years later.

On July 5, the Archbishop of York, Dr. Heath, was deprived of his see and committed to the Tower, but was soon released and permitted to live on his estate at Cobham in Surrey, where he was later to entertain the Queen more than once.

A week later, the abbot and monks of Westminster were again ejected from Westminster Abbey.

On July 26, Edmund Grindal, who had spent the previous reign in Strasbourg where he had listened to the lectures of Peter Martyr, was elected Bishop of London in place of the imprisoned Edmund Bonner. An ardent protestant, Grindal was said to entertain scruples as to the propriety of wearing episcopal attire.

On August 1, the election of the Queen's former tutor Matthew Parker as Archbishop of Canterbury took place. A shy scholarly man, he had spent the previous reign in hiding, changing his abode frequently and on one occasion falling off his horse while being pursued at night. He was to move into Lambeth Palace with his wife Margaret, who had borne him at least five children.

On September 28, the 85-year-old Bishop of Durham, Cuthbert Tunstall, who had remained loyal to the old religion, was deprived of his bishopric and placed in the custody of Archbishop Parker at Lambeth Palace, where two months later, on November 18, he died of exhaustion.

On December 21, Edwin Sandys, who had recently returned from Zurich and taken a second wife, was consecrated Bishop of Worcester. A zealous protestant, he was to embark on a visitation of his diocese 'before he was scarce warm in his seat'.

1560   The following June, the Rev. Bernard Gilpin, whose missionary journeys about his vast parish of Houghton-le-Spring, County Durham, had earned him the nickname 'Apostle of the North', entertained Sir William Cecil at his rectory.

A few weeks later, on July 29, Queen Elizabeth dined with Archbishop Parker at Lambeth Palace. It may have been on this occasion that the Queen, who still felt unhappy about clerical marriages, made her famous farewell remark to Mrs. Parker. 'Madam I may not call you. Mistress I am ashamed to call you, so I know not what to call you, but yet I do thank you.'

On August 8, the Dean of St. Paul's, William May, was elected Archbishop of York but, alas, he died the same day.

In November, Archbishop Parker complained to the Bishop of London, Edmund Grindal, that many of the clergy in his diocese were neither priests nor deacons and laymen had even been made prebendaries.

1561   On June 4, 1561, the spire of the eleventh-century St. Paul's Cathedral – 489 feet high and made of lead-sheathed wood – was struck by lightning. The building caught fire and the roof fell in.

Following this disaster, the new Dean of St. Paul's, Alexander Nowell, preached a sermon before the Lord Mayor which caused the City to take immediate steps to restore the damage. The Bishop of London's suggestion that lead should be taken from the nearby church of St. Bartholomew to repair the cathedral was, however, rejected.

On July 25, the Rev. Richard Bruherne, who had recently resigned his professorship at Oxford after being found guilty of gross immorality, was elected Provost of Eton. The Queen overruled the election, however, insisting on the appointment of the Rev. William Day, who was soon accused of cutting down the number of college chaplains and surrendering college plate.

1562   On January 1, 1562, the Dean of St. Paul's, Dr. Nowell, incurred the Queen's wrath when he put in her place at the cathedral a richly-bound prayer book containing pictures of the saints and martyrs. The Queen ordered the verger to remove the offending volume and after the service visited the Dean in his vestry and scolded him for having ignored her recent proclamation against 'pictures, images and Romish relics'.

Later that year, Dr. Nowell acquired the additional living of Much Hadham in Hertfordshire, where he was to spend much of his leisure time fishing in the River Ash. It was said that he refreshed himself with picnic lunches and unwittingly invented the idea of bottled beer.

1563   On February 13, 1563, the Lower House of Convocation considered a resolution demanding the total abolition of church organs. It was defeated by only one vote.

The same year, the Dean and Chapter of Worcester were accused of breaking up the large cathedral organ, which had cost £200. It was said that the pipes had been melted down to make plates for the wives of the prebendaries and the wooden case made into beds.

This year also saw the first appearance of the Rev. John Foxe's *Book of Martyrs*. The book was an instant success and its author, in spite of his objection to wearing the surplice, was given a prebend in Salisbury Cathedral together with the vicarage of the nearby village of Shipton.

1564   In Lent, 1564, the Dean of St. Paul's again clashed with the Queen. While Dr. Nowell was preaching slightly about the crucifix, the Queen called out from her seat, 'To your text, Mr. Dean. Leave that – we have heard enough of that.' The Dean was shattered by this interruption and unable to continue his sermon. He was taken home and later confronted by Archbishop Parker himself.

Some nine months later, on All Saints eve, a confrontation took place between the Rev. Melchior Smith, Vicar of Hessle in Yorkshire, and a seaman named Nicholas Laborn. Mr. Smith grabbed the man's beard and punched him in the face.

1565   In 1565, at Whitsuntide, Trinity Sunday and over the July Assizes.

Archbishop and Mrs. Parker provided lavish hospitality for the principal clergy and laity at their palace at Canterbury.

1566   On January 25, the following year, the Queen wrote to the Primate expressing her disquiet about the 'growing diversity of opinion' and scolding him for doing so little about the 'dangerous preaching abuse'. Parker responded by issuing, two months later, a set of 'Advertisements' designed to secure conformity by ordering, for example, the use of copes in cathedrals and surplices in parish churches.

Among those who refused to obey these 'Advertisements' was the puritanical Dean of Christ Church, Thomas Sampson. On his refusal to wear the square cap he was deprived of his deanery and placed in confinement.

Another consequence of this legislation was the arrival at Lambeth Palace of a party of 100 furious London clergymen. They were told by the Primate 'Be brief, make no words' and thirty-seven of them were instantly suspended and threatened with deprivation.

1567   In the spring of 1567, the fifty-year-old Dean of Gloucester, Dr. John Man, was sent to Spain as English ambassador. He was to outrage the Spaniards because he was married and was not a gentleman. He was sent home in disgrace.

Meanwhile, scandal had also been attached to the Rev. John Birkbie, Rector of Moor Monkton in Yorkshire, who was said to lead a very dissolute life and dress indecently in breeches of silk and taffeta and ruffles of gold lace. He was also accused of being a fornicator and drunkard and dancing offensively in ale houses.

1568   In 1568, the former Abbess of Tarrant in Dorset, a cousin of the Earl of Bedford, died leaving money, plate, jewels, silk gowns, velvet bonnets and a scarlet petticoat.

The same year, the death occurred of the Rev. Roger Ascham, a favourite of the Queen, an author and all-round sportsman, who in recent years had taken pleasure in cock-fighting. The Dean of St. Paul's preached at his funeral service and the Queen stated that she would 'rather have thrown £10,000 into the sea than have lost her Ascham'.

1569   In November 1569, Catholic rebels mustered under the Earls of Westmoreland and Northumberland. Their first step was to enter Durham Cathedral, tear up the Bible and other books, cast down the Communion table and restore the Mass. The insurgence failed to win popular support, however, and fizzled out with the Battle of Bramham Moor and some 600 people being hanged.

1570   On January 25, 1570, Robert Parsons, Gentleman of the Chapel Royal and a leading composer of church music, was drowned in the River Trent.

A few weeks later, on Easter Tuesday, the puritanical Rev. Thomas Drant, Archdeacon of Lewes, preached at St. Mary Spital denouncing the sensuality of the citizens of London.

In April, the Bishop of London, Edmund Grindal, was translated to the see of York. He was replaced at Fulham Palace by Edwin Sandys, who was to protest in a sermon at Paul's Cross that he was utterly unfit for 'an office full of danger and peril' and wishing, instead, for rest for his 'wearish body, full of diseases – and almost worn away like a clout'.

In May, the Papal Bull 'Regnans', excommunicating the Queen and absolving her subjects from allegiance, was secretly nailed to the door of the Bishop of London's house beside St. Paul's Cathedral.

On August 17, Mrs. Parker, wife of the Archbishop of Canterbury, died in London. Her remains were interred in the Duke of Norfolk's chapel at Lambeth Palace and her husband sank into a severe depression.

Meanwhile, the charitable and saintly Rev. Bernard Gilpin had spent £300 on improvements to his rectory at Houghton-le-Spring in County Durham. It was now large enough for him to give dinner every Sunday between Michaelmas and Easter to anyone who cared to call.

1571 In May 1571, the new Archbishop of York, Dr. Grindal, issued a set of Injunctions forbidding popish practices, such as the ringing of bells for a superstitious purpose and advising unmarried clergy of his diocese 'not to keep in your house any woman under three-score years' unless she happened to be a close relation, such as mother or niece.

Three months later, an Exeter clergyman named Blackall did penance at Paul's Cross for his scandalous life. It was said that he had four wives all alive and had moved from town to town, changing his name and frequently accompanied by strumpets. On August 10, the disreputable man was set in the pillory at Cheapside for forging a commission to preach from the Archbishop of Canterbury.

1572 On Easter Tuesday, 1572, the Rev. Thomas Drant, Archdeacon of Lewes, preached at St. Mary Spital on almsgiving.

A few weeks later, John Leslie, Bishop of Ross and ambassador for Mary Queen of Scots, was placed in the custody of the Bishop of Winchester, Dr. Horne, at Farnham Castle. Dr. Horne protested at this imposition and described his prisoner as a 'devil'.

Later this year, the St. Bartholomew's Day massacre of French protestants shocked Europe. In England, there were immediate demands for revenge. The Bishop of London, Dr. Sandys, told the Queen to 'forthwith cut off the Scottish Queen's head' and Archbishop Parker gave the same advice in more circuitous words. Staider bishops poured out their fears to the Lord Treasurer Burghley.

Meanwhile, Archbishop Parker, who was said to venerate the past, had published a massive volume entitled *De Antiquitate Ecclesiae* emphasizing the Primate's ancient rights over his suffragans. In particular, it stated his rights to the Bishops' seals and second-best rings on their deaths. It also claimed that the executors of the Bishop of Rochester must furnish him with a silver

1573 cup and hunting dogs. On May 9, 1573, a de luxe volume of this book, decorated with illuminated coats of episcopal arms, was presented to the Lord Treasurer Burghley.

In September this year, the ailing Archbishop received a visit at Canterbury from Queen Elizabeth and her courtiers. The Primate used this occasion to present his royal guest with a massive gold salt cellar valued at over 200 marks.

1574 The following year, Robert White, master of the choristers at Westminster Abbey, his wife and three daughters died of the plague. They were all buried in the churchyard of St. Margaret's, Westminster.

1575 On March 10, 1575, the Queen visited the Mortlake home of Dr. John Dee, a leading astrologer who had been given the livings of Upton and Long

Leadenham, though he was not in fact in holy orders and was even suspected by his enemies of dabbling in the black arts. The Queen was evidently well pleased with him because she signified shortly after this visit that Dr. Dee should hold his two livings for life.

Two months later, on May 17, Archbishop Parker died of what he had described as 'rheumatic tempis'. He was buried in the private chapel at Lambeth built by his predecessor, Boniface, in the thirteenth century and, a large monument was erected inscribed with Latin elegiacs. In his will, he is said to have left Dr. Sandys, Bishop of London, his walking stick.

On June 20, there was an encounter between the Rev. Mr. Lammynge, Rector of Caenby in Lincolnshire, and a local fishmonger named Henry Cooke. Calling the Rector 'a fool, a doltish fool, a doty-pole priest and a knave priest' the shopkeeper struck him across the face with a staff.

Meanwhile, a bell foundry had been opened in Whitechapel Road which was soon to supply bells for many London churches, including Westminster Abbey.*

1576   Early in 1576, Edmund Grindal, staunchly protestant Archbishop of York, was enthroned as Archbishop of Canterbury. A clean-living bachelor, he had been considered more suitable for the post than the other main contender Dr. Cox, Bishop of Ely, whom the Queen had recently threatened to 'unfrock', for resisting her demands on Ely House in Holborn which she wanted for her favourite, Sir Christopher Hatton.

On May 26, the Rector of Sherington, Buckinghamshire, was accused of immorality on the highway.

Before the end of the year, the Queen had clashed with her new Primate over his refusal to prohibit 'prophesyings' – meetings of moderate puritan clergy to discuss the scriptures which somewhat undermined the authority of the bishops. On December 20, Grindal wrote boldly to the Queen saying, 'Bear with me, I beseech you, Madam, if I choose rather to offend your earthly majesty than to offend against the heavenly majesty of God.'

1577   The following March, Dr. John Aylmer was consecrated Bishop of London amidst a quarrel with his predecessor Edwin Sandys over the question of revenues to the see and dilapidations. A believer in a sort of patriotic messianism – he is attributed with the saying 'God is English' – Dr. Aylmer was to rule the diocese with great severity.

In May, the Queen issued letters to all the bishops ordering them to put down 'prophesyings' in their dioceses. On his refusal to comply with these orders, the Archbishop of Canterbury was suspended for six months and there was talk of possible deprivation. Dr. Yale, the Vicar-General, was appointed to act on his behalf and Grindal was only permitted to discharge spiritual functions, the prestige of his office now much diminished.

1578   A year later, on May 31, 1578, Eton scholar the Rev. Robert Wolfall, Vicar of Westharptree in Somerset, abandoned his wife and children to accompany explorer Martin Frobisher as official chaplain on a voyage in search of the North-West Passage. He was to conduct Holy Communion several times inside the Arctic Circle.

* The Whitechapel Bell Foundry is still in existence and operates on almost the same site. Telegraphic address CHIMINGS LONDON.

Three months later, on August 24, the Rev. John Stockwood, stern moralist and headmaster of Tunbridge Grammar School delivered a stinging attack on the contemporary theatre from the pulpit at Paul's Cross. He branded plays and players as immoral, wasteful and sabbath-breaking.

1579 On May 10, 1579, the same man preached at the same place on the Christian Ministry and deplored the scarcity of 'faithful and painful labourers'. In a long, violent and repetitive sermon, Mr. Stockwood exhorted his listeners to go to church rather than attend filthy plays.

Ten days later, Norfolk ploughman Mathew Hamont had his ears cut off and was then burnt to death after being charged in the Consistory Court with 'denying Christ' by the Bishop of Norwich, Edmund Freake.

Shortly afterwards, on May 31, Marmaduke Middleton, who had left Oxford without a degree, was created Bishop of Waterford and Lismore. He was soon to be charged with being 'a man of bad life' and plundering his own cathedral.

1580 The following February the eighty-year-old Bishop of Ely, Dr. Cox, who had now been accused with his wife of covetous and corrupt practices, was obliged to resign his see. The Queen, who had already obtained the spacious Ely House at Holborn, for her favourite Hatton, was to keep the see vacant for the next nineteen years and pocket its revenues for herself.

Four months later, on June 1, John Horne, Bishop of Winchester, who was said to be dwarfish and deformed, died at Winchester House, Southwark. Following his death, his goods were seized on account of his debts to the Crown.

Queen Elizabeth I, who detested excessive religious zeal and liked to be known as the Supreme Governor of the Church of England

Later that month, the Anglican church was threatened by the arrival of Jesuit missionaries Robert Parsons and Edmund Campion on a soul saving mission intent on winning people back to the Old Faith.

Meanwhile, the Rev. Mr. Levitt, Vicar of Leaden Roding, in Essex, had been branded a swearer, dicer, carder, hawker, hunter and 'very careless person'. It was said that he had had a fight with a local parson at an inn at Chelmsford.

1581   In May 1581, a disgraceful plot was perpetrated against the Archbishop of York, Dr. Sandys, when a woman was smuggled into his bedroom by Sir Robert Stapleton, who was anxious to blackmail the Archbishop into giving him an advantageous lease of lands. The plot was disclosed to the Council and the conspirators punished.

Meanwhile, parliament had passed more stringent rules for the punishment of Roman Catholics, the penalty for concealing a Catholic priest or tutor, for example, being a year's imprisonment. In the anti-Catholic holocaust that followed a certain Lady Neville was frightened to death at Holborn while, at York, a certain Mrs. Vavasour was 'deprived of her reason'.

In November, Edmund Campion and twelve others were put on trial accused of a plot to murder the Queen and overthrow church and state. On December 1, Campion and other Catholic divines were executed at Tyburn, after first being savagely treated on the rack.

1583   Some fourteen months later, on March 4, 1583, the saintly and hospitable

Queen Elizabeth's favourite Archbishop, John Whitgift. A man of considerable private means, he was to restore much feudal magnificence to the Primacy. He also found time for sporting activities, killing twenty-eight bucks on a single outing in Lord Cobham's park

Rev. Bernard Gilpin, Rector of Houghton-le-Spring, died after being knocked down and fatally injured by a runaway ox in Durham market.

Four months later, on July 6, Archbishop Grindal, disgraced and suffering from a cataract on both eyes, died at his house at Croydon. He was buried in the local church and left gifts to the Queen and plate to Pembroke College, Cambridge and Queen's College, Oxford.

Five weeks later, on August 14, John Whitgift, Bishop of Worcester, was nominated the new Archbishop of Canterbury. A wealthy bachelor, he was to restore feudal magnificence to the Primacy and also establish an intimate relationship with the Queen, who was playfully to call him her 'little black husband' and confide in him 'the very secrets of her soul'.

At the end of the year, Archbishop Whitgift preached at Paul's Cross on the Royal Supremacy and obedience to those in authority. Taking the text 'Railers shall not inherit the kingdom of heaven', he stated that there were three types of people prone to disobedience: 'papists, anabaptists and our wayward and conceited persons'.

1584   The following year, Whitgift issued a stringent list of twenty-four articles, which any clergyman suspected of not conforming was required to answer on oath and which were to be administered by the Court of High Commission, whose powers were extended to punish heretics and schismatics. Some three or four hundred clergymen refused to subscribe and there were many suspensions. Among those to protest was a deputation of Kentish ministers who descended upon the Archbishop at Lambeth uninvited. Whitgift received them politely but suddenly lost his temper and shouted down an interrupter with the words, 'Thou boy, beardless boy, yesterday bird, new out of shell!'

This controversy was still raging when on September 27, 1584, Thomas Watson, deprived Bishop of Lincoln, died at Wisbech Castle, where he had been imprisoned since the beginning of the reign.

A month later, on October 27, the Rev. Samuel Harsnett preached at Paul's Cross against the Calvinistic doctrine of predestination. He was immediately denounced as a papist and commanded by Archbishop Whitgift to 'preach no more'.

1585   Early in 1585, the appointment of the Rev. Richard Hooker as Master of the Temple caused violent scenes at the Temple Church where Hooker's moderate puritan views were repeatedly denounced by the fanatical afternoon-lecturer Walter Travers.

1586   In the summer of 1586, the Archbishop of York, Edwin Sandys, conducted prayers at Paul's Cross for the Queen's safety following the failure of the Babington plot to raise a rebellion in favour of Mary Queen of Scots. 'Thou knowest, O Lord, that she hath not deserved this treachery at their hands, being most mild and merciful doing good unto all, hurting no one.'

That winter saw the arrest of puritans John Greenwood and Henry Barrow. On November 27, Barrow underwent a lengthy examination by a synod of bishops and deans at Lambeth Palace, during which Archbishop Whitgift lost his temper. 'Where is his keeper?' shouted the Primate. 'You shall not prattle here! Away with him! Clap him up close, close!' Barrow and Greenwood were then moved to the Fleet prison.

1587   On February 8, 1587, Mary Queen of Scots was executed at Fotheringay

Castle. She was attended on the scaffold by Dr. Fletcher, Dean of Peterborough, who harangued her mercilessly, ending with the words, 'So perish all the Queen's enemies!' Her body was later taken to Peterborough, where it was met by a convoy of ecclesiastics and lodged temporarily in the thirteenth-century bishop's palace. On August 2, there was a burial service in Peterborough Cathedral, which was hung with black braid for the occasion. The Bishop of Lincoln, William Wykeham, preached a sermon in which he tried to gloss over the circumstances in which the Scottish Queen had died. After this service, ecclesiastics and courtiers joined in an elaborate and festive banquet at the bishop's palace, incurring heavy pantry and buttery charges.

1588   The following year, shortly after Michaelmas, a series of anonymous pamphlets began to appear on the London streets aiming to make the episcopacy look ridiculous. Satirical and scurrilous, the bishops were described in these tracts as 'swinish rabble' and the Primate himself as 'the Beelzebub of Canterbury'. Bishop Cooper of Winchester issued a ponderous refutation entitled *Admonition to the People of England*, while Dr. Robert Some, chaplain to the Earl of Leicester and famous for his fooleries, answered them in kind.

In August 1588, Alexander Nowell, eighty-year-old Dean of St. Paul's, preached a sermon of thanksgiving at Paul's Cross following the defeat of the Spanish Armada. Three weeks later, he preached again on the same subject and the Spanish flags were displayed to his audience. Some thirteen naval chaplains had taken part in this successful operation.

Meanwhile, the Queen had taken vengeance on the Papists and a vigorous search was organized for concealed Catholic priests. In all, some sixty clergymen were to be put to death.

1589   On February 9, 1589, the Rev. Richard Bancroft, Canon of Westminster and right-hand man to the Archbishop of Canterbury, preached a sermon at Paul's Cross in which he described the episcopacy as near divine and condemned the puritans as false prophets.

The same year saw the downfall of the new Bishop of St. David's, the already notorious Marmaduke Middleton, who was now accused of having two wives, publishing a forged will, attempting to settle episcopal land on his son, misusing a charity and speaking disrespectfully of the Queen. After being fined by the Court of Star Chamber, the Bishop was handed over to the High Commissioners, who formally degraded him by divesting him of his episcopal robes and priestly vestments in a ceremony in Lambeth Palace.

Meanwhile, the Rev. Anthony Hoggett, puritanical incumbent of Northill, Bedfordshire, had sold his church's organ for forty shillings.

1590   On September 1, 1590, puritan minister Thomas Cartwright, who had been deprived of his fellowship of Trinity College, Cambridge, for pointing out defects in the church, was summoned before the Court of High Commission and committed to the Fleet prison.

1591   In February, 1591, puritan minister John Udal was condemned to death at Southwark Assizes for publishing, anonymously, a book called *A Demonstration of Discipline*, in which he had denounced bishops, lord bishops and other governors of the Church of England. He was to thwart the executioner by dying in prison before the sentence was carried out.

Three months later, the trials of fellow puritans Barrow and Greenwood, now in their fourth year of custody, were transferred to the Court of High Chamber. The use of corporal punishment was now contemplated to force them into conformity.

1592 In November, 1592, the Bishop of Bristol, Dr. Richard Fletcher, who had attended Mary Queen of Scots on the scaffold, laid claim in his capacity of High Almoner to the goods and chattels of wealthy goldsmith Nicholas Herrick, who had committed suicide. The matter was referred to arbitration and the self-seeking Bishop had to content himself with £220 out of an estate worth £5,000.

On Boxing Day, 1592, the three witches of Worboys, who were charged with, among other things, bewitching Lady Cromwell and members of the Throckmorton family, appeared before the Bishop of Lincoln at Buckden Palace, his ancient seat in Huntingdonshire. They were later passed on to the local Assizes where death sentences were pronounced.

1593 On March 22, 1593, John Penry, fugitive author of the Marprelate Tracts, was arrested after being spotted by the Vicar of Stepney and thrown into the Poultry Compter where he continued to denounce the episcopy in the strongest possible language.

Within the next few weeks, Penry, Barrow and Greenwood were all hanged and puritanism was for a time driven underground.

In September this year, the Rev. Adam Hill, Prebendary of Salisbury, delivered a broadside attack on sin from the pulpit at Paul's Cross. In his sermon he attacked the idolatry of the papists, blasphemy, swearing, the profanation of the sabbath, murder, sodomy, whoredom, the oppression of the poor, rebellion, atheism, pride in apparel, idleness, sacrilege, drunkenness, the corruption of magistrates, seditious talk, simony and covetousness. The sermon ended with a cry for repentance.

1594 The following spring, Dr. John Dove of Christ Church, Oxford, preached at the same spot on the Second Coming of Christ.

On Easter Eve, the Rev. Mr. Knight, Rector of Worlingham in Suffolk, struck a parishioner in his churchyard, drawing blood. He was subsequently excommunicated for this action.

1595 On June 11, 1595, the Eton-educated Bishop of Winchester, William Wykeham, died at his eleventh-century palace on the Thames at Southwark which had its own wharf and landing place known as the Bishop of Winchester's stairs.

In July, the Rev. Richard Hooker, whose massive eight-volume work in defence of Anglicanism, *Ecclesiastical Polity*, had now begun to be published, was presented with the Crown living of Bishopsbourne near Canterbury. Here, he was to receive admiring visitors, dressed in a coarse gown or canonical coat.

The same month, Dr. William Chaderton was enthroned as Bishop of Lincoln. He was to complain that the revenues of his see had been much impoverished and he was to allow Buckden Palace, the scene of the trial of the witches of Worboys three years earlier, to fall into decay.

In November, the Rev. William Day, scandalous provost of Eton, paid £1,000 to obtain the vacant see of Winchester but he was to die after only eight months' possession of his honours.

Meanwhile, the Rev. Nicholas Bound, Rector of Norton in Suffolk, had published *The True Doctrine of the Sabbath*, which demanded that Sunday activities should be confined to church-going, bible-study and visits to the sick. Feasting should not be permitted on Sundays except for 'noblemen and great personages'.

1596   In February, 1596, twelve-year-old Orlando Gibbons entered the choir of King's College, Cambridge, and soon became its chief chorister.

Four months later, on June 15, the self-seeking Richard Fletcher, now Bishop of London, died while smoking a pipe.

The same month, the Rev. William Alabaster accompanied the Earl of Essex on his expedition against Cadiz. While in Spain, Alabaster was to be converted to Romanism and he was placed in the Tower of London on his return to the country. He was later reconverted to Anglicanism and was appointed a prebendary of St. Paul's and Rector of Therfield in Hertfordshire.

Meanwhile, the Bishop of St. David's, Anthony Rudd, had ruined his chances of promotion by including in a sermon preached before the Queen a tactless reference to her age and wrinkles and the approach of death.

1597   The following year, there were disorderly scenes in the churches of Suffolk and Norfolk. It was said that drunkenness, gambling, swearing and immorality were rife among the clergy. At Cantley, the Rector William Phillips was often 'overtaken by drink', at Aldeburgh, the Rev. Paul Berbeck had allowed his chancel to become 'utterly ruinated', and at Blythburgh, a certain Mary Knights had brought mastiffs into the church, preventing other parishioners from worshipping.

1598   On February 15, 1598, the Bishop of Carlisle died of the plague. His body was quickly taken from his episcopal seat, Rose Castle, and buried in Carlisle the same day.

Nine months later, on Novembr 12, William Cotton was consecrated Bishop of Exeter, where he was to be remembered for his kindness to the cathedral's cat, arranging that money should be put aside for it and special holes should be made in the cathedral's doors to give the animal access to different parts of the building.

Meanwhile, the Rev. William Lee of Calverton in Nottinghamshire had presented the Queen with a pair of silk stockings made on his newly invented stocking-loom. The Queen had refused to give her approval of this machine on the grounds that it would discourage hand-knitters and Mr. Lee went abroad to die of grief and disappointment.

1599   On May 26, 1599, the Rev. John Darrel, who had claimed to be able to cast out devils and evil spirits, was examined at Lambeth Palace and found to be an impostor. He was henceforth degraded from the ministry and imprisoned in the Gate House prison in Westminster.

Two months later, there was a public dispute between Dr. Some, Master of Peterhouse and Dr. John Overall, regius professor of divinity, on the thorny subject of Christ's descent in to hell.

1600   On November 2, 1600, the Rev. Richard Hooker died at Bishopsbourne near Canterbury 'meditating on the number and nature of the angels'. Within days of his death, instructions were issued that his manuscripts were to be kept out of the clutches of his ignorant relatives.

1601   Two months later in January 1601, the aged Archbishop Whitgift sent out an army of forty horsemen and forty footmen to protect the Court and apprehend the rebellious Earl of Essex. This arrest was soon effected and the Earl was conducted to Lambeth Palace, where he spent the night. The following day he was sent to the Tower where a few weeks later he was executed.

On February 13, the ninety-five-year-old Dean of St. Paul's and keen amateur fisherman Dr. Alexander Nowell, died in London.

1602   Some fifteen months later, on May 16, 1602, the Rev. Mr. Sanders preached at Paul's Cross on the subject of riches. 'God made some rich and some poor', he explained, 'that two excellent virtues might flourish in the world: charity in the rich and patience in the poor.'

The same year, adventurer George Waymouth's attempt to find the North-West Passage had to be abandoned at Labrador when the chaplain, the Rev. John Cartwright, led a mutiny on board one of his ships.

At the end of the year, the Queen's strength began to desert her and the elderly Archbishop of Canterbury, Dr. Whitgift, was soon in constant attendance at the royal palace at Richmond. On March 24, 1603, the Primate remained in a kneeling position, conducting long fervent prayers, as the Queen finally breathed her last.

1603

THE EARLY STUARTS

1603–1642

Within weeks of the accession of James I, the religious tensions driven underground by Elizabeth had come out into the open. From the pulpit at Paul's Cross and elsewhere, a brilliant new generation of preachers of varying sympathies hurled abuse at each other and the seeds of the future revolution were sown. In 1611, King James, mainly concerned with preserving the Royal Supremacy, attempted to placate the puritans by appointing one of their number, George Abbot, Archbishop of Canterbury. He was soon in disgrace however – after a terrible hunting accident on July 24, 1621 – and before the end of the reign the High Church William Laud had emerged as the most powerful figure in the Church of England. During the following reign, Laud worked closely with King Charles in imposing a new order on the Church, suppressing parliament, silencing the puritans and using the Court of High Commission to inflict savage and degrading penalties on anyone, rich or poor, who stood in his way. Not surprisingly, thousands fled abroad to escape 'the prelate's rage' and establish new colonies where they could worship in peace. The period ended with the mob howling against the bishops in Palace Yard, the bishops quarrelling among themselves, the arrest of Laud and the flight of the King from London.

1603   On April 5, 1603, King James I began his slow journey south. En route, he paused to hear sermons from the Bishop of Durham in Durham Cathedral, from the Bishop of Limerick at York Minster and from the Bishop of Lincoln in the chapel of Burghley House. Finally approaching London, he was greeted in person at Theobalds by the aged Archbishop of Canterbury, Dr. Whitgift.

One of the King's first moves was to instruct the rebellious Sir Walter Ralegh to vacate Durham House in the Strand, which he had occupied for the past twenty years, and return it to Toby Matthew, Bishop of Durham, a jovial man who was said to enjoy the King's salty sense of humour.

On July 25, Westminster Abbey was hung with tapestries and banners and the Lord Mayor was in crimson velvet for the coronation of the new monarch.

Eleven days later, on August 5, the King ordered morning and evening prayers and sermons to drive away the plague, which was currently seizing several hundred victims a week.

The same week saw the arrest of the Rev. William Watson, following the failure of a far-fetched plot to seize the Tower of London, capture the King and install himself as Lord Chancellor. This eccentric parson, who, according to one historian, had such an appalling squint that he appeared to be looking nine ways at once, was executed before the end of the year.

1604   On January 14, 1604, a conference was convened at Hampton Court to give the puritans a chance to discuss the reformation of the church with the bishops. Archbishop Whitgift attended but the chief conduct of the conference was in the hands of Richard Bancroft, Bishop of London. It was to prove a triumph for the High Church party, and the King boasted afterwards that he had 'peppered the dissenters soundly' and Bishop Bancroft flung himself on his knees declaring that his heart melted with joy.

The following month, Archbishop Whitgift caught cold while travelling on his barge up the Thames for a consultation with the Bishop of London at Fulham Palace. A few days later he was stricken with paralysis at a dinner at Whitehall and soon became speechless, only able to ejaculate the words 'Ecclesia Dei'. On February 29, he died at Lambeth Palace.

On March 21, Orlando Gibbons was appointed organist of the Chapel Royal.

The previous day, the Convocation of the clergy of the diocese of Canterbury had assembled under the leadership of Richard Bancroft, soon to be nominated the new Primate. They were to inaugurate a sweeping reconstruction of the church and prepare a set of 141 canons. The clergy were commanded to use the Prayer Book, wear the surplice and hood and a new translation of the Bible was commissioned. Canon 74 laid down strict rules about the sleeves of gowns. Permissible variations ranged from straight sleeves slightly puffed at the shoulders to pudding sleeves where the wrist band was pushed slightly up the arm.

Before the end of the year, several hundred clerics had been harassed and victimized for refusing to obey these canons. In the diocese of Lincoln for example ninety-three clergy had refused to wear the surplice. The Rev. Thomas Wooll, Vicar of Boston, had his surplice made into a cushion. The deprivations that followed met with vigorous opposition. At Northampton, the deprived Vicar, Mr. Catlyn, locked the door of his pulpit and took away the key.

Meanwhile, bells were coming back into fashion despite puritan criticism and at Shillington in Bedfordshire over £48 had recently been spent on repairs and recastings of the church bells.

1605   The following year, the Rev. Gabriel Powel, domestic chaplain to the new Bishop of London, Dr. Vaughan, and Rector of a sinecure parish in Montgomeryshire produced a large Latin tome, which included over 400 pages of notes on the Antichrist.

On November 5, 1605, a papist plot to annihilate the King and Parliament was foiled when Guy Fawkes was discovered in a corner of the cellar of the parliament house armed with three matches, coal and firewood. Early the following year, the conspirators were put to death in a brutal manner in St. Paul's churchyard.

1606   Meanwhile, puritan feeling against the establishment was also increasing and, in November 1606, Scottish presbyterian Andrew Melville grabbed Archbishop Bancroft by his robes at a Privy Council meeting, describing them as 'Romish rags and part of the beast's mark' and at the same time

Paul's Cross beside the old St. Paul's Cathedral: a famous debating place from medieval times up to the Civil War. Among churchmen who held forth from the outdoor pulpit here were Thomas Cranmer, William Laud and John Donne

35

calling King James 'God's silly vassal'. He was promptly thrown into the Tower.

1607   A year later, on November 5, 1607, Martin Fotherby, Archdeacon of Canterbury, preached at Paul's Cross on the second anniversary of the discovery of the Gunpowder Plot. 'The dew of God's blessing has fallen on our land, when all our neighbour countries have been destitute of it', he declared.

The same year, the churchwardens of St. Mary's, Colchester, had been obliged to sell two bells to pay for repairs to their church's roof.

1608   The following year, work began on a fine fan vault to the nave of Bath Abbey, the Bishop of Bath and Wells, Dr. Montagu, contributing £1,000 towards the cost.

On December 8, 1608, the Rev. William Wheatlie preached at Paul's Cross on covetousness, which he described as 'the dropsie of the mind, an horse-leach humour after wealth'. He concluded his sermon by ordering the congregation to 'go home and purge'.

1609   The following May, the Rev. Daniel Price, chaplain to the young Prince Henry, held forth at the spot on the evil state of the world, which he described as 'a dry, heathy, thorny, bare, barren wilderness wherein Satan the serpent doth inhabit'.

A month later, on June 25, Dr. Lancelot Dawes, Fellow of Queen's College, Oxford, preached at the same place on the abominations of Rome and the sins of the English Catholics – 'the very scum and excrement of the land'.

On September 3, the Rev. Robert Johnson, chaplain to the Bishop of Lincoln, preached, again at Paul's Cross, on the sins of the puritans who, he said, 'wring the scriptures as a nose of wax'.

At the end of the year, the Rev. Charles Butler, Vicar of Wotton St. Lawrence in Hampshire, produced a best-selling book on bees, *The Feminine Monarchy*. Mr. Butler, later known as 'the father of British bee-keeping', warned his more slovenly parishioners that his bees would sting them. 'Thou must be chaste, cleanly, sweet, sober, quiet and familiar', he ordered.

1610   At the end of the following year, Archbishop Bancroft died at Lambeth Palace after suffering from a painful gallstone for many years. A lover of fine books and manuscripts, he bequeathed his great library to his successors on the strict condition that it should never be split up.

1611   The following March, George Abbot, Bishop of London and a popular figure among the puritans, was appointed new Archbishop of Canterbury. The King advised him to dispense generous hospitality at Lambeth Palace to secure the favour of the Court and Council.

Meanwhile, the new and magnificent Authorized Version of the Bible was ready to appear. The work of a large body of scholars, it included a fulsome dedication to 'the most high and mighty prince' King James and was marked 'Appointed to be read in churches'. It sold at thirty shillings a copy.

1612   The death of the eighteen-year-old Prince of Wales on November 6 the following year was interpreted by Roman Catholics as a punishment to the royal family for the persecution of their church. In a two hour funeral sermon, Archbishop Abbot dwelt on 'the fragility of human life and hopes'.

1613   On January 29, 1613, the Primate gave a lavish banquet to celebrate the

36

The unfortunate George Abbot, whose career as Archbishop of Canterbury went into a decline when he accidentally killed a game-keeper while out hunting

engagement of the King's daughter Elizabeth to the Elector Palatine Frederick V.

Eight months later, Abbot clashed with the King by declining to support the Countess of Essex's divorce petition. The matter was then referred to a commission of bishops and lawyers, who overruled the Archbishop and pronounced for the nullity of the marriage. Abbot stuck to his guns, however, drawing up a paper describing the evils of divorce, for the King's benefit.

Meanwhile, a handsome new organ had been installed in Worcester Cathedral at great expense. It was a two manual instrument, designed by the cathedral organist Thomas Tomkins and constructed by Thomas Dallam.

1614 On May 24, 1614, the Bishop of Lichfield and Coventry, Dr. Neile, made an emotional speech in the House of Lords in which he viciously attacked the House of Commons and declared for the Royal Prerogative. He later apologized for these tactless remarks in tears.

Four weeks later, the Rev. Lionel Sharp, Eton-educated royal chaplain, was committed to the Tower of London for trying to stir up trouble between the English and Scottish factions at court.

In August this year, Archbishop Abbot was responsible for the meeting between the King and the handsome George Villiers, who early the following year was appointed a Gentleman of the Bedchamber and was to become one of the most notorious favourites in European history.

1615 On January 23, 1615, poet and former man-about-town John Donne, who had been repeatedly thwarted in his attempts to find state employment, was ordained a priest at a ceremony in St. Paul's Cathedral.

Five months later, on June 2, the Rev. William Worship, Vicar of Croft in Lincolnshire, preached at Paul's Cross on the theme that 'all men are dogs without Christ but there are dogs within the circuit of the church which annoy her'.

1616   A year later, on June 19, 1616, the Bishop of Carlisle, Dr. Robinson, died of the plague at his episcopal seat, Rose Castle. A prelate 'of great gravity and temperance', he left both plate and linen to Queen's College, Oxford.

Six months later, on December 8, puritan Lewis Bayly, author of the best-selling *Practice of Piety*, was consecrated Bishop of Bangor.

1617   On January 5 the following year, the Rev. Immanuel Bourne, energetic preacher at St. Christopher's, London, exhorted his congregation at Paul's Cross in the following words: 'Get ye to the bible, that most wholesome remedy for the soul.'

The same month, the Bishop of Chichester, Dr. Harsnett, ordered the removal of Thomas Weelkes, organist at Chichester Cathedral and one of the greatest of the English madrigalists, on the grounds that he was 'a common drunkard and notorious swearer and blasphemer'.

On March 15, King James set off on a leisurely journey north to inspect his Scottish kingdom. His vast retinue included the Bishop of Ely, Lancelot Andrewes the Bishop of Winchester, Dr. Montagu, and the newly-appointed Dean of Gloucester, Dr. William Laud. During the journey, the great procession paused at Bishopthorpe Palace on the River Ouse, where the King was entertained by his old friend Toby Matthew, now Archbishop of York.

On October 9, Bishop Neile was translated to the see of Durham. He was to repair the palaces of the see and dispense great hospitality at Durham House in the Strand, providing a home there for many visiting churchmen.

A more minor event this year was the appearance before a Church Court at Hawton in Nottinghamshire of a Mr. Thomas Tailer, who was accused of 'misbehaviour' with his dog during divine service.

1618   The following May, the death occurred of the tobacco-hating Dean of Windsor, Dr. Maxey, who had recently made an unsuccessful bid for the see of Norwich. A few months earlier, this worldly man had instructed composer Orlando Gibbons to set to music his funeral text 'Behold thou has made my days' scored for counter-tenor solo, five part choir and instrumental accompaniment.

The same month, King James issued his Declaration of Sports. To the distress of puritans in general and Archbishop Abbot in particular, the King declared that recreations such as dancing, archery, leaping and vaulting were lawful Sunday activities. Following this declaration, the puritanical Rev. Gerard Prior, Vicar of Elsfield, Oxfordshire, was suspended by his bishop after praying that the King 'might be turned from profaneness, vanity and popery'.

1619   Early the following year, Archbishop Abbot and the Bishop of London, Dr. King, paid a surprise visit on Queen Anne, who was dying at Hampton Court and was still thought to be a strong Catholic sympathizer. 'We hope your majesty does not trust to your own merits, nor to the merits of the saints but only to the blood and merits of our saviour', said the two prelates sternly.

On March 12, Archbishop Abbot attended the Queen's funeral, at which her effigy was carried on a chariot drawn by six horses.

On April 11, the Bishop of London preached at a service of thanksgiving at Paul's Cross for the recovery of the King from a serious illness. After praising the monarch's noble conduct at death's door, the Bishop went on to meditate on death itself 'in the grand manner of the age'.

On June 17, Dr. Samuel Harsnett, Bishop of Chichester, obtained the see of Norwich. During his occupancy of this see, he was to spend some £2,000 on rebuilding and enlarging the episcopal residences at Norwich and Ludham.

In October, the buffoonish Bishop of Lincoln, ex-naval chaplain Dr. Mountain, entertained the King at his episcopal palace at Buckden in Huntingdonshire.

1620   On June 24, the following year, the foppishly-dressed Rev. Richard Corbet, famous for his practical jokes on butlers and college servants, was installed as Dean of Christ Church.

Five days later, Orlando Gibbons, organist and composer, was found brawling with a certain Mr. Eveseed, Gentleman of the Chapel Royal.

On September 6 the *Mayflower* set sail for America carrying a number of dissatisfied puritans, later named the 'Pilgrim Fathers'.

1621   The following summer, on July 16, 1621, the ambitious Bishop of Lincoln, John Williams, was made Lord Chancellor. This appointment, which he had obtained through his friendship with the mother of the King's favourite, Buckingham, astonished the legal profession and brought discredit to the church.

Eight days later, on July 24, a worse calamity occurred when Dr. Abbot, Archbishop of Canterbury, while out hunting in Bramzil Park in Hampshire shot at a buck with a cross-bow, missed and killed a game-keeper. Hearing of the incident, the King remarked, 'None but a fool or knave would think worse of a man for such an occurrence', but the Primate was overwhelmed with grief and retired to his native Guildford, feeling distraught.

The same month, the Dean of Exeter, Dr. Matthew Sutcliffe, was arrested and held in custody after expressing his opposition to the proposed marriage between the young Prince Charles and the Infanta Doña Maria, sister of King Philip IV of Spain.

On November 22, the poet and former man-about-town John Donne was appointed Dean of St. Paul's. With this job went a house fit for a bishop, with gatehouse, porter's lodge and spacious courtyards. Donne was soon established as the most powerful preacher of the day, his sermons being described as the most brilliant public entertainment London had to offer.

1622   Meanwhile, following the eclipse of Archbishop Abbot, William Laud, Bishop of St. David's and the tenth child of a Reading clothier, had emerged as one of the most powerful figures in the church. On March 22, 1622, he preached before the Court at Whitehall on the doctrine of the Divine Right of Kings. 'No prince hath ever kept more firm to religion', he declared.

Three months later, on June 30, Robert Harris, Vicar of Hanwell, Oxfordshire, preached at Paul's Cross on the theme of good order. 'Happy that state wherein the cobbler meddles with his last, the tradesman with his shop,

John Donne, a former man-about-town to whom the church offered a career. His appearance in the pulpit was said to resemble that of 'an angel preaching from a cloud'

the student with his books, the counsellor with state, the Prince with the sceptre and each creature lives in its own element.'

On September 15, the new Dean of St. Paul's, John Donne, explained to an enormous congregation at Paul's Cross the new *Directions to Preachers* recently issued by King James forbidding preachers to 'meddle with matters of state and differences between prince and people'.

On Christmas Day, Lancelot Andrewes, now Bishop of Winchester, preached before the ailing King James at Whitehall. 'Christ is no wild cat,' he declared – apparently a rebuke to puritan zealousness.

1623   The following spring, work began on the Queen's chapel at St. James's Palace, designed by Inigo Jones for Prince Charles's intended bride the Infanta of Spain. The royal pew in this beautiful building was to be fitted with a large and elegant fireplace.

At Easter, the Vicar of Storrington in Sussex clashed with parishioners who claimed an ancient right to have bread, cheese and a barrel of beer in church after Evening Prayer.

Before the end of the year, fifteen-year-old John Milton, a pupil at St. Paul's School, had written his famous hymn 'Let us with a gladsome mind'.

1624   The following year, the Rev. Richard Montague, Canon of Windsor, Rector of Petworth and Archdeacon of Hereford, published *A new gag for an old goose*, which attempted to prove the Church of England's divine right to tithes.

1625   On March 27, King James I died at Theobalds. His funeral some five weeks later in Westminster Abbey was the greatest event of its kind known in

40

England, with music written by Orlando Gibbons and the hearse designed by Inigo Jones. In the absence of Archbishop Abbot, Bishop Williams of Lincoln preached a high-flown sermon full of baroque images and ending with the compelling words, 'Dormivit Salamon'.*

Meanwhile, the Dean of St. Paul's, Dr. Donne, had preached his first sermon before the new King. 'The almighty hand of God hath shed and spread a text of mortification over all the land', he declared and then went on to remind the new monarch of his duty to the Church of England.

On June 5, royal composer Orlando Gibbons died suddenly of an apoplectic seizure while attending ceremonies in Canterbury to welcome the new King's wife, Queen Henrietta Maria of France. Rumours that he had died of the plague were hotly denied by his doctors and his body was quickly buried in Canterbury Cathedral.

1626 On February 2, 1626, the Archbishop of Canterbury, Dr. Abbot, in seclusion since his hunting accident five years earlier, re-emerged to officiate at the coronation of the new King in Westminster Abbey. During this service, there was a difficult moment when the congregation failed to respond to the Primate's call for a general acclamation and Lord Arundel was obliged to step into the breach and explain that everyone should shout 'God save King Charles'.

Four days later, William Laud, Bishop of St. David's, who had become the new monarch's intimate friend and closest ecclesiastical adviser, preached a sermon before Parliament in which he magnified the King's authority in both church and state.

In June, churchmen at Cambridge were alarmed when a large cod was cut up by a local fish merchant and a book entitled *A Preparation for the Cross* was found in its belly. Dr. Samuel Ward, Master of Sidney Sussex College, wrote to the Archbishop of Armagh, James Ussher, 'It may be a special admonition to us.'

In July, blue-blooded poet and courtier George Herbert was appointed prebendary of Leighton Bromswold in Huntingdonshire with his own stall in Lincoln Cathedral, though he had not yet been ordained a priest.

On September 26, Lancelot Andrewes, Bishop of Winchester, died at his twelfth-century palace beside the Thames at Southwark.

On Sunday November 21, the evening service at Graffham church in Sussex was disturbed by a potter, William Munnery, being violently sick.

1627 On February 22, the following year, Royalist extremist Dr. Robert Sibthorpe, Vicar of Brackley, preached an assize sermon at Northampton in support of a loan desired by King Charles and taking the text 'Render therefore to all their dues'. The Archbishop of Canterbury, Dr. Abbot, subsequently refused to give his *imprimatur* to the printing of this sermon and, on July 5, was visited by Lord Conway, Secretary of State, with a message from the King that he must 'withdraw to Canterbury and meddle no more with the High Commission's affairs'. The Archbishop replied that this was impossible as he was involved in a law suit with the citizens of Canterbury. He agreed instead to retire to a small house at Ford, near Canterbury.

On July 7, the Rev. Roger Mainwaring, Rector of St. Giles-in-the-Fields,

* Solomon slept.

Lancelot Andrewes, bachelor
Bishop of Winchester and one of
the leading preachers of his day.
His private chapel was said to be
adorned with popish furniture

preached before the King at Oatlands arguing that the King's subjects could
not refuse him money 'without peril of damnation'.

On October 9, the King transferred the authority of Archbishop Abbot to
a committee of five bishops, headed by William Laud, now Bishop of Bath
and Wells. The King sent the Primate a hand-written letter telling him not to
attend parliament.

A few weeks later, however, the unfortunate Archbishop was again
summoned to Court being received from his barge by the jovial Dr.
Matthew, Archbishop of York, and the Earl of Dorset and escorted to the
King's presence where he kissed the royal hand and a hollow reconciliation
took place.

At the end of the year, the elegant and courtly Dr. Mountain, Bishop of
London, was translated to the see of Durham, to make room for Laud as new
Bishop of London. Dr. Mountain, described by John Milton as a 'canary-
sucking, swan-eating' prelate, protested that this move was 'the worst kind of
banishment, next neighbour to a civil death' and obtained permission to
reside at Durham House in the Strand and thus remain in 'the warm air of
the court'.

In due course, the strict disciplinarian William Laud moved into Fulham
Palace where he was to occupy the small oak-panelled rooms in the Tudor
quadrangle.

1628   The following June, the House of Lords condemned Dr. Mainwaring,
Rector of St. Giles-in-the-Fields, for encouraging royal absolutism in his
sermons and he was placed in the Fleet prison for several days. Bishop Laud
was also censured for licensing similar sermons.

On July 27, the Rev. Peter Smart, prebendary of Durham and a zealous protestant, preached a violent sermon attacking fellow prebendary John Cosin accusing him of encouraging popish practices, elaborate ceremonial, and complex liturgical music in the cathedral. Smart was swiftly suspended by the Court of High Commission in York, fined £500 and imprisoned for non-payment.

1629   On February 11, the following year, young M.P. Oliver Cromwell accused Dr. William Alabaster of preaching 'flat popery' at Paul's Cross. A month later, further disagreements over religious doctrine and discipline compelled Charles to dissolve parliament. For the next eleven years, he was to reign without it, assisted by William Laud, who in December this year issued a series of injunctions aimed at preserving 'the settled continuance and doctrine and discipline of the Church of England as now established'. Bishops were ordered to live in their sees unless they had special business at Court.

    Meanwhile, parson-poet Robert Herrick had been admitted to the living of Dean Prior near Ashburton in Devon. Here, he was to share his life with a spaniel named Tracy, a pet lamb, a cat, a goose and a hen. Herrick was also said to have a favourite pig, which he taught to drink out of a pint tankard.

1630   The following April, the aristocratic George Herbert was admitted to the living at Fugglestone with Bemerton near Salisbury. Here, he was to pay for the rebuilding of the rectory which was in a sorry state of repair and perform the duties of his office with saint-like devotion. He was not ashamed of the humble status of parish priest, remarking, 'The domestic servants of the King of Heaven should be of the noblest families on earth.'

This portrait of Archbishop Laud is said to flatter him. He had a flushed face and was unattractive to women. Clever, fussy, irritable and occasionally rude, he shared his life at Lambeth Palace with a Smyrna cat and a tortoise

The same month, Bishop Laud was appointed Chancellor of the University of Oxford, where he was to carry out considerable improvements. At St. John's College, he was to spend some £5,000 of his own money on a fine new quadrangle with Italianate colonnades and elegant bronze statues of the King and Queen. At Balliol, he was to give refuge to Canopius, a member of the household staff of the murdered Patriarch Cyril of Constantinople and supposedly the first man to drink coffee in England.

Meanwhile, the Rev. Alexander Leighton had been thrown into a verminous cell in Newgate prison after publishing a book entitled *Sion's Plea against Prelacie*, in which he had called the Queen 'a daughter of Heth, a Cannanite and an idolatress' and counselled Parliament to kill all the bishops 'by smiting them under the fifth rib'.

On June 4, this uncompromising puritan appeared before Star Chamber and was sentenced to be degraded, twice whipped and pilloried, have his ears cut off, both sides of his nose slit, to be branded with the letters *S.S.*, sower of sedition, fined £10,000 and be imprisoned in the Fleet for life. As this cruel judgement was pronounced, William Laud is said to have held up his hands in joy and given thanks to God for giving him victory over his enemies. The terrible sentence was subsequently carried out in full.

On July 2, Laud baptized the infant Prince Charles, son and heir to the King, and composed a special prayer for the occasion. The ceremony took place in the Private Chapel at St. James's Palace with the font being placed on a platform in the middle of the aisle so that all present could see and hear what rites were being used.

On October 20, the Rev. William Slater, Rector of Otterden in Kent, appeared before the Court of High Commission dressed in riding habit, a careless ruff and deep sleeves, clothing described by Laud as 'not fit for a minister'.

1631   The following year, on February 25, John Donne, Dean of St Paul's, who was already preparing for death and was in the habit of wearing his shroud, preached his last sermon. It was called 'Death's Duel' and contained a reference to semen as 'excremental jelly'.

On March 27, Bishop Laud preached at Paul's Cross on the loyal theme that kings are ordained of God for the good of the people. 'The age is so bad', he said, 'they will not allow a good king to be commended for fear of flattery. I hope I shall offend no one by praying for the king.'

A few days later, on April 10, Laud obtained a commission under the Great Seal of England to look into the dilapidation of the ancient St. Paul's Cathedral. Repair work began later that month, with King Charles contributing £10,000. Stained glass, pictures, surplices, lawn sleeves and embroidered capes were re-introduced and it was said that Laud was bent on making the cathedral a rival to St. Peter's in Rome.

Meanwhile, the Bishop of Salisbury, John Davenant, had incurred the King's anger with a Lenten sermon on predestination. After appearing before the Council on his knees and being scolded by Dr. Harsnett, Archbishop of York, for half an hour, he was dismissed with a warning not to preach on such subjects again.

In May, two men named Young and Broughton were hauled before the

44

Court of Star Chamber and fined £100 each after being found fighting over a pew in Eccleston Chapel in Lancashire.

1632   A year later, on May 7, 1632, the amiable and easy-going Richard Corbet, former Dean of Christ Church, was appointed Bishop of Norwich, where he was to lock himself in his wine cellar at Ludham Palace along with his chaplain Dr. Lushington – provoking an angry response from puritan lecturer Samuel Ward, who delivered a sermon called 'Woe to Drunkards'.

The following month, Robert Wright was appointed new Bishop of Lichfield and Coventry, where he was to reap large profits from the sale of episcopal timber on the Eccleshall estate.

On August 23, Dr. John Bancroft, nephew of the former Archbishop of Canterbury was appointed Bishop of Oxford. He soon acquired the grant of the vicarage of Cuddesdon, where he was to build a fine palace for himself and his successors, with the aid of a grant of timber from the royal forest at Shotover.*

1633   Early the following summer, King Charles visited Scotland accompanied by the loyal Bishop Laud. En route, Laud inspected the close at York and cathedral at Durham and was horrified by their condition and ordered a general cleaning-up operation.

A few weeks later, on August 4, the unfortunate and almost forgotten Archbishop of Canterbury, Dr. Abbot, died at his palace at Croydon. He had spent the last few years in enforced inactivity and had suffered many blows to his prestige. Not long before his death, his coach had been 'incommoded' by a group of women who, recalling the Archbishop's hunting accident twelve years earlier, had shouted, 'Ye had best shoot an arrow at us!'

Two days later, the King greeted fifty-nine-year-old Bishop Laud at Court with the words, 'My Lord Grace of Canterbury, you are welcome.'

The following month, the new Primate moved into Lambeth, after an alarming journey across the Thames, during which his ferry had capsized and his coach and horses submerged. Laud moved into the twelfth-century palace accompanied by two pets, a tortoise and a Smyrna cat, the latter presented to him by Lady Roe, wife of the ambassador to the Court of the Mogul Emperor.

Shortly after his arrival at Lambeth, Laud wrote to his colleague Thomas Wentworth, 'I have had a heaviness hang over me ever since I was nominated for this place' and he is said to have preferred living at his previous residence, London House, beside St. Paul's Cathedral.

On September 19, at the instigation of his new Primate, the King wrote to the bishops, ordering them to restrict ordination to those who intended to undertake the cure of souls, in a bid to stop the supply of puritan lecturers now flooding the market.

1634   On February 17, 1634, puritan William Prynne, who had published a thousand-page book attacking stage plays, of which the Queen was especially fond, was sentenced by Star Chamber to be fined £5,000 and have both his ears cropped in the pillory.

* Cuddesdon Palace was badly damaged by a fire in 1958 and subsequently demolished. See page 217.

A contemporary cartoon showing Archbishop Laud dining off the ears of puritans

Meanwhile, Archbishop Laud had begun a visitation of seven dioceses, the first such visitation since the time of Cranmer, and had encountered immediate resistance from the Bishop of Lincoln, John Williams, who claimed that his diocese was originally part of the Kingdom of Mercia and thus not under the Archbishop's jurisdiction. On March 28, Bishop Williams appeared before the Attorney General, who, after a two day hearing decided against him on all points.

Laud's visitations continued throughout the year, unearthing many examples of crippling poverty among the clergy. At Lyddington in Rutland, for example, the Rev. Robert Ludd was found helping a thatcher carry out repairs to the roof of his vicarage.

1635 The following year, the new Bishop of Sodor and Man, Dr. Parr, announced that the extreme cold and ruinous condition of his episcopal house compelled him to live in England.

1636 On March 6, 1636, to the surprise and murmuring of many Dr. Juxon, the new Bishop of London, was appointed Lord High Treasurer. He was the first churchman to hold this position since the reign of Henry VII and in the years ahead had to cope with the reckless extravagance of the Court.

Five months later, at the end of August, the King and Queen paid a state visit to Oxford. They were met a mile from the city by Archbishop Laud, in his capacity as Chancellor of the University, who was now at the height of his power and travelling in a coach-and-six with fifty attendants. That night, a great feast – costing the immense sum of £2,666 1s. 7d. – was held in Laud's newly-built library at St. John's College.

While in the neighbourhood, the King also attended a splendid reception at the Bishop of Oxford's newly-built palace at Cuddesdon.

On November 5, the Rev. Henry Burton, incumbent at St. Matthew's Friday Street in London, preached against the bishops as 'blind watchmen, dumb dogs, ravening wolves, anti-christian mushrooms, robbers of souls, limbs of the beast and factors of Antichrist'. He was promptly summoned to appear before Dr. Duck, a commissioner for causes ecclesiastical, and ordered to be apprehended. Early the following year, Burton barricaded himself in his house but, on February 1, his doors were forced, his study ransacked and he was thrown into the Fleet prison.

1637 Meanwhile, puritan pamphleteer William Prynne, imprisoned in the Tower of London, had issued a tract describing the prelates as 'Bishops of Lucifer, devouring wolves and excreble traitors'.

On June 4, Prynne, Burton and fellow puritan John Bastwick appeared before the Court of Star Chamber and were sentenced to have their cheeks branded, ears cropped – in Prynne's case for the second time – followed by life imprisonment. These sentences were subsequently carried out in front of an audience of 100,000. 'Cut me, tear me, I fear thee not' Prynne told the executioner, 'I fear the fire of hell but not thee!'

On June 6, the rebellious Bishop of Lincoln, John Williams, appeared before Star Chamber charged with 'scandalizing' the government. He was fined, suspended and imprisoned in the Tower, where he was to continue to plot against the establishment.

On July 23, there was a riot in St. Giles's Cathedral, Edinburgh, when the Dean started reading from the new Scottish Prayer Book. A certain Jenny Geddes hurled a stool at him and Archbishop Spottiswood and Bishop Lindsay were assailed with other missiles. After the rioters had been evicted, the service continued with a much diminished congregation.

1638 In February the following year, the Bishop of Ely, Francis White, died at Ely House in Holborn, which had been seized by Queen Elizabeth fifty years earlier but had now been regained by the see.

He was to be succeeded as bishop by Dr. Matthew Wren, who was to preach against the draining of the Fens on the grounds that it would be tampering with Creation.

Meanwhile, the growth of puritan emigration to New England and the Bermudas had reached new proportions. In March, this year, it was noted that there were fourteen ships lying on the Thames, ready to sail by Easter.

Six months later, on September 27, the consecration took place of St. Paul's Church, Covent Garden, which had been built by Inigo Jones for the 3rd Earl of Bedford. It was said that the Earl had been anxious to cut costs and had asked the architect to design 'something in the nature of a barn', to which Inigo Jones had replied that he should have 'the handsomest barn in England'.

The following month, the King's mother-in-law Queen Marie de Medici arrived in London, causing more rumours of the spread of Romanism at Court.

Meanwhile, the Bishop of Lichfield and Coventry, Dr. Wright, who had been busy amassing a fortune out of the sale of church timber, apologized to Archbishop Laud for neglecting his see on the grounds that it was 'but a slip of forgetfulness'.

1639 In February 1639, the Bishop of Lincoln, Dr. Williams, was brought from the Tower of London to answer charges in Star Chamber of encouraging the Rev. Lambert Osbaldeston, headmaster of Westminster School, to call Archbishop Laud 'a little meddling hocus pocus' and other libels. The Bishop was found guilty of *scandalum magnatum*, fined £8,000 and sentenced to three more years in the Tower. Osbaldeston was fined £5,000 and sentenced to stand in the pillory, nailed by his ears in front of his pupils. He escaped before this sentence was carried out, however, leaving a note for his pursuers saying, 'If the Archbishop enquire after me, tell him I am gone beyond Canterbury.' Laud quickly sent messengers to the sea-ports to apprehend him but Osbaldeston had gone into hiding in a friend's house in Drury Lane.

A few months later, on July 9, the Rev. Obadiah Sedgwick became Vicar of Coggeshall in Essex. In hot weather it was said that Mr. Sedgwick would unbutton his doublet in the pulpit so that 'his breath might be longer'.

In September, Thomas Wentworth was recalled from Ireland to become the King's chief adviser and Archbishop Laud's long era of power and influence came to an end.

1640 In February 1640, Joseph Hall, Bishop of Exeter, published an enthusiastic defence of the Divine Right of Episcopacy.

Two months later, on April 13, eleven years of personal rule by the King ended with the reassembling of parliament. Many of the bishops rode to Westminster on horseback though the standard of apostolic horse-flesh was not high, many animals being bob-tailed and 'unsuited to an ecclesiastical baron's gravity or reverence'. Within a few weeks this parliament had been dissolved and many citizens directed their indignation against Archbishop Laud. 'So odious has he grown in the eyes of men', declared one poster, 'that we believe he stinketh in the nostrils of almighty God.'

On May 11, hundreds of apprentices, reinforced by seamen from the London docks, marched on Lambeth Palace, calling for Laud, that they 'might tear him to pieces', but the Archbishop had already fled to Westminster where he was protected by cannon. The riot lasted for three days and ended with one participant being tortured on the rack and then executed and another, nineteen-year-old Thomas Bensted, being hung, drawn and quartered.

The same month saw the deprivation of the Bishop of Gloucester, Godfrey Goodman, who had been absent from his see for several years preferring to reside at Windsor, where he was said to have become more and more papist in his views. He soon submitted and was restored – but asked permission to resign his see as soon as his debts were paid.

On October 23, a crowd of some 2,000 burst into the Court of High Commission and tore down the benches declaring that they would have no bishops and no High Commission.

The following Sunday, October 28, there was an ugly scene at Halstead church in Essex when a parishioner, John Pool, took the parish clerk by the throat, pushed him into the vestry, stripped off his hood and surplice and tore them to pieces. Meanwhile, another man had knocked the prayer book out of the hands of the curate while he was conducting a baptism at the font.

Six days later, parliament again assembled, its members now in a very determined mood. During the next few days, Prynne and his colleagues were recalled from their distant prisons, the impeachment of their oppressors got under way and arch-puritan John Vicars described the ceremonies of the Church of England as 'a stinking heap of atheistical and Roman rubbish'.

Meanwhile, John Atherton, Bishop of Waterford and Lismore, and former Rector of Huish Combe Flower in Somerset, had been convicted of whoredom and 'unnatural crime' and sentenced to death. On the morning of his execution day, December 5, he asked for 'a little salt butter and brown bread, cheerfully hoping to be invited to the supper of the lamb in the next world'. His elaborately elegant speech on the scaffold was rudely interrupted by enemies of the episcopacy.

Six days later, on December 11, a petition for the complete abolition of the episcopacy was presented in parliament for the first time.

A week later, Archbishop Laud was formally impeached and committed into the custody of Maxwell, Gentleman of the Black Rod, while a committee was set up to 'investigate' him. One of the members of this body, Sir Harbottle Grimston, was to describe the Primate as 'the very sty of all that pestilential filth'.

On January 22, 1641, parliament resolved that the proceedings against Dr. Peter Smart thirteen years earlier in the Court of High Commission were illegal and unjust and that he ought to be restored as a prebendary of Durham.

The following day, some ten ministers of the Church of England appeared at the bar of the House of Commons and presented another petition against the whole government of the church.

On February 26, fourteen articles of impeachment against Archbishop Laud were presented in the House of Lords. Among other things he was charged with trying to subvert the constitution, bringing popish articles into the church and alienating the mind of the King from his people. On March 1, there was much clamour and revilings as the Archbishop's coach made its way through the streets of London to the Tower, where Laud was to join his old colleague, Thomas Wentworth, the Earl of Strafford.

The same day, a Grand Committee of Religion was set up by the House of Lords under the chairmanship of Bishop Williams of Lincoln, who had recently been released from captivity. A sub-committee was appointed to enquire into the immoralities of the clergy and replace them with puritan ministers, under the chairmanship of John White, M.P., who was soon to inform the House of Commons that 8,000 of the clergy were 'unworthy and scandalous' and 'deserved to be cast out'.

In April, parliament resolved that the savage sentence passed on the Rev. Alexander Leighton eleven years earlier was illegal. He was released from prison, his sight and hearing badly impaired, most of his hair gone and in a revengeful mood.

On May 12, Archbishop Laud watched as his colleague Lord Strafford was led to his execution on Tower Hill. After blessing him from the window of his cell, Laud collapsed in a faint. Strafford was attended on the scaffold by James Ussher, Archbishop of Armagh, who declared that he 'never saw so white a soul return to its maker'.

On May 27, the Root and Branch Bill to eradicate bishops, deans, chapters and all church officials was given its first reading in the House of Commons. It passed at its second reading but made no progress in the House of Lords.

The same month, a poster was pinned to the entrance of parliament denouncing the bishops as 'limbs of Antichrist'.

On Midsummer's Day, June 24, the keys were torn off the great organ in Durham Cathedral.

In September, a fighting sermon was preached before the House of Commons by the Rev. Jeremiah Burroughs. 'God hath begun a work that he will never leave till he hath brought it to perfection', he said. 'God forbid that any of you should now give in'.

Shortly after Christmas, armed demonstrators gathered at Westminster, crying, 'No bishops!', 'No popery!' and 'No popish lords!' The stairs from the river Thames to Palace Yard were crowded with citizens aiming at preventing the bishops taking their seats in the House of Lords. An attempt was made to drag Bishop Morton of Durham from his coach and hands were laid on Dr. Williams, now Archbishop of York. The rabble also entered Westminster Abbey and would have pulled down the organs and ornaments but met with resistance from scholars and choir-men. In the affray, a knight was killed by a tile.

Fearing further violence, Dr. Williams and eleven other bishops swiftly absented themselves from the House of Lords and informed the King that any legislation passed in their absence would be illegal. These twelve bishops were at once accused of trying to subvert the fundamental laws of the kingdom and ten of them were thrown in the Tower of London. The two oldest ones were put into the hands of the Gentleman of the Black Rod.

The Bishop of London, Dr. Juxon, who had not joined in the protest, had meanwhile gone into retirement at Fulham Palace unmolested.

1642 On January 3, 1642, the King was attempted to impeach Pym and five others for treason but was defied by both houses of parliament and fled from the capital a week later.

On February 23, the popular puritan divine Stephen Marshall struck a savage note when he advocated the killing of popish children in a sermon before the House of Commons. 'If his work be to avenge God's church against Babylon, he is a blessed man that takes and dashes the little one against the stone,' he declared.

The same month the King, currently at Canterbury seeing off his wife to the safety of Holland, reluctantly gave his assent to the Bishops Exclusion Act. A few weeks later, the episcopacy was replaced with an Assembly of Divines.

During the summer, the Rev. John Barwick, Fellow of St. John's College, Cambridge, conveyed money and treasures from the university to the King's new headquarters. On August 11, he was arrested along with Dr. Richard Sterne, former chaplain to Archbishop Laud and now Master of Jesus College, Cambridge, and Dr. Beale, Master of St. John's, and conveyed to London amidst general reviling and thrown into the Tower.

On August 22, the King raised his standard at Nottingham and the Civil War had begun.

THE CIVIL WAR

1642–1649

A trail of ruin was now blazed across the country. Churches and cathedrals were entered, organs hacked to pieces, ornaments and stained glass smashed, surplices burnt and prayer books torn out of the hands of preachers. During the next seven years, some 2,500 clergy were evicted from their livings, many being barbarously treated. Bishops and clergy alike were dragged from their beds, their possessions plundered and their homes set on fire. Some were taken prisoner. Some fled abroad. Others joined the Royalist strongholds. In the battles that followed, clergymen distinguished themselves on both sides and there were many awe-inspiring examples of heroism.

1642   On the day the war broke out, the Rev. Thomas Newcomen, Vicar of Holy Trinity, Colchester, who had assisted Sir John Lucas in raising forces for the king, was arrested as he was setting off for Nottingham. An infuriated mob tore off his clothes and beat him with cudgels and halberds.

Five days later, on August 27, soldiers entered Canterbury Cathedral, overthrew the communion table, violated the monuments of the dead, damaged the organ, broke down ancient seats and rails, forced opened cupboards containing surplices and gowns, tore up prayer books and smashed various figures of Christ. The same day, soldiers broke into the house of the Dean of Canterbury, Dr. Isaac Bargrave, roused his wife from her bed and forced her to attend them. The Dean himself was subsequently arrested at Gravesend and thrown into the Fleet prison.

On August 30, the Bishop of Ely's palace was searched for hidden ammunition by a troop of horsemen and the Bishop, Matthew Wren, was brought to London and placed in the Tower.

Meanwhile, many puritan clergymen had reported for duty at the headquarters of the Earl of Essex, parliamentary commander at Northampton, and been posted to the regiments.

The first big battle of the war took place on October 23 at Edgehill. The Rev. John Sedgwick and other puritan clergy were present participating in the fighting and riding up and down giving encouragement. Among clergy on the Royalist side were the future Bishop of Worcester, Dr. Fleetwood, who after this inconclusive battle carried twelve-year-old Prince Charles to safety, and the Archdeacon of Coventry, William Higgins, who was taken prisoner.

On the same day, the Rev. Robert Chestlin, Rector of St. Matthew's, Friday Street, preached a sermon loyal to the King. He was quickly grabbed by guards armed with pistols and committed to the Compter and thence to Colchester gaol, from which he was to make a daring escape.

The following month, the Rev. Daniel Featly, D.D., had his church and rectory at Acton plundered by parliamentary soldiers who were defending London against a possible attack from the King.

On December 28, the Rev. Thomas Fuller, popular new curate at the Savoy Chapel, preached a sermon exhorting both sides to peace. 'There be drunkards on both sides and swearers on both sides, pious on both sides and profane on both sides' he pointed out.

1643 On New Year's Day 1643, a party of parliamentary soldiers headed by a certain Captain Buck broke into the rectory at Minchinhampton in Gloucestershire, seized the elderly and lame Rev. Henry Fowler at his fireside, called him an 'old knave', beat him with pole-axes and took away all that was portable or valuable.

Later that month, Lambeth Palace was made into a prison for Royalist clergy and the famous Rev. Alexander Leighton, who had been savagely punished by Archbishop Laud thirteen years earlier was appointed gaoler. Ely House, the Bishop of Winchester's palace at Southwark and the spacious Deanery of St. Paul's were also converted into prisons.

On February 19, soldiers again disturbed Dr. Daniel Featly, now ministering in a church at Lambeth. On this occasion, one worshipper was shot dead, another wounded and Dr. Featly escaped only to die later of his sufferings.

Meanwhile, Lichfield Cathedral had been converted into a fortress by Royalist troops and was besieged by the Roundheads. On March 2, a sharpshooter stationed in the central tower killed the parliamentary commander, Lord Brooke. Two days later, the cathedral surrendered and its new occupants were in due course besieged by Prince Rupert.

On March 31, parliament officially recognized the sequestration of clergymen's estates.

In April, commissioners arrived in Norwich, wrecked the eleventh-century cathedral, entered the episcopal palace, insulted the Bishop, Joseph Hall, and put up his books and other possessions for public sale. Bishop Hall bravely endured these ordeals and remained in his palace.

On May 1, the chapel at Lambeth Palace, built by Archbishop Boniface in the thirteenth-century, was defaced and the steps to the communion table torn up.

On June 29, the parsonage of St. Augustine's-by-St-Paul's was plundered and the frail old Rector, Ephraim Udal, who had remained loyal to the established liturgy and the episcopacy, was taken off to prison. His books were stolen and his elderly wife was dragged from the house by force and left lying in the street.

The same month, puritan divine Stephen Marshall had informed the House of Commons that the parliamentary armies were destroying the Antichrist. 'Christ has always had an army of saints to war against the beast', he said.

On August 11, the heads of three Cambridge colleges, Drs. Sterne, Martin and Beale, already deprived of all ecclesiastical preferments, were placed on board a ship at Wapping and held with other prisoners of distinction beneath the hatches. It was said that an attempt was made to sell them off as slaves to Algiers or the American islands.

On August 20, the Rev. Samuel Kem, Rector of Albury in Oxfordshire,

Ætatis Suæ.72

An͏° Dͫñ͏ 1632

Robert Wright, Bishop of Lichfield and Coventry who amassed a large fortune through the sale of episcopal timber. He later apologized for neglecting his see on the grounds that it was 'but a slip of forgetfulness'. He died a noble death in 1643 defending Eccleshall Castle for the King

preached in St. Peter's church in the precincts of the Tower of London on the righteousness of the parliamentary cause. He wore a buff coat and scarf.

On August 28, parliament gave its formal approval of the demolition of altars, removal of candle-sticks and the defacement of pictures and relics now under way.

The following month, the eighty-three-year-old Bishop of Lichfield and Coventry, Dr. Wright, died during the siege of his episcopal seat, Eccleshall Castle, which he was attempting to hold for the King.

In October, the Rev. Henry Wilkinson, Vicar of Epping, Essex, informed the House of Commons that the Royalist forces were 'the militia of hell and the trained bands of Satan'.

On December 9, the Rev. William Chillingworth, a leading theologian who had joined the Royalist army, was taken prisoner after the fall of Arundel Castle. He was in a delicate condition after the deprivations of the siege and was placed in the bishop's palace at Chichester where he was soon 'pestered to death' by a puritan clergyman named Francis Cheynell.

Meanwhile, the Rev. Thomas Campbell, ejected Rector of Swafield in Norfolk, was found in an unheated cottage in a neighbouring village living off ice-cold barley dumplings. He was said to be facing his predicament 'with courage and contentment'.

1644   On January 6, 1644, parliamentary commissioners led by William Dowsing made havoc in the parish church of Clare in Suffolk, taking down twenty cherubins, twelve carved apostles and some 200 relics.

Three weeks later, on January 29, Dowsing mutilated eleven churches near Ipswich in the space of a few hours.

On March 12, the long awaited trial of Archbishop Laud, now in his fourth year in the Tower of London, opened before the depleted House of Lords. The seventy-year-old primate was to defend himself against charges of treasons with considerable vigour, being rowed back to the Tower each evening, his shirt wet with sweat.

Meanwhile Dr. John Cosin was ejected from the Mastership of Peterhouse, Cambridge, after sending his college plate to the Royal Mint at York. He was to flee to Paris where he became Anglican chaplain to the household of Queen Henrietta Maria and had lodgings assigned to him in the Louvre.

At the end of the month, the famous antiquary Rev. Thomas Fuller served with the Royalist forces at the battle of Cheriton Down. After this defeat, Fuller briefly took up residence at the Royalist stronghold of Basing House, home of the Marquess of Winchester, where there was a fine library in which to pursue his studies.

On May 9, parliament issued further orders for the demolition of all organs and banned the use of copes, surplices and all superstitious vestments.

Two months later, on July 2, the Battle of Marston Moor gave parliament complete control of the north. Among the fleeing churchmen was John Bramhall, Archbishop of Armagh, who reached Hamburg on July 8 accompanied by the Marquess of Newcastle.

Meanwhile, the lengthy trial of Archbishop Laud had dragged on before the House of Lords, which was under great pressure from the Commons to find the Primate guilty of treason. On October 28, a petition for the execution of Laud was presented to the House of Commons by a large body of Londoners. A full pardon signed by the King with the Great Seal of England was ignored and the seventy-one-year-old Archbishop was eventually sentenced to death. On January 4, 1645, the House of Lords reluctantly passed the necessary ordinance.

Six days later, Laud met his death on Tower Hill 'with serenity and courage'. From the scaffold he preached a lengthy farewell sermon, full of sub-divisions, quotations and allusions. He spoke of the 'clamours and slanders' he had endured for 'labouring to keep a uniformity in the external service of God' and ended by praying for God to 'bless this kingdom with peace and plenty and with brotherly love and charity'. His remains were later deposited in the ancient church of All Hallows-by-the-Tower.

The same day, the Book of Common Prayer was officially abolished and replaced with the prosaic Directory of Public Worship.

The following month, royal chaplain Jeremy Taylor was taken prisoner by the Roundheads. After being held briefly in Cardigan Castle, where his captors referred to him as 'a most spruce neat formalist, a very ginger-bread idol', he found refuge as chaplain to the Earl of Carbery at Golden Grove, where he was to write his immortal prose works *Holy Living* and *Holy Dying*.

In April, eighty-one-year-old Dr. Morton, small and sprightly Bishop of Durham who had hitherto been permitted to reside unmolested at his house in the Strand, was brought before the House of Commons and charged with baptizing the infant daughter of the Earl of Rutland according to the rites of the Church of England. He was to spend the next six months in the custody of the Serjeant-at-Arms.

In June, the Rev. Richard Baxter joined the parliamentary army as chaplain to Colonel Whalley's regiment of horse, in which position he was to be unfairly accused of killing a man in cold blood and stealing a medal from him.

The same month, the Royalist infantry was annihilated by the New Model Army at the Battle of Naseby. Following this defeat, the Rev. Thomas Swift, Vicar of Goodrich near Hereford and father of thirteen children, rode off to the King and gave him a waistcoat into which were sewn 300 guineas.

In August, the Rev. John Lowes, Vicar of Brandeston in Suffolk for the past fifty years, was sentenced to death after being found guilty of bewitching a ship near Harwich, which had gone down with all hands. On his way to his execution, eighty-year-old Mr. Lowes, who was said to have been marked with teats on the crown of his head and under his tongue after making a covenant with the Devil, quietly read his own burial service.

On August 15, Sherborne Castle fell after being attacked by Fairfax with new demi-cannons. Among those taken prisoner was the Rev. Mr. Wake, Vicar of Wareham in Dorset. He was stripped naked and led with others through the town.

On September 10, the Bishop of Bristol, Dr. Howell, was one of the chief sufferers when his city surrendered to Fairfax. The episcopal palace was stripped of its lead roof and turned into a malt-house and both the Bishop and his wife, who was expecting a baby, died of their ordeal. Their surviving children were to be brought up by the citizens of Bristol.

A few days later, the city of Chester was besieged by the Roundheads and the elderly bishop, Dr. Bridgeman, left his palace and fled to the wilds of Wales. Among those killed in the seige was William Lawes, one of the greatest composers of the day, famous for his psalm settings for the Chapel Royal.

At the end of that month, the seventy-one-year-old Bishop of Winchester Dr. Curll, played a part in the unsuccessful defence of the town of Winchester. He was subsequently deprived of his private and episcopal property and left to die in poverty.

In October, the great Royalist stronghold of Basing House was at last overwhelmed by Cromwell's forces. Royal chaplain Matthew Griffith, Rector of Bladon in Oxfordshire, helped to defend the house and lost his daughter in the siege. Another famous inmate was architect Inigo Jones, who was stripped naked when the house was overrun and carried off in a blanket.

In December the city of Hereford also fell into the hands of the Roundheads. The clergy of the city were turned out in bitterly cold weather, the bishop's palace was rifled and occupied by a certain Colonel Birch, and the Deanery was given to a certain Dr. Nathaniel Wright. From the pulpit of the cathedral, the ejected Dean, Dr. Croft, boldly condemned the sacrileges which had taken place causing soldiers among the congregation to start fingering their muskets.

1646   Four months later, on April 26, 1646, King Charles left Oxford disguised as a servant and headed for London guided by one of his chaplains, Dr. Michael Hudson, who was said to know the intricacies of the roads. Within a fortnight, the King had given himself up to the Scots at Newark and Hudson was later arrested at Sandwich trying to escape to France.

On June 20, Oxford surrendered and Royalist parsons who had harboured there were dispersed. Among them was the Rev. Robert Sibthorpe, Rector of Brackley, who was to remark during these years, 'I have as much as I desire, if I have as much as I want; and I have as much as the most, if I have as much as I desire.'

On July 23, the city of Worcester capitulated. The cathedral was closed, its organ removed and the Bishop, John Prideaux, fled, selling linen, pewter and books to provide subsistence for himself and his family.

On October 10, the Dean of Wells, Dr. Walter Raleigh, who had been imprisoned in his own house, died after being stabbed in the back by his keeper while he was writing a letter to his wife.

The following month, parliamentary parson the Rev. Samuel Kem preached at Bristol, wearing full military dress and placing two pistols on the cushion of his pulpit.

Meanwhile, the Rev. Thomas Fuller, one of the first cavaliers to win the patronage of his political opponents, was spending the winter with his old school friend, Lord Montagu, at Boughton Castle, Northamptonshire.

The following year a degree of peace descended on the country. On January 30, the King was conducted to Holmby House, Northamptonshire, where he was to enjoy a few months' rest, ministered to by his chaplains, who were given special permission to use the banned Book of Common Prayer. By the end of the year, he had begun his long captivity at Carisbrooke Castle on the Isle of Wight, where it was said he sustained himself by reading the poems of the Rev. George Herbert.

Early in 1648, parliamentary visitors descended upon Oxford. In April, Dr. Gilbert Sheldon, warden of All Souls was committed into custody after refusing to leave his lodgings and was removed to Wallingford Castle along with the devout Rev. Henry Hammond, sub-dean of Christ Church. The Dean of Christ Church, Dr. Samuel Fell, had also had his lodgings broken into, Mrs. Fell refusing to stir and being eventually carried off in her chair. On April 15, a placard was fixed to the gates of several colleges forbidding the use of the Book of Common Prayer and ordering the use of the Directory of Public Worhsip.

Early in the summer, hostilities again erupted when Royal Chaplain Michael Hudson, who had escaped from the Tower of London disguised as an apple vendor, raised a troop for the King and seized Woodford House in Lincolnshire. On June 6, while defending this house, he was flung over the battlements and after clinging onto a spout or projecting stone-work, fell into the moat. He was fished out and killed with a blow from a musket. His tongue was cut out and exhibited as a trophy.

Eight days later, on June 14, soldiers entered the church at nearby Boothby Pagnell and tore the prayer book out of the hands of the vicar, the Rev. Robert Sanderson.

Five months later, on November 29, the Rev. Henry Ferne preached before the King at Carisbrooke Castle on the theme 'Comfort in adversity'. Later that day, a certain Colonel Cobbett arrived on the island with troops for the removal of the famous captive.

On December 11, Hugh Peters preached in St. Margaret's, Westminster taking the text 'Bind your king with chains, and your nobles with fetters of iron'. In the course of his discourse he described the King as a murderer, tyrant and traitor.

The Rev. Hugh Peters, puritan divine who was said to be one of the masked executioners at the death of King Charles I

1649   A few weeks later, on January 30, 1649, King Charles was attended on the scaffold at Whitehall by the Rev. Jeremy Taylor, to whom he gave a few pearls and rubies from the case of his bible, and the Bishop of London, Dr. Juxon. The latter informed him, 'You are exchanging a temporal for an eternal crown – a good exchange.'

The following day Bishop Juxon helped carry the King's coffin through driving snow for burial at St. George's Chapel, Windsor.

THE COMMONWEALTH

1649–1660

Superficially, the Church of England was now extinct. Its liturgy was illegal, many of its bishops were dying in poverty, Lambeth Palace chapel was in the process of being turned into a dance hall and the famous London pulpits were soon filled with what John Evelyn describes as 'novices and novelties'. Secretly, the life of the church went on. From his house at Richmond, Dr. Duppa, Bishop of Salisbury, corresponded with his colleagues, referring to the church as 'our expiring mother', Bishop Skinner of Oxford conducted hundreds of clandestine ordinations and, at a house in Fleet Street, Dr. Wild continued to conduct the Anglican service and administer the Holy Communion. Not all the bishops were in great straits. At his estate in Gloucestershire, the wealthy Bishop of London hunted with his fine pack of hounds and, on his death in 1656, the Archbishop of Armagh was given a state funeral in Westminster Abbey. Rules were strict, however, and any parson active for the Royalist cause was severely punished.

649 Within a week of the King's death, the Bishop of Rochester, Dr. Warner, preached a sermon, later published as a pamphlet, expressing his abhorrence at the execution. He only avoided sequestration of his property for this boldness by the payment of some £5,000 in fines.

At the end of the winter, the popular Rev. Thomas Fuller moved into the parsonage at Waltham Abbey in Essex, to which he had been given the living by the Earl of Carlisle. 'How good it is, especially in sad times, to keep home and not be gadding abroad', he reflected.

On July 11, Oliver Cromwell set off for Ireland accompanied by his chaplains Hugh Peters, John Owen, and Thomas Patient, who invoked God's blessing on the trip. During this campaign, Cromwell was to inform the Irish bishops that the distinction between clergy and laity was unchristian.

650 The following April, the Rev. John Barwick, who had rendered great services to the royal cause, was charged with high treason and thrown into the Tower of London. Here, he was to live on herbs, fruit and thin water gruel and become a living skeleton.

Two months later, on June 23, twenty-year-old Prince Charles arrived in Scotland and immediately fell into the hands of the staunchly presbyterian Marquess of Argyll, who was to keep him a virtual prisoner and subject him to four-hour sermons. Charles secretly informed the Dean of Tuam, Dr. King, 'I am a true child of the Church of England and a true Cavalier and shall remain firm to my first principles.'

The following month Dr. Prideaux, ejected Bishop of Worcester, died in poverty.

On October 1, Dr. Beale, ejected Master of St. John's College, Cambridge, died in exile in Madrid. He left instructions for the instant disposal of his body, in a deep pit and covered in quicklime, lest it should fall into the hands of his enemies.

Four days later, the Rev. Ralph Josselin, who had amassed a large fortune as a chaplain in Colonel Hackenden's regiment, preached at St. Paul's Cathedral by order of the Lord Mayor.

1651   On January 1, 1651, Charles was crowned King at the ancient palace of Scone. The crown was placed on his head by the Marquess of Argyll and three long sermons were preached during the eight-hour ceremony.

A few months later, on May 24, a religious fanatic named John Robins, who was attempting to collect an army of 144,000 men to liberate the Holy Land, was arrested at a meeting in Long Alley, Moorfields and thrown into the Bridewell prison in Clerkenwell.

On August 22, the Rev. Christopher Love, pastor at St. Lawrence Jewry, was executed on Tower Hill after being found guilty of writing treasonable letters to Charles Stuart and his mother Queen Henrietta Maria, in which he had plotted against the Commonwealth. This episode was known later as 'Love's Plot'.

The same day, Charles's army reached Worcester, where the new King was welcomed by the Lord Mayor and leading citizens. Two days later, on August 24, he attended a service in the cathedral and listened to an Anglican sermon.

On September 3, Charles watched the Battle of Worcester from a tower of the cathedral. After the defeat and dispersal of his army he fled by a circuitous route to France, assisted by, among others, a certain Father Huddleston. En route, he passed through Charmouth in Dorset where the puritan vicar Mr. Westley joined in the pursuit informing his congregation, 'Charles Stuart is somewhere in this district. You will merit from Almighty God if you will find him out.'

On September 30, one of Prince Rupert's chaplains Dr. Hart was among the 330 people who perished when his ship, the *Constant Reformation*, was lost in a gale.

At the end of October, the fugitive Charles Stuart eventually arrived at Rouen where his old tutor, the Rev. John Earle, failed to recognize him on account of his shabby, dishevelled appearance and burst into tears. Charles promptly appointed him his chaplain and Clerk of the Closet.

1652   On February 5, the following year, religious fanatic John Robins, lingering in the Bridewell Prison, was visited by fellow prophets John Reeve and Lodowicke Muggleton, who passed a sentence of eternal damnation on him.

Later that year, an attempt was made to set up a national church on a congregational plan. Among those serving on the committee was the Rev. Francis Rous, pious Provost of Eton and author of *The Art of Happiness* but the plan proved abortive.

1653   In April 1653 London clergy gathered to express their anxiety about the threatened expulsion of the Rump Parliament and its replacement with a military dictatorship. In a remarkable interview, Dr. Edmund Calamy, distinguished presbyterian divine, informed Cromwell that public opinion would not support him if he took the supreme power.

The following month, the Rev. Joseph Sedgwick preached a sermon at St.

Mary's, Cambridge, attacking devout puritan William Dell, who had expressed the view that degrees were unchristian.

On July 17, the Council of State passed an order permitting Major Packer, Captain Empson and other officers said to be 'eminent for their godliness' to have the free use of any pulpit they wanted providing the regular minister was not using it at the time.

Five months later, on December 22, Oliver Cromwell was proclaimed Lord Protector in the streets of London. Among the many to protest at this development was Christopher Feake, Vicar of Christ Church, Newgate, and father of eight, who spoke of the new dictator as 'the most dissembling and perjured villain in the world'. Feake was promptly brought before the Council of State, deprived of his preferment and committed to Windsor Castle. The pronouncement had also caused a breach in the army, where there were accusations that Cromwell had taken the crown from Christ and put it on his own head.

1654   The following May, there was a dispute over a living at Whitchurch in Shropshire. Cromwell had originally approved the order giving the living to a Mr. Porter but another candidate, a Dr. Bernard, had emerged appointed by the patron of the living, Lord Bridgwater. In the end, Cromwell changed horses and plumped for the landed interest.

Later that summer, new commissions were established for the examination of all clergymen offering themselves for any incumbency and for the expulsion and disqualification of scandalous ministers.

In the autumn, the Rev. Samuel Oates, chaplain to Colonel Pride's regiment, was thought to be the brains behind a plot to oust General Monck and was dismissed from his post.

In November, the Protector's mother, old Mrs. Cromwell, died in her ninetieth year and was given an elaborate funeral in Westminster Abbey, which was lit for the occasion with hundreds of torches.

1655   The following March, a Royalist rising under a certain Colonel Penruddock was quickly foiled. Among those to take defensive measures was the new Dean of Christ Church, Oxford, Dr. Owen, who made himself responsible for the security of the town, riding at the head of a troop of horses armed with pistol and sword.

On April 15, Old Etonian John Pearson, newly appointed lecturer at the small and unpretentious church of St. Clement's, Eastcheap, was preaching when there was an alarm of fire.

In September, a series of orders was issued forbidding Anglican clergy to preach and forbidding evicted parsons from acting as chaplains, schoolmasters, tutors or lecturers.

On Christmas Day, Dr. George Wild delivered a sermon at St. Gregory's by St. Paul's which was described by John Evelyn as 'the funeral sermon of preaching' and reduced many of those present to tears. After this date, Dr. Wild continued to conduct the Anglican service and administer Holy Communion at a house in Fleet Street.

Meanwhile, an eccentric named Thomas Tany, who had declared that 'all religion is a lie and a cheat' had set off for Jerusalem in a small boat he had built himself and been drowned.

1656   On March 21, 1656, the death occurred of the Archbishop of Armagh, Dr.

Ussher, who during his long reign had acquired the Book of Kells for Trinity College Dublin and worked out that the world was created in the year 4004 B.C. On Cromwell's orders, he was given a state funeral in Westminster Abbey and his burial in St. Erasmus's chapel was carried out according to the Anglican burial service. Cromwell's chaplain Peter Sterry later gave advice about which books should be purchased by the State from Ussher's extensive library.

Six months later, on September 8, the death occurred of the Bishop of Norwich, Dr. Joseph Hall, whose possessions had been seized some thirteen years earlier. Eighty-one year-old Dr. Hall had never left his see and died in the village of Higham near Norwich where he had rented a house which later became the Dolphin Inn.

On November 16, the Rev. Robert Leonard, chaplain on board the ship *Constant Warwick*, was charged with drunkenness and dismissed from the service. It was said that he had been so incapacitated by drink that he had to be hoisted on board his ship with the tackles.

Meanwhile, a prediction by the Rev. Robert Gell that there would be a repetition of Noah's flood this year had proved incorrect.

1657   On April 5 the following year, a rising of Fifth Monarchy men demanding 'no king but Christ' was quickly suppressed.

In July an unholy row erupted at Westminster School between the Head-master, Richard Busby, D.D., and the second master, Dr. Bagshawe, both ordained priests. The dispute, one of the greatest quarrels between school-masters of all time, ended with Bagshawe, who had been accused of wearing his hat in church and taking 'a strange delight in whipping', being dismissed and appointed vicar of Ambrosden in Oxfordshire.

In November, Cromwell's chaplain, the Rev. Jeremiah White, sparked off another row when he spoke disparagingly about the proposed marriage between the Protector's daughter Mary and Viscount Fauconberg. The indignant bridegroom cornered the waggish chaplain in his room and attacked him with a cane.

On Christmas Day, the Rev. Peter Gunning conducted an Anglican service in the chapel of Exeter House in the Strand. While he was giving the illegal holy sacrament, the building was suddenly entered by armed soldiers who seized all the communicants and kept many of them prisoner.

1658   On March 23, the following year, there was a secret collection at Covent Garden church for persecuted and sequestered ministers of the Church of England.

Two months later, Dr. Hewett, preacher at St. Gregory's by St. Paul's an indefatigable advocate of a Royal Invasion, who had made open collections for the exiled King, urging his congregation to 'remember a distressed friend', was found guilty of plotting against the government and was sentenced to death. On the scaffold on June 8 he was attended by Dr. Wild, Dr. Warmestry and Dr. Barwick, leading loyalist divines, and, at his funeral a week later, Dr. Nathaniel Hardy preached on the text 'The righteous perisheth'.

Four months later, on September 3, Oliver Cromwell died at Whitehall. After lying in state at Somerset House, his body was given a state funeral in

Westminster Abbey, for which the hearse alone cost £4,000, and was finally buried in Henry VII's chapel.

Power passed briefly into the hands of the Protector's son Richard, who preferred a quiet country life and was quite happy, the following May, to sign a formal abdication in favour of government by the army.

1659

Meanwhile, Dr. Brownrigg, former Bishop of Exeter, who had conducted hundreds of secret ordinations during the past few years, had been appointed chaplain to the Temple and been given handsome lodgings near the Temple Church, where he had already begun to preach to large congregations.

On September 22, the sprightly ninety-four-year-old Bishop of Durham, Dr. Morton, who had been thrown out of Durham House many years earlier, died at the home of Sir Christopher Yelverton at Easton Maudit in Northamptonshire.

On December 9, ardent Royalist the Rev. Peter Gunning, preacher at the Exeter Chapel, gave a dinner for Dr. Fearne, Dr. Henchman, Dr. Thrisco, Dr. Wild and other worthy figures, several of whom were to become bishops in the next reign.

1660

On March 25, 1660, Royalist divine Dr. Matthew Griffith preached at the Mercers' Chapel in Cheapside on 'the Fear of God and the King'. He was immediately arrested and sent to Newgate prison, but his stay there was not long.

Dr. Isaac Barrow, who was secretly ordained in 1659. One of the greatest preachers of the day, his only failing was the excessive length of his sermons. Once the vergers in Westminster Abbey were forced to set the organs playing till they had 'blowed him down'

63

THE RESTORATION

1660–1688

The King, the bishops, the Prayer Book and the Anglican attitude towards religion were now welcomed back with a vengeance. Puritan intruders were harassed out of the parsonages, their style of preaching was ridiculed and terrible indignities were inflicted on the corpse of Oliver Cromwell. In the years that followed, a new upper-class style of Anglicanism was enforced by the Clarendon Code and hopes of a truly national church were dashed. The bishops resumed their grand life-styles and took part in the extravagances of the day. Extremist groups such as the Quakers suffered acutely and the popular hatred of Rome was soon exploited by the infamous Titus Oates. A new scientific spirit was in the air. The Royal Society was founded, theatre was revived and the Bible began to lose its authority. Following the Great Fire of 1666, a new dignity was lent to the London scene by the churches of Sir Christopher Wren while in the depths of the country the bishops' palaces were also improved and adorned. Meanwhile, the royal family was drifting towards Rome. In 1685, Charles II died a Roman Catholic. In the stormy reign that followed, his brother attempted to undermine the protestant supremacy and the period ends with seven bishops being sent to the Tower and an invitation being extended to Prince William of Orange to come and rescue the nation.

1660   On May 8, 1660, Charles II was solemnly proclaimed King in Westminster Hall. Two days later, the Book of Common Prayer was read in the House of Lords.

A few days later, a large deputation arrived at The Hague to collect the exiled monarch and congratulate him on his restoration. Among this party was the Rev. Thomas Case, who suffered the humiliation of his boat capsizing.

On May 26, the new King arrived at Dover on board the *Naseby* and began a triumphant journey to London. En route, the procession paused at Canterbury, where a private meeting took place between Charles and Gilbert Sheldon, who had been quietly reinstated as Warden of All Souls and was soon to emerge as a leader of the Church of England.

After his triumphant entry into the capital on May 29, the new King immediately re-established the Chapel Royal, empowering the choir-master, Henry Cook, to raid cathedral and collegiate choirs for the best possible choristers.

On July 29, Dr. Robert South viciously attacked the puritan style of preaching in a sermon at St. Mary's, Oxford. He ridiculed those who practised strange new postures such as 'shutting the eyes, distorting the face and speaking through the nose'. He also attacked the use of rich allegories and rhyme, which he said were 'such pitiful embellishments of speech as serve for nothing but to embase divinity'.

The following month, the parsonage at Kibworth in Leicestershire was damaged in a brawl between the in-going and out-going families.

On September 13, 78-year-old Dr. William Juxon, Bishop of London, who had attended Charles I on the scaffold and spent the Commonwealth on his comfortable estate at Little Compton in Gloucestershire, was elected Archbishop of Canterbury.

Nine days later, the Bishop of Lichfield and Coventry, Dr. Frewen, was made Archbishop of York. A wealthy bachelor, who was said to preserve his chastity by having no female servants in his house, he was to restore and rebuild the medieval Bishopthorpe Palace beside the River Ouse, creating a splendid dining-room with an elaborate plaster ceiling.

The following month saw the execution of Thomas Scott, who had signed the late King's death warrant and occupied Lambeth Palace in the years that followed, turning its chapel into a dance hall.

On November 25, Dr. Edward Rainbow preached before the new King taking the text 'Glory to God in the highest and on earth, peace, goodwill to all men' and laying special stress on the glory to be given to God for restoration of the Church and Government.

Five days later, the Rev. John Fell, who had been in arms for the King during the war, and had continued to perform the rights of the church throughout the Commonwealth, was appointed Dean of Christ Church.*

On December 30, a new organ designed by the great organ-builder Bernard Smidt was unveiled in Westminster Abbey.

A month later on January 29, 1661, the Abbey was the scene of a less cheerful event when the corpse of Oliver Cromwell was solemnly exhumed from its resting place, taken to the Red Lion Inn in Holborn, then dragged through the streets on hurdles to Tyburn where, along with the corpses of two of his comrades, it was strung up on the gallows. It was then hacked down and beheaded by the common hangman, the body being thrown into a deep pit and the mummified head was placed on public display outside Westminster Hall.

Three months later, on April 15, twelve Anglican bishops and twelve puritan divines gathered at the lodgings of the Master of the Savoy to discuss the re-introduction of the Prayer Book and other aspects of worship. These discussions were to prove pointless as the bishops were unwilling to give any ground.

On April 23, the coronation of Charles II took place in Westminster Abbey. The elderly Archbishop of Canterbury, Dr. Juxon, was too weak to preside over the whole ceremony but managed to officiate at the unction and blessing of the sword, to place the crown on the King's head, the ring on his finger and present him with two sceptres. Assisting at the rite was the King's

---

* One of the students to come under Dr. Fell's care was a certain Tom Brown, to whom is attributed the following verse:

'I do not love thee Dr. Fell,
The reason why I cannot tell,
But this alone I know full well,
I do not love thee Dr. Fell.'

old tutor Dr. Earle, now Dean of Westminster. Many of those presiding wore copes of scarlet and purple cloth of gold, with heavy gold and silver embroidery.

On August 15, the much loved Rev. Thomas Fuller, who had been made a Doctor of Divinity the previous summer, died of a fever at his lodgings in Covent Garden. At his funeral the following day at Cranford in Middlesex, 200 clergy rode behind his cortège.

The following month, the remains of the puritan divine Stephen Marshall were taken from Westminster Abbey and thrown into a pit at the backdoor of the prebendary's lodgings in St. Margaret's churchyard.

On December 20, Westminster Abbey was the setting for the funeral of Dr. Monck, Bishop of Hereford and brother of the famous general. The Bishop's silver mitre and episcopal robes were borne by a herald in front of the hearse.

1662   On March 26, 1662, the Bishop of Winchester, Dr. Duppa, a one time tutor to the King, died at his home in Richmond. His former pupil had visited him the previous day and knelt beside his bed and asked for his blessing. The body was taken later to York House in the Strand, where it lay in state before burial in Westminster Abbey.

He was succeeded as Bishop of Winchester by the Bishop of Worcester, Dr. Morley, who in spite of his ascetic habits – he got up at five o'clock in the morning throughout the year and often sat without a fire on winter mornings – was to greatly improve the amenities of the see. During his episcopate, he was to repair Farnham Castle, where he often entertained the King and the Duke of York, employ Christopher Wren to rebuild Wolvesey Palace at Winchester and purchase, for £4,000, a house in Chelsea.

The Bishop of Winchester, Dr. Morley, who used to get up at 5 a.m. throughout the year and often sat without a fire on winter mornings

On May 19, the Act of Uniformity received the Royal Assent. It ordered all clergy to declare their absolute loyalty to the King, accept the rule of the bishops and the new revised Prayer Book. It also ordered that everyone holding public office must be a communicant member of the Church of England.

When this act came into force on St. Bartholomew's Day, August 24, some 2,000 clergy chose to resign or be ejected rather than comply with these regulations.

Three months later, on November 30, judges, nobility, bishops and clergy flocked to a sumptuous dinner, given by the Dean of Westminster, Dr. Earle, to celebrate his consecration as Bishop of Worcester. This event was said to have cost £600 and was described by John Evelyn as 'one of the most plentiful and magnificent dinners that in my life I ever saw'.

On Christmas Day, there was laughter when the new Bishop of Winchester, Dr. Morley, preached at Whitehall attacking 'the common jollity of the court' and its 'excess in plays and gaming'.

1663 On January 6, 1663, the fashionable presbyterian divine Dr. Edmund Calamy, one of the first clergymen to refuse to comply with the new Uniformity Act, was committed to Newgate Prison. During his short incarceration, it was said that Newgate Street was blocked with the coaches of his visitors.

Six weeks later on February 23, the marriage took place between the Rev. John Tillotson, preacher at Lincoln's Inn, and Cromwell's niece Elizabeth French. The bride was apparently reluctant to wed Mr. Tillotson but was overruled by her father with the words: 'You shall have him, Betty, for he is the best polemical divine in England.'

On June 4, the death occurred of the eighty-year-old Archbishop of Canterbury, Dr. Juxon. He had spent his short primacy restoring St. Paul's Cathedral and re-erecting the great hall at Lambeth Palace with a magnificent hammerbeam roof but had played little role in matters of state. Injunctions that his funeral service should be unostentatious were ignored and his body was laid in state in the Divinity School at Oxford and then buried with great pomp in the chapel of St. John's College. The remains of Archbishop Laud were later brought from All Hallows by-the-Tower and re-interred close by him.

On August 31, the translation of Gilbert Sheldon, Bishop of London, to the see of Canterbury was celebrated with a mighty feast for the nobility in the Great Hall at Lambeth Palace.

In September the Dean of Christ Church, Dr. Fell, entertained the King, Queen and many courtiers at his college, where he was currently rebuilding the great quadrangle.

1664 The following summer, Dr. Edward Rainbow, Dean of Peterborough, was consecrated Bishop of Carlisle. On arrival in his diocese he found the official residence, Rose Castle, much dilapidated and was to begin lengthy litigation with his predecessor, Dr. Sterne, now Archbishop of York

Meanwhile, another inter-episcopal quarrel was raging between Dr. Lucy, Bishop of St. David's, who claimed to be 'the poorest bishop in England and Wales' and his neighbour William Nicholson, Bishop of Gloucester, who claimed the right to visit Dr. Lucy's diocese and correct faults in the clergy.

On October 8, a stormy confrontation took place between the two prelates and the Bishop of London was called in to arbitrate.

A few days later, on October 15, the Bishop of Winchester, Dr. Morley, was found dining with the Lord Chancellor at Worcester House in the Strand.

1665   On February 23, 1665, the new Archbishop of Canterbury, Dr. Sheldon, and the Bishops of London and Winchester were present at a great feast given by Mr. Rich, reader at Lincoln's Inn.

Meanwhile, the Rev. Samuel Speed, who had been a pirate in the Civil War and taken part in much fighting, plundering and drunkenness, had renounced his past and become Vicar of Godalming. In June this year, he felt the lure of the sea again and set off with the Earl of Ossory on his expedition against the Dutch, where he was to win much acclaim for his gallant seamanship. 'He prayed like a Christian and fought like a Turk', wrote a contemporary poet.

The same month, the Great Plague hit London and raged until September, causing some 100,000 deaths. Archbishop Sheldon bravely remained at Lambeth Palace throughout the period and the Bishop of London, Dr. Humphrey Henchman, warned runaway clergy that they would be replaced. The Deanery of St. Paul's was fumigated twice a week with brimstone, hops, pepper and frankincense, though the Dean himself, William Sancroft, was already at Tunbridge, whither he had apparently been advised to go 'long before any plague was heard of'. Of the London parsons who braved the pestilence, eleven died agonizing deaths.

On October 14, the famous Royalist parson Dr. Matthew Griffith died of a ruptured blood vessel while preaching at Bladon in Oxfordshire.

On November 17, Dr. Earle, now Bishop of Salisbury, died at Oxford, whither he had accompanied the King at the outbreak of the plague in London.

1666   The following year, the eleventh-century St. Paul's Cathedral, eighty other churches and fifty-five parsonages were destroyed in the Great Fire of London, which began on September 2 and lasted five days. During the blaze, the Dean of Westminster, Dr. Dolben, organized the scholars of Westminster School to douse the fire. After it was all over the learned Dean Harding declared in a sermon that London had been 'reduced from a large folio to a decimo-tertio'.

On September 12, thirty-four-year-old Christopher Wren laid before King Charles a sketch plan for the restoration of the city and was immediately appointed 'surveyor general and principal architect for rebuilding the whole city, the cathedral church of St. Paul's, all the parochial churches, with other public structures'.

On October 14, the wealthy Bishop of Rochester, Dr. Warner, died leaving money and instructions for the erection of a spacious almshouse for the widows of loyal and orthodox clergy to be built at Bromley.

At the end of the year, Lewis Evans, celebrated harpist at the Chapel Royal, who had not been paid for five years, died of starvation and was buried that night in a pauper's grave.

Meanwhile, the Rev. Thomas Daffy had been installed as vicar of Redmile in the vale of Belvoir, where he was to invent a soothing elixir, said to be specially suitable for the treatment of flatulent colic, dyspepsia and diarrhoea, which was soon on sale at his son's apothecary's shop in Nottingham.

1667   In July 1667, Dr. Creighton, Dean of Wells, preached a sermon before the King 'against the sins of the court and particularly against adultery'. He also bemoaned the fact that most English castles were without both 'ammunition and powder'. Curiously, this boldness did not offend and he was shortly afterwards made Bishop of Bath and Wells.

The following month, the death of Dr. Jeremy Taylor, Bishop of Down and Connor, inspired fine words from his colleague, George Rust, Bishop of Dromore. 'He had the good humour of a gentleman, the eloquence of an orator, the fancy of a poet, the acuteness of a schoolman, the profoundness of a philosopher, the wisdom of a chancellor, the sagacity of a prophet, the reason of an angel and the piety of a saint.'

1668   Thirteen months later, on August 23, 1668, the Bishop of Chester, George Hall, died after accidentally wounding himself with a knife in his pocket when he fell in his garden at Wigan.

He was succeeded as bishop by John Wilkins, an ingenious, mechanically-minded man who in early life had tried to prove that the moon was habitable and had even invented a locomotive which would sail there.

1669   On March 1, 1669, the venerable Bishop of Hereford, Dr. Herbert Croft, was found dining at Lord Arlington's new residence, Goring House, off Piccadilly.

A few days later, on March 13, Archbishop Sheldon gave a lunch party at Lambeth Palace at which guests were entertained by a certain Cornet Bolton, who stood behind a chair and gave a parody of a presbyterian sermon.

On July 9, the opening of the new Sheldonian Theatre at Oxford designed by Christopher Wren and said to have cost Archbishop Sheldon some £25,000, was celebrated. The inauguration ceremony was attended by many leading churchmen but the Primate himself was absent.

1670   The following year saw the erection of the new Deanery of St. Paul's, a simple but spacious building, designed by Christopher Wren and featuring a staircase with heavily twisted balusters.

1671   In March 1671, the Bishop of Worcester, Dr. Blandford, attended the Duchess of York on her deathbed and was warned by her husband before he entered her chamber that she had been reconciled with the Roman Catholic faith. Dr. Blandford made 'a short Christian exhortation' at her bedside and left.

1672   Ten months later, on January 15, 1672, the seventy-seven-year-old Bishop of Durham, Dr. Cosin, died after a long illness aggravated by his insistence on attending church in bad weather. A magnificent funeral followed at Bishop Auckland at which the Archdeacon of Northumberland stated that Dr. Cosin had spent some £2,000 a year on charitable works.

On October 16 this year the first stone was laid of Wren's St. Stephen's Walbrook, a majestic little church later described as 'a miniature St. Paul's Cathedral'.

At Christmas, the Duke of York's conversion to Romanism was publicly demonstrated when he refused to take the Anglican sacrament with the King.

1673   In March 1673, the Test Act, which ordered that only members of the

Church of England should hold public office, was quickly rushed through both Houses of Parliament.

That Easter, the Duke of York again refused to take the Anglican communion, causing, in the words of John Evelyn 'exceeding grief and scandal to the whole nation'.

Meanwhile, the young Rev. Titus Oates had been installed as Vicar of Bobbing in Kent where he was soon to disgrace himself by making a false charge against a local school-master. He was put in prison and ordered to pay £1,000 in damages.

1674   On March 25, 1674, the Bishops of Salisbury, Lincoln and Chester dined together at Knightsbridge, near London.

Four weeks later, on April 25, the new Master of Trinity College Cambridge, Dr. Isaac Barrow, who was said to be uncouth in appearance and over-fond of tobacco and fruit, preached before the royal household on love and charity to our neighbours.

1675   On February 3, the following year, the King issued orders that all those failing to appear for communion at their parish church should have their names passed on to their bishops for ecclesiastical action. Among those soon arrested was forty-six-year-old unlicensed puritan preacher John Bunyan. Unable to pay £60 in fines, he was thrown into Bedford County Gaol, where he was to complete his book *Pilgrim's Progress*.

On June 21, the foundation stone of the new St. Paul's Cathedral was laid.

Six days later, there was a magnificent feast at Ely House in Holborn to celebrate the consecration of sixty-eight-year-old Thomas Barlow as Bishop of Lincoln. Barlow was to seriously neglect his diocese and was even accused of never entering his cathedral.

On December 19, the new St. Bride's Church, off Fleet Street, was formally opened. The Vicar, Dr. Henry Dove, preached before the Lord Mayor and a crowded congregation. Designed by Christopher Wren, the church featured oval clerestory windows but did not yet possess its 226-foot spire.

1676   The following year, the same architect began work on St. James's Church, Piccadilly, which was designed to hold a congregation of over 2,000:

Meanwhile the great hall at Farnham Castle, one of the Bishop of Winchester's several residences, was being restored and repaired at a total cost of £10,000.

1677   On October 4, 1677, the death occurred of Dr. Lucy, Bishop of St. David's who had spent the last five years confined to his house owing to mental illness and had permitted his diocese to become filled with non-resident parsons.

A month later, on November 4, the marriage of Princess Mary and Prince William of Orange took place in the bride's apartment in St. James's Palace conducted by the new Bishop of London, Dr. Henry Compton. The King was impatient to get the proceedings over and at one moment called out, 'Come, Bishop, make all the haste you can!'

Five days later, the Archbishop of Canterbury, Dr. Sheldon, died at Lambeth Palace. He had been seriously ill for several months and every attempt to save him, including the prescription of an *aurum potabile* by a German physician, had failed.

Within a month, Dr. William Sancroft, Dean of St. Paul's, had been

The Rev. Titus Oates, one of the most scandalous clergymen in history. Expelled from Merchant Taylors school, he 'slipped' into Holy Orders and became Vicar of Bobbing in Kent, but was soon in disgrace after making a false charge against a local schoolmaster

chosen to be the new Primate, in spite of his protests that he was unfit for the post having led a very solitary life. It was said that he had been chosen because he stood outside the political and religious strife of the day.

1678   On February 18, 1678, the library of the late Rev. William Greenhill, a former Vicar of St. Dunstan's in the East, was auctioned in Stable's Coffee House in Bread Street.

Three days later, Archbishop Sancroft and Bishop Morley of Winchester visited the Duke of York at St. James's Palace and tried to persuade him to return to the Church of England. They were received politely but their ministrations failed to have any effect on the Duke, who told them that he was in no doubt about his faith and his conscience was clear.

Six months later, in the middle of August, the already scandalous Rev. Titus Oates, along with Dr. Israel Tonge, Rector of St. Michael's, Wood Street, released details of a fictitious plot to assassinate the King and re-establish Romanism. Oates was quickly summoned before the Privy Council who readily accepted his tale. The mysterious murder of Sir Edmund Berry Godfrey, a well-known magistrate, some weeks later fanned the flames and a reign of terror for Roman Catholics began. In the course of the next few months, eight clergymen suspected of a part in this plot were executed and five others were to die in prison.

1679   On February 2, 1679, the Dean of Windsor, Dr. Durrell, preached before the royal household at Whitehall, reading his entire sermon from notes.

At the end of the month, the Rev. John Gostling, possessor of a phenomenal voice with immense range and power, was sworn a member of the Chapel Royal.

On May 3, the Archbishop of St. Andrews, James Sharp, who was notorious for his use of the thumb-screw to intimidate his political opponents, was dragged out of his coach and murdered.

1680   Seventeen months later, on October 8, 1680, the Rev. Thomas Tenison was appointed to the living of St. Martin-in-the-Fields where he was to establish a reputation for devoted pastoral care, gathering around him a team of assistant curates and founding the first public library in London.

The following month, the Rev. Titus Oates was the principal witness against Lord Stafford at his trial in Westminster Hall. In spite of the King's comments that he would not have hanged a dog on the evidence presented, the Earl was executed for high treason before the end of the year.

1681   On March 3, 1681, the Rev. Edmund Hickeringill, half-crazy rector of All Saints, Colchester, appeared at Chelmsford Assizes to answer twenty-four charges of indulging in vexatious litigation. The parson conducted his own defence with such skill that the prosecution broke down.

Four months later, on July 1, the Roman Catholic Archbishop of Armagh was executed after further corrupt evidence from the Rev. Titus Oates.

1682   On January 14, 1682, the majestic looking Dr. Dolben, Bishop of Rochester and Dean of Westminster, celebrated his twenty-fourth wedding anniversary with a dinner party at his home in Westminster.

Two months later, on March 8, the Rev. Mr. Hickeringill was again in court this time being prosecuted for slander and *scandalum magnatum* by the Bishop of London, Dr. Compton. He was initially fined £2,000 but this was cancelled when he made a full public confession of his guilt in the court of the Dean of Arches.

In June, royal chaplain the Rev. Thomas Ken preached a memorable sermon at the funeral of Lady Margaret Maynard, during which he made a sharp distinction between men and women. 'Women are made of a temper more soft and frail, are more endangered by snares and temptations, less able to control their passions and more inclinable to extremes of good and bad', he stated firmly.

1683   A year later, when the Court visited his home town of Winchester, Thomas Ken refused to permit the King's mistress Nell Gwynn to occupy his house. 'A woman of ill repute', he explained, 'ought not to be endured in the house of a clergyman and especially the King's chaplain.'

On August 26, the corpulent but lively Dr. Dolben was enthroned as Archbishop of York amidst much popular acclaim.

Meanwhile, the penniless Rev. John Thomas, former curate at Stalbridge in Dorset, was to be found in Chelmsford Gaol, where he had been placed for cursing and swearing while drunk.

1684   At Easter, 1684, the new Bishop of Rochester, Dr. Sprat, preached at Whitehall before the King, who was accompanied to the altar by three of his illegitimate sons, the Dukes of Northumberland, Richmond and St. Albans.

Three months later, on Sunday July 13, the Bishop of London, Dr. Compton consecrated the newly-built church of St. James's Piccadilly which had been paid for by Henry Jermyn, Lord St. Alban, who was currently developing this new suburb of London.

On November 5, Dr. Gilbert Burnet of the Rolls Chapel in Chancery Lane preached a vehement and offensive two-hour sermon against popery, taking the text 'save me from the lion's mouth' and making a disloyal reference to the lion and the unicorn. Although this sermon was greeted with bursts of applause, Burnet was deprived of his chaplaincy and fled abroad.

Early in 1685, it became known that the King was dying. His bedside was soon surrounded by Anglican bishops imploring him to receive the sacrament of the church of which he was head. Among them was Thomas Ken, now Bishop of Bath and Wells, who kept up an unbroken vigil of three whole days and nights in the King's bedchamber. However, shortly before the King's death on February 6, Father Huddleston, who had helped him escape after the battle of Worcester, was smuggled into the room and received him into the Catholic church.

Eight days later, on February 14, King Charles II was buried in a small private service at Westminster Abbey, which was conducted under the cover of darkness, on the instructions of the new King, a declared Catholic, who did not want his brother publicly subjected to Anglican rites.

On April 23, King James II was crowned by Archbishop Sancroft in Westminster Abbey. A sermon was preached by the Bishop of Ely, Dr. Turner, and the musical arrangements were in the hands of the abbey's organist, Henry Purcell. The service ended with Purcell's great anthem 'My heart is Inditing' ending with an Alleluya coda in swinging three-time.

Two weeks later, on May 7, the Rev. Titus Oates was brought before Judge Jeffreys on the King's Bench and charged with perjury. He was fined 2,000 marks and sentenced to be stripped of his clerical habit and be whipped from Aldgate to Newgate and, two days later, from Newgate to Tyburn, followed by imprisonment for life.

On June 11, the late King's illegitimate son, the Duke of Monmouth, arrived in England. In the commotion that followed, public orator Dr. Robert South offered to change his priest's cassock for a buff coat and join in the fighting. The rebellion soon ended in disaster and on, July 15, Monmouth was executed in London, his painful death – it took five chops to remove his head – being witnessed by Bishop Turner of Ely, Bishop Ken of Bath and Wells and Dr. Tenison, vicar of St. Martin-in-the-Fields.

On November 14, diarist John Evelyn dined with the Archbishop of Canterbury, Dr. Sancroft, being taken across the Thames to Lambeth in the Primate's private barge.

Meanwhile, the Bishop of Lichfield and Coventry, Dr. Thomas Wood, had been suspended for non-residence and scandalous living.

On April 15, 1686, the Archbishop of York, Dr. Dolben, died of small-pox at Bishopthorpe Palace. It was said that he had caught the disease while staying at an inn on his way from London to York the previous year.

Three months later, the Court of High Commission was revived, presided over by the cruel Judge Jeffreys. Archbishop Sancroft declined to serve on it, on the grounds of his age and infirmities and was henceforth forbidden to appear at Court.

One of the first people to appear before the new court was the Bishop of London, Dr. Compton, who, on September 6, was suspended for refusing to discipline Dr. Sharp, Dean of Norwich, for preaching a sermon attacking the Roman Catholics. Dr. Compton, brother of the Earl of Northampton, retirted to Fulham Palace and his botanic pursuits.

Two months later, on November 16, Dr. Samuel Johnson, Rector of

'It is a foolish sheep that makes the wolf her confessor': an anti-Catholic satire published at the end of the seventeenth century

Corringham, Essex, appeared before the King's Bench, after printing an anti-papist tract entitled *An Humble and Hearty Address to all English Protestants in the Army*. He was sentenced to be degraded from the priesthood, to stand four times in the pillory, pay a fine of 500 marks and be whipped from Newgate to Tyburn.

Four days later, his defrocking ceremony took place in the Chapter House of St. Paul's. Bishop Sprat of Rochester, Bishop Crewe of Durham and Bishop White of Peterborough stripped the thirty-seven-year-old Rector of his bible, cap, gown and girdle.* Two days later, he appeared for the first time in the pillory and, on December 1, he received 317 stripes with a whip of nine knotted cords. In spite of his ordeal, Dr. Johnson's spirit apparently remained unbroken.

This Christmas, a new chapel for the performance of the Roman Catholic service was opened in Whitehall Palace. The building featured an organ by Renatus Harris and magnificent carvings by Mr. Grinling Gibbons.

1687   In January 1687 the Archbishop of Glasgow, Dr. Cairncross, was deprived of his see after failing to act decisively against Dr. James Canaries who had preached against Popery before a large congregation in the High Kirk in Edinburgh the previous year.

A few weeks later, on March 20, Dr. Ken, Bishop of Bath and Wells, preached at St. Martin-in-the-Fields on the Beloved Saviour's agony and lunched afterwards with the Vicar, Dr. Tenison.

Five days later, on Good Friday March 25, Dr. Tenison himself was preaching at St. Martin's when several men entered the church with their swords drawn, throwing the congregation into confusion.

On August 24, Michael Wise, master of the choristers at St. Paul's Cathedral and composer of some thirty-seven anthems, died of a fractured skull after a fight with a night-watchman in the precincts of Salisbury Cathedral.

On November 17, Dr. Thomas Tenison conducted the funeral of Nell Gwynn at St. Martin-in-the-Fields. Tenison had nursed the late King's mistress through her last illness and in his funeral address represented her as a penitent.

1688   On May 4, the following year, the Council ordered all clergy to read in their parish churches the King's new Declaration of Indulgence which dispensed with the laws discriminating against anyone not a member of the established church.

Two weeks later, a petition, hand-written by Archbishop Sancroft, was presented at Court to the effect that the bishops could not give their support to this order. The King was insistent but the bishops stood their ground and, declaring 'God's will be done', respectfully withdrew.

On June 8, Archbishop Sancroft and six episcopal colleagues were arrested, charged with seditious libel and taken by barge to the Tower of London. The banks of the Thames were crowded with supporters seeking their blessings and as the bishops entered the Tower the bell of the church of St. Peter ad Vincula on the precincts was tolled.

On June 29, the trial of the bishops took place in Westminster Hall.

---

* But not his cassock, which was later held to invalidate the degradation.

The Seven Bishops are taken by barge to the Tower of London. The banks of the Thames are crowded with supporters asking for their blessings

The following day, the Not Guilty verdict was greeted with shouts of joy and a letter signed by, among others, the suspended Bishop of London, Dr. Compton, was despatched to Prince William of Orange offering him the throne and inviting him 'to come and rescue the nation'.

On September 21, King James attempted to quieten things down by issuing a proclamation that he would guarantee the privileges of the Church of England and do nothing inimical to it.

Over the next few weeks, there were a number of interviews between the panic-stricken King and the aged Archbishop Sancroft. Although the King was now prepared to give some ground, the situation was too advanced to be remedied.

On November 5, Prince William of Orange landed at Torbay, accompanied by the swarthy Dr. Gilbert Burnet, who had fled the country four years earlier after making a violent attack on popery in the Rolls Chapel. The party made their way to Exeter, where Dr. Burnet annoyed the local clergy by preaching in the cathedral. The Bishop of Exeter, Dr. Lamplugh, had already fled to London to warn the King of the invasion and was rewarded with the Archbishopric of York.

At the end of November, the Bishop of London, Dr. Compton, put on his sword-belt and escorted the King's daughter, Princess Anne, to join the rebels at Nottingham.

On the morning of December 18, the King finally left London and later the same day Prince William arrived in the capital.

THE REVOLUTION SETTLEMENT

1688–1714

This bloodless revolution was swiftly followed by the passing of the Toleration Act, which removed the worst disabilities that had been inflicted on the dissenters and ended the Church of England's monopoly of the nation's religious life. This settlement won wide support and reflected the growth of intellectual freedom. By 1700, over a thousand chapels and meeting houses had been put up by the newly emergent sects and Archbishops Tillotson and Tenison had begun to root out some of the ancient evils of the Church and impose a stricter discipline on the bishops. A reaction to the licentiousness of the Restoration period set in and trade began to unite the nation and gloss over religious differences. Hymns began to appear, the new St. Paul's Cathedral was completed, the charity schools were opened, the Society for the Propagation of the Gospel was founded and, in 1704, Queen Anne handed over a portion of her income to aid poorer clergy. At the end of the period, the extreme high church party came into power and attempted to undermine the revolution settlement with savage pieces of legislation against dissenters but Archbishop Tenison and others worked away quietly in the background to secure the Hanoverian succession.

88   On December 23, 1688, the burly Dr. Gilbert Burnet preached at St. James's chapel on the text 'It is the Lord's doing and it is marvellous in our eyes'.

A week later, the Bishop of London, Dr. Compton, administered the sacrament to the new ruler.

89   On January 15, 1689, there was a meeting of bishops and lay peers at Lambeth Palace, at which Archbishop Sancroft declared his willingness to appoint William regent but refused to go back on his oath to King James.

On January 30, the reinstated Dean of Norwich, Dr. Sharp, preached an unexpected sermon before the Convention Parliament in which he condemned the deposing of kings as a popish practice. He then caused hot debate by praying for King James.

On April 11, the new monarchs were crowned in Westminster Abbey. The Bishop of London stood in for the Primate, Dr. Gilbert Burnet, now Bishop of Salisbury, preached a sermon and there was powerful singing from the amazing John Gostling.

On May 24, parliament passed the Toleration Act, which recognized as legal other churches besides the Anglican and introduced an element of freedom into the nation's religious life.

On June 11, parliament resolved that the judgement passed on Dr. Samuel Johnson, who had been defrocked and savagely whipped three years earlier for treasonable activities, was illegal. He was reinstated as a clergyman and was offered – but refused – the Deanery of Durham.

On August 1, under the terms of an act of parliament requiring certain oaths to be taken to the new government, the Archbishop of Canterbury, Dr. Sancroft, eight other bishops and some 400 clergy were suspended. The bishops were leniently treated for a while and permitted to reside in their sees and occupy their palaces.

On November 21, the Rev. John Tillotson, already Clerk of the Closet to the new King, was made Dean of St. Paul's. On kissing hands, the king intimated to Tillotson, said to be the first parson to wear a wig, that in due course he should follow Archbishop Sancroft as Primate.

In December, parliament passed the Bill of Rights, which ordered that no Catholic should become King or Queen of England and imposed a new oath of allegiance to be taken on all office-holders, M.P.s and clergy.

1690   On February 1, the following year, Archbishop Sancroft, Bishop Ken of Bath and Wells and other bishops who felt unable to take this oath to the new King and Queen were deprived of their sees. Bishop Ken was to go quietly into retirement at Longleat House, where his old friend Lord Weymouth provided him with a spacious upper room, but Archbishop Sancroft was to cling on at Lambeth Palace for many months.

On March 7, the new Dean of St. Paul's, Dr. Tillotson, preached a sermon before the Queen in which he attempted to demolish the terrifying doctrine of the eternity of hell torments.

Later this year, the deprived Bishop of Ely, Dr. Turner, was found to be engaging in treasonable correspondence with the former King and on **1691**   February 5, 1691, a warrant was issued for his apprehension. The bishop, educated at Winchester, fled to France before the arrest could be affected.

On April 22, the nomination of Dr. Tillotson as new Archbishop of Canterbury compelled the elderly Dr. Sancroft to begin at last to pack up his books at Lambeth Palace and tell his chaplains and servants to leave, though he himself remained in occupation of the great house.

On May 20, the elderly Archbishop received a curt order from the Queen to leave Lambeth in ten days, which only served to stiffen his determination to remain there till forced out by law.

Meanwhile, Dr. Tillotson was consecrated archbishop in a splendid ceremony at the newly built church of St. Mary-le-Bow in Cheapside. Absent from this event was the bachelor Bishop of London, Dr. Compton, who had been bitterly disappointed not to receive the primacy himself and had gone into a sulk at Fulham Palace, unwilling to go to Court or make any approach to the King or Queen.

The following month, the vacant Deanery of St. Paul's was given to former non-juror William Sherlock, provoking a savage outcry about his apparent change of face.

On June 23, judgement was at last given against Dr. Sancroft by the Barons of the Exchequer and that evening he finally left Lambeth by barge. His first port of call was the Palsgrave's Head coffee house at Temple Bar and he later retired to a small house near his birthplace at Fressingfield in Suffolk.

Five months later, on November 26, the new Archbishop moved into

Lambeth Palace, where a special apartment had been constructed for his wife, niece of the late Oliver Cromwell and the first archbishop's wife seen at Lambeth since the death of Mrs. Parker in 1570. During his period at Lambeth, Tillotson's son-in-law was to build a furnace for the palace's greenhouse.

Meanwhile, the popish chapel at Whitehall had been dismantled and Queen Mary had given the organ – built by Renatus Harris – to the new Church of St. James's, Piccadilly.

1692   The following Easter, the new Dean of St. Paul's, Eton-educated William Sherlock, preached before the Lord Mayor at St. Bride's Church on the 'charity of lending without usury'. He suggested the setting-up of a charitable bank, provided with funds by rich men who could afford to lend money for no interest. 'It would enlarge your hospitals, clear your streets of beggars, maintain those who can't work, employ those who can and put poor children at apprentice', he explained.

A few weeks later, on May 7, the Bishop of Rochester, Dr. Sprat, was arrested and charged with conspiring to restore King James II to the throne, after the discovery of incriminating papers at his palace at Bromley. After five weeks' confinement under guard in the Deanery at Westminster, it was discovered that Dr. Sprat had been 'framed' and he was immediately released.

On October 20, Dr. William Lloyd was appointed Bishop of Lichfield and Coventry following the death of the scandalous Bishop Wood. During his short occupation of the see, he was to build a spacious L-shaped house with a thirteen bay façade in the enclosure of Eccleshall Castle.

Meanwhile, the new Vicar of Codrington in Gloucestershire had found his parishioners playing cards on the communion table and the church-wardens smoking and drinking in the sanctuary. The pipe-smoking parish clerk informed him that this had been the practice for the past sixty years.

1693   The following year, Queen Mary appointed the learned Rev. Samuel Wesley to the Crown living of Epworth in Lincolnshire. His high churmanship was to lead to quarrels with his parishioners, who stabbed three of his cows and threw lighted flares at the thatch of his ancient rectory.

1694   On March 20, 1694, the Bishop of Down and Connor, Dr. Hacket, was deprived of his see. It was said that, for the past twenty years, he had been notoriously negligent of his pastoral duties, openly selling livings to the highest bidders and residing most of the time at Hammersmith, where he had been mockingly nicknamed the 'Bishop of Hammersmith'. No action had been taken against him for so long because the Primate of Ireland, Archbishop Boyle, had been incapacitated, deaf and almost blind.

At the same time, the Dean of Connor, the Rev. Thomas Wood, was deprived for adultery.

Meanwhile the Rev. John Mason had been preaching the Second Coming of Christ, which he proclaimed would occur in his own parish of Water Stratford in Buckinghamshire. In April the village became crowded with onlookers and there was continuous dancing and singing, day and night, in the parsonage. In the midst of these celebrations, Mason died suddenly of a quinsy.

In July, commissioners were appointed to visit the Welsh diocese of St.

David's following charges against its bishop, Thomas Watson, of simony, extortion, perjury and saying 'God damn!' in his cathedral.

Four months later, on November 18, the Archbishop of Canterbury, Dr. Tillotson, was suddenly struck down by an apoplectic stroke while worshipping in the chapel at Whitehall. Four days later he died in the arms of an old friend, religious writer and non-juror the Rev. Robert Nelson. Following his death, Mrs. Tillotson was offered £2,000 for the copyright of her husband's sermons.

The first task of the new Primate, Thomas Tenison, former Vicar of St. Martin-in-the-Fields, was to attend thirty-two-year-old Queen Mary when she died of small-pox at the end of the year.

1695   On January 28, 1695, twenty-seven-year-old Jonathan Swift was ordained in Christ Church Cathedral, Dublin. He was given the post of prebend at Kilroot near Belfast but obtained a licence for non-residence.

On February 3, the King issued a set of injunctions drawn up by Archbishop Tenison for restoring and preserving the discipline of the church and carefully defining the duties of the bishops and clergy.

On April 6, the death occurred of the eighty-eight-year-old Rev. Richard Busby, D.D. who had ruled as headmaster of Westminster School for the last fifty-five years and had once boasted that he had educated sixteen bishops.

On May 16, Dr. Tenison was formally enthroned in Canterbury Cathedral, the first archbishop to be enthroned there since Thomas Cranmer. Immediately afterwards, he embarked on a primary visitation of his see, confirming nearly 4,000 people.

Three months later, on August 23, Tenison summoned the Bishop of St. David's to appear before him at Lambeth to answer the grave charges made against him the previous year. This complicated case was to drag on for many years with the Bishop using his position as a member of the House of Lords and his ownership of temporal estates to go from one court to another.

Meanwhile a new edition of Dr. Thomas Ken's *Manual of Prayers* had appeared, to which were now added two magnificent hymns, 'Awake my soul and with the sun' and 'Glory to thee, my God, this night'.

1696   On May 6, 1696, Archbishop Tenison gave a dinner for the Countess of Sutherland and other ladies. They dined in Mrs. Tenison's special apartment at Lambeth Palace.

Seven months later, the elusive Bishop of Ely, Dr. Francis Turner, was at last arrested for his Jacobite sympathies. On December 15, he was discharged from custody on the condition that he again left the country.

1697   The following March, thirty-eight prominent clergy of the diocese of St. Asaph charged their bishop, Dr. Edward Jones, with corruption, negligence and oppression. The Primate acted promptly, suspending the offending prelate and ordering two bishops and his Dean of Arches to conduct a visitation.

Eight months later, on November 21, there was a musical festival in St. Paul's Cathedral, still in the process of construction but now enriched with choir stalls carved by Grinling Gibbons and an organ built by Father Bernard Schmidt. On this joyful occasion, the choirs of St. Paul's, Westminster Abbey and the Chapel Royal were combined and a string ensemble was supported by two trumpeters.

In March 1698 a reaction to the easy-going obscenity of the Restoration period was shown by the publication of the Rev. Jeremy Collier's *Short View of the Immorality and Profaneness of the English Stage.*

The following month, thirty-four-year-old Thomas Wilson landed on the Isle of Man as its new bishop. In his first few years in office, he was to rebuild the dilapidated espicopal seat, Bishop's Court, and set up drug shops giving free advice and medicine for the island's poor.

On May 30, the death occurred of Dr. Thomas White, deprived Bishop of Peterborough. At his funeral at St. Gregory's by St. Paul's on June 4 there was friction when the Dean of St. Paul's, Dr. Sherlock, refused to allow Dr. Turner, deprived Bishop of Ely – who was officially in exile – to officiate at the grave. 'Is not this a precious mannikin of a dean?' Turner asked afterwards.

Thomas Wilson, appointed Bishop of Sodor and Man in 1698. He was to impose stringent discipline on the island, ordering slanderers to wear the bridle and prostitutes to be dragged through the sea after a boat

Ten months later, on March 27, 1699, the handsome Dr. Edward Stillingfleet, Bishop of Worcester, who had been known as 'the beauty of holiness', died at his house in Park Street, Westminster. His valuable library was later purchased by the Archbishop of Armagh, Dr. Narcissus Marsh, for £6,000.

On December 16, this year Dr. Thomas Bray, active force behind the newly formed Society for Promoting Christian Knowledge, set off for North America to see about the possible establishment of the English Church there.

1700   On February 23, 1700, the deprivation of the scandalous Bishop of St. David's, Thomas Watson, was officially confirmed by the Court of Delegates, though this ruling did not prevent him from continuing to sit in the House of Lords.

The same month, the Rev. Jonathan Swift acquired the living of Caracor near Trim. Here, he was to rebuild the parsonage, make a fish pond and plant willows, though his congregation consisted of only fifteen people and he continued to spend most of his time in Dublin.

On August 22, the execution took place at Edinburgh of the Rev. Thomas Hunter who had murdered two children who had discovered he was having an affair with a maid-servant. On the scaffold, Hunter declared himself to be an atheist. 'There is no God', he said, 'or if there be, I hold him in defiance'. Before the death sentence was carried out, this infamous clergyman had his right hand cut off with a hatchet.

Meanwhile, Dr. Daniell Phillips, newly appointed Vicar of Much Marcle, near Ross-on-Wye, had begun building a stately new vicarage in keeping with the architectural principles of the day. The house was to include a fine staircase with barley-sugar slide bannisters and tall, wide sash windows.

1701   On June 16, the following year, the King gave the Society for the Propagation of the Gospel its first charter.

Eight days later, the scandalous Bishop of St. Asaph, Dr. Edward Jones, was suspended by Archbishop Tenison after a formal hearing during which Jones declared that he had only acted 'pursuant to the example or under the instructions of his predecessor'. He was later to make a grovelling admission of his guilt and was reinstated.

1702   On March 8, 1702, King William III died in the arms of Bishop Burnet and the Primate. Burnet subsequently broke the news to the good-natured but indolent Princess Anne.

Some six weeks later, on April 23, Archbishop Tenison crowned the new Queen in Westminster Abbey but, as a staunch whig, he was out of favour with the new Court and was soon to be isolated at Lambeth Palace. Preaching at the service was Dr. Sharp, former Dean of Norwich, now Archbishop of York, who was to become the new monarch's principal adviser on matters ecclesiastical.

The same month, the Rev. George Keith, the first missionary of the new Society for the Propagation of the Gospel sailed off for America, landing in Boston six weeks later.

Meanwhile, the Queen had declared war on France and the Earl of Marlborough had left to take command of the British forces in Europe. It was recorded that he had a Chaplain General at his headquarters and a chaplain on the establishment of each regiment.

In November, extreme Tories introduced the Occasional Conformity Bill, which threatened to overthrow the Toleration Act and impose savage penalties on anyone who attended a dissenting meeting. The bill was carried in the House of Commons with an overwhelming majority but was thrown

1703   out the following year by the House of Lords after vigorous opposition from most of the bishops. 'I have long looked on liberty of conscience as one of the rights of human nature', declared Bishop Burnet.

In November 1703, some 8,000 people died in a great storm which swept the south of England. Among them were the seventy-year-old Bishop of Bath and Wells, Dr. Kidder, and his wife who were killed in their bed when a chimney stack collapsed at their medieval palace at Wells.

1704   On February 7, the following year, Queen Anne announced her intention of giving up for the benefit of the church the revenue from the First Fruits and Tenths appropriated by the Crown in 1534. She proposed that this money, known later as Queen's Anne's Bounty, should be devoted to the augmentation of small livings.

Seven months later, on September 7, there was a thanksgiving service at St. Paul's Cathedral to celebrate the victory of the Battle of Blenheim. Queen Anne arrived at the nearly completed cathedral with the Duchess of Marlborough, in a coach drawn by eight horses.

1705   On January 23, 1705, the scandalous Bishop of St. David's, who had fought a ten-year battle to keep his see, was finally ejected from the House of Lords.

Three months later, the Rev. Jonathan Swift, whose masterpiece *A Tale of a Tub* had been published the previous year, and gone through four editions, paid a brief visit to London and was welcomed by the leading wits of the day. His quaint behaviour in the coffee houses was to earn him the name 'The mad parson' and his romance with Miss Esther Johnson became the talk of society.

In June this year, the Rev. Samuel Wesley, Vicar of the royal living of Epworth in Lincolnshire and father of nineteen children, was confined in Lincoln Castle for debt.

The same year, the Rev. Benjamin Hoadly preached before the Lord Mayor at St. Lawrence Jewry a sermon in which he maintained that only rulers who governed for the good of the people should be obeyed. Mr. Hoadly had been crippled as an undergraduate and had to preach from a kneeling position.

1706   The following year, the Rev. John Wade, curate of Hammersmith, was found living in style at his handsome parsonage. In his orchard he grew apples, peaches, apricots, cherries, plums, nectarines, strawberries, raspberries, currants and vines. His flowerbeds contained roses, violets, auriculas, tulips, gillyflowers, jonquils and hollyhocks.

1707   On February 7, 1707, the elderly new Bishop of St. David's, Dr. Bull, was found smoking a pipe in the lobby of the House of Lords.

In July, this year, the young Isaac Watts, who had protested against the dullness of the psalms and their lack of New Testament content, published his *Hymns and Spiritual Songs*. This volume contained 'When I survey the wondrous cross' and other masterpieces.

In August, the colourful Rev. Edmund Hickeringill, Rector of All Saints Colchester and now seventy-six-years-old, was convicted of altering the rate books of a neighbouring parish and fined £400.

At the end of the year, Jeremiah Clarke, master of the choristers at St. Paul's Cathedral and composer, shot himself with a small screw pistol at his house in St. Paul's churchyard. Mr. Clarke, composer of the famous *Trumpet Voluntary*, was said to have been depressed after a disappointment in love.

1708   The following year, the new Tory Bishop of Exeter, Dr. Blackall, enraged the Whig government when he preached a sermon before the Queen in which he argued that rulers were ministers of God and 'none upon earth had the right to question or resist them'.

1709 In February 1709, villagers again set light to the Lincolnshire rectory of the high church Samuel Wesley. In the blaze that followed the Rector's five-year-old son John was rescued while his father was commending his infant soul to God.

Three months later, on May 17, the Rev. Francis Atterbury preached before the clergy at Sion College on the High Tory theme that when subjects were treated badly they must suffer in silence.

On November 5, fellow Tory cleric Dr. Henry Sacheverell viciously attacked the Whig government in a sermon in St. Paul's Cathedral entitled 'The Perils of False Bretheren in Church and State.' Impeachment proceedings were quickly instituted against him though his lodgings were surrounded by fans, some 40,000 copies of the sermon were sold and crowds even followed the Queen's coach 'hoping that Her Majesty was for Dr. Sacheverell'.

1710 On February 27, the following year, Sacheverell's trial opened in Westminster Hall amidst widespread rioting and attacks on leading Whig houses, including that of Dr. Burnet, Bishop of Salisbury. On March 20, the outspoken cleric was found guilty of malicious libel but he was let off lightly, being sentenced only to three years' suspension from preaching. An admirer had meanwhile given him the living of Aston in Shropshire and he soon set off on a triumphant journey across the country amidst rumours of the break up of the Whig ministry.

On September 7, Dr. Jonathan Swift arrived in London again and was welcomed by the Tory government now in power. He took lodgings in Bury Street, off Pall Mall and within easy reach of the St. James's Coffee House, where two months later he was to baptise the proprietor's child.

On December 14, the bachelor, heavy pipe-smoking Dean of Christ Church, Dr. Aldrich, died at Oxford. His priceless antiquarian library was bequeathed to the college and he was succeeded, the following year, by the High Tory Francis Atterbury, a close friend of the Queen.

1711 On April 26, 1711, Dr. Swift moved to lodgings in Chelsea, where he was to bathe in the River Thames and begin a flirtation with Miss Esther Vanhomrigh, whose family lived nearby.

At the end of this year, the Occasional Conformity Bill at last received the Royal Assent. This savage measure barred all officials from attending dissenting meetings and inflicted heavy penalties on anyone breaking the law.

Meanwhile, parliament had declared that the work on St. Paul's Cathedral, now adorned with a magnificent dome, gold ball and cross was complete and much praise was heaped on its architect, Sir Christopher Wren, now seventy-nine-years-old. At the same time, parliament authorized the building of more churches in the suburbs of London and Sir Christopher was again called in to advise.

1712 On March 27, the following year, Dr. Jonathan Swift was found dining sumptuously in Ozinda's Chocolate House in St. James's Street with Dr. John Arbuthnot, one of the leading physicians of the day.

Three months later, on June 30, the Bishop of Worcester, Dr. Lloyd, now

The new St. Paul's Cathedral took thirty-six years to complete and was later described as 'God's Railway Station'

eighty-five-years-old and suffering from apocalyptic visions, informed the Queen of a religious war which, he said, would soon engulf the world.

1713 On Palm Sunday, 1713, Dr. Sacheverell's suspension from preaching came to an end and he delivered a sermon at St. Saviour's, Southwark, on 'the duty of praying for enemies'. A few days later, on April 13, he was presented with the rich living of St. Andrew's Holborn where he was to continue to harp on about the wickedness of Whiggery and the duty of passive obedience to the Crown.

On May 20, the Bishop of Rochester, Dr. Sprat, died of apoplexy at his palace in Bromley.

On June 13, Dr. Jonathan Swift, now suffering from dizziness and shingles, was consecrated Dean of St. Patrick's in Dublin. He had been seeking an ecclesiastical honour for several years but the Queen had been warned off him by her intimate adviser on these matters, the Archbishop of York, Dr. Sharp. With his new post went a large gloomy house near the cathedral, where he was soon besieged by official callers.

A few weeks later, on July 7, the elderly Bishop of London, Dr. Compton, who had been constantly thwarted in his desire for the Primacy, died at Fulham Palace, where he had consoled himself planting exotic plants and trees.

1714 On February 2, 1714, the Archbishop of York, Dr. Sharp, died at Bath, now a fashionable watering place.

Meanwhile, the Rev. Richard Welton, Rector of St. Mary's, Whitechapel, had commissioned a new altar-piece of the Last Supper, ordering the artist to make the portrait of Judas Iscariot resemble the Whiggish Bishop of Peterborough, Dr. White Kennett. On April 26 this year, the Bishop took proceedings in court to have the offending detail removed.

On June 10, the strength of the High Church party was demonstrated by the passing of the Schism Act, which ordered that no one should keep a school who did not subscribe to the beliefs of the Church of England and thus barred dissenters from bringing up their children according to the religion of their choice.

The same month, Dr. Bentley, Master of Trinity College, Cambridge, was hauled before the Bishop of Ely, Dr. Moore, at Ely House in Holborn accused of encroaching on the rights of his fellows. Alas, the Bishop caught cold during these long sessions and died on July 31 before giving judgement.

The following day, Sunday August 1, Queen Anne died at Kensington Palace.

In spite of the keenness of the part of Francis Atterbury, now Bishop of Rochester, and others present at her deathbed to proclaim James Stuart the new monarch and re-introduce Catholicism, the Crown was to pass to the staunchly protestant House of Hanover.

THE EIGHTEENTH CENTURY

1714–1793

A reaction to the religious and social upheavals of the past two centuries now set in. The church was now no longer torn apart by destructive enthusiasms and instead sank into a state of slumber, becoming closely identified with the aristocracy and conservatism. In spite of the rapid increase in the population, only a handful of churches were built in London in the years that followed. Musically, the church became dependent on visiting foreign composers, and ecclesiastics themselves became notoriously lax. At Lambeth Palace, the Archbishop of Canterbury, whose income by the end of this period was to reach £7,000 a year, kept a ducal household, dispensed lavish hospitality, kept a coach and six horses and a private state barge with liveried crew. Most of the bishops under him, who no longer had a direct part to play in the running of the nation, had aristocratic connections. Many of them had been pluralists at some stage in their careers and most of them died rich. Many shamefully neglected their duties, indulging themselves in luxuries and worldly pleasures in the great houses in which they now guarded their inheritance. 'Our modern superior clergy', declared a contemporary, 'are driven about, lolling in superb vehicles and drawn by fiery steeds to places of diversion'. Many of the parish clergy were equally corrupt. Though many now had fine pulpits to preach from, equipped with sounding board, hourglass, wig holder, cushions and candlestick, the name of Christ was often never heard in the eighteenth century sermon. Many tailored their sermons to please their smart congregations. Others were 'four or five bottle' men, given over to hunting, gambling and irregular sexual behaviour. In London, a specially degraded type of parson conducted marriages in the Fleet taverns or sat about in the coffee houses plying for the odd burial or sermon that might come his way. Many were absentee, some parishes being left unattended throughout this period. The laxity of these 'shepherds of the flock' was matched by the behaviour of members of the congregation. Gambling, drunkenness – by 1742 the annual consumption of gin had risen to seven million gallons – and immorality permeated every level of society. Into this idle and soporific world came the Wesley brothers and their great religious movement. To the dismay of their friends, a number of social leaders 'turned Methodist' and attempts were made to persuade them out of their 'new-fangled beliefs'. By the outbreak of the Napoleonic war, the Evangelical movement had also taken root and this scandalous phase of church history was over.

1714 On October 20, 1714, Archbishop Tenison emerged from enforced retirement in Lambeth Palace to crown King George I in Westminster Abbey. The seventy-seven-year-old Primate was assisted during the ceremony by the treacherous Bishop Atterbury, who was soon to refuse to sign a declaration of confidence in the new Whig government. In London, there were no disturbances but in the provinces there were high church riots and disloyal cries of 'God bless Dr. Sacheverell!'

On December 11, the clergy were ordered not to meddle with state affairs in their sermons or act as tutors.

1715 On March 17, the following year, parliament assembled and swiftly passed the Riot Act, to control the mobs currently being encouraged to pull down chapels and disturb dissenters' meetings by High Church preachers.

Five months later, on August 12, Nahum Tate, author of the celebrated hymn 'While shepherds watched their flocks by night', died in the Mint at Southwark, a sanctuary for debtors, where he had been hiding from his creditors.

The same month, a Jacobite rebellion erupted in Scotland which was to rage throughout the autumn. On its suppression, there was a new vote of confidence in the government which Bishop Atterbury, among others refused to sign.

On December 14, Dr. Tenison, Archbishop of Canterbury, died at Lambeth Palace. He was replaced as Primate the following month by the
1716 wealthy William Wake, Bishop of Lincoln, who was a strong supporter of the House of Hanover and said to be a descendant of Hereward the Wake. His reign began with an embarrassing dispute with his predecessor's nephew which nearly developed into a law-suit.

Six months later, on June 15, 1716, the Rev. William Paul, Vicar of Orton-on-the-Hill in Leicestershire, was sentenced to death for his part in the Jacobite rebellion of the previous year. A month later, on July 13, he duly appeared at Tyburn dressed in the canonical habit of the Church of England and was hung, drawn and quartered.

On December 1 this year, strange noises were heard at the newly built Epworth Rectory, home of the Rev. Samuel Wesley. Groans and knockings in every part of the house were accompanied by the rattling of metal pans and the latches of doors and windows. From under the stairs came the sound of breaking glass and the gobbling of a turkey cock. These sounds were to continue for two months and are said to have led the rector's thirteen-year-old son, John, to believe in spiritualism.

Meanwhile, the Bishop of Exeter, Dr. Blackall, had died after falling from
1717 his horse. In January 1717, he was replaced by Dr. Lancelot Blackburne, a boisterous man, who had served as a chaplain on a ship and engaged in buccaneering and who was to shock his vicars by calling for pipes and liquor in the vestry after a confirmation service.

On March 31, the crippled Dr. Benjamin Hoadly, now Bishop of Bangor but never to set foot in his diocese, preached before King George taking the text 'My kingdom is not of this world' in which he argued against the necessity of any sort of organized church. This sermon, said to have been suggested by the King himself, threw the church into confusion and caused such fierce disputes in Convocation that it had to be prorogued.

On August 30, the Bishop of Worcester, Dr. Lloyd, now ninety years old and said to be half-crazy, died at his ancient episcopal seat, Hartlebury Castle.

Three months later, in November, the christening of the infant son of the Prince of Wales caused a fierce quarrel between the King and his heir which lead to the ejection of the Prince of Wales from St. James's Palace. The Archbishop of Canterbury, Dr. Wake, was called in to arbitrate.

On December 1, Dean Swift preached in St. Patrick's Cathedral, Dublin on brotherly love, which he described as 'the very bond of peace and all virtues'.

1718 A year later, in December 1718, bills were introduced to repeal the infamous Occasional Conformity and Schism Acts and cancel out the Test Act. In spite of the opposition of both the Archbishops of Canterbury and York, the bills were carried early the following year.

The Fleet Prison was situated on the east side of Farringdon Street. Among many clerics imprisoned there over the centuries were the Bishop of Gloucester, Dr. Hooper and the Dean of Canterbury, Dr. Isaac Bargrave

1719 In July 1719, the newly ordained Joseph Butler was appointed preacher at the Rolls Chapel in London, where he was to deliver sermons composed of sentences of labyrinthine length and containing lugubrious references to the brevity and frustrations of life.

Meanwhile German composer George Frederick Handel had been appointed director of music at Canons, country home of the Duke of Chandos
1720 near Edgware, Here on August 29, 1720, the opening of a new private chapel was celebrated with a performance of Handel's first English oratorio *Esther*.

Later this year, bishops and clergy were among investors who suffered in the collapse of the scandalous South Sea Company.
1721 On January 21, 1721, Dr. Francis Hutchinson, author of a learned history of witchcraft, was consecrated Bishop of Down and Connor.

Three months later, on April 28, the King issued a proclamation for the suppression of the Hell Fire Club, a company of profligate young men under the leadership of the twenty-three-year-old Duke of Wharton, who was to defend himself against accusations of blasphemy by quoting to the House of Lords from an old family bible in a sanctimonious voice.

Meanwhile the Archbishop of Canterbury, William Wake, who had been deluged with letters deploring the current malaise, had co-operated with the Earl of Nottingham in the introduction of a bill 'for suppressing blasphemy and profaneness' imposing penalties of up to three months' imprisonment for anyone who spoke against the being of God. This proposed legislation failed to win the full support of the bishops, however. Dr. White Kennett, Bishop of Peterborough, declared that its effect would be to set up an inquisition while another prelate went as far as to issue a pamphlet against it.

1722 On May 21, 1722, the Rev. George Kelly, secretary to the Bishop of Rochester, Dr. Atterbury, was arrested at his lodgings in Little Ryder Street and charged with carrying treasonable letters between his master and the Jacobite Pretender. He was thrown into the Tower of London where, on August 21, he was joined by Bishop Atterbury himself.

Meanwhile, the Bishop of Sodor and Man, Dr. Wilson, had been thrown into the island's Castle Rushen after sentencing the wife of the governor to do penance for slander. Loyal crowds gathered outside the gaol and were blessed by the Bishop from a window. On August 31, he was released but the dampness of his cell had crippled his fingers and he now had to write by grasping his pen with his whole hand.

1723 On January 7, the following year, Dr. Henry Sacheverell broke two ribs when he fell in hard frost on the stone steps outside his house in Holborn.

A few weeks later, on February 25, ninety-year-old Sir Christopher Wren died at his house in St. James's Street after catching a chill. He was later buried in St. Paul's Cathedral and on his tombstone was written in Latin 'Reader, if you seek his monument, look around you'.

On June 18, Bishop Atterbury was banished from the realm for his loyalty to 'the king over the water'. He was placed on a man-of-war and deposited at Calais. His chaplain, the genial George Kelly, remained in the Tower of London, where he was often to be found dining with the officers at the coffee house on the premises.

1724 On January 6, 1724, the Bishop of London, Dr. Edmund Gibson, delivered a sermon protesting against masked balls and masquerades which had recently been 'imported' from France and which many people felt led to drunkenness and promiscuity. This sermon was followed by an episcopal petition to the King, which resulted in a Royal Proclamation being issued banning public masquerades. Private ones continued, however, and a further petition of protest to the King, signed by Archbishop Wake and sixteen colleagues, was firmly rebuffed.

Meanwhile, on March 23, the handsome new church of St. George's, Hanover Square, had been completed featuring a magnificent portico of six Corinthian columns and sixteenth-century stained glass taken from a church in Antwerp, and a richly carved pulpit with a cast-iron stair rail.

On April 30 this year, the Archbishop of York, Dr. Dawes, died of an inflammation of the bowels and his see was promptly given to the boisterous Bishop of Exeter, Dr. Blackburne, who, it was rumoured, had obtained the

Dr. Lancelot Blackburne, the buccaneering sea chaplain who rose to become Archbishop of York. At Bishopthorpe Palace, he is said to have kept a harem

promotion by secretly marrying the King to his mistress, the Duchess of Munster.

On June 5, Dr. Sacheverell died of the complications of his fall the previous year and was buried at St. Andrew's Holborn. In his will he left £1,000 to fellow Tory cleric Francis Atterbury, now living in exile in Paris.

1725   Fifteen months later, on September 19, 1725, the neatly-dressed twenty-two-year-old John Wesley was ordained a deacon by the Bishop of Oxford, Dr. Potter. The following month he preached his first sermon, at South Leigh, near Witney.

1726   The following year, the new church of St. Martin-in-the-Fields was completed, featuring a magnificent temple front with a portico of giant Corinthian columns and concave-sided obelisk spire with four tiers of circular openings and surrounded by fine, cast-iron railing. It had cost £36,891 10s. 4d. to build.

1727   On May 19, 1727, the Bishop of London, Dr. Gibson, preached a sermon in support of the ownership of slaves and the unfair distribution of wealth. 'Christianity and the embraces of the Gospel do not make the least alteration in civil property', he said firmly.

Three weeks later, on June 11, King George I died suddenly. Three days later, the new King George II held his first council meeting at Leicester House, at which the Archbishop of Canterbury produced the late King's will, expecting that it would be read. However, the King placed it in his pocket and it was seen no more.

Four months later, on October 11 the new King was crowned in Westminster Abbey. A sermon was preached by Bishop Potter of Oxford and an anthem by Handel was sung. While attending this ceremony, Dr. Leng, Bishop of Norwich, caught small-pox and died before the end of the month.

At the end of the year, the serious young John Wesley, now an ordained priest, acted as a steward at an annual dinner to celebrate Charterhouse Founder's Day, at which roast pike, fried whitings, venison patties, pigeons, sirloins of beef, asparagus, roasted lobsters, almond tarts, custards, florentines, jellies and other dainties were consumed to the musical accompaniment of two French horns.

1728 A year later, in December 1728, a new note was struck by the publication of *A Serious Call to a Devout and Holy Life* by the Rev. William Law, a devout Northamptonshire school-teacher.

A detail from Hogarth's Midnight Modern Conversation showing bogus priest John Henley presiding at the punch bowl

Meanwhile, the indignation of the clergy had been excited by a certain John Henley who had donned priest's robes and set himself up in a booth in Leicester Fields, from which he preached and administered a primitive form of eucharist. On January 18, 1729, Henley appeared before a grand jury charged with profaning the character of a priest but was later to resume his practices, with such success that his pulpit was soon enriched with velvet and gold decorations.

1729

The same month, the Rev. Thomas Kinnersley was found guilty of forging a promissory note for £1,260 and was sentenced to stand in the pillory in Fleet Street and at the Royal Exchange followed by two years' imprisonment. Kinnersley duly appeared in the pillory, clad in his canonical robes but died of fever in the press-yard of Newgate Prison three months later.

In November, this year, a group of religious enthusiasts gathered at Oxford under the leadership of the young Rev. John Wesley, now a fellow of Lincoln College. Dedicated to bible-reading, prison-visiting and strict personal habits such as getting up at four o'clock in the morning, these studious and pious young men were to provoke much ridicule and indignation and were nicknamed 'The Holy Club' and 'The Bible Moths'.

Meanwhile, the Rev. James Miller, lecturer at the Trinity Chapel in Conduit Street, had taken up dramatic writing to supplement his income. **1730** On January 9, 1730, his satirical comedy *The Humours of Oxford* opened at the Drury Lane theatre, offending his bishop and spoiling his chances of preferment.

Lambeth Palace, ancient seat of the Archbishops of Canterbury, acquired in the year 1183 and still the home of the Primate

Eleven months later, on November 21, the translation of Dr. Chandler, Bishop of Lichfield, to the wealthy see of Durham was confirmed amidst rumours that he had paid £9,000 for this advancement.

1731 On June 4, 1731, the learned Rev. Samuel Wesley, Vicar of Epworth, whose sons John and Charles were now creating a religious stir at Oxford, was thrown from a waggon and permanently disabled.

1732 In February 1732, the Rev. George Berkeley returned from an evangelical mission to America and preached an important sermon in support of foreign missions before the Society for the Propagation of the Gospel at St. Mary-le-Bow in Cheapside.

1733 Fifteen months later, in May 1733, the Rev. Thomas Secker, a regular guest at Queen Caroline's philosophical parties, was appointed Rector of St. James's Piccadilly, where he delivered sermons of 'discreet warmth', to a fashionable congregation, which often included Frederick Prince of Wales.

The following autumn, the Rev. Dr. Gainham conducted a clandestine marriage at the Rainbow Coffee House beside the Fleet Ditch. Giving evidence at the Old Bailey bigamy trial which followed this marriage. Dr.

Gainham, nicknamed 'The Bishop of Hell', refused to admit to any shame at the unorthodoxy of the procedure and claimed that his marriage register was 'as fair as any church in England can produce'.

1734 The following year, Dr. Secker was nominated Bishop of Bristol but was permitted to remain Rector of St. James's, Piccadilly, because the Bishopric was said to be the poorest in England.

1735 In August 1735, the neatly-dressed Rev. John Wesley presented a copy of his father's last work *Dissertations on Job* to Queen Caroline, whom he found romping with her maids of honour when he entered the room. On receiving the volume, she remarked, 'It is very prettily bound' and put it down on a window seat without opening it.

On October 14, Wesley and his brother Charles, also a parson, set sail for Georgia, where the founders of the colony required new men to preach the gospel. Before their ship left Gravesend, the Wesleys had denounced the use of flesh and wine and resolved to live on water, rice, vegetables and biscuits. The mission was to prove marked by hazards. On one occasion, John Wesley was attacked by a certain colonial wife named Mrs. Hawkins, who fastened on the sleeve of his gown with her teeth, ripping it to shreds.

Meanwhile, London had been honoured by a visit from the popular Dr. Wilson, Bishop of Sodor and Man since 1698. On his appearance at Court, the Queen remarked, 'Here is a bishop who does not come for a translation', and the King asked for his prayers. Dr. Wilson's coach was surrounded by crowds crying, 'Bless me too, my Lord.'

1736 On February 16, a freak high tide caused flooding in the Houses of Parliament and the lords spiritual were taken to their coaches by boat.

In July, the devoutly orthodox Rev. Joseph Butler was appointed Clerk of the Closet, in which capacity he was expected to spend two hours each evening discussing theology and philosophy with the Queen.

On October 25, the genial Rev. George Kelly, former secretary to Bishop Atterbury, escaped from the Tower of London where he had been held for the past twelve years and made his way to France to join the Pretender.

1737 On January 24, 1737, Archbishop Wake died at Lambeth Palace, leaving a considerable fortune, largely derived from patronage. He bequeathed his library and valuable coin collection, together worth £10,000 to Christ Church, Oxford. He was the last Primate to use a state barge, with liveried crew, to carry him across the Thames each time he attended parliament.

A month later, linen draper's son John Potter, the scholarly but arrogant Bishop of Oxford was translated to Canterbury. One of his first duties as Primate was to attend Queen Caroline, who was now dying of a stomach rupture.

At the memorial service which followed the Queen's death on November 20, Dr. Thomas Secker preached a sermon which impressed the King and prompted him to ask Secker to intervene in his long-running quarrel with the Prince of Wales. This enterprise was a flop, however, and Secker only succeeded in annoying the King.

1738 On May 24, 1738, the Rev. John Wesley, back from his unsuccessful mission to Georgia, attended a religious meeting in Aldersgate Street, at which he felt 'a warming of the heart'.

94

Hogarth's caricature of the Sleeping Congregation

Eleven days later, on June 4, Archbishop Potter was present at the birth of the future King George III at Norfolk House, St. James's Square, where the Prince of Wales's family had found refuge after being turned out of St. James's Palace. Such was the feeble condition of the baby boy that baptism was quickly performed by Dr. Secker.

On August 20, twenty-four-year-old Laurence Sterne, great-grandson of a former Archbishop of York, was ordained by Dr. Peploe, Bishop of Chester and given the living of Sutton-on-the-Forest. Sterne was said to be quite unsuitable for the priesthood and was to spend much of his time in nearby York, at coffee houses, concerts and other galas.

Meanwhile, the Rev. Charles Wesley was spending the summer ministering to the occupants of the condemned cells at Newgate, some of whom were children, and subsequently escorting them to the gallows.

The same year, the first of the famous bells for St. Mary-le-Bow in Cheapside was cast at the Whitechapel Bell Foundry.

1739   On February 17, the following year, newly-ordained preacher George Whitefield, already barred from every London pulpit on account of his excessively enthusiastic preaching style, addressed an open air audience of 200 miners at Kingswood, near Bristol. Three weeks later, he preached to an audience of 10,000. Much of his thundering was directed at the clergy of the day, whom he described as 'blind, unregenerate, carnal, lukewarm and unskilful guides'.

Two months later, on March 31, the Rev. John Wesley arrived in Bristol and four days later addressed his first open air audience. His preaching style was calmer than that of Whitefield but produced equally remarkable results. People dropped to the ground, roared like beasts, and were agitated by unsightly convulsions – symptoms which were subsequently interpreted as the true phenomena of conversion.

These intruders into his diocese caused deep distress to the new Bishop of Bristol, the orthodox Joseph Butler, who summoned Wesley and informed him, 'The pretending of extraordinary revelations and gifts of the Holy Ghost is a horrid thing. Yes, sir, it is a very horrid thing.' Then he added, 'You have no business here. You are not commissioned to preach in this diocese – therefore I advise you to go hence.'

On June 5, there was an ugly clash in the elegant city of Bath between John Wesley and the city's ageing dandy Beau Nash, which left the sixty-five-year-old fop deflated.

Meanwhile, George Whitefield had been preaching to vast outdoor audiences in London, his congregation at Hyde Park Corner on June 1 being assessed at 80,000, and had angered many eminent clergy. 'Go not after these imposters and seducers', urged the orthodox Dr. Joseph Trapp. 'Shun them as you would the plague!'

On June 9, an interview took place at Lambeth Palace between Archbishop Potter and the Wesley brothers after which the Primate forbade his clergy to admit the brothers to their pulpits.

The movement quickly gained ground, however, and six months later, at Christmas 1739, the first Methodist Society was formed in London with the wealthy thirty-two-year-old Countess of Huntingdon one of its staunchest adherents. Attempts by this devout and exceedingly plain woman to introduce the 'new light' into aristocratic circles had a mixed reaction. The elderly Duchess of Marlborough wrote, 'God knows we all need mending and none more than myself', but the Duchess of Buckingham, illegitimate daughter of James II, responded: 'Their doctrines are most repulsive, strongly tinctured with impertinence and disrespect towards their superiors. It is monstrous to be told you have a heart as sinful as the common wretches that crawl the earth'.'

Meanwhile, the Rev. Charles Wesley had published his first collection of hymns, including 'Hark! the herald angels sing' and other masterpieces.

1740 In the winter of 1739–40, severe weather conditions hit the British Isles. In London, bishops' coaches were driven on the Thames while, in Ireland, Bishop Berkeley of Cloyne dosed the sick with tar water, which he believed to be a cure for fevers, diseases of the lungs, scrofula, throat infections and apoplexies as well as a general drink for infants.

Later in 1740, the young Rev. Edmund Keene was presented with the fat living of Stanhope, near Durham. It was said that he had only obtained this appointment by promising to marry an illegitimate daughter of the patron of the living and had subsequently jilted her, satisfying his conscience by paying her £600.

Meanwhile, the Rev. John Wesley faced mob violence while preaching in London. Stones were flung at him in Marylebone Fields and at Hoxton the rabble attempted to drive an ox among the congregation. Wesley faced these incidents with composure.

1741 In May, 1741, the Rev. Stephen Hales, an all-round pioneering scientist who had built a laboratory at his vicarage at Teddington where he was often visited by the Prince of Wales, addressed the Royal Society on the subject of ventilators.

Six months later, a new bond was formed between the Methodist Movement and the aristocracy when the Yorkshire evangelist the Rev. Benjamin Ingham married Lady Margaret Hastings, sister-in-law of the devout Countess of Huntingdon.

1742 On April 13, 1742, the first public performance of Handel's *Messiah*, which had been written the previous year in only twenty-three days, took place in a music-hall in Dublin.

A few weeks later, on Whit Monday, the Rev. George Whitefield preached before an audience of 10,000 at Moorfields and was pelted with stones, rotten eggs and dead cats.

The same year, evangelist William Grimshaw was appointed to the living of Haworth in the West Riding of Yorkshire, where he was to bring about a religious revival single-handedly. A man of gigantic build, who was said to possess only one shabby coat and one pair of shoes, he was to be described as 'the mad parson of the Yorkshire moors', whipping his flock to church and openly rebuking inattentive members of the congregation.

1743 On March 8, 1743, the Bishop of Worcester, Dr. Hough, died at the ripe old age of ninety-one and was replaced by Dr. Isaac Maddox who was said to look more like a butcher than a bishop and had once trained as a pastry-cook.

A few days later, on March 23, the jolly old Archbishop of York, Dr. Blackburne, who was said to have kept a seraglio at Bishopthorpe Palace, died of a heavy cold and was replaced by Dr. Thomas Herring, who claimed to have confirmed 30,000 people during his first few months in office.

On May 5, Dr. Thomas Secker, now Bishop of Oxford, preached an austere sermon at an anniversary meeting of the Charity Schools. Explaining how pupils of the school should live, he declared, 'If they are fed, their food should be of the coarsest sort.'

Meanwhile, the Rev. William Bridges, Rector of Gotham in Nottinghamshire had complained that his parsonage had 120 windows, 8 staircases and 100 doors.

1744   On May 2, 1744, the secret runaway marriage of footman's son Henry Fox and Lady Caroline Lennox, daughter of the Duke of Richmond, took place in the house of Sir Charles Hanbury-Williams, conducted by an unknown parson recruited from the disreputable Fleet area of London.

The same month there was much excitement over a new book by Bishop Berkeley of Cloyne, extolling the many virtues of tar water, which he had now set up a special apparatus to manufacture.

On June 25, the first Methodist Conference opened at the movement's headquarters in Moorfields. The six regular clergy and six lay preachers present decided against separation from the Church of England and also affirmed the duty of canonical obedience to the bishops. They also divided the country up into different Methodist 'circuits'.

1745   Eleven months later, on May 9, 1745, the pious Bishop of Bristol, Dr. Butler, preached on the education of poor children, at the parish church of Christ Church, Newgate Street. 'Children have as much right to some proper education as to have their lives preserved.'

Later that summer, the Young Pretender landed in Scotland and quickly seized Perth and Edinburgh. In London, the old popery scare was revived and, in Cornwall, where John Wesley was on a preaching tour, rumours were put about that the Methodists were agents of the the rebels and attempts were made to arrest him by the half-crazy Rev. William Borlaise, a local clergyman and magistrate.

On September 21, the defeat of Sir John Cope's army at Prestonpans inspired the Archbishop of York, Dr. Herring, to raise many volunteers and some £40,000 for the Hanoverian cause.

In the midst of this upheaval, on October 19, seventy-seven-year-old Jonathan Swift who had been suffering from mental decay for the last few years, died at his Deanery in Dublin, declaring, 'I am dying like a poisoned rat in a hole'. In his will, he left his horses and mares and harness to an old friend, the Rev. John Jackson, Vicar of Santry.

The following month, the Young Pretender took possession of the city of Carlisle, turning the cathedral into a prison and attempting to install the Rev. Thomas Coppock, former curate at Snave in Kent as the new Bishop.

1746   The following February, the unworldly Rev. James Hervey published his *Meditations among the Tombs*, based upon his thoughts in the churchyard at Kilkhampton in Devon. In spite of its inflated language and surfeit of truisms, the book was to run through many editions, with all its profits going to charity.

On April 16, the Jacobite rebellion was finally suppressed at the Battle of Culloden and the miscreants were duly punished. On St. Luke's Day, on

October 18, the would-be Bishop of Carlisle, the Rev. Thomas Coppock, who had taken part in the march on Derby, was hung, drawn and quartered at Harraby, on the outskirts of Carlisle.

1747   On Good Friday, April 17, the following year the Rev. Laurence Sterne, desperately thin since an attack of pulmonary tuberculosis in early life, preached a sermon before the Lord Mayor of London at the church of St. Michael le Belfry which brought in a collection of £64 for the charity schools of York.

Three months later, on July 26, the sexton at St. Andrew's, Holborn, was gaoled for stealing the lead coffin of the late Dr. Sacheverell who had been buried at the church twenty-three years earlier.

On October 11, Archbishop Potter died at Lambeth Palace, leaving a fortune which some estimates placed at £100,000. His oldest son, the Dean of Canterbury, had recently been disinherited for marrying a domestic servant and the fortune went to the Archbishop's younger son, Thomas, who was to become a member of Sir Francis Dashwood's scandalous brotherhood at West Wycombe and rapidly dissipate the money in 'the relentless pursuit of every type of vice'.

The death of the Primate was followed by several weeks of embarrassment for the King and his chief minister, Newcastle, as they searched for a successor. Dr. Gibson, Bishop of London, and Dr. Sherlock, Bishop of Salisbury, quickly refused this high office on the grounds of their old age and gout and Bishop Butler of Bristol declined on the grounds that it was too late for him 'to try and support a falling church'. Finally Dr. Herring, fifty-four-year-old Archbishop of York, accepted under pressure from the Lord Chancellor and was duly translated. He later congratulated himself on being appointed primate 'at a time when we breathe the benign and comfortable air of liberty and toleration'.

1748   The following year, the Rev. George White, belligerent and heavy-drinking curate at Colne in Lancashire, who was in the habit of carrying a large pistol about with him, rallied a private army for the defence of the Church of England against Methodism. In August, a violent encounter took place between White's 'army' and John Wesley and William Grimshaw. The Methodists were beaten with clubs and pelted with clods and stones.

The same month, the Countess of Huntingdon, or 'Pope Joan Huntingdon' as she was known in certain circles, appointed the Rev. George Whitefield her private chaplain. During the winter that followed there were big gatherings at the Countess's house in Chelsea and at her mansion in Park Lane to hear Whitefield preach. Among the aristocratic converts to the cause were the Earl of Buchan, Lady Dartmouth and Lady Chesterfield. Many others merely found Methodism a fashionable amusement.

While these events were continuing in London, the Rev. Edward Stokes, Rector of Blaby in Leicestershire, was causing a stir by riding to hounds in spite of the fact that he was totally blind. This aged parson was accompanied by a groom who rang a bell whenever there was a hedge to jump.

1749   In June the following year keen cricketer Henry Venn became a priest. A week before his ordination he threw down his cricket bat saying that he had no further use for it. 'I will never have it said of me "Well struck, parson",' he explained.

The Rev. George Whitefield was capable of addressing an audience of 20,000 out of doors. He believed in Original Sin and employed every oratorical device to save men from hell. It is estimated that he preached 18,000 sermons during his life

Six months later, on December 3, the Rev. Thomas Hayter, who was rumoured to be an illegitimate son of the late Archbishop Blackburne of York, was consecrated Bishop of Norwich.

Meanwhile the wealthy Bubb Dodington had founded a 'joke' monastery at his house on the Thames at Medmenham, where obscene parodies of the rites of Rome were carried out. Among welcome guests here was Thomas Potter, debauched son of the late Archbishop of Canterbury.

The same year, the hot-tempered Bishop of Exeter, Dr. Lavington, had published a treatise in which he had described the Methodists as people with 'sanctified singularities, low fooleries and high pretensions'.

1750   On February 8 and March 8, 1750, there were earthquakes in London. Clergymen were quick to take advantage of the situation and exploit people's terror. The new Bishop of London, Dr. Sherlock, issued a twelve-page pamphlet in which he gave a grim description of popular morals and Methodist leader John Wesley published *A Collection of Hymns Occasioned by the Earthquake*. Among the churches and chapels soon full of groaning penitents was St. George's, Hanover Square, where the fearsome morning preacher the Rev. William Romaine, who was said to possess accurate knowledge of the geography of Hell, drew large crowds of ragged people, to the annoyance of the genteel regular congregation who wished to keep the elegant new church for their own exclusive use.

On July 20, this year, the Bishop of Durham died in London, according to one observer 'shamefully rich'. He was succeeded by the pious and prematurely aged Joseph Butler, Bishop of Bristol, who in his charge to the clergy of his new diocese spoke of 'the general decay of religion in this nation'.

1751   February 1751 saw the appearance of *Elegy Written in a Country Churchyard* by thirty-four-year-old Thomas Gray. It was an instant, popular success.

The same month, John Wesley embarked on a disastrous marriage to a certain Mrs. Mary Vazeille, a former domestic servant. Mrs. Wesley was to become acutely jealous of her husband's absorption in his work and of his female converts, to whom he was in the habit of writing 'devotional endearments'. On one occasion the founder of Methodism was discovered on the floor, where his wife had been dragging him by his hair, plucking out some of his locks by the roots.

1752   On June 16 Bishop Butler died at Bath, where he had been transported by his doctors. It was said that the Bishop had summoned a chaplain to his deathbed and confessed that he was afraid to die. On being reminded that Christ was a saviour, Butler had apparently replied, 'True. But how shall I know he is a saviour for me?'

A few weeks later, on August 30, the Bishop of Gloucester, Dr. Benson, who had looked after Dr. Butler in his last illness, died himself, worn out by the strain and anxiety.

Meanwhile, the Society for the Propagation of the Gospel had sent its first chaplain to the Gold Coast.

1753   In March, 1753, the Rev. Samuel Ogden became preacher at the Church of the Holy Sepulchre in Cambridge. His huge, scowling figure, topped with a sable periwig, and uncouth rustic manner was to draw huge crowds of undergraduates. He was to become famous for his remark that the goose was a silly bird: too big for one dish and not enough for two.

Meanwhile, public indignation had at last been excited by the irregular marriages being performed at a minute's notice in the Fleet prison and elsewhere in return for as little as a dram of gin or a roll of tobacco. Among guilty parsons were the notorious 'Bishop of Hell' the Rev. Dr. Gainham and the Rev. Alexander Keith who was said to marry 6,000 couples a year and was fond of quoting the proverb 'Happy is the woo-ing that is not long a-doing'.

An irregular wedding takes place within the precincts of the Fleet prison, where unscrupulous parsons were prepared to perform the marriage service in return for a dram of gin or a roll of tobacco

In May 1753, the Clandestine Marriages Bill was presented introducing much stricter rules and enacting that any person solemnizing marriage in any place other than a church or chapel and without banns or licence was guilty of a felony and should be transported for fourteen years. After some opposition, the bill passed, infuriating the Rev. Mr. Keith, who declared : 'God damn the bishops! I'll be revenged. I'll buy two or three acres of land and, by God, I'll bury them all!'

The same year, a careless gardener at Lambeth Palace had accidently killed the old tortoise which had once been a pet of Archbishop Laud, outliving him by over a hundred years. Its shell was later exhibited at Laud's centenary celebrations.

1754   In the spring of 1754, the Rev. Stephen Hales, scientifically minded author, Vicar of Twickenham and a member of the Royal Society, was found working on the installation of a decent water supply to his parish.

That summer, the Rev. John Swinton, absent-minded chaplain to Oxford gaol, preached before three men on the eve of their execution. At the end he told the prisoners that he would give them the rest of the sermon the following Sunday.

The remains of Archbishop Laud's tortoise, kept behind glass in the Guard Room at Lambeth Palace

Meanwhile, the ardent evangelist Henry Venn had been appointed a curate at the village of Clapham near London, where a number of wealthy merchants had their country seats. A parishioner was soon to ask Mrs. Venn to suppress the 'disgusting earnestness' of her husband.

1755 On March 7, 1755, the longest episcopate in history ended with the death of the ninety-one-year-old, Dr. Wilson, Bishop of Sodor and Man for the last fifty-seven years. He died at his residence on the island and his coffin was made from an elm tree he had planted himself.

The same year, the Rev. Gilbert White settled as curate at Selborne in Hampshire. He immediately began to take careful notes of the natural history of the area and correspond with the leading scientists of the day.

1756 On February 28, 1756, the death occurred of Dr. Wilcocks, Bishop of Rochester and Dean of Westminster, who had been responsible for the building of the new west front of Westminster Abbey, with its towers by Nicholas Hawksmoor.

Some six weeks later, on May 11, the death occurred of the Rev. Mr. Mickleburgh, Rector of Landbeach and Impington, a professor of chemistry at Cambridge University and a keen conservator of the River Cam.

Meanwhile, contrary to the recently passed Clandestine Marriages Act, the Rev. John Grieson and his colleague Dr. Wilkinson had continued to conduct irregular weddings at an unlicensed chapel in the Savoy. This summer, both men appeared at the Old Bailey and were sentenced to be shipped off to the Colonies.

On November 7 this year, the Rev. George Whitefield's handsome tabernacle in Tottenham Court Road, soon to be known as 'Whitefield's Soul Trap' opened its doors to the public.

1757 The following February, the Rev. Mr. Porter, Vicar of East Hoathly, was found in a crowd of drunken revellers.

A few weeks later, on March 13, the Archbishop of Canterbury, Dr. Herring, died at Croydon, where he had retired some years earlier concentrating his diminishing energies on gardening and minor repairs to the old house, originally given to Lanfranc by William the Conqueror.

On April 13, Matthew Hutton, Archbishop of York, was nominated the new primate. He had hesitated to accept the job, because of the enormous cost of entertaining at Lambeth and after a clash with his predecessor's executors over dilapidations at the palace decided to reside at his own house in **1758** Duke Street, Westminster, where he died on March 18, the following year, of a stomach rupture.

On the day of Hutton's death, the Duke of Newcastle wrote to the royal family's old friend, Dr. Secker, Bishop of Oxford, ordering him to accept the primacy. He did so reluctantly but was to play a prominent role in the nation's life for the next few years, frequently attending parliament, speaking often and taking notes in shorthand which he had taught himself while Bishop of Bristol.

Meanwhile, the London social scene was enriched by the arrival of the Rev. Charles Churchill, a rowdy individual who had supplemented his income as a West Country curate by keeping a cider cellar. On arrival in London, he was appointed lecturer at St. John's, Westminster. Here, he was to preach long tedious sermons to sleeping congregations and concentrate his energies on his flamboyant social life and exotic literary activities.

1759 In May, 1759, extraordinary scenes began at Everton church in Bedfordshire. While the powerful-looking Methodist Vicar, John Berridge, was preaching, members of the congregation fainted, screamed, and shrieked

The Rev. John Berridge, Vicar of Everton, who used to preach in the open fields

and fell down in terrible contortions. These events were dismissed by many as a case of 'spiritual influenza' and Berridge was branded as 'insane'.

A few months later, on September 27, the Bishop of Worcester, Dr. Maddox, died at Hartlebury Castle, where he had added an extremely pretty fan vault to the Great Hall.

On January 1, 1760, the publication of *Tristram Shandy* by Yorkshire parson Laurence Sterne was announced and it instantly became the talk of London. The easy-going Bishop of Gloucester, Dr. Warburton, recommended it to one and all, while others were shocked by the brazen innuendos or indecency of certain passages.

At the beginning of March, the controversial spider-legged author visited London and took rooms in Pall Mall, where he was overwhelmed with callers. For the next few weeks, he partook in all London's pleasures, being given a box at Drury Lane by David Garrick and being seen often at Ranelagh Gardens. After nights of debauchery it was said that he dosed himself with Bishop Berkeley's famous all-purpose tar water.

On October 25, King George II died of a burst ventricle of the heart, after visiting the water-closet at Kensington Palace. His funeral in the candle-lit Henry VII chapel at Westminster Abbey was marked by the Duke of Newcastle going into hysterics and being ministered to with smelling salts by Archbishop Secker.

On October 31, the serious twenty-two-year-old King, who saw it as his duty to purge public life, issued a Royal Proclamation 'for the encouragement of piety and virtue and for the preventing and punishing of vice, profaneness and immorality.'

Meanwhile Dr. Robert Plumptre had been elected president of Queens' College, Cambridge, Dr. Plumptre, who already held the rectory of Wimpole in Cambridgeshire, the vicarage of Whaddon and a prebendal stall at Norwich, was to sit for his portrait by Benjamin Wilson and ask that his motto should be inscribed in large letters: *Non magna loquimur, sed vivimus*, or in other words, 'We don't say much but we hold good livings'.

On April 17, 1761, the eminent Whig prelate Dr. Hoadly, Bishop of Winchester, died at the spacious Winchester House in Chelsea.

Five months later, on September 22, the coronation of the new King and Queen took place in Westminster Abbey. The pious young monarch asked Archbishop Secker if he and his wife should not take off their crowns for the communion service, but this proved impossible as the Queen's crown was in some way attached to her head-dress.

Preaching at this ceremony was the worldly Dr. Robert Hay Drummond, son of the 7th Earl of Kinnoull, who, a fortnight later, was elected Archbishop of York. He was to make great improvements at Bishopthorpe Palace, adding a fancy new gatehouse, fashionable ogee-headed windows and other gothic decorations.

Meanwhile, the Rev. Timothy Shaw, in whose parish at Medmenham was sited Bubb Dodington's notorious joke monastery, had drowned himself in a fit of melancholia.

On June 5, 1762, twenty-one-year-old Augustus Toplady was ordained a deacon by the Bishop of Bath and Wells and appointed curate at the village of Blagdon, where, according to local tradition he wrote his famous hymn 'Rock of Ages'. Toplady soon received other West Country livings but soon abandoned them in favour of the more fashionable congregations of London.

Five months later, on November 7, the jovial Frederick Keppel was consecrated Bishop of Exeter, where he was to spend large sums improving the episcopal palace. It was rumoured that he had only been given this promotion because of the recent successful capture of Havana by his brother the Earl of Albemarle.

1763   In January 1763, there were protests against the improprieties of the Rev. Charles Churchill, lecturer at St. John's, Westminster, who wore gold lace on his hat and waistcoat and was the author of a number of scandalously satirical poems. He was soon persuaded to resign his lectureship and give himself over completely to the life of a rake.

Six months later, on Sunday July 3, the formal opening of St. Lawrence's Church on the estate of Churchill's friend, the dissolute Sir Francis Dashwood, took place. The building was equipped for banquets with wine bins and mahogany armchairs instead of a pulpit and lectern. At the opening ceremony the Vicar, the Rev. William Wroughton, preached a sermon on 'charity'.

Later that month, the famous Dr. Samuel Johnson commented on preaching by women, now being permitted by certain dissenting sects. 'A woman's preaching is like a dog's walking on its hind legs. It is not done well, but you are surprised to find it done at all.'

At Christmas this year the Rev. Charles Wesley published his *Hymns for Children*, including the famous 'Gentle Jesus, meek and mild'.

1764   On June 17, the following year, John Newton, who had gone to sea as a child and ended up as a captain on a slave ship but been 'converted' during a storm, was at last ordained a priest. Several biships had refused to perform this service, Dr. Gilbert, a former Archbishop of York, even suggesting that Newton was a fool to leave a lucrative profession.

On November 4, the Rev. Charles Churchill, only thirty-three-years-old, died of his debaucheries at Boulogne. 'What a fool I've been', were his last recorded words, but on his tombstone at St. Martin's Church, Dover, was written 'Life to the last enjoyed, here Churchill lies'.

1765   On March 24, 1765, Dr. Keppel, Bishop of Exeter, ordained a negro priest in the Chapel Royal at St. James's Palace. The devout behaviour of the ordinand deeply impressed the congregation.

A few weeks later, on April 23, a luminous arch of bright white colour was seen in the sky at Oxford by the absent-minded Rev. John Swinton, chaplain to the local gaol.

On August 20, at the Twenty-Second Methodist Conference, held in Manchester, John Wesley forbade his preachers to touch tobacco or alcohol 'on any pretence' and ordered them to denounce the use of these substances from their pulpits.

Meanwhile, Lady Huntingdon had been selling her jewels to erect Methodist chapels across the country.

1766   On January 9, 1766, the Rev. Thomas Birch, Secretary to the Royal Society and said to be 'as brisk as a bee in conversation', had a fit of apoplexy while riding in Hampstead Road, fell from his horse and was killed.

Three months later, a North American Indian who had been converted to Christianity preached to a large congregation at the Old Jewry where the broad-minded Dr. Samuel Chandler had been minister for the past forty years.

On July 19, the death occurred of the Bishop of Salisbury, Dr. John

Selina, Countess of Huntingdon embraced Methodism and sold her jewels to build chapels up and down the country. Her enemies called her 'Pope Joan Huntingdon'

Thomas. He had been married four times, outliving all his wives and was looking for a fifth wife when he died.

1767   Fourteen months later, in September 1767, the celebrated Rev. Laurence Sterne, who had been in poor health throughout his life, was found bathing in the sea at Scarborough. He was staying in the lodgings of Dr. Browne, Bishop of Cork, along with two ladies and a gentleman.

A few weeks later, there were impressive scenes at Bath following the death of the Methodist Earl of Buchan, who had come to the city for his health. His body was taken to a chapel recently erected by his friend Lady Huntingdon and lain in state, covered in black baize and 'the usual funeral concomitants'. Nobility and gentry were issued with 300 tickets for the funeral at which the Rev. George Whitefield preached a sermon.

1768   On February 18, the following year, the thirty-eight-year-old Rev. Frederick Augustus Hervey was given the Bishopric of Derry, the richest see in Ireland. He was to take a somewhat frivolous approach to his episcopal duties, travelling frequently abroad, and on one occasion arranging a curate's race on the sea-shore and rewarding the winners with vacant benefices in his diocese.

Three weeks later on March 11, six students were expelled from St. Edmund Hall, Oxford, for 'having too much religion'. It was alleged that they had held conventicles and preached extempore. This incident was to inspire Lady Huntingdon to open her own theological college in South Wales.

On Friday March 18, the Rev. Laurence Sterne died at his lodgings above a shop in Old Bond Street, his last moments witnessed only by a nurse and a footman. His body was buried in a burial ground in Bayswater Road but was quickly dug up by body-thieves who sold it for dissection purposes to the Professor of Anatomy at Cambridge, where, according to one story, it was recognized on the dissection table by an old friend of Sterne's.

Five months later, on August 3, the Archbishop of Canterbury, Dr. Secker, died of a caries of the thigh bone. He was buried in a passage at Lambeth Palace and, at his own request, no monument was placed over his remains.

Within a month, the Bishop of Lichfield and Coventry, Dr. Cornwallis, had been elected to succeed him. The first Old Etonian to occupy this high office, he was to turn Lambeth Palace into a place of revelry and dissipation, holding frequent routs there with his wife and drawing furious protests from the Countess of Huntingdon, who begged the King 'to interpose his authority and see what that will do towards reforming such indecent practices'.

1769   The following year, eccentric divine John Trusler, a former curate at St. Clement Danes in the Strand, sent circulars to every parish in England and Ireland proposing to print, in imitation handwriting, about 150 sermons at the price of one shilling each. This scheme, designed to save clergy the bother of studying, met with considerable success and enabled Trusler, son of the proprietor of a tea gardens in Marylebone to move to Bath and, later, buy an estate in Middlesex.

1770   On September 30, 1770, fifty-six-year-old George Whitefield died in Massachusetts, worn out after a life-time of preaching during which it was

Laurence Sterne and Death: the celebrated author-parson cordially confronts the Reaper

estimated he had preached 18,000 sermons. In his will he left his friend Lady Huntingdon all his negro slaves.

The same month, there were alarming scenes at Kingswood School near Bristol following a visit from the Rev. John Wesley. Terrified children ran across the playground to their teacher, asking 'what they must do to be saved'. At night, they prayed and cried on their knees, deeply disturbed. This strange behaviour was interpreted as a case of 'infantile conversion'.

The same year saw the publication of the *Botanical Dictionary* by the Rev. Colin Milne, non-resident Rector of North Chapel, Petworth. Dedicated to the Duke of Northumberland, the book contained an impartial examination of the doctrine of the sex of plants.

Meanwhile, the Rev. Charles Wesley and his wife had moved into a comfortable new home, 1 Chesterfield Street in Marylebone, lent to them by Lady Gumley and possessing a wine-cellar well-stocked with wine and table beer. Although he had now retired from active life, Charles Wesley continued to preach regularly at the Methodist headquarters in Moorfields, travelling there on a white pony and reading a book or scribbling verses as he ambled along.

1771 On July 8, 1771, Dr John Egerton was appointed Bishop of Durham, where he was to make fanciful additions to his ancient episcopal seat, Auckland Castle, adding Tudor arches, battlements and a gothic gatehouse.

Two months later, on September 8, the Rev. Brownlow North, half-brother of Lord North, was consecrated Bishop of Lichfield and Coventry at the age of only thirty.

1772 The following year, the Bishop of Ely, Dr. Edmund Keene, poured some of the proceeds of the recent sale of his historic Holborn property into the building of a fine, new West End residence at 37 Dover Street, Piccadilly,

A caricature pouring scorn on the would be sporting macaroni parson

with a magnificent Palladian façade and a glazed dome over the staircase well.

1773 On January 14, 1773, Dr. Richard Richmond was consecrated Bishop of Sodor and Man in a ceremony at the Whitehall Chapel. He was to prove a peculiarly secular bishop, undoing much of the good work done by his predecessors.

Eight months later, the death occurred at Christchurch, Hampshire, of the ninety-year-old Rev. Luke Imber, who a few years earlier had caused a sensation by marrying a thirteen-year-old village girl.

1774 In August 1774, Dr. William Dodd was struck off the roll of royal chaplains after attempting to bribe Lady Apsley, wife of the Lord Chancellor, to get him the living of St. George's, Hanover Square. A foppish man, known as the 'macaroni parson', Dodd had been ruined by love of luxury and ostentation and had run up terrible debts. He was now obliged to flee the country.

The following month, Dr. William Bell, domestic chaplain to the King's daughter Princess Amelia, was robbed of his watch and eighteen pence on the highway near Gunnersbury Lane. His attacker, a notorious ruffian known as 'Sixteen String Jack', was later hung at Tyburn.

On November 28, Dr. James Johnson, Bishop of Worcester, died after falling from his horse at Bath. A wealthy and hospitable man, he had embellished Hartlebury Castle with gothic decorations and had also spent an estimated £5,000 on improvements to his thirteenth-century palace in Worcester.

1775 The following May, the Archbishop of Canterbury, Dr. Cornwallis – whose parties at Lambeth Palace had continued to attract criticism – vigorously opposed a bill to license a playhouse at Manchester on the grounds that theatres had an 'immediate and pernicious effect' leading to idleness in manufacturing towns.

1776 In March 1776, the Bishop of Exeter, Dr. Keppel, preached before the King, urging him to make peace with the American colonies.

The same month, the Rev. Augustus Toplady, author of 'Rock of Ages', wrote an article in *Gospel* magazine in which he tried to explain that each human being commits 630,720,000 sins by the age of thirty.

Two months later, on May 24, the Rev. James Woodforde moved into the parsonage at Weston Longueville in Norfolk, of which he had been given the living some fifteen months earlier. A thirty-six-year-old bachelor with a taste for good living, he was to attend to his parish duties in a somewhat skimpy manner concentrating his main energies on his meals and entertainments. A few days after moving into the parsonage he was racked with toothache and had to summon a man to draw the offending tooth at five in the morning.

The same year, royal chaplain James Smith was appointed Vicar of Lambourn in Berkshire. He was to design a portable sentry box from which he could conduct burial services in rainy weather without getting his wig wet.

1777 January 1777 saw the appointment of Dr. William Markham as Archbishop of York. This tall, portly man with a magnificent presence and almost martial bearing, was the son of a penniless schoolmaster.

The following month, the scandalous Dr. Dodd, who had been struck off the roll of royal chaplains three years earlier, was arrested and charged with forging a bond for £4,200 in the name of Lord Chesterfield. This once fashionable clergyman, a friend of Dr. Johnson, was committed to the Compter prison in Southwark and thence to the Old Bailey where he was found guilty of the offence and sentenced to death.

On June 27, immense crowds thronged the streets leading to Tyburn where Dr. Dodd was to be executed. 'I am now a spectacle to men and soon shall be a spectacle to angels', he remarked as he was led to his death. Attending him on the scaffold was the Rev. Dr. Dobey, minister at the Magdalen Chapel where Dodd had once been a popular preacher. After the execution, it is said there was an attempt by surgeon John Hunter to bring the clergyman's body back to life.

A few days later, on July 4, the Eton-educated Rev. John Horne, son of a poulterer to the late Frederick Prince of Wales, was accused of trying to raise a subscription on behalf of the American rebels and was sentenced to a year's confinement in the King's Bench prison. The terms of his incarceration were generous: he was permitted to have a weekly dinner with his friends at the nearby Dog and Duck Inn, drink claret to cure himself of gaol fever and have his portrait painted by Richard Brompton, who was in the same prison for debt.

On October 16, the Eton-educated Bishop of Durham, Dr. Egerton, gave a large dinner party at his London residence, 17 Albemarle Street, at which the guests included actor David Garrick.

At the end of the year, John Holmes and Peter Williams, grave-diggers at St. George's, Bloomsbury, were found guilty of stealing corpses from their own graveyard. They were both sentenced to be whipped on their bare backs from Kingsgate Street, Holborn to Dyott Street, St. Giles, followed by six months' imprisonment.

1778   On April 9, 1778, ex-soldier Jonathan Shipley, now Bishop of St. Asaph, was to be found dining with Sir Joshua Reynolds, Mr. Gibbon, and Dr. Samuel Johnson. The last named had recently declared, 'No man can now be made a bishop for his learning and piety; his only chance for promotion is his being connected with somebody who has parliamentary interest.'

A month later, on May 14, Sir George Savile introduced a bill repealing some of the harsher laws against Roman Catholics. It quickly passed both houses of parliament, in spite of the opposition of the Bishop of Peterborough, Dr. Hinchliffe, who correctly prophesied that it would produce an outburst of anti-Catholic hysteria.

On June 14, the thirty-eight-year-old Rev. Augustus Toplady, now dying of consumption, was carried from his sick-bed to the pulpit of the Orange Street chapel to contradict rumours that he had modified his hostile views of John Wesley and wished to have a meeting with him. 'I sincerely hope', he declared, 'that my last hours will be better employed than in conversing with such a man.' Toplady died two months later in a sort of ecstasy of happiness. 'No man could endure such manifestations of God's glory as I have done and live', he said on his deathbed.

1779   On January 14, John Powel was found guilty of stealing dead bodies from the burial ground of St. George's Hanover Square, and was sentenced to be publicly whipped.

Later that spring, the Bishop of Llandaff, Dr. Shute Barrington, introduced a bill in the House of Lords to discourage adultery. He stated that as many divorces had occurred in the first seventeen years of the present reign as during the entire recorded history of the country. The bill was passed by the House of Lords but thrown out by the Commons.

On April 7, the Rev. James Hackman, Vicar of Wiveton in Norfolk and 'a victim of insane love', shot and killed the mistress of the Earl of Sandwich as she emerged from the Covent Garden theatre and was about to step into her coach. Nine days later, this unfortunate parson appeared before Mr. Justice Blackstone at the Old Bailey, explaining, 'A momentary frenzy overcame me and induced me to commit the deed I now deplore.' But he added, 'I have no wish to avoid the punishment which the laws of my country appoint for my crime.' Three days later, he was hung at Tyburn.

On June 7, Bishop Warburton, who had never fully recovered from a bad fall in his library several years earlier died at his palace at Gloucester. His lively wife, Gertrude, who was said to have had an affair with Thomas Potter, dissolute son of the late Archbishop of Canterbury, went on to make a second marriage.

Six months later, on December 23, Frederick Hervey, Bishop of Derry, succeeded to the title of Earl of Bristol. This genial, popular and extremely wealthy man, who had already built two vast houses in Ireland, now began work on the construction of a house at Ickworth in Suffolk with a façade of 600 feet and a giant rotunda.

Meanwhile, a new collection of hymns had been published by the Rev. John Newton, former slave-trafficker who had been 'converted' during a storm at sea and become curate at Olney in Buckinghamshire. The collection, known as *The Olney Hymns* included Newton's own compositions such as 'How sweet the name of Jesus sounds' and 'Glorious things of thee are spoken', and several contributions from poet William Cowper, who lived in the same parish, including 'God moves in a mysterious way'.

1780   On June 2, the following year, vast crowds gathered in London claiming to be protectors of the Church of England, and protesting aainst the recent legislation giving relief to Roman Catholics. After a stirring speech by twenty-nine-year-old eccentric Lord George Gordon, they made their way to Westminster with many cries of 'No popery!' Here, they attacked Dr. Markham, the Archbishop of York, tearing off his lawn sleeves and flinging them in his face, and demolished the coach of Dr. Thurlow, Bishop of Lincoln, who first sought refuge in a friend's house, then escaped across the roof-tops dressed as a woman. A separate group of some 500 marched on Lambeth Palace with drums and fifes and cries of 'No popery!' Archbishop Cornwallis and his family had already fled, leaving the house in the hands of 300 soldiers, whose officers were handsomely entertained by two chaplains. These disturbances continued until June 8 when the King at last called out the militia and order was restored with the loss of 285 lives.

The following month wealthy philanthropist and proprietor of the *Gloucester Journal*, Robert Raikes, opened the country's first Sunday school. Cynics said that he had only done so because he had been annoyed by noisy children playing near his newspaper office on Sundays.

Meanwhile, Archbishop Cornwallis had ceased to make use of the old palace at Croydon, probably because it was too far from London for his party-loving wife, and a private Act of parliament was passed to place the estate in the hands of commissioners.

On February 5, 1781, trouble-making eccentric Lord George Gordon was acquitted at the Old Bailey on charges of high treason. He was later to adopt the Jewish faith.

Later that spring, the Bishop of St. Asaph, Dr. Shipley, gave a big party attended by Sir Joshua Reynolds, Lord and Lady Spencer, Mr. Gibbon and other celebrities. After dinner, James Boswell was found to be disgustingly drunk and he was sharply rebuked by poetess Hannah More.

A few days later, on April 12, in the middle of Passion Week the wealthy Bishop of Chester, Dr. Porteus, gave a dinner in London attended by Sir Joshua Reynolds, Dr. Samuel Johnson and many others. Dr. Porteus was currently campaigning for a stricter observation of Good Friday and other religious festivals and his Sunday Act was to be passed later that year.

The following month, the Hon. Brownlow North, forty-year-old Bishop of Worcester and half-brother of the Prime Minister, was appointed Bishop of Winchester. He was to greatly dilapidate the revenues of the see, providing his relatives with some thirty livings and often travelling abroad where he acquired mosaics, marble chimney-pieces and a bust of Bacchus for his house at Chelsea.

The vacant see of Worcester was given to wealthy bachelor Richard Hurd, who was to install new bookcases in the marble-columned library at

Hannah More, who blamed the immorality of the lower-classes on the bad example set by the upper-classes

Hartlebury Castle, in which to house the books he had recently purchased from the executors of the late Bishop Warburton.

On June 8, the bachelor Norfolk Vicar, James Woodforde, served his friends a dinner consisting of two boiled chickens, a tongue, a leg of mutton, two ducks, green peas, artichokes, blancmange, almonds and raisins, oranges and strawberries. The meal was rounded off with port wine.

A few weeks later, on June 25, the Rev. Henry Bate, who had founded the *Morning Post* newspaper to supplement his meagre income as a clergyman, was committed to the King's Bench prison in Southwark for libelling the Duke of Richmond. Mr. Bate, an intimate friend of many of the wits of the day, did not let this set-back stand in his way and he went on to purchase lucrative livings.

Six months later, on December 17, Mrs. Cornwallis, fun-loving wife of the Archbishop of Canterbury, was found playing whist with Mr. Gibbon and Horace Walpole at a party given by Lady Lucan.

1782 On May 26, the following year, twenty-two-year-old Charles Simeon who had been a notably lively pupil at Eton, performing such stunts as jumping over half a dozen chairs in succession and snuffing out a candle with his bare feet, was ordained a deacon in Ely Cathedral. Within a few months he was appointed incumbent at Holy Trinity Cambridge where his dramatic preaching style attracted huge congregations but infuriated the old-fashioned church wardens who shut and bolted the doors against him when he tried to hold a special service for 'instructing the poor'.

On June 18, the Rev. Mr. Allen killed a Mr. Lloyd Dulany in a duel.

Charles Simeon preaching

In August, George Crabbe, unsuccessful doctor and poet and a familiar figure in the taverns of Aldeburgh, was ordained a priest by the Bishop of Norwich and appointed chaplain to the Duke of Rutland at Belvoir Castle where he was to be snubbed by both servants and guests.

On October 20, the Rev. Dr. Richard Watson a former chemistry professor at Cambridge and inventor of the black bulb thermometer was consecrated Bishop of Llandaff. He was never to reside in his diocese, blaming the lack of a suitable house, and spent most of the time in London, where he continued to devote his energies to scientific activities.

1783   On March 19, next year, the Archbishop of Canterbury, Dr. Cornwallis died at Lambeth Palace after a few days illness. The Primacy was first offered to the Bishop of Worcester, Dr. Hurd, who turned it down as 'not suited to his temper and talents' and was eventually accepted by the Bishop of Bangor, Dr. Moore, a grazier's son who had been tutor to the young sons of the Duke of Marlborough. He was duly translated to the see on April 26.

Five months later, on September 4, the new bishop of Norwich, Dr. Bagot, entertained twenty guests to lunch at his palace at Norwich. The fare included stewed carp and tench, a haunch of venison, a turkey, partridges, pigeons, sweetmeats, mulberries, melons, currants, peaches, nectarines and grapes. The meal was accompanied by Madeira, red and white wines and the table was adorned with a miniature garden.

Two months later, the celebrated Earl-Bishop of Derry, Frederick Hervey, attended a convention of volunteers in Dublin, entering the city in an open landau drawn by six horses and accompanied by a troop of dragoons. He was dressed in purple, with diamond knee and shoe buckles and white gloves fringed with gold lace, fastened by long gold tassels.

Meanwhile, the Eclectic Society had been formed in London, dedicated to 'religious intercourse and improvement'. The main person behind it was the former slave trafficker John Newton, now Rector of the lovely Hawksmoor church of St. Mary Woolnoth. Its first meetings took place at the Castle and Falcon Inn in Aldersgate Street at which members were to refresh themselves with tea from a silver teapot.

1784   Early the following year, the Rev. James Ramsay, a former naval surgeon, who had become vicar of Teston near Maidstone, where he was attended by a black servant named Testor, published his *Essay on the Treatment and Conversion of Slaves in the British Sugar Colonies* which proposed steps toward their total emancipation.

Meanwhile, Charles Wesley's son Samuel had become a Roman Catholic, to the distress of his father and uncle. On May 22, 1784 he publicized his conversion by dedicating a specially composed mass to Pope Pius VI.

In October, young M.P., man-about-town and atheist, William Wilberforce left for a holiday in the South of France, accompanied by his mother and sister and the Rev. Isaac Milner, lively and dashing tutor of Queens' College, Cambridge. While in Nice, now a popular resort among the English, Wilberforce slowly began to be 'converted' to Christianity.

1785   On April 4, 1785, the Rev. Edmund Cartwright, Rector of Goadby Marwood in Leicestershire, took out a patent for a primitive power loom he had invented. This innovation was to be vigorously opposed by weavers with

116

some 50,000 petitions against its use being received by the House of Commons.

At the end of the summer, Dr. Samuel Parr, a hot-tempered, coarse-featured Old Harrovian, was appointed perpetual curate at Hatton in Warwickshire, where he was to enlarge the parsonage and build a library capable of housing 10,000 volumes. A heavy smoker, Dr. Parr would even light up his pipe in the vestry during breaks in the service.

Clergymen demand Easter offerings from a reluctant John Bull

On the evening of December 15, the impecunious Rev. Robert Burt conducted the secret marriage of the twenty-three-year-old Prince of Wales and his friend Mrs. Fitzherbert, which took place in the latter's house in Park Street. It was said that Burt hoped to be rewarded with a bishopric but, in fact, he was to die soon afterwards in utter oblivion.

1786   On June 2, the following year, the Rev. James Woodforde, Rector of Weston Longueville, dined off mackerel, spring chickens, tongue, a roast leg of mutton, gooseberry tarts and custards, followed by both tea and coffee. A few days later, he was struck down by earache, which he treated successfully by taking rhubarb.

The following month, the Bishop of Chester, Dr. Beilby Porteus, visited Sir Charles Middleton, head of the Navy Board at his home near Maidstone to discuss the abolition of the Slave Trade. One outcome of the meeting was a letter from Sir Charles to young M.P. William Wilberforce, who had recently been 'converted' to Christianity, suggesting that he raise the matter in parliament.

1787   In January 1787, thirty-seven-year-old George Pretyman was appointed both Bishop of Lincoln and Dean of St. Paul's. The King had originally objected to this appointment, declaring, 'Too young, too young. Can't have it!' but was won over by the Prime Minister Pitt who had been tutored by Pretyman at Cambridge. For the next nineteen years the bulk of ecclesiastical patronage was to be exercised on Bishop Pretyman's advice.

A country parson enjoying his tithes . . .

The same month, the Rev. James Woodforde conducted the funeral of a five-week-old infant in blizzard conditions at Weston Longueville. He was protected against the biting wind and snow at the graveside by an umbrella: a recent innovation still regarded as somewhat effeminate.

On June 1, King George was persuaded to re-issue his proclamation against Vice and Immorality, requesting all persons of honour to set an example to help reform 'persons of dissolute and debauched lives'. With the encouragement of Bishop Porteus and William Wilberforce a society was formed to promote the proclamation's objectives.

1788   Twelve months later, on June 13, 1788, seven clergymen assembled at the Temple Church, Bristol, to dispossess a certain Mr. George Lakins of seven devils.

Two months later, on August 2, the King and Queen and several of their children visited the wealthy bachelor Bishop of Worcester, Dr. Hurd, at his episcopal seat, Hartlebury Castle.

Before the end of the year, the King was struck down with his first major attack of insanity. In the constitutional crisis that followed the Archbishop of Canterbury, Dr. Moore, rushed to the royal sick-bed at Windsor Castle anxious 'to make a humble offer of my personal attendance and services in any possible situation in which they may be acceptable'.

1789   In January 1789 the publication of *The Natural History of Selborne* by the sixty-nine-year-old Rev. Gilbert White was announced. This book, subse-

118

quently described as 'one of the most delightful books in the English language' received immediate, general acclamation.

The following month, parson-poet George Crabbe was appointed Rector of Muston and Allington near Belvoir Castle. On one of his first journeys through his new domain he had a bad attack of vertigo, collapsing in a street and was thought by passersby to be drunk. His digestive organs were later found to be at fault and opium was prescribed.

Meanwhile, the King had recovered from his mental illness and on March 18, at Weston Longueville in Norfolk, Parson Woodforde gave his servants a bottle of gin with which to celebrate the news.

On April 23, a great thanksgiving service was held at St. Paul's Cathedral for the restoration of the King's health. The monarch was welcomed at the door the new Bishop of London, Dr. Porteus, and the Bishop of Lincoln, Dr. Pretyman. Five thousand children from the charity schools of London sang the Hundredth Psalm as the King made his way to his seat while outside a military band played martial music.

Later that summer, poetess Hannah More, now devoting her life to good works, was to be found staying with Bishop Porteus at Fulham Palace, where she was to pen a poem about her host's famous predecessor which she entitled 'Bishop Bonner's Ghost'.

On July 24, the Rev. James Woodforde learnt of the Fall of the Bastille while staying with his sister near Bath. The same day, he purchased a large four-pound crab from a travelling fisherman, priced at one shilling.

On November 4, nonconformist minister Dr. Richard Price preached at the Meeting House in Old Jewry on 'the love of our country'. He declared that the French Revolution was a glorious event. 'I could almost say "Now lettest thou thy servant depart in peace for mine eyes have seen thy salvation"', he declared.

1790   Thirteen months later, in December 1790, the small but corpulent Rev. Joshua Brookes was appointed chaplain of the Collegiate Church in Manchester, where he was to conduct twenty weddings and a hundred baptisms a day and once interrupt a funeral to buy some horehound drops at a local confectioner's. He spoke in a broad dialect and was nicknamed by some 'the knave of clubs'.

Meanwhile, Miss Hannah More had published her *Estimate of the Religion in the Fashionable World*, in which she blamed the immorality of the lower classes on the bad example set by the upper classes.

1791   On March 2, 1791, veteran Methodist John Wesley died at his chapel house in City Road, whispering 'Farewell' to his friends. It was calculated that he had travelled over a quarter of a million miles preaching the gospel. He died a devout member of the Church of England though the movement he had founded had already begun to split with the established church.

In May, a bill to bring further relief to Roman Catholics was introduced and carried by both Houses of Parliament. The Archbishop of Canterbury Dr. Moore, supported this measure but pointed out that he was not prepared to 'destroy the wholesome regulations respecting the protestant religion'.

In July there were riots in Birmingham against Unitarian minister Dr. Joseph Priestley and other dissenters who had expressed sympathy with the

A confrontation between High and Low church or 'A Fruitless Application'

French revolutionaries. With cries of 'Church and King!' the rioters descended upon Dr. Priestley's home, desecrated his library and smashed his furniture. Following this upheaval, Dr. Porteus, Bishop of London, remarked, 'The mob may sometimes think right but they always act wrong.'

A few weeks later Dr. Porteus's wife was in an over-turning carriage but escaped unhurt.

On December 6, the Rev. James Woodforde held his Tithe audit dinner at his Norfolk parsonage. The company consumed a roast sirloin of beef, a boiled leg of mutton with caper sauce, a couple of rabbits served with onion sauce, boiled salt fish, plum puddings and other fine fare washed down with six bottles of rum, four bottles of port and several gallons of home-brewed beer.

1792   Six months later on June 8, 1792, the Rev. John Venn was installed as Rector of Clapham, now a popular suburb of London with a newly-built church with a three-decker pulpit, and many city businessmen among its inhabitants. In spite of his poor health, Venn was to become leader of a vigorous group of philanthropists dedicated to a new, reinvigorated Anglicanism.

THE NAPOLEONIC WARS

1793–1815

The self-confidence of the eighteenth century could not last for ever. The French Revolution and the war which followed was to transform the English church into a bulwark against atheism. Many parsons became super-patriotic and some played an active role in recruiting forces. The new problems created by the Industrial Revolution, the increasing population, the slum towns without sanitation and the horrors of the Slave Trade also pricked the church's conscience. Much of the old complacency continued, however. Scandalous bishops survived, the delightful but self-indulgent Rev. Sydney Smith arrived on the scene, the Clergy Residence Act of 1803 failed to drive the clergy back to their livings and Lambeth Palace was only lukewarm in its support of the new missionary movement. Throughout this period, many leading churchmen looked upon the evangelical movement, based on the 'Holy Village' of Clapham, with contempt. The lower orders, too, were suspicious of the columns of carriages now to be found outside the churches and wondered what was the matter.

1793 On February 1, 1793, France declared war on England. That evening, at his rectory at Weston Longueville in Norfolk, the Rev. James Woodforde played at cribbage with his niece Nancy, losing sixpence.

Later that year, the Rev. Richard Burgh, domestic chaplain to the Duke of Leinster, was charged with attempting to set fire to the King's Bench prison in Southwark, where he had been confined for debt. He was found guilty of the offence and sentenced to a further three years' imprisonment.

1794 The following spring, the ambitious young Wykehamist Sydney Smith was compelled to take Holy Orders in order to support himself. He was immediately appointed curate at Netheravon on Salisbury Plain, where he made a brave effort to stamp out poverty and ignorance. 'Nothing can equal the profound, the immeasurable, the awful dullness of this place,' he grumbled to a friend.

A few weeks later, on May 16, the Rev. John Horne, who had now taken the additional name of Tooke, was arrested after expressing sympathy with the French revolutionaries and committed to the Tower of London. A flamboyant man, who flaunted gold lace and scarlet clothing and made no secret of his two illegitimate children, he was triumphantly acquitted on charges of high treason later in the year.

Meanwhile, sea battles were raging and on June 1, the Rev. Dr. Richard Caddick, Rector of St. Mary-de-Castro with All Saints, Canterbury, and a noted Hebrew scholar, was present on board the *Impregnible* during a furious action in the Atlantic.

Four clergymen found enjoying a fast day

1795 On April 8, 1795, the Archbishop of Canterbury, Dr. Moore, presided over the marriage of the Prince of Wales and Princess Caroline of Brunswick, after first satisfying himself that the Prince was not legally bound in wedlock to Mrs. Fitzherbert. The service took place in the hot and crowded Chapel Royal at St. James's Palace and ended with the choir singing 'Happy, happy, happy, happy, happy shalt thou be' and church bells being rung throughout the country.

1796 Twelve months later, in April 1796, the Bishop of Durham, Dr. Shute Barrington, William Wilberforce and others subscribed together to present the parish of Marylebone with a soup kitchen to feed the poor.

That summer, the Rev. Charles Simeon held a series of house parties for evangelical clergy and their wives at the Manor House at Shelford near Cambridge which had a spacious garden running down to a river.

On September 23, a royal warrant announced the creation of the Army Chaplain's department with the Rev. John Gamble to act as the first Chaplain-General. On taking office, Gamble discovered that 340 army chaplains were on leave and he ordered them to report for duty by Christmas or be retired.

The following month, the energetic new Dean of Westminster, Dr. Horsley, whose favourite sport was rowing, objected to the use of Tothill Fields, just south of Westminster Abbey, as the site for a new, model humane gaol.

Meanwhile, the Rev. William Moreton had been installed as Vicar of the large parish of Willenhall in Staffordshire. A keen cock fighter and heavy drinker, said to be capable of drinking three bottles of wine at a meal, he was

A late eighteenth-century caricature showing a priest-ridden village

to rule the district for the next fifty years. Rumour had it that he was an illegitimate scion of the royal family.

1797 The following year, a dispute began over the valuable living of Bradwell-juxta-Mare in Essex when the Bishop of London, Dr. Porteus, refused to institute journalist-parson the Rev. Henry Bate, who claimed to have purchased the living some years earlier and had already spent some £28,000 on repairs and improvements to it and, as a leading member of the local hunt, had once killed a fox on the roof of Bradwell church itself. The living was eventually bestowed upon Mr. Gamble, the newly appointed Chaplain-General.

Meanwhile, the Rev. Lord George Murray, son of the Duke of Atholl and holder of livings in Essex and Kent, was playing an active role in recruiting forces to oppose the threatened French invasion but was thwarted by a meeting of bishops at Lambeth Palace who decided to check 'the arming influenza of their inferior brethren'.

1798 On March 2, 1798, the Bishop of Durham, Dr. Barrington, intervened in a debate in the House of Lords on the Divorce Bill to criticize the dancers at the Opera and accuse the French government of sending agents to England to corrupt our manners. The following night, dancers at the opera appeared in white stockings instead of the usual titillating flesh-coloured silk. This move was reinforced by a series of Lenten addresses by the Bishop of London, Dr. Porteus, at St. James's Piccadilly aimed at counteracting what he described as 'the growing relaxation of public manners'.

On April 21, Thomas Morgan, D.D., chaplain on board the 74-gun battleship *Mars*, which had fought a desperate action in the Bay of Brest, attended her captain Alexander Hood as he lay dying after being shot in the thigh by a musket-bullet. Dr. Morgan was later presented with a ring by the Hood family.

Later this year, the Rev. Thomas Malthus published his *Essay on the Principle of Population* in which he argued that vice and human misery were necessary to control the rapidly expanding population and argued that the lot of the majority of men could never be bettered. Though published anonymously, this pamphlet made Malthus, a former curate at Albury in Surrey, the target for bitter abuse.

1799   On April 12 the following year some sixteen clergymen met at the Castle and Falcon Inn in Aldersgate under the chairmanship of the Rev. John Venn, Vicar of Clapham, and formed themselves into the Society for Missions to Africa and the East. Shortly afterwards, letters seeking official recognition from the Church of England were delivered to the Archbishop of Canterbury, Dr. Moore, and the Bishop of London, Dr. Porteus, but the reactions of these prelates was only lukewarm and representatives failed to obtain audiences at either Lambeth or Fulham Palace.

The following month, the Religious Tract Society was founded.

Seven months later, on December 10, the Rev. James Woodforde held his annual tithe dinner at Weston Longueville. This year the fare consisted of two legs of mutton, capers, salt fish, a sirloin of roast beef followed by both plain and plum puddings. The company also consumed two bowls of punch, four bottles of wine, four bottles of rum, and some six gallons of beer. After dinner, the parson's nephew, Bill, entertained his guests with a song.

Meanwhile the church of St. Martin-in-the-Fields had been enriched by the addition of a new pulpit approached by a dainty staircase with three twisted balusters to each step.

1800   On Easter Tuesday 1800, the hot-tempered Dr. Samuel Parr, Vicar of Hatton in Warwickshire, preached a controversial sermon at Christ Church, Newgate, in which he attacked the theory of universal benevolence. Among other things, he said that the current agitation against the Slave Trade was 'utopian'.

Three months later, on July 2, the marriage took place in the parish church at Cheam between the twenty-nine-year-old Rev. Sydney Smith and Miss Catherine Pybus. The bridegroom, now acting as tutor, promised to endow his bride with all his worldly goods, which at that time consisted of six worn silver teaspoons.

Meanwhile, a friendship had blossomed on the hunting-field between the Prince of Wales and the Rev. Billy Butler, Rector of Frampton in Dorset, who was said to know the haunts of every fox in the neighbourhood. The Rector was to become a welcome guest at Crichel, nearby stately home where the Prince had set up his love-nest with Lady Jersey.

1801   In January the following year there were protests over the election of the Rev. John Horne Tooke as M.P. for Old Sarum and the Clergy Incapacitation Act was swiftly introduced banning clergymen from sitting in parliament. Old Etonian Tooke was allowed to retain his seat for the short duration of the current session.

In March, ardent evangelical the Rev. Charles Simeon ministered to a Cambridge chimney-sweep who was under sentence of death for receiving stolen property.

Later this year, the more devout clergy were shocked by the appearance of a two volume work entitled *Rural Sports* by the Rev. William Daniel, covering

Raeburn's famous painting of the skating parson strikes a tranquil note after the indignities of the eighteenth century

hunting, shooting, coursing, angling, and wild fowling as well as such matters as the inter-breeding of dogs and foxes. Mr. Daniel, who held no benefice, later tried to make amends by publishing a series of discourses entitled *Plain Thoughts upon the Lord's Prayer*.

1802   The following year, the Proclamation Society was reformed under the name the Society for the Suppression of Vice. It was to carry on a vigorous warfare against brothels, fortune-tellers, and obscene publications and even consider using dishonest methods to secure convictions.

Meanwhile, the Rev. James Woodforde, now sixty-three years old, had been struck down by a serious throat infection and had been unable to conduct his parish duties or pursue his usual pleasures. He grew weaker and

1803   weaker and finally died on January 1, 1803, leaving harness, clothes and cash worth £437.

Five months later, on June 3, the Bishop of St. David's, Lord George Murray, died at his house in Cavendish Square after catching a chill waiting for his carriage outside the House of Lords.

The same month, the Bishop of Lincoln, Dr. Pretyman, assumed the additional name of Tomline after inheriting an estate from an admirer, Marmaduke Tomline of Riby Grove, Lincolnshire, with whom he was only slightly acquainted.

1804   In January 1804, the Rev. Lockart Gordon and his brother were charged with abducting Mrs. Lee, daughter of the late Sir Francis Dashwood, from her home in Bolton Row, Piccadilly. The brothers pleaded that they had only done so to prevent her spreading her vehemently atheistic views and both were acquitted.

Two months later, on March 7, the first meeting of the British and Foreign Bible Society was held in the luxuriously carpeted banqueting hall of the London Tavern in Leadenhall Street, where the cellar vats were said to be stocked with live culinary turtles.

On November 10, the Rev. Sydney Smith, who had little time for evangelical activity, began a series of lectures on Moral Philosophy at the Royal Institution in Albemarle Street. The instant success of this venture, which he modestly described as 'the most successful swindle of the season', enabled him to take a house, 18 Orchard Street, Portman Square where he was to hold noisy dinner parties each week for some two dozen guests at a time. In the wake of these lectures, Smith also became a habitué at Holland House where Lady Holland held sway over the most powerful personalities of the day. He was soon so well established there that he could help himself to butter from his hostess's own special dish.

1805   On January 18, 1805, the death of the Archbishop of Canterbury, Dr. Moore, was followed by an ugly clash between the King and his Prime Minister. Pitt was anxious that his old tutor, George Pretyman Tomline, Bishop of Lincoln, should be given the Primacy but he was by-passed by the King, who quickly rode over to the Deanery at Windsor, interrupted a dinner party and offered the job to the Dean, Dr. Manners Sutton, grandson of the 3rd Duke of Rutland, and father of twelve children. 'My Lord Archbishop of Canterbury, I wish you joy', said the King, adding, 'Not a word. Back to your guests.' A furious exchange later took place between monarch and Prime Minister.

Nine months later, on October 21, the Rev. Alexander Scott was present on board the *Victory* when Lord Nelson was fatally wounded during the Battle of Trafalgar. This imperturble chaplain, who could speak eight languages and had a library of 650 books on board, nursed the Admiral through his last hours. 'I have not been a great sinner', Nelson told his chaplain before expiring.

1806   Three months later, on January 9, 1806, Scott rode in the procession to Nelson's funeral in St. Paul's Cathedral. He later retired to a living at Southminster in Essex taking with him a mirror, wardroom table, bureau, and fireplace from the famous ship in which he had served.

Two weeks after Nelson's funeral, William Pitt died in the arms of the Bishop of Lincoln, thanking him for all his kindnesses. Two of the many services that the Bishop had rendered the Prime Minister were to advise him about his debts and personally loan him £1,000. The Bishop's control of ecclesiastical appointments now came to an end.

1807   On February 24, the following year, a bill for the abolition of the Slave Trade was at last passed by the House of Commons amidst great excitement. At his spacious town house in St. James's Square, the elderly Bishop Porteus noted that the act had put an end to 'the most execrable and inhuman traffic that ever disgraced the Christian World'. Also joining in the celebrations was eighty-one-year-old Rev. John Newton, former captain of a slave ship, who had become one of the greatest hymn-writers of the day.

On September 28, Dr. George Pelham, Bishop of Bristol, who was said to be greedy for lucrative office, was translated to the see of Exeter, where he was to prove disgracefully lax, dealing with ordination candidates by sending his butler to tell them to write an essay.

Two months later, on November 3, the grand old Archbishop of York, Dr. Markham, died at his house in South Audley Street in his eighty-ninth year.

Meanwhile, the new Archbishop of Canterbury, Dr. Manners Sutton, had acquired Addington Palace and its 1,200 acre estate near Croydon. This quiet rural retreat was paid for out of funds accumulated by the recent disposal of the Old Palace nearby.

1808   The following year, the Rev. William Lewis Rham became Vicar of Winkfield in Berkshire where he was to devote much of his time to agricultural experiments, and contribute many articles to the *Royal Agricultural Society Journal* including 'An Essay on the Simplest and Easiest Mode of Analysing Soil'.

1809   In June, 1809, the Rev. Edmund Cartwright was voted £10,000 by the Commons for his services to the community in inventing the power loom, which had revolutionized the weaving industry. Mr. Cartwright was now applying his inventive skills to the agricultural processes on the Woburn Abbey estate of the Duke of Bedford.

Two months later, Dr. John Randolph was appointed Bishop of London following the death of Dr. Porteus. A professor of divinity and man of great learning, Dr. Randolph was to annoy the Prince of Wales by becoming the first bishop to dispense with his wig.

The same summer, the popular Rev. Sydney Smith, was forced to forsake the delights of London and take up residence in the obscure parish of Foston-le-Clay in Yorkshire. There had not been a resident parson here since the reign of Charles II, the parsonage was a tiny hovel and when Smith thumped the cushion of his pulpit he claimed that the accumulated dust of 150 years made such clouds that he could not see his congregation for several minutes. Smith soon commissioned the building of a new rectory and became absorbed in the delights of gardening, ploughing, baking, brewing, churning and fattening poultry.

Meanwhile, evangelical leader the Rev. John Venn had personally installed a water closet at his rectory at Clapham.

1810   The following February the wealthy Rev. John Mitford was installed in the Crown living of Benhall in Suffolk. Here he was to build a handsome new parsonage, surrounded by a splendid arboretum of ornamental shrubs and foreign trees, and to excite much gossip by taking under his wing a twelve-year-old village girl named Eliza. Rumours were to circulate that Mitford, who also rented permanent lodgings in London's Sloane Street, had dealings with 'his satanic majesty'.

The following month, the new Chaplain General to the Forces, Archdeacon John Owen, noted a conspicuous absence of brigade chaplains.

Eight months later, in October 1810, King George III was struck down by his mental illness again and was placed in the care of a committee of which the Archbishop of York, Dr. Vernon, was a leading member.

Meanwhile, the Archbishop of Canterbury, Dr. Manners Sutton, and six other bishops had voted against a bill to remove the death penalty for the pilferage of goods up to the value of five shillings.

1811   On February 6, 1811, the Duke of Wellington expressed his concern about the conspicuous absence of brigade chaplains and said he knew of only one chaplain doing his duty.

The same year, English hymnology was enriched by two new compositions: 'Lead us, heavenly father, lead us' written by architect James Edmeston for the children of the London orphan asylum, and 'Brightest and best of the sons of the morning' by the Rev. Reginald Heber, Vicar of his family living of Hodnet in Shropshire. Certain people were to refuse to use the latter hymn on the grounds that it involved the worshipping of a star.

1812   On May 13, 1812, the Bishop of Ely, Dr. Dampier, died suddenly at his magnificent house in Dover Street. The bishopric passed into the hands of Dr. Edward Sparke, Bishop of Chester, a somewhat scandalous figure who was to provide his relations with the best livings in the Fen country and who himself derived revenues from his see calculated at £200,000.

A few weeks later, the Luddite riots, inspired by the cost of the war, came to a head. At Hartshead in Yorkshire, where the rioting was particularly bloody, the Vicar, thirty-five-year-old Patrick Brontë, purchased a pair of pistols for his own protection.

1813   In February 1813 thieves broke into Old Hummums Coffee House in Covent Garden. At two in the morning, the Rev. H. Byron, who was temporarily lodging at the establishment, apprehended a coloured man under his bed, who later appeared at Bow Street Court.

Five months later, on July 1, the Rev. John Venn, who had recently ridden over to visit the Bishop of Winchester at his house in Chelsea in spite of his poor health, died at his vicarage in Clapham. During his twenty-year ministry there, the parish had become the most important in England.

An early nineteenth-century caricature showing a master parson and his journey-man

1814   The following January, the infant heir to the House of Rutland was baptized in the chapel of Belvoir Castle by the Archbishop of Canterbury, Dr. Manners Sutton. The ceremony was followed by magnificent entertainments at the castle and was attended by the Prince of Wales, who had now been appointed Regent following his father's final collapse into apparent lunacy.

    Two months later, on March 20, the Rev. Sydney Smith moved his family into his comfortable new rectory at Foston-le-Clay near York on which he had spent some £4,000. The coach carrying the clergyman's family got stuck in a field and Mrs. Smith lost a shoe in the mud.

    Meanwhile, the new diocese of Calcutta had been founded by an act of parliament. On May 8 this year Dr. Thomas Middleton was consecrated its first bishop in a service at Lambeth Palace, at a salary of £5,000 a year, and six months later on November 28 he arrived in his diocese and soon afterwards embarked on a 5,000 mile primary visitation.

    Meanwhile, the good-natured Rev. R. H. Barham had been presented with the livings of Snargate and Warehorne on the Romney Marsh. His church here was soon revealed to be a depot for smugglers, a large seizure of tobacco being made in the belfry and a keg of gin being discovered under the vestry table.

1815   On June 18, the following year, the Battle of Waterloo effectively ended the Napoleonic Wars and brought peace to England. Many officers now found themselves without an occupation and decided to take Holy Orders.

AGITATION AND REFORM

1815–1833

The ranks of the church were now expanded to make room for a large number of ex-officers: unpriestly figures who were to combine their military half pay with the stipend of rural livings. The Anglican establishment, with its vast but ill-distributed wealth, was to become increasingly unpopular. Plump red-faced bishops and wordly-wise parson-magistrates who suppressed the mob were lampooned in the radical press. The erection of cheap unattractive churches, with hideous towers and porches, to cater for the nation's new urban population did little to mollify the critics. The once powerful Evangelical movement could no longer be depended upon to champion the under-privileged. The movement was now confined mainly to fashionable watering places such as Cheltenham and Tunbridge Wells and, in 1827, one of its former leaders Charles Simeon had the cheek to ask a friend to send him another consignment of game for his next dinner party. Meanwhile the income of the bishops was soaring. At the end of this period the Bishop of Winchester was earning £50,000 a year. The church's unpopularity came to a head in October 1831 when twenty-one bishops voted against the Reform Bill. In the violence that followed, their palaces were stoned, their coaches burnt and a dead cat was thrown at the Archbishop of Canterbury's chaplain. It was left to the newly formed Oxford Movement to pick up the pieces.

1815   Peace began with a controversy over the appointment – in June 1815 – of the Rev. Henry Ryder as Bishop of Gloucester, the first evangelical to receive a bishopric and brother of the reformer Lord Harrowby. Though not welcomed initially by the clergy of his diocese, he soon won them over by his devotion to duty, often preaching three times on Sundays.

1816   On March 24, 1816, the death occurred of William Cowherd, a former Anglican clergyman who had formed an obscure sect at Salford in Lancashire, whose members denounced animal food and intoxicating drink.

Four months later, on July 4, the elderly Bishop of Llandaff, Dr. Richard Watson, died at Calgarth Park in Westmoreland where he had been living in rural retirement, concentrating his energies on estate improvements and only visiting his diocese once every three years.

On October 30, a general order was issued forbidding army chaplains from marrying without the permission of their field marshal.

1817   At the spring Assizes at Bedford the following year Sir Montague Burgoyne was prosecuted for having been absent from his parish church for several months. He was saved from the penalty of his 'misdeeds' by producing evidence that he had been ill.

That summer, the Rev. George Crabbe, who had now received proper recognition as a poet and taken on a new lease of life as a result, arrived in London to partake in the delights of the Season. On June 24, he was to be found dining at Holland House with the Duchess of Bedford, the Countess of Bessborough and other celebrities, and on July 11 he was present at a breakfast party at the house of Mr. Samuel Rogers in St. James's Place. He attended scores of social events in between.

In November, sixteen-year-old John Henry Newman, an undergraduate at Trinity College, Oxford, received his first communion. One of his black silk gloves got stuck as he was about to receive the bread and he was obliged to rip it off, tearing it to shreds. The young Newman had been warned against religion by his father: 'Religion, when carried too far, induces a softness of mind. Take care, I repeat.'

A few weeks later, on December 17, bookseller William Hone was charged with issuing pamphlets parodying the Anglican liturgy and the Cabinet. He conducted his own defence before a jury and secured a triumphant acquittal.

1818   The following summer, the worldly Bishop of Exeter, Dr. Pelham, was a daily attendant at the dinners given by the Prince of Wales at the Brighton Pavilion. Also partaking in these festivities was the Bishop's wife, a haughty woman who was said never to rise from her seat when receiving guests at the episcopal palace at Exeter.

On September 8, former naval chaplain Lawrence Halloran was transported for forging a ten-penny postage frank. This unfortunate man, who claimed to be a doctor of divinity but in fact possessed only deacon's orders, had served in the 100-gun battleship *Britannia* at the Battle of Trafalgar.

Meanwhile, the Rev. Robert Taylor, a curate at Midhurst in Sussex, who was said to have fallen under the influence of a local tradesman with non-Christian views, had preached a sermon which scandalized the orthodox in the congregation. He had resigned his living on conscience grounds but before the end of the year he published a recantation, written in Latin, and wrote a penitent letter to his former parishioners. He then applied to the Bishop of Chichester, Dr. Buckner, for a new living but was rebuffed with the reply, 'My dear Taylor, the background is the place for you.'

The same year, parliament had passed the Church Building Act providing for the expenditure of one million pounds on new churches in London and the provinces. Most of the 218 churches built as a result were in Gothic style: cheap, unattractive and dreary.

1819   On May 24, 1819, the Duchess of Kent gave birth to a baby girl in Kensington Palace. The Archbishop of Canterbury, Dr. Manners Sutton, subsequently officiated at the christening and held the infant in his lawn sleeved arms while the Duke of Kent and Prince Regent argued about what names she should be given. The Bishop of London, Dr. Howley, eventually pronounced her Princess Alexandrina Victoria.

Meanwhile, agitation for reform was reaching new heights, with several clergymen haranguing the masses. On July 21 this year, the Rev. Joseph Harrison was arrested on the platform of a public meeting at Smithfield and, the following month, the eccentric Dr. Healey led a band of protesters to the celebrated meeting at St. Peter's Church, Manchester, which was broken up by the militia with the loss of eleven lives.

In September, work began on alterations and rebuilding at 32 St. James's Square, new town house of the Bishop of London, Dr. Howley.

1820   On January 29, 1820, the death of the mad, old King George gave the Crown at last to the Prince Regent and presented the Archbishop of Canterbury with the embarrassing problem of how to deal with the new monarch's wife, Queen Caroline, who had been living on the Mediterranean for several years in somewhat scandalous circumstances.

The following month, the Rev. Patrick Brontë was appointed to the living of Haworth, high up on the Yorkshire moors. This scattered parish, once ruled over by the mad parson William Grimshaw, included three hamlets and numbered in all some 500 souls. Brontë was to live at his grim parsonage with his daughters Charlotte, Emily and Anne and his son, Patrick Branwell.

Four months later, on June 4, the arrival of Queen Caroline in London met with confused reactions in Anglican circles. William Wilberforce wrote to the King asking him to restore his wife's name to the Prayer Book, while the Rev. Robert Landor, former chaplain-in-ordinary to the Prince Regent, published extraordinarily vituperative letters attacking her. 'The country is in danger', he stated. 'A set of scoundrels have undermined the government, abused the church and calumniated all honest men.'

Meanwhile the Queen had settled into a house in Piccadilly and appointed the pipe-smoking Old Harrovian Dr. Samuel Parr as her chaplain.

On July 12, the deaf but amiable Dr. Brownlow North, Bishop of Winchester, who had provided his relatives with no fewer than thirty livings, died after a long illness. The lucrative bishopric passed into the hands of Dr. Pretyman Tomline, who was to arrange for the disposal of the episcopal house in Chelsea, which had been an official residence of the Bishops of Winchester since the reign of Charles II.

On November 10, the failure of the King to prosecute the Queen was greeted with church bells being rung throughout the country and, on November 29, the Queen went in state to St. Paul's Cathedral to give thanks for her deliverance from her enemies. The Bishop of Llandaff, Dr. Van Mildert, condemned this event as 'a mockery of a religious ceremony at which every serious Christian must shudder'.

On December 15, the popular Rev. Sydney Smith was a guest at Lambton Castle, County Durham, where he was excited by the new gas lighting which had been installed.

Meanwhile, an important book had appeared entitled *The Black Book, or Corruption Unmasked*, containing details of poverty to be found in the church. Among other things, it claimed that twenty-five daughters of Welsh clergy were to be found among the prostitutes of Liverpool.

1821   On February 23, 1821, the tall and aristocratic Archbishop of York, Dr. Edward Vernon, entertained the King and the Dukes of Wellington, Cumberland and Cambridge at his house in Grosvenor Square while in a nearby house, the Cato Street conspirators were planning the murder of the entire Cabinet.

By the middle of the summer, Queen Caroline's popularity had faded away and on July 19, a swelteringly hot day, she was refused admission to her husband's coronation in Westminster Abbey. After going from door to door and failing to get into the building she fled to the accompaniment of derisive

Hot-tempered Old Harrovian pedagogue Dr. Samuel Parr, who was appointed chaplain to the unfortunate Queen Caroline. A heavy smoker, his pipe has been carefully obliterated from this portrait

hoots. A few weeks later, on August 7, she died, partly from the effects of her ordeal.

Meanwhile, the Coronation had been followed by a magnificent banquet in Westminster Hall, which got off to a slow start owing to the absence of the Dean of the Chapel Royal, who was supposed to say grace. He eventually appeared so out of breath that no one could hear his words.

1822   On April 7, the following year, the new St. Pancras Church was consecrated by the Bishop of London, Dr. Howley. The building featured a magnificent pulpit consisting of a square substructure on four Ionic columns with an octagonal sounding board above.

Three months later, on July 8, Dr. Middleton, first Bishop of Calcutta, died of a fever. He was to be succeeded as bishop by the aristocratic Reginald Heber, author of the hymn 'From Greenland's icy mountains'.

Eleven days later, on July 19, the Rt. Rev. Percy Jocelyn, Bishop of Clogher and nephew of Lord Roden, was discovered in the back room of the White Lion public house in St. Alban's Place, St. James's, committing sodomy with a private in the footguards. He was immediately arrested and taken to Vine Street watch-house, where he spent the night in prayer. The following day, on presentation of sureties valued at £1,000 he was released and fled to the Continent. In his absence, he was sentenced to be deprived and deposed by the Primate of Ireland.

1823   On August 8, 1823, a gang of thieves broke into Lambeth Palace and made havoc in several of the principal rooms. Archbishop Manners Sutton was away at the time but his bedroom was plundered and letters from the King were found strewn across the floor. A wardrobe containing valuable dresses belonging to Mrs. Sutton was untouched, however, and the Archbishop had fortunately sent off eight chests of valuable plate to the safekeeping of Messrs. Rundell and Bridge before going away.

1824   On February 14, the following year, the Rev Thomas Viall of Twickenham appeared at Bow Street court accused of assaulting his sister-in-law, a Mrs. Marshall. It was stated that Mr. Viall had ridden alongside her carriage and struck at her through the window with his whip.

Meanwhile, cholera had replaced small-pox and the plague as the major killing disease, but caused just as much alarm. In 1824 it raged through the moorland parish of Haworth, causing the death of, among others, the Rev. William Weightman, who had recently become curate to the Rev. Patrick Brontë.

1825   On January 20, 1825, the British and Foreign Temperance Society was formed.

The same week, seventy-eight-year old pedagogue Dr. Samuel Parr, whose only form of exercise had been bell-ringing, caught cold while conducting the funeral of a parishioner at Hatton in Warwickshire and died two months later.

1826   On April 2, 1826, the pious forty-two-year-old Bishop Heber died suddenly at Trichinopoly, worn out by the strain of travelling around his vast diocese of Calcutta.

The same month, the Rev. Sydney Smith paid his first visit to Paris, where he was introduced to high society and taken by the Duke of Bedford to dine at the house of Prince Talleyrand, where the cook was said to be the best in France.

A few weeks later, on May 30, the young Rev. Jack Russell, famous for his feats of endurance in the boxing and wrestling rings, was married to admiral's daughter, Penelope Bury. The couple's first home was at Iddesleigh in North Devon, where Jack Russell quickly built up a pack of foxhounds.

1827 On October 8, 1827, the aristocratic Hugh Percy, son-in-law of the Archbishop of Canterbury, was appointed Bishop of Carlisle. Here, he was to spend some £40,000 restoring and rebuilding his official residence, Rose Castle, and hiring the famous Mr. Paxton to re-design the gardens, though the house remained an uncomfortable place to live in, with no heating apparatus and not a single curtain on any window. Not surprisingly Bishop Percy travelled often to London, driving his coach and four himself and keeping permanent lodgings at Usher's Hotel, 16 Suffolk Street, off Pall Mall.

Meanwhile, the Rev. Robert Taylor, who had resigned his curacy at Midhurst in scandalous circumstances nine years earlier, had opened a chapel next door to the Mansion House in Cannon Street and been charged with blasphemy and 'attempting to overthrow the Christian Religion'. On October 24, he appeared in the High Court before Lord Justice Tenterden, wearing an eye-glass, flowing clerical robes, and sumptuous rings and carrying a neat clerical hat and a pair of light kid gloves. For three hours he defended himself, quoting Greek, Latin and Hebrew. 'The motive for my infidelity is the most ardent piety', he told the jury, 'I fear God and therefore I dare not be a Christian because Christianity seems to be unworthy of him.' The jury took thirty minutes to find him guilty and he was sentenced to twelve months' imprisonment in Oakham gaol.

The same month, the elderly evangelical leader Charles Simeon received a parcel of game from his old friend, anti-slavery campaigner Sir Thomas Fowell Buxton. Simeon thanked his friend warmly but had the impertinence to ask for a second consignment of game for a dinner party he was to give the following week.

Two months later, on December 12, handsome Old Etonian Dr. Charles Sumner was translated to the immensely lucrative see of Winchester – its income was now estimated at £50,000 a year – at the suggestion of the King's mistress Lady Conyngham. One of his first steps as Bishop was to purchase a town house, 21 St. James's Square, out of the funds of the see.

Meanwhile, unassuming Oxford don, the Rev. John Keble, who was said to be a man of shining goodness in constant communion with God, had published a collection of poems entitled *The Christian Year* and intended to be read as daily spiritual refreshment. The book was an instant and unexpected success and its ideas quickly infiltrated the religious world.

The same year, the Rev. John Darby had given up his curacy in County Wicklow and become a founder member of the new Plymouth Brethren group, which denounced all ecclesiastical forms and denominational distinctions. He was later to break away again and found his own sect, the 'Darbyites'.

1828 On January 2, 1828, the Rev. Sydney Smith was made a Canon of Bristol.

135

The King declared that he had never met such a profligate parson but nevertheless gave the appointment his approval. One of Smith's first sermons in Bristol Cathedral in favour of a more tolerant attitude towards Roman Catholics was greeted with furious glares from the Mayor and Corporation of the city.

The following month the newly ordained John Henry Newman, now twenty-seven years old, was presented with the living of St. Mary's Oxford. Here, his four o'clock sermons, delivered in an entrancing voice with silvery intonation were to mould the new generation of clergy. It was said that while preaching Newman would sometimes pause for half a minute between sentences.

Five months later, on the death of Archbishop Manners Sutton, the Bishop of London, Dr. Howley, was raised to the primacy. A deplorable public speaker, Howley had been educated at Winchester, where he had once knocked down fellow pupil Sydney Smith with a chess-board.

The see of London, now rapidly increasing in population, was given to Dr. Blomfield, Bishop of Chester, who was to prove indefatigable in building new churches and schools and sponsoring charities.

In August, thirty-three-year-old Thomas Arnold – who had confessed to being 'one of the most ambitious men alive' – took up his appointment as headmaster of Rugby School. 'My object will be, if possible, to form Christian men, for Christian boys I can scarcely hope to make', he declared. A man of great religious fervour, he was to issue frequent warnings of death and hell and would often break down in the pulpit and weep openly in front of the entire school.

On November 23, the ranks of the priesthood were enriched by the ordination of wealthy twenty-eight-year-old Edward Bouverie Pusey, who was said to be a first rate horseman, shot, swimmer and whip and the last pupil at Eton to learn dancing.

Meanwhile, the living of Redbourn in Hertfordshire had been given to the Rev. Lord Frederick Beauclerk, younger son of the Duke of St. Albans and one of the most famous cricketers of the day. He had taken sixty-six wickets in one year and in 1826 had become president of the M.C.C.

1829   In January, 1829, work began on the re-furnishing and enlarging of Lambeth Palace at the expense of its new occupant, Archbishop Howley. Small medieval rooms, corridors and passages were swept away and the building – which had belonged to the see since the twelfth century – took on a new, forbidding nineteenth-century appearance. The Great Hall, rebuilt by Archbishop Juxon, in the 1660s, was converted into a library by the addition of neo-Jacobean bookcases.

The following month, the death occurred of the eccentric Rev. Francis Egerton, who had recently inherited the Bridgwater earldom. This wealthy bachelor, son of a former Bishop of Durham, held livings in Shropshire but had spent the last few years in Paris living in a house in the Rue St. Honoré which he kept full of cats and dogs, some of which were dressed as men and women, and were taken for drives in his carriage and fed at his table.

On March 29, Sir Robert Peel's bill to give Roman Catholics the right to sit in Parliament, vote and own property without restrictions was passed by the House of Commons, in spite of the objections of the Archbishop of

136

Canterbury, Dr. Howley. On April 13, the Bill received the Royal Assent and on May 4, for the first time since the Reformation a Roman Catholic took his seat in the Commons.

A few weeks later on June 10, the first Oxford and Cambridge boat race was held. Three-quarters of the undergraduates who took part in this event were to become clergymen.

On June 15, Dr. Edward Drax Free, Rector of Sutton near Lincoln, appeared before the Arches Court accused of having 'illicit connections' with a succession of maid-servants, owning indecent books and prints, drunkenness, using profane language, stripping his church roof of lead and turning cattle and swine into the churchyard. He was sentenced to suspension and deprivation.

The same summer, the Rev. Sydney Smith acquired the living of Combe Florey near Taunton. Here he found the rectory in a dilapidated state and at once started building with a band of twenty-eight workmen. The new house was to feature a library crammed with volumes lusciously bound in blue and red and an apothecary shop filled with drugs and groceries for needy parishioners.

1830   A year later, on June 26, 1830, King George IV died at Windsor Castle attended during his last hours by the Bishop of Chichester, Dr. Carr, who had read out a prayer for his recovery to which the dying King had responded 'Amen, amen, amen'. He was buried in St. George's Chapel and succeeded by his popular brother William who was said to have been a 'devout believer' since surviving a storm at sea many years earlier.

One of the dying King's last tasks had been to give the Royal Assent to the Duke of Wellington's beer bill. This act proved abortive and in October this year the Rev. Sydney Smith, who had more sympathy for beer-drinkers than wine-drinking moralists, declared, 'Everybody is drunk. Those who are not singing are sprawling.'

On November 22, Dr. Henry Phillpotts, son of a former proprietor of the Bell Inn, Gloucester, was appointed Bishop of Exeter. In preparation for the move to his diocese, he gave advance orders that several dozen bottles of port, sherry and claret should be bought and laid down in the cellar of his palace – while other wine should be ready for immediate consumption on his arrival. He also gave instructions that his bed should be 'thoroughly well aired'.

1831   On January 15, 1831, the impressive-looking Archbishop of York, Dr. Vernon, assumed the surname of Harcourt on inheriting the huge estates of his cousin, Field Marshal Earl Harcourt.

Three days later, a Tithe Audit dinner was held at Brightstone on the Isle of Wight, where William Wilberforce's son Samuel had recently been appointed rector. The twenty-three people present drank eleven bottles of wine, twenty-eight quarts of beer, two and a half quarts of spirits, and twelve bowls of punch, 'and would have drunk twice as much, if not restrained', noted the twenty-five-year-old rector.

Five months later on June 29, the London Temperance Society held its first meeting in Exeter Hall under the chairmanship of the Bishop of London, Dr. Blomfield. Dr. Blomfield, champion of many good causes including sanitary reform and the abolition of the episcopal wig, had privately suggested to his incumbents that 'a good deal of port wine is a sovereign remedy for the ague'.

On July 4, former Anglican clergyman Robert Taylor, who had recently served a twelve-month sentence for blasphemy and had now removed himself even further from his mother church by branching out into the strange field of 'astro-theology', was arrested after preaching at the Rotunda in Blackfriars Road. He was again charged with blasphemy, brought before the Surrey Court of Sessions and sentenced to two years' hard labour in the Horsemonger Lane gaol.

Meanwhile, the new Bishop of Exeter, Dr. Phillpotts, had begun to grapple with the fox-hunting clergymen in his diocese. On July 18, he confronted the popular Rev. Jack Russell, accused him of neglecting his cure and begged him to give up his hounds. The following day, he visited the notorious Rev. John Foude, Vicar of Knowstone in Devon, who was said to be 'guilty of every crime in the calendar', and found six foxes' brushes hanging in his dining-room. Other unruly parsons with whom Bishop Phillpotts was to cross swords included the Vicar of Wellclose, the Rev. Jack Hannaford, a famous clerical bruiser who was said to have arms like oak saplings, the Rev. John Radford, brutal Rector of Lapford, and the Rev. C. F. Bampfylde, who was known as 'the Devil of Dunkerton' and once described by a fellow cleric as 'the worst man in the West of England'.

On September 27, the Rev. Sydney Smith, now Rector of Combe Florey in Somerset, acquired the additional post of Canon of St. Paul's Cathedral. This involved three months a year duty in London and occasional appearances at Court, where he was to draw attention to himself by wearing shoe laces instead of buckles.

A few days later, on October 8, the Archbishop of Canterbury, Dr. Howley, and twenty other bishops voted against Lord Grey's Reform Bill infuriating the populace and causing anti-clerical riots across the country. Dr. Howley was designated a Judas Iscariot and, after being pelted in the streets of Canterbury, and a dead cat being thrown at one of his chaplains, had to ask the Home Secretary for armed protection. The Bishop of Bristol, Robert Gray, had his palace burned to the ground and, on November 5, effigies of the Bishops of Exeter and Winchester were burned outside their respective homes. 'The church as it now stands no human power can save', commented the Rev. Thomas Arnold sadly.

1832 The following year, many bishops changed their tactics and on June 7, 1832, the Reform Bill at last received the Royal Assent.

At the end of the same month, the Rev. John Keate, headmaster of Eton for the past twenty-three years, dealt with a rebellion at the school by flogging eighty boys in one day. A small man with bright red hair, Keate was cheered by the rest of the school after his marathon was over.

On July 10, Samuel Sebastian Wesley, great nephew of the founder of Methodism, was appointed organist at Hereford Cathedral where he was soon to cause a scandal by running off with the Dean of Hereford's sister.

Nine days later, cholera broke out at Exeter and the unpopular Bishop Phillpotts, currently on a confirmation tour outside the city, was accused by his enemies of having 'run away'.

On Christmas Day, newly-ordained Old Etonian George Denison was

The much-loved Rev. Sydney Smith, who once observed that there were three sexes – 'men, women and clergymen'. He is also remembered for his remark, 'My idea of heaven is eating pâté de foie gras to the sound of trumpets'

officiating at Cuddesdon Church near Oxford when the building caught fire. The submissive congregation remained in their seats until Denison announced: 'I see there is a little accident. You had better go and get ladders and plenty of water.'

The same month, the holy young Rev. John Henry Newman and his equally devout and devoted friend, The Rev. Hurrell Froude, both deeply impregnated with the ideas of John Keble, left for a long holiday abroad for the sake of Froude's health. Together they visited France, Gibraltar, Malta, the Ionian islands, Sicily, Naples, and Rome. Sailing back alone from Palermo to Marseilles the following June on board an orange-boat, Newman penned his famous hymn 'Lead kindly light, amid the encircling gloom'.

1833

THE VICTORIAN ERA

1833–1890

This period of British mercantile supremacy and the rapid expansion of the empire was accompanied by an unprecedented upsurge of religious activity at home. The revival was triggered off by the Oxford Movement but later inspired by a mixture of philanthropic types, including Gladstone, Lord Shaftesbury, Charles Kingsley, Angela Burdett-Coutts and Queen Victoria herself. These busy years saw the growth of Christian Socialism, muscular Christianity, sanitary reform, the Temperance Movement, hymn-writing, church-building, the public schools and the expansion of the Church of England onto a global scale. Between 1840 and 1876, eight theological colleges and some 7,000 churches were built, at a total cost of more than £25 million. Simultaneously, Acts of Parliament removed the worst ecclesiastical abuses, bridged the gap between rich and poor clergy, stripped the bishops of some of their grandeur and cut their salaries. In 1861, Hymns Ancient and Modern *became a national institution almost overnight. During his first term of office, Prime Minister Gladstone appointed twelve new bishops and eight new deans. Meanwhile, a string of new overseas bishoprics were being founded and the new railway network linked up the parishes and dioceses like never before. In 1867, the bishops of the Church of England gathered for the first Lambeth Conference and by the end of the period representatives of the new religious-minded aristocracy had begun to gather round the Archbishop of Canterbury and pledge him their support. This enthusiasm was not easily achieved or readily accepted by either the establishment or the populace, as the hysterical fuss over ritualistic practices shows. Beneath the passionate philanthropy, the church remained intensely conservative. In 1848, Chartist theologian Jacob Cadley described the Church of England as 'the Conservative Party at prayer', a sentiment echoed by Matthew Arnold in 1877 when he declared that the church was 'devoted above all to the landed gentry and to the propertied and satisfied classes generally'. Many Victorian parsons lived in vast vicarages, ate off massive dining-room tables, mixed in the best County circles, continued to pursue the fox – in the 1860s no fewer than twenty Devon parsons still kept packs of hounds – took long holidays abroad and employed curates to do their dirty work.*

1833 On Sunday July 14, 1833, the Rev. John Keble ascended the pulpit of St Mary's Church, Oxford and called for a great revival of true churchmanship. He argued that the Church of England had been progressively abdicating its authority to secular powers and influences and spoke of the urgent need for the clergy to preserve their divine heritage and trust handed down to them through the ages.

A few days later, inspired by this sermon, a meeting took place at Hadleigh Rectory in Suffolk, headed by the frail-looking Rev. John Henry

Newman, at which it was resolved that the church should be defended by the publication of cheap tracts, the contents of which were to be reinforced by Newman's powerful sermons from the pulpit of St. Mary's.

On August 5, the funeral of the great William Wilberforce, who had been a keen admirer of this new movement, took place in Westminster Abbey amidst widespread mourning. Two royal dukes, the Lord Chancellor, the Speaker and four peers supported the pall.

1834 Seven months later, on March 18, 1834, the sentence of transportation on the Tolpuddle Martyrs inspired Dr. Arthur Wade to lead a procession of 50,000 people to protest. 'To withhold God's bounty from those who want is the highest treason against heaven', he declared.

On December 31, that year, the Rev. Stephen Hawker was installed as Vicar of Morwenstow on the rocky, north Cornish coast, where there had not been a single resident vicar for the past century. An eccentric and autocratic man, who wore crimson gloves during divine service, he was to attempt to modernize the church by taking down the ancient curtained family pews. One well-to-do farmer objected to this innovation but the Vicar took the matter into his own hands, smashing up the pew with an axe and scattering the bits outside the church.

Meanwhile, in protest at the election of the Duke of Wellington as Chancellor of the University of Oxford, the Archbishop of Dublin, Dr. Whately, had applied for the command of the Horse Guards.

1835 On February 4, 1835, Ecclesiastical Commissioners were appointed to enquire into the distribution of the church's finances. A mixed body of laymen and clergy, they set about putting the church's house in order in the most determined manner.

Three days later, sixty-three-year-old Sydney Smith and the young M.P. William Gladstone were among the guests at the house of historian Henry Hallam. Smith told Gladstone that the new generation of clergy was a great improvement on the last one. 'Whenever you meet a clergyman of my age you may be sure he is a bad clergyman,' he said.

Five months later, on July 7, the young Rev. Henry Manning delivered a sermon in Chichester Cathedral in which he spoke of the office of the priest as 'invested with a dignity of unequalled brightness'; twenty-seven-year-old Manning, who had played cricket for Harrow two years running and had taken Holy Orders only in order to further his career, had now become a model parish priest at Lavington in Sussex.

Meanwhile, the Rev. Charles Tennyson, curate of Tealby in Lincolnshire, had become addicted to opium, which he had originally been given as a treatment for emotional and nervous tension. He now went around dressed in rabbit's skins, looking like 'the dog's meat man', his drug-addiction scandalizing the neighbourhood.

The same year, the Dean of Westminster, Dr. Ireland, had appointed Lord John Thynne, son of the Marquess of Bath, as his sub-dean. Thynne, who already held a handful of livings in the Home Counties, was soon to distress his superior by permitting free admission to the Abbey. 'Now we shall have people eating their luncheons in every corner and scattering their sandwich papers over the nave', grumbled the elderly Dean.

On March 9, 1836, the shy but celebrated John Keble, originator of the Oxford Movement, was instituted as Vicar of Hursley near Winchester, where he was to share his house with his wife Charlotte and sister Elizabeth, who had an artificial leg.

Meanwhile, the question of church tithes, which had been a source of bitterness and friction since before the Reformation, was being debated in parliament: The outcome was the Tithe Commutation Act, which was passed on August 11, putting an end to the payment to the local parson of one-tenth of everything produced by local farmers, and replacing it with a simple rent charge on land.

Two months later, the young Rev. Christopher Wordsworth, nephew of the poet, was appointed headmaster of Harrow, where the school had sunk into a state of drunkenness and lawlessness under his easy-going predecessor, the Rev. Charles Longley. Wordsworth, who had won renown for his severity as a monitor at Winchester and his prowess on the cricket field, once catching out Henry Manning in a Winchester–Harrow match, was soon to find he was fighting a losing battle at the school and his health began to fail.

Four months earlier, another link between the church and public schools had been forged with the appointment of the Rev. Samuel Butler, Head-master of Shrewsbury, as Bishop of Lichfield and Coventry. In his address to his successors at Shrewsbury, Butler had urged them to 'labour faithfully, zealously and happily in their calling, training those who are confided to their care in the principles of religion and sound learning and endeavouring to make them good Christians, good scholars and honourable and useful members of society. Amen!'

Meanwhile, the Rev. Sydney Smith was spending the autumn in Paris, where he took great delight in French food, which he compared most favourably with 'the Stonehenge masses of meat with which we feed ourselves'. He rejoiced particularly over a *matelote*, an almond tart and a *poulet à la tartare*.

On November 12, this year, former evangelical leader Charles Simeon, who had continued to dress in the style of the clergy of his youth and had shown marked hostility to the new Oxford Movement, died of a chill he had caught when paying his respects to the new Bishop of Ely in the draughty Ely Cathedral.

On April 5, 1837, the ninety-three-year-old Bishop of Norwich, Dr. Bathurst, died in his residence, 12 Hereford Street, off Oxford Street. An anachronistic figure, he had been frequently absent from his diocese, winter-ing at Bath and indulging in card games with his ancient lady friends.

Two months later, on June 20, the Archbishop of Canterbury, Dr. Howley, and the Lord Chamberlain, Lord Conyngham, were present at the deathbed of King William IV at Windsor Castle. The King died in the early hours of the morning and the Archbishop and Lord Chamberlain im-mediately ordered a carriage and drove post haste through the night to Ken-sington Palace. They arrived there at 5 a.m. but were not finally admitted by the new young Queen, in her dressing-gown, for almost an hour.

A few days later, the Rev. Sydney Smith preached a sermon in St. Paul's

Cathedral in which he urged the new monarch to keep her people in a state of peace. 'Extinguish in your heart the fiendish love of military glory', he ordered.

Meanwhile the tall and muscular Rev. Walter Hook, who was said to believe that bishops should be as poor as Saint Augustine, had been appointed Vicar of the vast and rapidly expanding parish of Leeds. Shortly after his induction, in August 1837, he faced a mob of 3,000 complaining about the half-penny church rates but won them over with the force of his personality.

1838 In May 1838, an imposter named John Thom caused riots at Canterbury and Brighton after announcing that he was the Messiah. Eventually, two companies of the 35th Regiment were called in and Thom was killed in the battle that followed.

A few weeks later, on June 28, the splendid coronation of the new monarch was slightly marred by clerical blunders. Archbishop Howley attempted to force the ruby ring onto the Queen's fifth rather than fourth finger, the Bishop of Bath and Wells, Dr. Law, accidentally turned over two pages of the service book at once and another participant Dr. Maltby, Bishop of Durham, was, in the Queen's own words, 'remarkably maladroit'. Archbishop Howley admitted afterwards, 'We ought to have had a full rehearsal'.

The same month, the dynamic new Vicar of Leeds, Dr. Hook, preached a highly controversial sermon before the Queen in the Chapel Royal in which he argued that the church had an authority entirely separate from its connection with the state.

Meanwhile, far away in Leicestershire, the Rev. Hugh Costobadie, who had been a pupil at Harrow with Sir Robert Peel, had been made Vicar of Hallaton. Here he was to set up the remarkable record one day by riding forty miles, taking four services, jumping four gates and shooting a couple of wild duck.

1839 On May 26, 1839, Mrs. Edward Pusey, whose husband had become one of the leading lights of the Oxford Movement, died of consumption. Dr. Pusey never recovered from this sadness and, though he zealously continued his religious work, retired from the world, leading a more and more austere life, laying stripes on himself, wearing hair cloth next to the skin and deliberately eating repulsive food.

The following autumn, the good-living Sydney Smith purchased 56 Green Street, off Grosvenor Square as a London residence, which he was to beautify with marble chimney-pieces and other decorations to please his wife. He was also to be found at the newly opened Athenaeum Club in Pall Mall, where he would button-hole bishops and make them laugh.

1840 On February 10, 1840, the marriage of Queen Victoria and Prince Albert of Saxe-Coburg-Gotha took place in the Chapel Royal, St. James's Palace. Archbishop Howley again blundered during the ceremony, trying to make the exquisitely-uniformed bridegroom place the wedding ring on the Queen's right hand. At the end of the service, there was fresh confusion when the Earl Marshal the Duke of Norfolk insisted on signing the register first and held everybody up while he fumbled with his spectacles.

Three months later, on May 12, the Rev. G. Grantham, a much respected

A detail of Sir George Hayter's painting of Queen Victoria's wedding at which Archbishop Howley tried to make the bridegroom force the ring on the bride's right hand

senior fellow of Magdalene College, Cambridge, over-balanced as he opened his second floor window at the college and fell to his death.

The same spring, the Church Discipline Act strengthened the control of the bishops over their clergy, enabling them to call in the secular arm of the law to punish contumacy.

1841   On March 10, the following year, the wife of the Rev. Samuel Wilberforce died suddenly. After suffering 'paroxysms of convulsive anguish' her husband rallied his forces and, in his own words, made the church his bride.

Meanwhile, the Dean of York had been found guilty of 'the foul crime' of selling ecclesiastical preferments and, on April 2, 1841, he was formally deprived in a ceremony in York Minster conducted by the Archbishop of York, Dr. Vernon Harcourt. The Dean was absent from this event, and remained unrepentant, declaring, 'If I had a hundred livings I would sell them all.'

Six months later, on October 17, Old Etonian George Selwyn was consecrated first Bishop of New Zealand in a ceremony at Lambeth Palace. A few weeks later the thirty-two-year-old Bishop set sail for his new diocese, acquiring almost perfect mastery of the Maori language during the long voyage.

Meanwhile, the aristocratic Bishop of Norwich, Dr. Stanley, had infuriated teetotallers by challenging them to give up sugar on the grounds that it was chemically linked with alcohol.

1842   The following April, the Rev. John Henry Newman, who had begun to have doubts about the Anglican religion and had handed over the leadership of the Oxford Movement to the devout Dr. Pusey, retreated to Littlemore, near Oxford, where he had fitted up a set of cottages as a refuge, to think about his future.

Two months later, on June 12, forty-six-year-old Dr. Thomas Arnold, whose loathing of the Oxford Movement had known no bounds, died suddenly at the height of his fame.

Meanwhile, the arrival of the railways in the West Country had brought great joy to the Rev. Sydney Smith who could now travel between his rectory at Combe Florey in Somerset and his house in Green Street, Mayfair, in a matter of hours. 'Railroad travelling is a delightful improvement in human life', he declared, though he was to fiercely oppose the fashion of locking carriage doors between stations.

1843   On February 1, 1843, the Rev. William Bailey, a fashionable preacher at St. Peter's, Queen's Square, appeared in the dock at the Old Bailey, charged with forging a promissory note for £2,875. He was found guilty of the offence and was sentenced to transportation for life.

On May 14, Dr. Pusey preached a sermon before Oxford University on the Holy Eucharist and was subsequently condemned by the Vice-Chancellor and six Doctors of Divinity for having preached false doctrine and was suspended from preaching for two years.

Four months later, on September 18, the frail John Henry Newman, said by some to look 'like an old lady washed in milk', resigned the incumbency of St. Mary's Oxford which he had held for the last fifteen years. A week later, he preached on 'The Parting of Friends' at the nearby Littlemore Church. The building was decked out for the occasion with flowers and friends remarked that this lent a funereal air to the proceedings. Newman was now to withdraw for two years of prayer and fasting.

On December 2, the former Bishop of Clogher, Percy Jocelyn, who had been defrocked for sodomy twenty-one years earlier, died in Edinburgh, where he had been reduced to working as a domestic servant and living under an assumed name.

1844 On May 16, 1844, the Archbishop of Armagh, Lord John Beresford, was proceeding in his carriage across Westminster Bridge when his horses bolted. The carriage hit a cab, then an omnibus and then went over on its side, the coachman being thrown from his box and taken to hospital. The Archbishop, head of the Anglican church in Ireland, was not injured but had to be removed from the vehicle by a window.

The same month, the Rev. Charles Kingsley, who had been torn between a career in the army or the church, was appointed Rector of Eversley in Hampshire, where it was said not one labourer in the parish could read or write and sanitation was non-existent. Kingsley was to preach the doctrine of 'fresh air and cold water' and express a horror of saintliness: 'a poor pitiful thing, not God's idea of man, but a poor shaveling idea'.

Meanwhile, the Rev. Sidney Godolphin Osborne, Vicar of Durweston in Dorset, had begun publicizing the grinding poverty of agricultural workers in a series of letters to *The Times*, causing splutters of rage from rich farmers and local landowners, who branded him a popularity-hunting parson.

On November 20, the Bishop of Exeter, Dr. Phillpotts, caused an outcry against 'romanizing tendencies' by ordering the clergymen of his diocese to wear the surplice. In December, people left churches where the minister 1845 wore a surplice and, on January 12, 1845, the Rev. Francis Courtenay, high church Vicar of St. Sidwell's Exeter, was followed from his church by a yelling mob of 600 who pelted him with filth and rotten eggs and struck at him with sticks. The following week, the mob had swollen to 2,000 and Courtenay was obliged to ask for official protection. Indignation had also been excited across the country and there were demands for Phillpotts' resignation as bishop.

On February 22, the Rev. Sydney Smith died at 56 Green Street, Mayfair, leaving London society grief-stricken. In his last sermon in St. Paul's Cathedral he had said, 'I never take leave of anyone for any length of time without a deep impression on my mind of the uncertainty of human life and the probability that we may meet no more in this world'.

Eight months later, on October 9, John Henry Newman was received into the Roman Catholic Church at his house at Littlemore near Oxford, leaving Dr. Pusey, who was to declare his intention of dying in the bosom of the Church of England, to guide the Anglican revival.

Five days later, Samuel Wilberforce was offered the Bishopric of Oxford. 'My soul is penetrated with a thrilling sense of it', he confided in his diary. During the long episcopate that followed, Bishop Wilberforce, known by some as Soapy Sam, was to make full use of the railway network to keep in touch with his diocese, write more than forty letters a day, and build a hundred churches, seventy parsonages and a picturesque looking theological college for ordinands.

The following month saw the suspension of the Rev. William Day, Rector of Hawridge in Buckinghamshire, after being found guilty of various acts of intoxication. He had frequently been found in the tap room of the local Rose and Crown inn, drinking with labourers and 'other low persons' and had recently spent six weeks in Aylesbury gaol for assault.

Meanwhile, the Rev. Charles Vaughan had taken over as headmaster of Harrow and begun to impose rigid discipline on the school, delivering terrifying sermons – one of them was on the text 'Cast forth that evil person from among you' – and was said to be so sarcastic that his smile was even more frightening than his frown.

1846   Early in 1846, the repeal of the Corn Laws was an additional burden for the poorer tenant farmers and many country parsons came to the rescue of their parishioners. Many gallons of nourishing broth were doled out from vicarages and the Rev. Sidney Godolphin Osborne asked Lord John Russell's government if it realized that it spent less on educating the nation's poor than on keeping the London opera house open.

In July this year, the unpopular Bishop of Exeter, Dr. Phillpotts, sued the Editor of the *Western Times* after the appearance of an editorial describing him as 'one who does no credit to the mitre which he is paid £200 a week or thereabouts to wear'. Phillpotts lost the case, church bells were rung throughout his diocese and a crowd formed outside his palace gates to give three resounding groans.

The same year, an earnest appeal to the nation on the subject of beer-shops was published by the Rev. Thomas Page of Virginia Water, in which he described beer-shops as 'hot beds of every species of iniquity' and claimed that the working-classes had become 'disaffected dissolute, impatient of superiority or control, reckless of family duties'.

1847   On November 5, the following year, the death occurred at Bishopthorpe Palace of the wealthy Archbishop of York, Dr. Vernon Harcourt, who had fathered some sixteen children during his long marriage.

Fifteen days later, the death occurred in the South of France of the Rev. Henry Lyte, author of the famous hymns 'Abide with me! Fast falls the eventide' and 'Praise my soul the king of heaven'. He had spent much of his life living abroad for health reasons and was buried in the English cemetery at Nice.

At the end of the year, a storm blew up over the offer of the see of Hereford to Dr. Renn Dickson Hampden, whose unorthodox views had aggravated both the high church and his university. Thirteen bishops joined in a demonstration against the appointment which they claimed would excite 'apprehension and alarm'. When these objections were brushed aside by the Prime Minister, Hampden's enemies instituted proceedings against him for **1848**   heresy. These were ultimately unsuccessful and on January 11, 1848, the election was officially confirmed and, in the words of one commentator, Hampden was 'buried alive' in his diocese.

Meanwhile, a separate controversy, which was to rage for several years, erupted over the appointment of the Rev. George Gorham, who was said to hold controversial views on baptismal regeneration, to the Crown living of Brampford Speke near Exeter. Bishop Phillpotts was to insist on examining him for fifty-two hours and eventually refused to institute him and the case went on to be disputed in the appropriate courts.

Dr. Howley, last of the Prince Archbishops and the last primate to wear a wig. He was educated at Winchester, where he once knocked down fellow pupil Sydney Smith with a chess board

In the midst of these troubles, on February 11, the eighty-two-year-old Archbishop of Canterbury, Dr. Howley, died at Lambeth Palace, repeating the words, 'Leave off from wrath and let go displeasure: fret not thyself else shalt thou be moved to do evil.' The last of the 'prince-archbishops' and the last Primate to wear a wig, he left £120,000 and was conveyed to his final resting place at Addington Palace, near Croydon, in a hearse drawn by six black horses with a plume of black feathers borne in front.

Following Howley's death, the new Ecclesiastical Commissioners slashed the income of the see of Canterbury to £15,000 and stripped the Primacy of much of its splendour. The new Archbishop, Old Etonian John Bird Sumner, who was enthroned at Canterbury on April 28, was to live the life of a country gentleman at Lambeth, walking over to the House of Lords with his umbrella, whereas his predecessor had ridden in a coach and four flanked by liveried outriders.

Meanwhile, Miss Frances Humphrey had launched her *Hymns for Little Children* containing the joyful 'All things bright and beautiful'.* and other more gloomy compositions apparently aimed at frightening children into being good.

1849 On September 6, 1849, the Bishop of Norwich, Dr. Stanley, died suddenly

---

* 'All things bright and beautiful' contains the controversial verse:
  The rich man in his castle,
  The poor man at his gate,
  God made them, high or lowly,
  And ordered their estate.

149

at Brahan Castle in Ross-shire where he was on holiday with his wife and daughters. His body was brought back to his diocese by sea, being landed at Great Yarmouth and buried in the nave of Norwich Cathedral.

Some six weeks later, Old Etonian Henry Hart Milman, author of the Palm Sunday processional hymn 'Ride on, ride on in majesty' was installed as Dean of St. Paul's.

1850   On June 24, the following year, the new £90,000 church of St. Stephen's, Rochester Row, was consecrated, along with a supporting parochial system of soup kitchen, temperance rooms and self-help club. This venture, paid for by wealthy philanthropist Angela Burdett-Coutts, was designed to bring Christianity to the slums of Westminster.

The following month, the up-and-coming William Ewart Gladstone surprised the House of Commons by suggesting that new bishops should be appointed wherever there was a demand for them, but they should be paid only £1,500 a year and not be given a seat in the House of Lords.

On November 1, the foundation stone of All Saints, Margaret Street, was laid by Dr. Pusey, head of the Oxford Movement. The interior of this church was to be adorned with garish frescoes, carvings, marble, mosaics, stained glass and gilding, with no surface being left uncovered.

On November 16, the philanthropic work of the Rev. William Queckett at Christ Church, Watney Street, in the East End was praised by Charles Dickens in a magazine article entitled 'What a London Curate can do if he Tries'.

Meanwhile, the papal bull, published on September 30, establishing a Roman Catholic hierarchy in England headed by Cardinal Nicholas Wiseman as first Archbishop of Westminster, had caused a surge of indignation and anti-Catholic hysteria. On December 5, on the eve of Wiseman's enthronement, there was a huge meeting at the Freemason's Hall and 320,000 people signed a protest to the Queen against 'papal aggression'. Much of the indignation was concentrated on the newly-built church of St. Barnabas, Pimlico, pioneer church of the Anglo-Catholic movement, prompting the Vicar, the Rev. W. J. E. Bennett to flee to the West Country, where he was appointed vicar of Frome Selwood by the Dowager Marchioness of Bath and became a habitué at Longleat House.

While these dramas were going on, the Rev. H. T. Ellacombe, Vicar of Clyst St. George in Devonshire, was devoting himself to the harmless study of church bells, visiting every belfry in his county in twelve months and finding rotten floor-boards, unsafe towers, broken bells, jackdaws' nests and quantities of guano. Ellacombe, who had studied engineering under Brunel, was the inventor of an ingenious system of chiming hammers, which enabled one man to chime all the bells in a steeple.

The same year, the Rev. Charles Kingsley, now spear-heading the Christian Socialist movement, had published an exposure of the grim conditions in the tailoring industry under the title *Cheap Clothes and Nasty*.

1851   On April 6, 1851, the medieval-looking Henry Manning, former Archdeacon of Chichester and a leader of the high church party, was received into the Church of Rome at the newly-built Farm Street Church, Mayfair.

Four months later, on August 6, after several years of controversy and litigation, and the publication of some sixty books or pamphlets on the

150

subject, the Rev. George Gorham was at last instituted as Vicar of Brampford Speke in Devonshire. A public subscription was arranged to pay his heavy legal costs, a small surplus from which was used to buy the controversial vicar a silver tea service.

1852   In January 1852, the newly ordained twenty-seven-year-old Brooke Westcott joined the staff of Harrow School, where he was to visit the churches in the neighbourhood on a tricycle.

Meanwhile, the ranks of the property speculators now buying up tracts of land on the outskirts of London were enriched by the unusual figure of Dr. Samuel Walker, Rector of St. Columb Major in Cornwall, who was said to be 'hungry for land and able to pay handsomely for it'. In March this year Dr. Walker paid £32,000 for twenty-five acres of North Kensington, on which he hoped to make immense profits. Alas, the venture was to prove a disaster and Walker lost his fortune and his Cornish living and was to die abroad in poverty.

The same spring, the Church Convocation, which had been suppressed by successive governments who did not care for clergymen debating in public, assembled again after a break of 135 years. Clergy travelled to the great meeting by the new railway network now covering the country.

On November 18, one and a half million people watched as the funeral procession of the eighty-three-year-old Duke of Wellington made its way through London to St. Paul's Cathedral, where a service took place of 'unexampled magnificence'.

1853   In August 1853, Old Etonian George Denison, uncompromisingly high church Archdeacon of Taunton, began to preach a series of sermons in Wells Cathedral in which he claimed that the Body and Blood of Christ were present in the sacraments and should therefore be worshipped. He was soon prosecuted for heresy by Mr. Ditcher, Vicar of the nearby parish of South Brent, and a new church battle began, which was not resolved for many years.

Meanwhile, the Rev. John Colenso, a former mathematics master at Harrow School, was consecrated first Bishop of Natal. A man 'without a

The Duke of Wellington's funeral car is drawn to St. Paul's Cathedral

spark of personal vanity', he sailed from Plymouth on December 15, and was to cause an outcry on his arrival in the diocese by tolerating polygamy among the Kaffir converts.

1854   On May 21, 1854, Dr. Tomlinson, Bishop of Gibraltar, was to be found at Scutari in the Crimea giving communion to 300 officers and men.

Some six weeks later, on July 2, the Rev. and Hon. Gerald Wellesley, nephew of the late Duke of Wellington, was installed as Dean of Windsor, in which position he was to form an intimate relationship with the royal family.

On October 24, the Society for the Propagation of the Gospel resolved that a further dozen chaplains should be despatched to the perils of the Crimean battlefield, where conditions were now complicated by cholera, typhus and dysentery. Already on his way to the troubled area was the militant Dorset vicar, Sidney Godolphin Osborne, who was to assist at the hospital set up by Miss Florence Nightingale at Scutari, dressing the wounds of the sick and dying with great skill and tenderness.

1855   The following year, the Rev. Jack Russell helped to inaugurate a hunting tournament at Dulverton in Somerset.

1856   In the spring of 1856, five children of the Dean of Carlisle, Dr. Tait, died from scarlet fever in the space of a month. 'Oh God, thou has dealt very mysteriously with us', Tait wrote in his diary. This appalling family tragedy aroused the sympathy of the entire nation, including the Queen, who in September this year gave her warm approval of the appointment of Dr. Tait as Bishop of London.

On November 12, the Rev. Alfred Nathanial Curzon, Rector of Kedleston, inherited the barony of Scarsdale and an estate of 10,000 acres, which had been in his family for the past 800 years. He soon ceased to officiate at his church but continued to retain responsibility for 'both the moral and material welfare of his flock'. A man of meticulous domestic habits, he was noted for his habit of keeping the gravy spoon warm in a silver bowl while carving the joint.

Meanwhile, the churchyard at Chipping Norton in Oxfordshire had been let to a local butcher as grazing land for his sheep. One old lady refused to buy mutton that had been grazed in the churchyard because it had 'a deathly taste'.

1857   Early the following year, the Bishop of Norwich, Dr. Hinds, was obliged to resign his see after marrying his cook. He moved to London and, through the influence of Lord Shaftesbury, the 'bishop-maker', the diocese passed into the hands of the zealous John Pelham, fourth son of the Earl of Chichester, who was to build a new episcopal palace beside the cathedral at Norwich, later described by Pevsner as 'a distressing building of flint and red brick'.

A few months later, on July 20, the Rev. Henry Polehampton, chaplain at Lucknow, who had rowed for Oxford in the 1846 boat race, died of cholera during the Indian Mutiny.

On October 22, the Archbishop of Canterbury, Dr. Sumner, sentenced fellow Old Etonian Archdeacon George Denison to deprivation for his high church heretical views. Archdeacon Denison, whose brothers included a former Bishop of Salisbury and a Governor General of Australia, was to appeal to the Privy Council and get the judgement reversed. In due course, he became an extreme ritualist, believing in 'costly and magnificent ceremonial'.

Meanwhile, the new rector at Colkirk in Norfolk, a pipe-smoking Balliol man the Rev. J. B. Sweet had begun extensive restoration work at his church, which had suffered from neglect for many years. It was said that a previous parson, an elderly man, had taken the unusual and distasteful step of installing his own sanitary system in his pew.

1858   On July 3, 1858, the first National Rose Show was held in London, organized by the Rev. Samuel Hole, who was said to know more about flowers and plants than any man alive. In his vicarage garden at Caunton in Nottinghamshire, Hole grew over 400 varieties of roses and on his frequent visits to London he spent many happy hours in Messrs. Veitch's nursery gardens and glass-houses in King's Road, Chelsea.

In December this year, Bishop Wilberforce of Oxford told students at the newly opened Cuddesdon Theological College, where high church teaching had been getting out of hand, not to 'walk with a peculiar step, carry their heads at a peculiar angle and read in a peculiar tone'.

Meanwhile, a madman named Thomas Pooley had appeared before Liskeard magistrates charged with blasphemously carving the words 'Jesus Christ' on the gate of the home of the local Vicar, the Rev. Paul Bush, and was sentenced to six months in Bodmin Gaol. Pooley was said to believe that the world was a living animal and that potato rot and other diseases could be cured if all bibles were burnt and their ashes spread over the fields.

1859   In January 1859, the Rev. Edward White Benson was appointed first Master of the newly instituted Wellington College. He was to rule this new model school by terror and was to be particularly remembered for the highly theatrical manner in which he would enter the school chapel. When chastising a pupil, it was said he would turn completely white.

The following month, Dr. Hook's long and successful pastorship as Vicar of Leeds ended with his appointment as Dean of Chichester. During his twenty-two years at Leeds, the city had become a stronghold of the Church of England and some twenty-one churches, twenty-seven schools and twenty-three parsonages had been built.

On April 27, the wealthy Rev. John Mitford died after collapsing in a London street. His lack of religious conviction and irregular personal life at his Suffolk rectory had excited much comment during his career and his cynical comments had often brought him into conflict with his bishop. During the summer that followed his death, his fine collections of Greek coins, cameos, miniatures, engravings and rare manuscripts came up for sale in Sotheby's auction rooms.

Meanwhile, rioting had begun at the mission church of St. George's-in-the-East where certain parishioners and church-wardens objected to the ritualistic practices of the resident clergy. The Rev. Charles Lowder counter-attacked by giving local boys sixpence each to throw rotten eggs at a sandwich man parading on behalf of a hostile church-warden and, by September 25, the situation had become sufficiently grave for the Bishop of London, Dr. Tait, to close the church.

The same month, the Rev. Charles Vaughan suddenly resigned as headmaster of Harrow, after the discovery that he had had a homosexual affair with one of his pupils. The parent of another boy had threatened to expose him publicly if he did not give up his post at once. Dr. Vaughan, one of the country's most able schoolmasters, meekly exchanged the great head-mastership for the humble post of Vicar of Doncaster.

On November 24, Charles Darwin's *The Origin of Species* was published, selling out on the first day and drawing a chorus of horrified criticism from leading churchmen. Among those to condemn the book was Darwin's old tutor, the Rev. Adam Sedgwick, who described it as 'grievously mischievous' and gave it a savage review in the *Spectator*.

Meanwhile, the easy-going Old Harrovian Rev. George Hustler had been given the living of Stillingfleet near York, where he was to hunt with all the neighbouring packs, especially the York and Ainsty and the Bramham Moor. Out hunting, Hustler fortified himself with a mixture of quinine and whisky, which he carried in a flask.

Another appointment this year was that of the Rev. William Kingsley as Rector of South Kilvington near Thirsk in North Yorkshire. Kingsley was to apply himself to improving the drainage systems in the village and set up a notice on the back gate of his rectory reading 'Man traps are set at night in these grounds' to deter village boys courting his housemaids.

1860   On February 16, 1860, the Bishop of Rochester, Dr. George Murray, who was said to be the last bishop to wear his wig in the House of Lords, died at his house in Chester Square. He was succeeded as bishop by Dr. Joseph Wigram, who was to criticize the wearing of beards and moustaches by the clergy.

Three months later, on May 28, the Rev. Henry Moule, Vicar of Fordington in Dorset, took out a patent for a lavatory he had invented which 'flushed' with dry earth. Marlborough-educated Moule had been shocked by the recent outbreaks of cholera and firmly believed that Cleanliness was next to Godliness.

On Saturday June 30, at a meeting of the British Association for the Advancement of Science at Oxford, Bishop Wilberforce, supported by a mass of clerical sympathisers, attempted to 'smash Darwin' but was himself demolished by Professor Huxley, who resented the Bishop's intrusion in a scientific matter.

On November 13, the death occurred at Hartlebury Castle of Dr. Henry Pepys, seventy-seven-year-old Bishop of Worcester. A popular man, bells were tolled for him in Birmingham, Worcester and other major and minor towns in his diocese.

The same month, the Rev. R. Burden gave a dinner for the thirty workmen who had built his new rectory at Haselbury Bryan in Dorset. The fare consisted of roast beef, plum pudding and home brewed ale.

1861   The following year saw the appearance of *Hymns Ancient and Modern* edited and promoted by the Rev. Sir H. W. Baker, Bart., a firm believer in the doctrine of the celibacy of the priesthood and himself the author of some distinguished hymns including 'The king of love my shepherd is'.

The same year, the Hon. Colin Lindsay proposed at the Church Congress that a further 130 bishops should be appointed to control the rapidly increasing number of clergymen.

On December 14 this year the great bell of St. Paul's tolled at midnight to announce the sudden death of the Prince Consort. A private funeral took place at St. George's Chapel, Windsor, and the distraught Queen was ministered to by the Bishop of Oxford, Dr. Wilberforce, who urged her to henceforth make Christ her 'spouse', advice she later dismissed as 'twaddle'.

Meanwhile, the new bishop of Central Africa, Charles Mackensie, who had been an enthusiastic oarsman and cricketer at Cambridge, was engaging in tribal warfare to establish his position. On January 31, 1862 these acts of violence came to an end when he died of fever.

Later that spring the Rev. Alexander Mackonochie was appointed first Vicar of the vice-infested parish of St. Alban's, Holborn, where a new church was being built along strict high church lines. This building was not yet ready for use and, on May 11, services began in a room over a fish-shop.

Four months later, the Archbishop of Canterbury, Dr. Sumner, who had tried to damp down theological controversy during the last few years, died at Addington Palace. He was succeeded as Primate by Charles Longley, Archbishop of York, who was himself succeeded by forty-three-year-old William Thomson, whose excitement on learning of his promotion was such

The Rev. Charles Kingsley, who spear-headed the Christian Socialist Movement and was said to be a 'lover of the north-east wind'

155

that his wife begged him 'Oh, *do* go and lie down.' Omitted from this re-shuffling of positions was Bishop Wilberforce of Oxford, who afterwards received many letters of sympathy for being denied promotion.

On December 1, the induction of the Rev. William Barnes as Rector of Winterborne Came in Dorset took place. Sixty-one years old and a poet of distinction, Barnes was to live in a quaint thatched parsonage with his study over-looking a fruit garden containing apricots and asparagus plants, and make the rounds of his parish dressed in cassock, knee-breeches, wide-brimmed hat and a home-made poncho of Scottish plaid.

Meanwhile, the Rev. Francis Cunningham, Rector of East Tisted near Petersfield, where scarlet fever, small-pox and typhoid were currently raging, had been reprimanded by the local doctor for visiting infectious parishioners and changing their surgical dressings.

1863 On March 10, the following year, the marriage took place between the Prince of Wales and the beautiful Princess Alexandra of Denmark. Protests by the Archbishop of Canterbury, Dr. Longley, that the wedding should not take place in Lent had been crushed by the Queen's reply, 'Marriage is a solemn, holy act *not* to be classed with amusements.'

Among those attending the service at St George's Chapel, Windsor, was the Rev. Charles Kingsley, who had written his famous book *The Water Babies* the previous year. Later that day, still in court dress, he was back in his parish at Eversley in Hampshire, where the royal wedding was being celebrated with a big bonfire, a roasted sheep and a flow of beer.

Meanwhile, the church had been shaken by the publication of a book by Bishop Colenso of Natal in which he had professed himself unable to use the baptismal and ordination services in the Prayer Book. Disciplinary measures had been taken against him by the Bishop of Capetown and the English bishops had unanimously inhibited Colenso from preaching in their dioceses. In February this year, forty-one bishops had urged him to resign his see. 'We will not abandon hope' they wrote, 'that through earnest prayer and deeper study of God's word you may, under the guidance of the Holy Spirit, be restored to a state of belief in which you may be able with a clear conscience again to discharge the duties of your sacred office.' The Bishop refused to budge however and, on December 16, Bishop Gray of Capetown pronounced sentence of deprivation. This, too, Colenso chose to ignore and he was to appeal later to the Privy Council and get the sentence reversed, remaining all the while in possession of his see and its property.

On December 30, the Rev. Octavius Pickard-Cambridge, curate at Blox-worth in Dorset and a firm believer in Darwin's new theories of evolution, set off from Southampton on the first step of a scientific grand tour of Europe and the Middle East. During his journey, he was to keep a meticulous inven-tory of all birds, spiders and scorpions he encountered.

1864 On January 9, 1864, the Rev. Arthur Stanley, who had accompanied the Prince of Wales on a journey to Egypt and Palestine two years earlier and married a lady-in-waiting to the Queen, was installed as Dean of West-minster. Speaking of Dean Stanley's close intimacy with the royal family, *Vanity Fair* wrote later that he 'makes tea on occasion for the highest per-sonage in the realm'.

A few months later, on Whitsunday, the exceptionally tall Sabine Baring-

The controversial Dr. Colenso, Bishop of Natal, who was said to be retiring and modest as a child and without a spark of personal vanity

Gould was ordained a deacon and the following day took up his appointment as curate in the small wool and coal-mining town of Horbury near Wakefield where he was to write a famous hymn for the local Sunday school, 'Onward, Christian soldiers'.

1865   Meanwhile a fresh controversy had blown up over the use of the confessional by certain high church clergy and, on May 28, 1865, the Rev. A. D. Wagner, curate at St. Paul's Brighton, who had refused to answer questions in court which would 'involve a breach of the confessional' was brutally assaulted in the street. His attackers were both sentenced to two months' hard labour.

Later that summer, a meeting took place between the Prince of Wales and hunting parson, Jack Russell, at the Royal Agricultural Society's meeting at Plymouth. These two keen sportsmen became good friends and Russell was soon invited to stay at Sandringham.

1866   The following February, the eighty-eight-year-old Bishop of Exeter, Dr. Phillpotts, emerged from seclusion to attend a meeting at Lambeth Palace to

The Rev. Jack Russell, M.F.H. in old age

discuss the possibility of a regular assembly of all Anglican bishops. The Church of Canada had been most vocal in campaigning for this scheme, Bishop Lewis of Ontario pleading with Archbishop Longley after dining at Lambeth, 'Your Grace, do we not all belong to the same family? Why should we not meet?'

1867   Some nineteen months later, on September 24, 1867, seventy-seven bishops gathered in the Guard Room at Lambeth Palace at the start of their first official conference, which began with a service of Holy Communion in the thirteenth-century chapel followed by a wordy and inadequate sermon by the Bishop of Illinois. A notable absentee from these proceedings was the Archbishop of York, Dr. Thomson, who had fiercely opposed the conference and even questioned its legality.

1868   On March 28, 1868, the solemn looking Rev. Alexander Mackonochie was found guilty of illegal practices at the new church of St. Alban's Holborn, where hired informers had provided evidence of the use of altar lights, incense, coloured silk vestments, the mixed chalice and the elevation of the elements. Mackonochie subsequently appealed to the Privy Council and got most of the judgement reversed but he was ordered to pay costs and went on to face further prosecutions.

Seven months later, on October 28, the death of Archbishop Longley caused the familiar difficulties over the appointment of a successor. Prime

Minister Disraeli wanted Dr. Ellicott, Bishop of Gloucester, but Lord Derby successfully opposed this idea on the grounds of Ellicott's 'foolish voice and manner'. Dr. Thomson, Archbishop of York, known as 'cod fish' in certain circles and also as 'the Archbishop of Society', was out of the question having blotted his copy book by treading on the Queen's train at a ceremonial function. Eventually, the primacy went to the Queen's own choice, Dr. Tait, who had been doing sterling work as Bishop of London in spite of his chronically poor health and club foot.

Meanwhile, the Bishop of Chichester, Dr. Gilbert, had laid the foundation stone of Lancing school chapel, the largest school chapel to be built in England.

1869   In February 1869, Dr. Christopher Wordsworth, former headmaster of Harrow and the author of some commonplace hymns, was consecrated Bishop of Lincoln, where he was to reside at a large and straggling house called Riseholme three miles from the city, with two lakes in its grounds. A man of unfailing courtesy, Dr. Wordsworth was to start work at six each morning and administer his diocese with single minded devotion.

Archbishop Thomson was nicknamed the Archbishop of Society but blotted his copy book when he stepped on Queen Victoria's train

159

Six months later, on August 11, the Bishop's Resignation Act was passed, providing for the appointment of coadjutors in the event of a bishop's infirmity permitting the Crown to declare any see vacant in the event of a bishop becoming incapable on the account of old age, mental or physical infirmity.

On September 18, ninety-one-year-old Bishop Phillpotts, father of eighteen children, was in the process of resigning the see of Exeter when he died at his house at Torquay. He was replaced by Dr. Frederick Temple, who had had a long and successful reign as headmaster of Rugby, and was to establish himself in the restored Bishop's Palace beside Exeter Cathedral.

On November 18, the new Archbishop of Canterbury, Dr. Tait, had a cataleptic seizure owing to overwork and anxiety and was obliged to petition the government for the appointment of a suffragan, Bishop Parry of Dover, to assist him at Lambeth.

The following month, the modernization of heating, lighting and sanitary arrangements at 21, St. James's Square – official London residence of the Bishops of Winchester – was carried out for the new, incoming Bishop Wilberforce who had been appointed to replace Dr. Sumner, who had been incapacitated by a stroke.

At the end of the year, parson's wife Mrs. Josephine Butler began agitating on behalf of prostitutes, founding with Miss Florence Nightingale the Ladies National Association for the repeal of the Contagious Diseases Act which had placed prostitutes under police supervision and subjected them to cruel masculine officialdom.

1870   Eight months later, on August 9, 1870, the Education Act was passed on its third reading. This provided for religion as part of the curriculum in the new state schools but ordered that there should be no 'denominational formulary'. Staunchly Anglican prime minister William Gladstone regarded this clause as 'a moral monster'.

In December, East End doctor, Dr. Thomas Barnardo, opened his first boys' home at 18, Stepney Causeway, under the patronage of leading Anglican layman Lord Shaftesbury.

Meanwhile, the Archbishop of Canterbury, Dr. Tait, was wintering at San Remo on the Mediterranean coast, after a series of heart attacks. The following spring he returned to his post, refreshed and full of vigour.

1871   In May 1871, the Rev. John Purchas, curate at St. James's Chapel Brighton, was condemned by the Privy Council for infringing the laws of the church by using a cope, chasubles, albs, stoles, birettas, wafer bread, lighted candles, crucifixes, holy water and other illegalities, including the hanging of a stuffed dove over the altar on Whitsunday. Purchas did not appear at the hearing on the grounds of ill-health and, having made his money over to his wife, did not pay costs either.

In August, sensitive Somerset vicar the Rev. Richard Church, who was said to detest controversy, reluctantly accepted the Deanery of St. Paul's from Mr. Gladstone. He came up to London 'with fears and repugnance' but was to become a leading influence on ecclesiastic affairs and to transform St. Paul's Cathedral into such a hive of activity that it merited William Morris's description – 'God's railway station'.

A few weeks later, on September 16, the Bishop of Melanesia, Dr. Patteson, was murdered by natives on the South Pacific island of Nukapu. A former captain of the Eton eleven, Dr. Patteson had become one of the most outstanding missionaries of the day, who according to those who knew him 'seemed to move on holy ground'. A chaplain, the Rev. Joseph Atkin, who was shot by an arrow on the same occasion, died afterwards of tetanus.

Two months later, in the middle of November, the church's help was called in when the Prince of Wales was suddenly struck down by typhoid after staying at Lord Londesborough's seat near Scarborough, where the drains were said to be bad. Archbishop Tait quickly drew up suitable prayers which were first used on December 10 and thereafter until the danger had passed.

Meanwhile, the Rev. John Ellerton, domestic chaplain to leading Anglican layman Lord Crewe, had published his book of *Church Hymns* which included his famous composition 'The day thou gavest, Lord, is ended'.

1872   On January 23, 1872, there were disorderly scenes at a meeting at Exeter to debate the new licensing bill to which a lot of people had gained admission with forged tickets. Temperance campaigner Wilfred Lawson and the new Bishop of Exeter, Dr. Temple – who had been converted to the cause after seeing 'that most degraded of all creatures, a drunken clergyman' – were pelted with bags of flour and the police were called. Dr. Temple's statement on this occasion that he was a teetotaller inspired the headline in a newspaper 'Bishop's Strange Confession'.

The same month, the elderly Rev. John Selby Watson of Stockwell appeared at the Old Bailey charged with murdering his wife. He was found guilty of the crime and sentenced to death by Mr. Justice Byles. He was later reprieved and was to spend the rest of his life in Parkhurst prison.

On February 7, the first agricultural labourers' union was launched at a rowdy meeting at Wellesborne, with the enthusiastic support of Canon Edward Girdlestone who had been promoting the idea of such a union at meetings up and down the country, winning himself the nickname 'The Agricultural Labourer's Friend'.

On February 27, the recovery of the Prince of Wales was celebrated with a service of thanksgiving at St. Paul's Cathedral. The Archbishop of Canterbury, Dr. Tait, preached a sermon and Arthur Sullivan's specially written joyful *Te Deum*, scored for soprano solo, chorus, orchestra and military band, was performed.

On April 24, a violent exchange took place in the Lower House of Convocation between high church firebrand Archdeacon Denison and the Dean of Westminster, Dr. Stanley, which led to Denison's temporary ejection from the chamber.

On May 2, the Bishop of Peterborough, Dr. Magee, offended teetotallers by attacking the Intoxicating Liquors Bill in the House of Lords, 'I declare, strange as such declaration may sound coming from one of my profession that – it would be better that England should be free than that England should be compulsorily sober.' In protest at this pronouncement, the Rev. R. M. Grier, Vicar of Rugeley in Staffordshire, wrote to the Bishop declaring,

The Bishop of Peterborough Dr.
Magee infuriated teetotallers by
voting against the Intoxicating
Liquors Bill

'Even as I write, my lord, a dear relative of my own is suffering from intense pain from a fearful blow inflicted by an educated man in a state of intoxication'.

On June 11, a certain Mark Tuck was put in the stocks at Newbury for four hours after being found guilty of drunken and disorderly conduct in the local church.*

The following winter, seventy-two-year-old Dr. Pusey, a champion of orthodoxy, was struck down by an illness which left him specially prone to attacks of bronchitis and he was to spend the rest of his life indoors – 'never dining out, never walking out' – and his voice soon became too husky for him to preach.

1873   On July 19, 1873, the elderly and overworked Bishop of Winchester, Dr. Samuel Wilberforce, was thrown from his horse while riding on Abinger Common. He died instantly and, in the whimsical words of *Vanity Fair*, was 'translated to a higher see'.

That autumn, the Bishop of Lincoln, Dr. Wordsworth, preached a sermon in which he protested that the Total Abstinence Pledge was often forced on young children, who subsequently broke it. This sermon produced a hail of angry sermons and pamphlets and shortly afterwards Dr. Frederick Lees, teetotaller campaigner, arrived in Lincoln and denounced the Bishop from the platform of the Corn Exchange. Words from the offending sermon were later taken out of context and found hanging in beer-shops and pubs.

On December 31, the Prince of Wales gave a New Year's Eve ball at Sand-

* This is believed to be the last time the stocks were used in England.

ringham, at which one of the most illustrious guests was the seventy-seven-year-old Rev. Jack Russell. An extrovert, but abstemious man, Russell was found leading the beautiful Princess of Wales out to dance in the early hours of the morning.

1874 The following July, the headmaster of Shrewsbury School, the Rev. Henry Moss was accused in the press of undue severity after giving a pupil eighty-eight strokes of the birch for repeatedly drinking ale and porter. Moss met the charge with an 'indignant denial'.

The same summer concern about the new ritualistic practices infiltrating the church had come to a head. On June 15, Queen Victoria told Archbishop Tait that something must be done about 'romanizing tendencies' and the Bishop of Bath and Wells, Lord Arthur Hervey, declared that ritualists were as fanatical as the Indian Mutineers or Scottish Covenanters. On August 5, the Public Worship Regulation Act, which laid down severe penalties for liturgical innovators, was passed to widespread protestant rejoicing. At Osborne, the delighted Queen, who had told Dean Wellesley that she would abdicate in favour of the Stuarts if the bill were rejected, 'glided about the room like a bird'.

Meanwhile, the Rev. John King, wealthy Vicar of Ashby Launde in Lincolnshire had been enjoying a spectacular season's racing with his horse Apology, winning the One Thousand Guineas, the Oaks and the St. Leger. This last win prompted the Bishop of Lincoln, Dr. Wordsworth, to accuse Mr. King of neglecting his parish duties and a lively exchange of letters followed between the two men which ended in October with Mr. King, whose racing colours were medium blue body and red sleeves and cap, resigning his living.

The same month, the death occurred of the aristocratic Rev. John Lucy, Rector of Hampton Lucy, who had been in the habit of giving out fox-hunting notices from his pulpit.

1875 On February 18, 1875, the Archdeacon of Exeter, Dr. Freeman, who was in London to attend a meeting of the Lower House of Convocation, fell from an Underground train at Chalk Farm station and died of his injuries. Fifty-seven-year-old Dr. Freeman was the author of *Principles of Divine Guidance*.

Four weeks later, on March 16, the former Bishop of Dunedin, Dr. Jenner, slipped and fell on Waterloo station, tearing a tendon in his leg. Railway officials carried him to the Gentlemen's Waiting Room where his leg was bound in a splint and he was then taken by carriage to a friend's house.

The same month, the Rev. Mandell Creighton, who had been noted as an undergraduate for his clever, flippant talk and taste in silk ties, good wine and Morris wallpapers, was appointed Vicar of the remote village of Embleton on the Northumbrian coast.

On April 9, the Rev. John Monsell, author of the famous hymn 'Fight the good fight', died after being injured while watching re-building operations at St. Nicholas's Church, Guildford.

On July 28, Mrs. Philpott, Spanish-born wife of the Bishop of Worcester, unveiled a statue at Kidderminster of the seventeenth-century nonconformist divine Richard Baxter who had fought on the Parliamentary side in the Civil War.

Five months later on December 23 yet another clerical railway accident

163

occurred when the Rev. John Cussons was killed at a level crossing on the Malton and Thirsk railway. A short-sighted man, the Rev. Mr. Cussons had apparently failed to see the approach of an express train from York.

Meanwhile, a dispute had blown up over Bishop Wordsworth's objection to the use of the word Reverend on the tomb of a Wesleyan preacher. Archbishop Tait thought the word acceptable and Dr. Wordsworth was **1876** finally overruled by a Privy Council decision on January 21, 1876, that the term was 'merely laudatory'.

Six months later, on July 24, a meeting of nonconformist ministers took place at Lambeth Palace, organized by the broad-minded Archbishop Tait. This event was widely criticised but was well received by its participants, one of whom wrote to the Primate afterwards thanking him for promoting 'the unity of spirit for which we all pray'.

In December, the National Rose Society was established, largely through the efforts of the high church Rev. Samuel Hole, whose *Book about Roses: How to Grow them and Show them* had been a best-seller. It was sold in America and translated into German.

The same year, the Rev. Osbert Mordaunt had opened a special pub in the Warwickshire village of Hampton Lucy. This was to be run on new 'improved' lines, with shorter opening hours, a ban on the sale of spirits and the installation of one of the rector's servants as salaried manager. Demands from women of the parish for medicinal gin and brandy were met by adding spirits to the simple store of medicines already kept at the rectory for the use of villagers.

1877 May 1, 1877, saw the enthronement of Dr. Edward White Benson, former headmaster of Wellington, as first bishop of the new diocese of Truro. He immediately started raising funds for the erection of a cathedral, the first to be built since the Reformation, driving about the diocese in a coach, dictating letters to a chaplain. Among those to respond to his appeal was the celebrated Lady Rolle of Bicton, who sent him a cheque for £40,000.

Meanwhile, the savage Public Worship Regulation Act had come into force, and in the summer of 1877, the Rev. Arthur Tooth, who had been suspended as Vicar of St. James's Hatcham in the Rochester diocese, spent twenty-eight days in the Horsemonger Gaol after breaking into his own church to celebrate Holy Communion. The experience apparently broke his health and he eventually resigned his benefice, though he was to live on well into the next century.

In November and December this year Archdeacon Farrar of Westminster, author of *Eric, or Little by Little* and a brilliant preacher, aroused a storm of anger with a series of sermons in Westminster Abbey in which he challenged the ancient doctrine of eternal punishment.

1878 The following summer, the Second Lambeth Conference took place attended by a hundred bishops. The proceedings began with a service in Canterbury Cathedral on St. Peter's Day at which Archbishop Tait addressed those present from St. Augustine's chair, 'The monuments which surround us speak of a chequered history', he said, 'They tell of dark times and great times – but they all testify to the superintending power of God.' Three days later, business began in the Great Library at Lambeth, interrupted each day by lunch in the Guard Room, presided over by the Primate.

The following year saw the appearance of the first volume of *Spiders of Dorset* by the Rev. Octavius Pickard-Cambridge, who had already published some eighty scientific papers on this subject and been in correspondence with scientists all over the world, including Charles Darwin, with whom he had discussed the spider's sex life.

Meanwhile, far away in Afghanistan, where war was raging, the spiritual welfare of the troops was in the hands of the athletic Rev. J. W. Adams, who, on December 11, 1879, was to rescue several badly injured Lancers under heavy fire, for which gallant action he became the church's first V.C. Padre Adams was described by a contemporary as 'a spare man as active as a cat' and on the day of his brave deeds had been 'as cool as a cucumber'.

Back in England the same month, the Bishop of Peterborough, Dr. Magee, caused further offence to teetotallers by vetoing a proposal by the Church of England Temperance Society for a day of humiliation and prayer against drunkenness. Dr. Magee, who was said rarely to touch alcohol until his day's work was done, declared that drunkenness was 'the vice of a small minority'.

On April 19, the following year, the athletic, thrice-married Rev. John Ryle, was appointed first bishop of the new see of Liverpool. A famous preacher who, according to *Vanity Fair* occasionally made his congregations 'creep with pictures of hell fire', was to rule over his diocese with a firm hand.

A few days later, on May 3, a controversy broke out in the House of Commons which was to continue for many years when newly elected M.P. Charles Bradlaugh, an ardent atheist, refused to swear the oath on the Bible. On more than one occasion, Bradlaugh was to be forcibly ejected from the chamber.

On May 20, the fun-loving Prince of Wales laid the foundation stone of the new grey granite, neo-gothic Truro Cathedral.

Later that summer, the Rev. William Wilks, secretary of the Royal Horticultural Society, discovered a new white poppy in the corner of the vicarage garden at Shirley in Surrey, which he successfully set about cultivating.

On September 7, the Burial Act, which permitted any Christian to be buried in a parish churchyard, was passed in spite of the protests from some 15,000 clergymen and 30,000 laymen. This piece of legislation was a triumph for Archbishop Tait, who needed all his powers of statesmanship to pilot it through parliament.

Six weeks later, on October 30, the ritualistic innovator Rev. T. Pelham Dale, Vicar of St. Vedast's, Foster Lane, was arrested under the terms of the new Public Worship Regulation Act and thrown into the newly built Holloway prison, where he remained until Christmas Eve.

In November, the Rev. R. W. Enraght, Vicar of Holy Trinity, Bordesley, who had also committed ritualistic offences under the new Act, was thrown into Warwick gaol, where he remained until early the following year.

On January 18, 1881, Dr. Anthony Thorold, delicate new Bishop of Rochester, was caught in a heavy snowstorm and struggled from Croydon Station to his episcopal residence, Selsdon Park, wading through snowdrifts which came up to his waist.

On February 9, the death occurred of the stately but courteous Rev. Lord John Thynne, who had served as sub-dean of Westminster for the past forty-six years as well as administering his considerable estates in Bedfordshire, from which he was said to derive some £13,500 a year. At his funeral, his coffin was covered in a dark violet pall with a white silk fringe.

A few weeks later, on March 19, the Rev. S. F. Green, Rector of St. John's, Miles Platting, was thrown into Lancaster Castle after a series of clashes with the Bishop of Manchester over the use of incense and other ritualistic practices at his church. During his long imprisonment – he was not released until November 4, 1882 – his goods and chattels were sold to pay his legal costs and his wife and five children were turned out onto the streets.

On November 12, the Deanery of Wells was given to the Rev. Edward Plumptre, whose celebrated hymn 'Thy hand, O God, has guided' with its famous refrain 'One Church, one Faith, one Lord' had attempted to gloss over the disunity currently prevailing in the church. While at Wells, he was to pen a distinguished biography of the great Bishop Ken.

1882   The following March, the Rev. Mr. Lee-Warner, Vicar and school-master of Tarrant Gunville in Dorset, was sued for assault by the father of one of his pupils, whom he had dragged from his home and given a sound hiding after learning that the boy had committed an indecent offence against a girl and then 'boasted of the same in filthy and disgusting language'. At the subsequent court case, the judge upheld the vicar's action, dismissed the assault charge and fined him the nominal sum of one shilling for fetching the boy from his home.

Meanwhile, the Archbishop of Canterbury, Dr. Tait, who suffered from sleeplessness and nervous weakness, was ordered by royal doctor, Sir William Gull, to take a holiday in the sun. On March 12, he left for the French Riviera but returned six weeks later very little improved.

During the Primate's absence, the great Charles Darwin, whose books had offended many churchmen, was buried in Westminster Abbey at the suggestion of Archdeacon Farrar, who acted as a pall bearer at the funeral and preached an important sermon on Darwin's work.

At the Convocation this summer an attempt was made to bring General Booth's militant Salvation Army under the wing of the Church of England. A committee of bishops was set up for this purpose but was never to turn in a report.

On September 16, the gentle old Dr Pusey, who had withdrawn from the world many years earlier, died at Ascot Priory, Berkshire, murmuring the words of the *Te Deum*.

The following day, the mild-mannered Very Rev. Gerald Wellesley, Dean of Windsor and intimate friend of the Queen, died at Hazelwood, near Watford.

On December 1, the uncompromising Rev. Alexander Mackonochie, who had fought a series of legal battles in defence of the use of ritualistic practices at his church in Holborn, resigned his living in response to an urgent request from the dying Archbishop of Canterbury.

The same day, Archbishop Tait died at Addington Palace, attended in his last hours by his devoted personal servant James Kersley. Queen Victoria asked for a lock of his hair and *The Times* commented, 'He has stood at the helm in troublous times; he has steered the ship past many a storm and he leaves it in comparatively tranquil waters.' Faced with the usual problem of

Dr. Pusey, who, in his youth, had been a first-rate shot, swimmer and horseman but later withdrew from the world, leading a more and more austere life

finding a suitable successor, Prime Minister Gladstone despatched the young Rev. Randall Davidson, the former primate's son-in-law, to ask Mrs. Browne, wife of the Bishop of Winchester about the state of her husband's health.

The Prime Minister's choice eventually fell upon Dr. Edward White Benson, Bishop of Truro. The nomination was officially confirmed in Bow Church on March 3, 1883 and on March 28, on the eve of his enthronement, he was formally received by the Mayor and Dean of Canterbury and greeted with blasts on the Wardmote horn, which caused irreverent laughter. The new Archbishop was said to have a horror of socialist ideas and was to take to the ceremonies surrounding the sixty-four-year-old Queen 'like a duck to water'.

On April 28, the Rev. Jack Russell, whose hunting territory had stretched from Bodmin to Torrington, died in his eighty-ninth year. His funeral took place in Swymbridge Church, near Barnstaple on May 3 and was attended by over a thousand people, lords and ladies, gypsies and rat-catchers.

The following month, the thirty-five-year-old Rev. Randall Davidson was

1883

installed as Dean of Windsor and domestic chaplain to the Queen, where his dealings with the royal family were said to resemble those of 'a cautious family solicitor'. His first tricky task came early the following year, when he felt it his duty to advise the Queen not to publish another volume of memoirs, the last such volume having been badly received in many quarters. The Queen was furious at this interference and demanded an apology, but Davidson felt unable to withdraw his advice and offered his resignation instead. The Queen then lapsed into silence, and nothing more was said of the proposed book and Davidson remained at his post.

In February 1884, Old Etonian Henry Scott Holland was appointed a Canon of St. Paul's Cathedral where he was to fascinate countless congregations with his magician-like flow of rhetoric, though *The Times* commented later that his speech 'was too rapid for a building which plays havoc with a hurried delivery'.

Ten months later, on December 4, the celebrated Canon Edward Girdlestone, champion of the agricultural labourer, died after catching cold on a visit to the Prince of Wales at Sandringham.

Meanwhile, a bell-ringer at Winterborne Kingston in Dorset had become entangled with the rope while ringing in a wedding peal and was lifted up by the bell, cracked his head on the ceiling, dropped to the floor and was killed.

On February 25, 1885, Dr. Frederick Temple, Bishop of Exeter, was called to the see of London. Such was the expense of entering this new office that he was obliged to borrow £5,000.

The following month, devout theologian Dr. Edward King was elected Bishop of Lincoln. Hearing of the appointment, his predecessor Bishop Wordsworth, who had resigned the see on grounds of failing health, telegraphed Prime Minister Gladstone with words *Deo gratias*. Bishop King quickly arranged to get rid of the large and straggling episcopal residence at Riseholme near the city and was to make his home at the tudor-style Old Palace beside Lincoln Cathedral. On taking up his appointment, Bishop King was informed that the clergy of his diocese could be divided into three categories: those who had gone out of their minds, those who were about to go out of their minds, and those who had no minds to go out of.

In August, the jovial Old Harrovian Rev. Robert Dolling was appointed in charge of the Winchester College mission in the slums of Portsmouth. Here he was to keep open house for soldiers and sailors, thieves, tramps, inebriate clergymen and Winchester College prefects.

Meanwhile, the Bishop of Equatorial Africa, Dr. Hannington, was making his way by a new route to Lake Victoria with a team of a hundred porters and a total caravan of 226. On October 21, he was seized by the King of Uganda and other chiefs, who feared that some sort of attack was taking place and, after being held captive for several days, Dr. Hannington, a former captain of the St. Mary Hall, Oxford, boat crew, was brutally murdered.

The following February, the new Archbishop of Canterbury, Dr. Benson, formally opened a new house of convocation consisting entirely of laymen. This innovation met with opposition in many quarters and one M.P. was even to question its legality and wonder whether the Primate should not be imprisoned. Benson jokingly noted in his diary that he had his barge ready in the event of his being committed to the Tower.

Four months later, on June 23, the Archbishop and his wife celebrated their wedding anniversary with a dinner party at Lambeth, at which turtle soup, whitebait, venison and other delicacies were served.

In the autumn, teetotallers were shocked to find temperance workers and clergymen among applicants for shares in the Guinness Brewery now a public company and the great nonconformist preacher Charles Spurgeon denounced brewery dividends accepted by fellow Christians as 'leprous and defiling gold'.

Meanwhile, the Archbishop of York, Dr. Thomson, had got into a conflict with the churchwardens of St. Mary's Beverley, who wanted to open all seats in their church to all parishioners. On January 10, 1887, the Archbishop wrote to the churchwardens ordering them to assign seats to parishioners according 'to their degree' and followed this with a circular to all parishioners inviting them to inform him of their 'rank, profession or occupation' so that he personally could arrange their seats. Dr. Thomson was widely criticized for this piece of arrogance and did not obtain the co-operation of the parishioners involved.

On May 4 this year, the Rev. James Bell Cox, Vicar of St. Margaret's, Toxeth Park, Liverpool, was thrown into Walton Gaol, after a clash with the Bishop of Liverpool, Dr. Ryle, over ritualist practices at his church. High churchmen were outraged by this imprisonment and Cox was released sixteen days later.

Meanwhile, the Church of England had plunged into the Queen's Golden Jubilee celebrations. On June 21, the carriage bearing Archbishop Benson to a great service of thanksgiving in Westminster Abbey was stopped by a policeman demanding to see the coachman's pass. The Primate leant out of the window and shouted, 'They can't begin till I get there!' Later, he recorded in his diary, 'Everyone feels that the socialist movement has had a check.'

On December 15, rebellious high church priest, Alexander Mackonochie got lost in the Mamore deer forest during a visit to the Duke of Argyll and, two days later, was found dead in a snow-drift, his body guarded by the two dogs which had accompanied him.

The same month, the famous horticulturist, Dr. Samuel Hole was appointed Dean of Rochester, where he was to appoint the famous Miss Jekyll to design a formal garden in which some 135 varieties of roses were to flourish.

The following summer, 145 bishops assembled in London for the Third Lambeth Conference. At all three services held during the gathering, a new hymn designed to defend orthodoxy 'The Church's one foundation' was sung. At a service in Westminster Abbey on July 2 Archbishop Benson preached for three-quarters of an hour but noted afterwards that 'the interest of the event kept people awake and *still* in the most marvellous way'.

Meanwhile, the saintly Bishop of Lincoln, Dr. King, had been accused of using altar lights, the mixed chalice, the sign of the cross, and other illegal procedures. On January 4, 1889, Archbishop Benson reluctantly summoned him to appear before him at his Court, which had not been in use since the trial of the Bishop of St. David's 200 years earlier. An initial hearing took place the following month at Lambeth Palace but soon came to a halt. Bishop Stubbs of Oxford declared, 'This is not a court. It is an archbishop sitting in his library', and the Dean of St. Paul's, Dr. Church, described the goings-on as 'fishy'.

On May 9, the death occurred of the militant philanthropist the Rev. Sidney Godolphin Osborne who had continued to write letters to *The Times* until his death. His last letter had concerned the Whitechapel murders now terrifying London.

Later that year, the new Bishop of London, Dr. Frederick Temple, returned early from his summer holiday to intervene successfully in the dockers' strike.

1890 1890 began with the Dean of Windsor, Dr. Randall Davidson, being elected a member of the Athenaeum Club in Pall Mall, for which he had been on the waiting list for the past fifteen years.

On February 4, the trial of the Bishop of Lincoln, which had been described as 'the ecclesiastical law-suit of the century' resumed in the library at Lambeth Palace. Archbishop Benson sat with five other bishops, whose wives were found flitting restlessly about the corridors of the palace during the long drawn-out proceedings, which ended with the Primate reserving his judgement.

On August 11, a chapter in the nation's religious life ended with the death of eighty-nine-year-old Cardinal Newman, which took place at the Oratory, Birmingham. The following day, Newman's famous hymn 'Lead, kindly light, amid the encircling gloom' which he had written as a young Anglican priest, was sung in churches throughout the country and, at Westminster Abbey, Canon Blore spoke of the Cardinal's 'singleness of heart and purity of purpose'.

Meanwhile, Archbishop Benson had left for a long holiday at the Rieder Furca Hotel near Bel Alp to consider his judgement in the Lincoln case. This was ultimately delivered on November 21, and was generally in favour of the Bishop and had the effect of declaring certain practices legal, such as having lighted candles on the altar. Extremists on both sides were annoyed but the majority, who longed for peace from ritualistic disputes, were well-pleased.

THE EDWARDIAN ERA

1891–1914

Queen Victoria was now living in semi-retirement, only to re-emerge briefly for her Diamond Jubilee festivities in 1897. The tone of the next two decades was set by the Prince of Wales, shortly to become King Edward VII, and his democratic and sporting attitudes were to permeate every level of society. During this period, protestantism was on the decline, the sharply defined religious beliefs of the past began to crumble and a movement away from church-going and family prayers in favour of race-going, gambling, motoring and other pleasures was detected. Many clergymen shared in these pursuits. In 1892, the Dean of Rochester defended moderate drinking and gambling at the Church Congress and in the years that followed at least two parsons met their deaths on the hunting-field. Meanwhile, church leaders coped with striking workers, suffragettes' bombs and other democratic eruptions. Among those who chose to swim with the new tide were Archbishop Temple, who in 1897 sold his stately home near Croydon declaring, 'The day is past when the Archbishops of Canterbury should appear as country gentlemen', and the new socialist Bishop of Worcester, Dr. Gore, who in 1901 refused to live in Hartlebury Castle. The period ends with a doctrinal crisis over the historicity of the miracles in the New Testament and the outbreak of the First World War.

1891 On March 3, 1891, Dr. Anthony Thorold was enthroned as Bishop of Winchester, amidst lamentations by the *Spectator* about his lack of spirituality. He was to make his home in the rambling and picturesque Farnham Castle, an official residence of the Bishops of Winchester since the twelfth century and occupied in their time by Bishops Gardiner, Andrewes and other notables.

A few weeks later, on March 26, the new Tithe Act, which made church tithes payable by the landowner and not the hard pressed tenant farmer, received the Royal Assent and brought peace to the countryside.

In June, the country was rocked by the Tranby Croft baccarat scandal and the Prince of Wales became the target for vicious attacks on the grounds of his moral conduct. Mistakenly believing that Archbishop Benson had instigated the campaign, the Prince summoned him to Marlborough House and defended himself against this abuse. The Primate gave his assurances that he had carefully avoided mentioning the subject and the two parted friends. Benson wrote later to the Prince asking him to publicly condemn gambling, but this the Prince declined to do.

On September 15, Dr. William Dalrymple Maclagan, a former officer in the Madras cavalry who, according to *Vanity Fair*, still walked 'as though he had his loins girded with a sword belt' was enthroned as Archbishop of York.

Dr. Anthony Thorold, Bishop of Winchester, whose entertaining at Farnham Castle absorbed two-thirds of the income of the see

In spite of his military past and bearing, he was said to be a strong objector to clergymen wearing moustaches.

1892   One of Dr. Maclagan's first duties was to visit on January 13, 1892, the dying Archbishop of Westminster, Cardinal Manning, who had been converted from Anglicanism to Rome some forty years earlier.

Later that spring, the seventeen stone Dean of Rochester, Dr. Hole, spoke at the Church Congress in defence of the playing of whist for small stakes and moderate drinking. The latter remarks infuriated teetotaller W. Kempster, who hit back with a pamphlet entitled *The Dean and the Drink*.

On June 1, the popular new Bishop of Durham, Dr. Brooke Westcott, was cheered at Auckland Castle for his role in bringing about the end of the Durham Miners Strike.

The same summer, the Rev. Cecil Legard, Vicar of Cottesbrooke in Northamptonshire, who was said to hunt four days a week with the Pytchley, was a judge at the Dublin Horse Show.

Meanwhile, another sporting parson, the Rev. Evelyn Burnaby, Vicar of Burrough-on-the-Hill in the Quorn country, was riding from Land's End to John o'Groats. Burnaby weighed sixteen stone and three horses were 'played out' during the marathon ride and the Royal Society for the Prevention of Cruelty to Animals was tempted to intervene.

At the end of the year, the Clergy Discipline Act was passed, making drunkenness one of the offences for which a parson could now be deprived of his living. The bill had had a difficult passage through parliament, Lord Grimthorpe complaining that it would make bishops 'more powerful than the pope'.

1893   On February 21, the following year a large number of witnesses were

172

called to support charges of intoxication against the Rev. Alfred Harris, Vicar of Stoke, near Rochester. The charges were found proved and Harris was deprived.

The same month, the vigorous young Bishop of Chester, Dr. Jayne, announced details of a bizarre new scheme under which the profits of publicly-owned taverns could be used to build 'bright and attractive temperance houses' to drive taverns out of business. The idea did not catch on, however, and parliament refused to pass the necessary legislation.

A few weeks later, on Saturday May 20, a missile was hurled at the train carrying Mr. Gladstone. It missed the elderly statesman but entered the next compartment in which the Dean of Chester, Dr. Darby, expert on microscopes and telescopes, was travelling.

On July 6, Archbishop Benson presided over the marriage of the Duke of York and Princess May of Teck at the Chapel Royal, St. James's Palace. The happy couple left the chapel to the strains of Mendelssohn's *Wedding March* and the enthusiasm of the crowds in the streets was such that three people were killed.

Meanwhile, the serious young Charles Gore had been appointed Vicar of Radley in Oxfordshire, where parish difficulties soon prompted him to write a long letter to the Bishop of Oxford, Dr. Stubbs, seeking episcopal advice. He was rebuffed with the reply, 'My dear Gore, don't be a bore.'

1894 The following summer, Archbishop Benson invited Abbé Fernand Portal of the Congregation of St. Vincent de Paul to Addington Palace to discuss a possible reunion between the Church of England and Rome. Informal talks soon revealed the vast gulfs that existed between these two branches of Christianity and the matter was taken no further.

1895 In May, 1895, the Rev. Stewart Headlam, founder of a Christian socialist movement and generally known as 'the outsider's friend' went bail for the unfortunate Oscar Wilde, whom he had met only twice. During the trial that followed Headlam accompanied the famous playwright to court each day and was punished for this gallantry by having his house in Upper Bedford Place stoned and his housemaids threatened. 'I knew very well', he reflected afterwards, 'that this action of mine would, with many people, damage my already damaged reputation.'

1896 A year later, on May 20, 1896, Archbishop Benson had a friendly discussion with the Prince of Wales covering a multitude of topics, including education, missionaries and bicycling.

The same month, the Bishop of Peterborough, Dr. Creighton, who had recently intervened successfully in a strike in the boot trade, was sent to Moscow to represent the English church at the coronation of the Czar Nicholas II. An urbane figure, Bishop Creighton was well received in Moscow and was invited to the state banquet after the coronation.

On Sunday October, 11, Archbishop Benson, who had recently completed an exhausting preaching tour of Ireland, collapsed and died in Hawarden Church. His host, Mr. Gladstone, declared, 'He died as a soldier. It was a noble end to a noble life.' His body was later taken to Canterbury where he was the first archbishop to be buried since Cardinal Pole.

A few weeks later, seventy-five-year-old Dr. Frederick Temple, Bishop of London, was named as the new Primate. A friend of the previous

Archbishop for forty years, he remarked, 'I do not think I shall find the work very new.' The appointment did not please everybody however and, on December 22, there was an ugly interruption at the confirmation service in Bow Church when the Rev. S. J. Brownjohn shouted out that Temple was 'a self-confessed believer in the full doctrine of evolution'.

1897 At his enthronement on January 8, Dr. Temple caused further controversy when he announced his intention of acquiring a home in the town of Canterbury and parting with the large and costly Addington Palace near Croydon, which had been used as a rural retreat by his predecessors since 1807. Among those opposed to this re-arrangement was Dr. Randall Davidson, now Bishop of Winchester, who was to telegraph the Queen's private secretary Sir Arthur Bigge begging Her Majesty to intervene when the matter came up for her approval at the Privy Council.

The sale went ahead, however, and the palace was sold to a South African diamond merchant for £70,000 and Dr. Temple commented, 'The day is past when Archbishops of Canterbury should appear as country gentlemen.'

On May 25, 1897, the Rev. C. H. Bousfield, Rector of Bratton St. Maur, was killed when the brake on his tricycle failed as he was going down a hill.

A few weeks later, on June 20, the sixtieth anniversary of Queen Victoria's accession was celebrated with a huge gathering of churchmen at St. Paul's Cathedral. The Archbishops of Canterbury and York wore their purple coronation robes, the elegant new Bishop of London, Dr. Creighton, was in a golden cope and the Dean of St. Paul's, Dr. Gregory, was in green, gold and white. After the service there was an unexpected delay on the steps of the cathedral as the Queen waited for her carriage. The elderly Archbishop Temple saved the situation by calling for three cheers for the Queen, after which the royal vehicle pulled up.

A fortnight later, the fourth Lambeth Conference began. Dr. Temple ran the proceedings with a firm hand, telling one bishop to keep his mouth shut and informing another, 'What you mean is all right but what you say isn't what you mean.'

1898 In January 1898, the young Vicar of Portsea, the Rev. Cosmo Gordon Lang, was invited to spend the weekend at Osborne and preach before the Queen. He was ill-equipped for such a visit and had to borrow an umbrella, tall hat and robes bag from one of his curates. During his visit, the Queen questioned him closely about the alleged lack of religion of the working-classes.

Two months later, work began on the construction of a large, rambling Tudor-style building on the site of the ancient episcopal palace at Canterbury, which was to become Archbishop Temple's second home. Asked if he expected his successors would wish to live at Canterbury, he replied with a sardonic smile, 'No I don't. I want to make 'em.'

Meanwhile, eighty-eight-year-old Mr. Gladstone was dying of cancer at Hawarden Castle. In spite of his almost unbearable pain, he insisted on climbing from his bed to take Holy Communion from his son, Stephen, Rector of Hawarden. On his death on May 19, preparations began at once for a state funeral in Westminster Abbey, at which the Prince of Wales acted as a pall bearer, the Primate officiated and Gladstone's two favourite hymns 'Rock of ages' and 'Praise to the holiest in the height' were sung.

174

In December this year another scandalous practice was rooted out when the U.K. Benefices Act forbade the sale of advowsons.

On May 24, 1899, the Queen's eightieth birthday was celebrated with a service of thanksgiving in St. Paul's Cathedral. In a sermon preached on this occasion, Archbishop Temple declared the fact that the great scientific advances during the century had not been matched by similar improvements in the nation's morals.

Five months later, on October 25, Dr. Temple took the chair at a special meeting of the National Temperance League at Mansion House. Protesting at the distribution of public houses throughout the country, he declared, 'It is almost impossible for any ordinary man to go from one place to another without having the temptation put directly in his way.'

The century ended with the Rev. James Bacon-Phillips, Rector of Crowhurst in Sussex, protesting about the use of passenger trains for the transportation of Christmas parcels. In a letter to *The Times* published at the end of December he revealed that he had been kept waiting for twenty-three minutes at Three Bridges Station while parcels were unloaded, though he added generously, 'It is only fair to add that the officials worked with the most praiseworthy energy'.

On March 29, 1900, the Rev. Robert Fillingham was convicted at Hadleigh Petty Sessions, Suffolk, of 'indecent behaviour' in the parish church of Kettlebaston in the same county. During the celebration of Holy Communion, Fillingham had stood up and shouted, 'This is idolatry! Protestants, leave the house of Baal!' He was dismissed with a twenty shillings fine.

In October, controversy surrounded Archbishop Temple's desire to give Lambeth Fields, adjoining his palace, to the London County Council for use as a public playing field. The scheme was opposed by Bishop Davidson of Winchester and the majority of the Ecclesiastical Commissioners but the aged Primate chose to overrule the flood of appeals and signed memorials on the subject and went ahead with his public-spirited plan.

On January 22, 1901, Bishop Davidson was among those present at the death of Queen Victoria at Osborne on the Isle of Wight. In London, news of this momentous event was broken to citizens by the tolling of the four and a half ton passing bell of St. Paul's Cathedral once a minute for two hours.

Two days later, the Archbishop of Canterbury informed the House of Lords, 'There can be no question that all society has been better because the Queen has reigned. She was a religious woman. She prayed for her people. She was a good woman. She set up a true standard of such lives as Christians ought to live.' These comments drew the comment from one person present, 'Well, your grace, you made us all cry.'

On February 2, the Queen's funeral took place in St. George's Chapel, Windsor, with the new King and his nephew, the German Kaiser, leading the mourners. The congregation joined in singing 'O God, our help in ages past'.

Three months later, the Anglican community was shocked to hear that congregationalist missionary the Rev. James Chalmers and his colleague the Rev. O. C. Tomkins had been killed and eaten by savages on the South Sea island of Dopima.

On May 1, the Rev. Cosmo Gordon Lang was consecrated Bishop of Stepney in a ceremony in St. Paul's Cathedral. Dr. Lang began his episcopate as 'a bus and bag bishop', travelling by train, tram and bus and carrying his own robes bag, but his friends soon presented him with a small motor-car, a Belsize Coupé, complete with chauffeur, which in the years ahead was to be involved in more than one collision.

In November, the Rev. Charles Gore, most outspoken of the new generation of high church clergy and a fierce critic of the government's treatment of the Boers, was nominated Bishop of Worcester. An ardent socialist, in spite of aristocratic connections, Bishop Gore was to refuse to occupy the ancient episcopal seat, Hartlebury Castle.

1902   Seven months later, on June 24, 1902, there came a dramatic announcement that the new King was seriously ill and his coronation must be postponed.

This great event eventually took place on August 9, presided over by the eighty-year-old Archbishop Temple, whose own frail condition caused concern to many of those present. At one moment, Bishop Davidson of Winchester was moved to offer the Primate a meat lozenge but this was rejected with the words, 'What's the good of that? My trouble's in my legs not in my stomach.' Later, the Archbishop placed the crown on the King's head back to front and required the King's help when he tried to get up after kneeling to do homage. The service ended cheerfully with an eight part anthem, *I was glad*, written by Old Etonian Sir Hubert Parry, using massive choral forces, organ and orchestra.

The Archbishop's health did not improve and on December 4 he collapsed while speaking in the House of Lords. He struggled to his feet and finished his speech but was afterwards hurried out of the House and back to Lambeth Palace, where two days before Christmas he died.

On New Year's Eve, Prime Minister Balfour scribbled a curt note to Bishop Davidson, 'I mean to propose your name to H.M. for Canterbury. From conversations I have had with him I have no doubt that he will agree.' On accepting the appointment Davidson, son-in-law of the late Archbishop Tait, told a close friend, 'I know I am not good enough but I do know the ropes better than others.' Among those to offer their congratulations was the Duke of Argyll, who wrote, 'You are one of the very few preachers who prevent me falling asleep.'

Meanwhile, the elderly Rev. F. J. Bleasby had entered Tiverton workhouse after making 470 unsuccessful applications for a curacy.

1903   On February 19, 1903, the Rev. Maurice Otho Fitzmaurice, Vicar of St. James's, Bolton-le-Moors, was found guilty of gathering alms under false pretences and was branded a rogue and a vagabond.

Eight months later, on October 24, the death occurred of the Rev. J. W. Adams, hero of the Afghan campaign and the first clergyman to win the V.C. His funeral at Ashwell in Leicestershire was attended by Lord Roberts and his widow later donated the portable altar her husband had used in battle to the local church.

The same month, the new Primate, Dr. Davidson, refused to add his signature to a letter to the press protesting against the opium traffic. 'I have no wish to promote the continuance of a trade which is undoubtedly

The Bishop of Stepney, Dr. Cosmo Gordon Lang, whose duties included vetting some controversial nude statues by Jacob Epstein before they were placed on public view

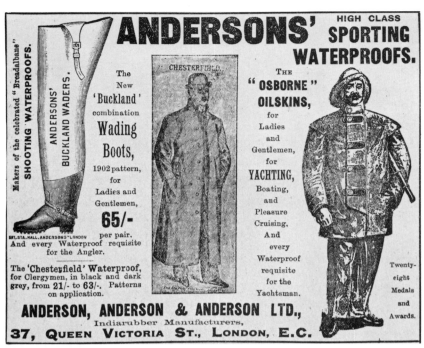

An advertisement, apparently aimed at sporting parsons, from the 1902 edition of *Crockford's Clerical Directory*

productive of much evil', he told the organizer of the anti-opium campaign, Mr. Broomhall, 'though apparently, in the opinion of many wise observers it is also all productive of a great deal that is wholesome and good.' The Archbishop's attitude drew a despairing response from one of Broomhall's sons, who had lived in China: 'Incredible – it's heart-breaking.'

1904   On March 17, the following year, the Rev. George Moore, popular Vicar of Cowley, appeared before the Consistory Court at Oxford and was found guilty of 'immoral intercourse' with a certain Miss Johnson and of having an immoral habit of 'swearing and ribaldry'. Moore subsequently appealed to the Judicial Committee of the Privy Council and got the judgement overruled.

Two months later, on May 4, the Royal Commission on Ecclesiastical Discipline began sitting in the ancient Church House of Westminster to look into 'the alleged prevalence of breaches or neglect of the law relating to the conduct of divine service'.

On September 14, the Bishop of Carlisle, Dr. Bardsley, who had never fully recovered from an attack of ptomaine poisoning while staying in a hotel in Egypt six years earlier, died at Rose Castle.

1905   On February 25, 1905, the death occurred of Old Harrovian parson Rev. George Hustler, when he fell from his horse Maccaroni while out hunting with the Ross Harriers.

A few weeks later, on April 5, famous cricketing parson the Rev. and Hon.

178

Edward Lyttelton, who had scored a century against Australia in 1878, was appointed Headmaster of Eton. Author of *Cricket, Training for the Young in the Laws of Sex*, and other books, he was to find organization at the school 'a nightmare'.

In July this year, the elderly and aristocratic Bishop of Ely, Lord Alwyne Compton, resigned his see, exchanging for a small house near Canterbury, the palatial Ely House in Dover Street, which was later disposed of by his conscientious successor, Dr. Frederic Chase.

1906

On February 3, 1906, the death occurred of old Tom Preston, squire of Moreby Hall in Yorkshire, whose horse-box style pew in the local Stillingfleet church was equipped with its own fireplace at which he would poke diligently if the sermon was not to his liking.

A few days later on February 22, the death occurred of ninety-one-year-old Rev. Edward Boys Ellman, who had served as parson of the Sussex parish of Berwick for the last sixty years 'I have much to be thankful for in having led this quiet life', he had reflected as he lay dying, 'I have not had the temptations other men have had. Looking back, I can't remember ever having wilfully committed sin.' Finally, milk and brandy had been held to his lips but he pushed them away with the words, 'No, prayers first.'

37 Dover Street, the stately town house built by the Bishop of Ely, Dr. Keene in the 1770s and occupied by his successors until 1905. It is now the Oxford University Press

179

Eight months later on September 16, the Bishop of Hong Kong, Dr. Joseph Hoare, was drowned when the boat carrying him to visit parishioners in Kowloon capsized in Castle Peak Bay.

1907   On January 5, 1907, the traffic was stopped to allow the funeral procession of the great philanthropist Baroness Burdett-Coutts pass from her house in Stratton Street, Piccadilly, to Westminster Abbey, where a full choral service was held.

The same day, the Archbishop of Canterbury, Dr. Davidson, joined with the Roman Catholic Archbishop of Westminster in issuing a joint manifesto in favour of the movement for the better observation of Sunday.

On April 30, the Rev. Thomas Colley, keen spiritualist and Rector of Stockton near Rugby brought a successful libel action against a professional entertainer named Maskelyne, who had issued a pamphlet trying to expose Mr. Colley's spiritualist activities.

Six months later on October 14 the Church of England Temperance Society was found guilty of causing an obstruction with a coffee stall outside St. Mary Butts church, Reading. A nominal fine of one shilling was imposed.

1908   The following July, the Anglican bishops gathered for the fifth Lambeth Conference. After dispensing 'warm and gracious' hospitality at their palace – assisted by forty domestic servants – and having many overseas bishops and their wives to stay, Archbishop and Mrs. Davidson left for a well-earned holiday at Courmayeur.

Four months later, on November 27, Dr. Davidson appeared in the House of Lords, leaning on a stick, to give support to the Government's Licensing Bill. To the great indignation of the House of Commons, the Lords threw it out.

Meanwhile, much gentle persuasion had been brought upon the elderly and mentally infirm Archbishop of York, ex-Cavalry officer, Dr. Maclagan, to get him to resign his see. On November 1, he had at last issued a statement announcing his decision 'to surrender the helm to a younger and perhaps more active man and give myself up to a life of quiet preparation for the world to come'.

He was succeeded as Archbishop by forty-four-year-old bachelor Dr. Cosmo Gordon Lang, Bishop of Stepney, who was duly enthroned at York **1909**   Minster on January 25, 1909, in the presence of some 600 clergy and more than 5,000 laymen. After the ceremony, Dr. Lang was escorted to his new home, the large and rambling Bishopthorpe Palace, official seat of the Archbishops of York since the thirteenth century. For the last stage of the journey, his coach was dragged by choir-men and sidesmen.

Among possessions that Dr. Lang was to purchase from his predecessor was a refectory table capable of seating twenty-two people. Lang gave £10 for this old table but was soon offered £1,000 for it.

Later that spring, the Bishop of London, Dr. Winnington-Ingram, led a midnight temperance march through the East End of London. In one mile alone, it was said that the bachelor Bishop encountered 200 men 'the worse for drink'. Among them was a group who when invited to join in singing 'Lead, kindly light' insisted on bellowing 'For he's a jolly good fellow'.

On April 29, the trial began before the Consistory Court at Hereford of the Rev. Frederick Lovibond, Vicar of How Caple, near Hereford, and a former chaplain at Amalfi in Italy. Lovibond was found guilty of immoral acts at a boarding house at Weston-super-Mare and with servants at his vicarage and of taking an immoral photograph some twenty-two years earlier. He was duly deprived of all ecclesiastical preferment in the diocese.

Eleven months later, on March 8, 1910, the saintly Bishop of Lincoln, Dr. Edward King, hero of the great ecclesiastical law-suit of the previous century, died at the Old Palace at Lincoln. Archbishop Davidson officiated at his funeral and he was succeeded as bishop by sixty-six-year-old Dr. Edward Hicks, a militant teetotaller.

The following month, a new chapter opened in the life of the parish of Thaxted in Essex with the appointment of the Rev. Conrad Noel, grandson of the 1st Earl of Gainsborough, as Vicar. A Christian communist, he was to dress in the full rig of a medieval priest and hoist the Red Flag in his parish.

On the morning of May 6, Archbishop Davidson rushed to the bedside of the dying King Edward VII. He returned to Lambeth Palace for luncheon but was back again at Buckingham Palace in the afternoon. In the evening, he was with the King when he died. 'I have seldom or never seen a quieter passing of the river', he noted.

The Rev. Conrad Noel, Vicar of Thaxted in Essex. A Christian Communist, he was to raise the Red Flag in his parish

On May 11, the Archbishop took a break from state affairs to sit for his portrait by the celebrated artist John Sargent.

On May 17, he conducted the King's lying-in-state in Westminster Hall. In an address to the royal mourners and members of both Houses of Parliament he stated, 'Here in the great hall of English history, we stand in the presence of death. But death is, to us Christians, swallowed up in a larger life. Our common sorrow reminds us of our common hope.'

At the end of this year, the over-worked Bishop of Winchester, Dr. Herbert Ryle, son of the former Bishop of Liverpool, who had recently suffered an attack of angina pectoris, appendicitis and an infection of the foot was forced to swap his bishopric for the less arduous position of Dean of Westminster.

1911   On April 18, 1911, the Deanery of St. Paul's was offered to the Rev. W. R. Inge, Old Etonian and former Eton master, who once described his academic career as 'mainly a record of scholarships and prizes'. Inge accepted the offer but the old Dean, ninety-two-year-old Dr. Gregory, refused to resign unless he was permitted to occupy the seventeenth-century Deanery until his death, so Inge and his wife were obliged to stay in a hotel for a while.

On June 10, Dr. Inge went to Windsor Castle to preach before, and dine with, the new King and Queen. He was met at the station by a royal carriage drawn by two white horses and followed by a huge vehicle to carry his robes bag. Going into dinner that night, Queen Mary asked her lady-in-waiting, 'What shall I talk about to this learned man?'

Twelve days later, the coronation of King George V was slightly marred by a disagreement between the King and the Primate about whether photographs should be taken during the service, in Westminster Abbey. The service ended on a triumphant note, however, with a rendering of Sir Charles Stanford's specially composed *Gloria in excelsis*.

Later that long, hot summer, soldier's son, Leopold Campbell-Douglas, who 'by some Freudian twist of the subconscious had become a clergyman of the Church of England instead of a colonel in the Scots Guards', was found lunching off delicious country fare in the garden of his vicarage at Frome in Somerset: juicy joints, Somerset cream and butter, home-made bread, peas and beans and raspberries.

1912   On April 19, 1912, there was a great service in St Paul's Cathedral for the victims of the *Titanic* disaster. The Lord Mayor of London, in his state robes of black silk and gold, joined in singing 'Rock of ages' and the newly appointed Dean Inge read the lesson. Many friends and relatives of the victims were present and several thousand members of the public were turned away.

Seven months later, on November 12, the elderly Rev. Charles Slingsby was killed while out hunting with the York and Ainsty Hunt. His horse had 'pecked' badly at a strong thorn fence and he was thrown off, breaking his neck. An impromptu service was held on the spot by the Rev. A. S. Crawley, also out hunting that day, who commended the soul of Mr. Slingsby to the care of 'the Great Unknown'. A stained glass window was later unveiled in his memory at Moor Monkton Church by the Archbishop of York, Dr. Lang. 'Hunting is a sport which develops some of the finest qualities of human courage and endurance', said the Archbishop on this occasion, 'There are many courtesies, both to man and beast, which spring naturally from the sport of the field.'

On February 14, the following year, the King and Prime Minister were present at the memorial service at St. Paul's Cathedral for Captain Scott of the Antarctic and his four gallant companions. Queen Alexandra followed the service in strict privacy from the Bishop's Closet. Some 10,000 people were unable to gain admission and at one stage the mob burst through a police cordon and entered a reserved part of the cathedral.

Three months later, on May 7, St. Paul's was again in the news when following the defeat of the Dickenson Bill, suffragettes placed a time bomb under the bishop's throne, designed by Grinling Gibbons, in the choir of the cathedral. Fortunately, it was discovered by a cleaner and defused and the Bishop of London, Dr. Winnington-Ingram scoffed, 'Those who set themselves to do the devil's work often cannot even do *that* right!'

On May 23, Dr. Winnington-Ingram and Dean Inge, who had recently been elected a member of the Athenaeum under Rule 2, were to be found playing tennis together. The fifty-five-year-old bachelor Bishop hopped about the court like a boy.

On October 27, it was announced that the British Undertakers' Association, in co-operation with the Royal Society for the Prevention of Cruelty to Animals, was to abolish the practice of fixing black plumes to horses' heads at funerals.

Meanwhile a doctrinal crisis had broken out over a new book written by a clerical don, the Rev. J. M. Thompson, denying the historicity of some of the miracles in the New Testament and enraging the Bishop of Oxford, Dr. Gore, and others. Archbishop Davidson had attempted to steer a middle course and, in February 1914, offered to resign to cool Gore down.

The same month, the Archbishop entertained the King and Queen to dinner at Lambeth Palace, the first time in history that a reigning King and Queen had visited the Archbishop's residence together. Also present on this occasion were the editor of *The Times* and Mrs. Benson, widow of the former Primate, who had recently set up house with Lucy Tait, daughter of Archbishop Tait, who called her Ben and shared her bed.

Four months later, at the beginning of June, while storm clouds gathered over Europe, the Dean of St. Paul's was to be found staying with the Bishop of Carlisle, Dr. Diggle, at Rose Castle, where the roses and rhododendrons were said to be at their best.

In July, thirty-four-year-old Rev. Dick Sheppard was appointed Vicar of the famous but ill-attended church of St. Martin-in-the-Fields. Friends had advised him, 'You mustn't go there. You'll be buried alive.'

On Sunday August 2, the Archbishop of Canterbury, Dr. Davidson, preached to a crowded congregation in Westminster Abbey. 'The thing which is now astir in Europe', he said, 'is not the work of God but the work of the Devil.'

The following evening, the conscientious Bishop of Ely, Dr. Chase, the Dean of Wells, Dr. Armitage Robinson, and the high church Canon Bullock-Webster sat up late into the night at Lambeth Palace drafting special war-time prayers.

THE FIRST WORLD WAR

1914–1918

During the next four violent years, over 3,000 Church of England clergymen were commissioned as chaplains. Several were to win the V.C. for feats of bravery. Eighty-eight were to die on active service. Back home, the over-worked Archbishop of Canterbury annoyed the government and the general public by condemning the use of poison gas and reprisal tactics against German civilians and refusing to allow the clergy to use their pulpits to appeal for men to enlist. The Archbishop of York also earned unpopularity by making some tactless remarks sympathetic to the Kaiser and by taking an extensive trip to America. This testing and emotional time also saw the birth of the Life and Liberty movement, which was to attempt to revitalize the church from within.

1914   Among those who spent the first night of the war at Lambeth Palace was the young Rev. George Bell, who was soon to accept an invitation from Archbishop Davidson to become one of his personal chaplains.

A few days later, the Rev. Dick Sheppard, newly appointed vicar of St. Martin-in-the-Fields, volunteered to go and fight. During the next two action-packed months, Sheppard ministered to the dying in Flanders, joined in an infantry attack and took part in the retreat from Mons.

At the end of the year, the Archbishop of York, Dr. Lang, caused a furore when he spoke, at the Empire Music Hall in York, of his 'sacred memories' of the Kaiser kneeling at the bier of Queen Victoria and his conviction that he would not have embarked lightly on war with England. Vast numbers of furious letters and some twenty-four iron crosses were sent to him and he was attacked in the gutter press and cold shouldered in the Yorkshire County Club.

1915   Meanwhile Archbishop Davidson and his wife had retired to their palace at Canterbury where on New Year's Day 1915, they entertained Prime Minister Asquith, his wife Margot and daughter Elizabeth to lunch.

After lunch, the Primate showed his guests round the cathedral, where the Prime Minister displayed a keen interest in the heraldic monuments.

Later that month, the marriage took place between the Primate's secretary Miss Amy Faithfull and the Dean of Wells, Dr. Armitage Robinson.

On March 4, the death occurred of sixty-nine-year-old Mr. John Parker, who had been a porter at Lambeth since 1883 and had become one of the Archbishop's inner circle of domestic staff.

Meanwhile, a Worcestershire clergyman had written an abusive letter to the King's aunt, Princess Helena, whose son was an officer in the German Army. The Princess forwarded the letter to Archbishop Davidson who wrote to the parson concerned on April 26, expressing his amazement that 'a letter so coarse and even brutal in its rudeness could have been addressed by a clergyman or a gentleman to a lady who from her position is absolutely helpless to reply.' The Vicar stuck to his guns, however, and wrote back to the Primate, 'The fact remains that she is a Princess of Germany having a son serving in that army of savages.'

The same month, the first Zeppelin raids began on the East coast of England. York was bombed twice and Archbishop Lang, fearing for the safety of the precious stained glass of the Minster, ordered the elderly Dean, Dr. Purey-Cust, to remove it from the windows and bury it in some safe place. At Scarborough, two shells crashed through the roof of St. Martin's Church but Archdeacon Mackarness, who was celebrating the Eucharist at the time, continued with the service undeterred.

On May 7, the Archbishop of Canterbury wrote a strongly worded letter to the Prime Minister deploring the use of asphyxiating gas by British troops.

Two days later, the Rev. and Hon. Maurice Peel, youngest son of Viscount Peel and one of the first clergymen to enlist, was badly wounded at the battle of Festubert. He was sent home to recuperate and later awarded the M.C.

In June, the Rev. William Kingsley, Rector of South Kilvington near Thirsk, celebrated his hundredth birthday. A flag flew on the village green, the church bells were rung and the ancient clergyman, who held the title 'England's Oldest Rector' for several years, received letters of congratulations from the King, the Archbishop of York and the Master of Trinity.

In July, the National Registration Act was passed which rendered parsons exempt from military service.

At the end of August the severely over-worked Archbishop Davidson was suddenly taken ill. He was to be carefully nursed back to health at Tremans, Horsted Keynes, where Archbishop Benson's widow had set up house with Archbishop Tait's daughter Lucy.

Meanwhile Archbishop Lang had accepted an invitation from Admiral Jellicoe to visit the fleet at Scapa, Invergordon and Rosyth.

At the end of November, Archbishop Davidson refused to agree to Lord Derby's request that the clergy should appeal from their pulpits for men to enlist.

On December 21, the Rev. G. Studdert-Kennedy was appointed a temporary chaplain to the forces. He was posted to the military base at Rouen where his generosity in dishing out cigarettes with Bibles earned him the nickname 'Woodbine Willie' which was to remain with him the rest of his life.

1916   On February 17, 1916, many members of the public were infuriated by a resolution by the House of Convocation condemning reprisal tactics and the killing and wounding of non-combatants.

The same month, the Council of the National Mission for Repentance and Hope, whose organizers believed that the Church of England had 'lost touch with the people', met for the same first time, with the Rev. William Temple, Rector of St. James's Piccadilly and son of the late Archbishop of Canterbury, acting as its secretary.

A few weeks later, on March 23, the eighty-three-year-old Rev. Lord Scarsdale, father of Lord Curzon, died at his stately home in Derbyshire. A country gentleman of the old school and Rector of Kedleston for the past sixty years, Lord Scarsdale had carried a gun till he was well past eighty and killed a brace of partridges on the last day he went out. He left a fortune of £218,000.

Four days later, the Rev. Edward Noel Mellish, chaplain attached to the Fourth Battalion of the Royal Fusiliers, rescued and tended several wounded men while under continuous artillery and machine gun fire. For this gallantry he was subsequently awarded the V.C.

In May, the Archbishop of Canterbury, Dr. Davidson, spent eight days with the troops in Belgium and France. He was accompanied by a chaplain, Old Etonian John Macmillan, later Bishop of Guildford, and the deputy Chaplain-General Bishop Gwynne and was shown round by Sir Douglas Haig. On May 17, the Archbishop visited the 'Toc H' headquarters at Poperinghe, recently established by the stocky and cherubic Rev. 'Tubby' Clayton, who wrote home afterwards, 'Cantuar was perfectly delightful'.

A fortnight later, eight naval chaplains died in the Battle of Jutland.

On July 23, the Bishop of London, Dr. Winnington-Ingram, conducted a confirmation service for 200 on board the flagship *Iron Duke* at Scapa Flow.

The same month, there was much agitation over a resolution carried by the newly formed council of the National Mission for Repentance and Hope,

The death of an Acton Vicar the Rev. W. M. Le Patourel in the Battle of Jutland makes front-page news

encouraging women speakers. Mr. Athelstan Riley protested that this was an attempt to 'claim the priesthood for women'.

On September 19, the Rev. Rupert Inglis, who had been unwilling to 'twiddle his thumbs' as Rector of Frittenden in Kent, was killed while rescuing wounded comrades during the Battle of the Somme.

The following month, the Rev. Dick Sheppard, who had been invalided out of the army early in the war, opened the church of St. Martin-in-the-Fields all night for the use of soldiers waiting for trains and anyone else in need of shelter.

Later that autumn, the Rev. Horace Wilkinson was appointed chaplain on board the battleship *Revenge*. A skilled handyman, he was to make a surplice out of sail cloth and repair a set of false-teeth belonging to the ship's paymaster, who until that moment had been noticeably hostile to all clergymen.

On Christmas Day, Archbishop Davidson fell ill again and was confined to his bedroom.

917 On January 10, 1917, a mighty explosion at Woolwich dockyard caused several ornaments to fall from chimneypieces at St. Paul's Deanery, nine miles away.

On March 9, the elderly and white-bearded Rev. Octavius Pickard-Cambridge, world expert on spiders, author of *Specific Descriptions of Trapdoor Spiders* and other works, died at his rectory at Bloxworth in Dorset, where he had lived for the last fifty years. In recent years he had been crippled by rheumatism and his parochial duties had been performed by a curate, the Rev. Ernest Benison, a dashing young man who owned a motorcar.

Two months later, on May 1, the Upper House of Convocation re-affirmed the resolution of the previous year condemning reprisal tactics and the killing of non-combatants. This move was violently attacked by the Duke of Argyll, who declared that 'the war is not going to be won by going back to coracles and arrows', and urged the bishops to 'stick to their belfries'.

On May 14, the Rev. and Hon. Maurice Peel, who had returned to the battle-front as chaplain to a Welsh regiment, was killed by a sniper's bullet while trying to rescue an injured man.

On May 29, the Dean of St. Paul's and Mrs. Inge were to be found staying with the wealthy Earl Beauchamp at his treasure-packed stately home, Madresfield in Worcestershire.

Meanwhile, a ginger group had taken form within the National Mission of Repentance and Hope, dedicated to freeing the church from the shackles of the Establishment. On June 20, this body, to be known as the Life and Liberty movement, announced its intentions in a letter to *The Times*. 'We wish to arouse the church to a sense of its vital need and to call on all who love it to demand for it the liberty which is essential to its life'. The Rev. William Temple was soon to give up his well-paid job as Rector of St. James's Piccadilly and devote himself full time to this new movement.

On July 9, the Dean of St. Paul's and Mrs. Inge gave a dinner-party at their deanery at which the Archbishop of Canterbury and Mrs. Davidson were the principal guests.

Meanwhile, the haughty and misunderstood Archbishop of York, Dr. Lang, visited all the fronts in France and Flanders. The strain of being the scapegoat of much of the nation's ill-humour had taken its toll and Dr. Lang had begun to lose his hair in handfuls. He was to wear a wig for a while but gave this up when it caught on a chandelier at Bishopthorpe Palace.

This autumn, services at St. Martin-in-the-Fields conducted by the charismatic Dick Sheppard, a leading light in the new Life and Liberty movement, became so popular that men had to be stationed at the doors, armed with poles to control the crowds.

On December 11, there was an uproar over the announcement that the controversial but hard-working Dr Hensley Henson, who was said to disbelieve in miracles and the apostolic creed, was to be the new Bishop of Hereford. The high church Bishop Gore of Oxford wrote a private letter to all the bishops of the southern province declaring that he was going to make a formal protest against the consecration. Other complaints poured in to Lambeth Palace and to the editor of *The Times*.

1918   On January 15, 1918, a meeting took place between the unorthodox Dr. Henson and Archbishop Davidson at Lambeth Palace, during which Henson convinced the Primate that he did not hold unacceptable beliefs. The appointment was duly confirmed on January 23 and the consecration took place on February 2. As Bishop of Hereford, Dr. Henson was to win the respect of many of the clergy and laity, carrying his dedication to work to the extent of refusing to have a telephone in his palace. When there were urgent calls to be made, he would send out a chaplain to a public kiosk with a pile of coins.

On April 11, Archbishop Davidson spoke in the House of Lords on the morals and health of British soldiers in France. He urged the authorities to take a more responsible line with regard to brothels in Le Havre and elsewhere and the prevalence of venereal disease. 'We owe everything to these men', he said. 'Are we doing everything for them that we can possibly do?'

Four days later, on April 15, the young Rev. Oswin Creighton, son of a former Bishop of London and whose mother was now living in a grace and favour apartment in Hampton Court Palace, was killed while serving with a brigade of the 29th Division.

The same day, the Haileybury-educated Rev. Ivor Hood was killed while conducting two wounded gunners to a dressing station.

The same month the Rev. Theodore Hardy, temporary chaplain to the 8th Battalion of the Lincolnshire Regiment, won the V.C. by rescuing a wounded officer from 400 yards beyond the front line.

Meanwhile, the controversial Archbishop of York, Dr. Lang, had been on an extensive tour of America, staying in New York at the mansion of financier, Mr Stuyvesant Fish, where he was given a bedroom 'fit only for a pope'. On April 28, he was back in Yorkshire, where he found the trip had brought him more unpopularity and a meeting he was to address at Middlesbrough was boycotted.

Six months later, on October 12, the Archbishop of Canterbury, Dr. Davidson, dined at Claridge's Hotel as a guest of the Prime Minister of Serbia, M. Paschitch. After dinner, he was decorated with the blue and white sash brooch of the 1st Class grade of the Serbian order of St. Sava.

On Saturday November 9, the Primate was driven in a royal carriage to the great banquet at the Guildhall at which the Prime Minister, Lloyd George, announced the abdication of the Kaiser.

The following evening, severe lumbago almost prevented the Primate preaching at a service in Westminster Abbey but he was given a soothing massage by a sister at St. Thomas's Hospital and managed to get through the service and have supper afterwards with the Dean of Westminster and the Archbishop of York.

The following morning, the Armistice was signed and St. Paul's Cathedral and Westminster Abbey were crowded throughout the day.

The crowd outside St. Paul's during the Armistice service

BETWEEN THE WARS

1918–1939

The evils and abuses of the past had now been remedied and the age of absentee clergy, wealthy ne'er-do-wells and nepotists was past. The next two decades see the advent of broadcasting, the coming of age of the Labour Party, the General Strike, a controversy over birth control, widespread unemployment and the rise of Fascism. The Church responded to these developments and took on a more mundane face. Cocoa-drinking bishops travelled by bus and tram, carried their own robes bags and made prim pronouncements on the changing morals of the time. Dean Inge began writing articles in the Evening Standard *and the great, spell-binding authoritarian sermons of the past were replaced by cosy, ten minute man-to-man chats, in which Christ was at last presented as a friend of the poor and oppressed. Two major sexual scandals involving clergymen and the somewhat princely behaviour of Archbishop Lang – whose effigy was publicly burnt by tithe-payers in 1935 – strike the only off-notes.*

1918 A month after the Armistice, the Bishop of London, Dr. Winnington-Ingram, made a public appeal on behalf of the poor clergy in his diocese, many of whom were said to be facing bankruptcy and starvation owing to the great increase in the cost of living. He cited the example of a married curate who was 'racked with anxiety about how to pay his very modest Christmas bills'.

On Christmas Day, King George and Queen Mary drove in an open carriage to a special service in Westminster Abbey. The royal party was met at the West Cloister entrance by a group of abbey clergy.

On Saturday, December 28, the Bishop of London took a break from his fund-raising activities to give a children's party at Fulham Palace.

The following day, Archbishop Davidson preached in Canterbury Cathedral on the gallant dead. 'Life is a school', he said. 'It is not a prison or a playground. It is a school.'

1919 Early in January 1919, the Bishop of Chelmsford, Dr. Watts-Ditchfield, was driving home from a confirmation service at Woodford when his car hit a stray horse in Epping Forest.

Later that spring, the Dean of St. Paul's, Dr. Inge, injured himself internally by carrying heavy coal boxes up to the nursery at his deanery. Dr. Inge kept no manservant and this was a task he had not wished to impose on his young housemaids.

On June 27, there was a memorial service in Westminster Abbey for the eighty-eight Anglican chaplains who had been killed during the war. The

Archbishop of Canterbury attended and a bugler sounded the Last Post followed by Reveille.

Six weeks later, on August 7, Dr. Henry Luke Paget, said by some to be the ugliest man in England, paid homage to the King on his appointment as Bishop of Chester.

On October 23, Dr. Cyril Garbett was enthroned as Bishop of Southwark. A cocoa-drinking bachelor, Dr. Garbett could not afford a car and was to travel about his un-glamorous diocese by tram, bus and train, carrying his heavy robes case himself.

Meanwhile, the efforts of the Life and Liberty movement to establish a working relationship between clergy and laity had been successful and, two days before Christmas, the Enabling Act, which laid down terms for a Church Assembly and Parochial Church Councils received the Royal Assent. In a jubilant letter to members of the movement, the Rev. William Temple declared, 'We enter the New Year with an unclouded hope'.

1920 On January 15, 1920, a West Country vicar appeared before Exeter Consistory Court, charged with selling a silver Elizabethan chalice and other items of church plate belonging to his church to a Torquay antique dealer. He was found guilty of the offence and was subsequently deprived of his living by the Bishop of Exeter.

Two months later, on March 21, the Vicar of All Saints, Cheltenham, was preaching by candle-light when the horrified expressions on the faces of his congregation drew his attention to the fact that his surplice was on fire.

On June 13, the Dean of St. Paul's and Mrs. Inge were to be found week-ending with Mr. and Mrs. Asquith at their Berkshire home. Others

The elderly Rev. Sabine Baring-Gould, author of the famous hymn 'Onward Christian soldiers' sets off on his morning round at Lew Trenchard in Devonshire

present included Mrs. Keppel, mistress of the late King Edward VII, and the newly married Lady Diana Cooper, whom Mrs. Inge later described in her diary as 'the most gloriously beautiful girl my eyes have ever seen, dressed very simply'.

The following month, Archbishop Davidson was still suffering from lumbago when the Sixth Lambeth Conference opened. One of the bishops present suggested an infallible cure – 'Tie a fiddle string round your waist' – to which the Primate replied, 'You are always very kind.'

On August 24, the Rev. Henry Herbert Williams was consecrated Bishop of Carlisle, where his bull-dog appearance and stubbly chin and cheeks were to earn him the unsavoury nickname 'Burglar Bill'.

In December, Lieutenant Geoffrey Woolley, who had won the V.C. for his exploits in the last war, was ordained a priest in Coventry Cathedral.

1921   On February 15, 1921, Dr. William Temple was enthroned as Bishop of Manchester: now a thriving diocese of three and a half million inhabitants and some 600 parishes. The hideous official residence, Bishopscourt, Higher Broughton, was not ready for his immediate occupation and the teetotal Dr. Temple was to stay for a few weeks with Canon and Mrs. J. J. Scott, whose eight-course dinner parties at their house at Fallowfield were the talk of the diocese.

Meanwhile, sixty-one-year-old Archdeacon John Wakeford had been found guilty of immorality with an unknown woman at the Bull Hotel, Peterborough, and stripped of his honours after sensational evidence by chambermaids at the hotel. He was to refuse to accept this verdict and appealed against the conviction to the Judicial Committee of the Privy Council. The case opened on April 7 in the presence of the Bishops of London, Ely, Rochester, and Gloucester, all of whom appeared for the hearing in top hats and gaiters, and after several weeks of re-examination of the evidence, the appeal was turned down.

Three months later, on July 28, thousands packed into Queen's Hall to hear the ex-Archdeacon plead his innocence. At first, he held the audience in the palm of his hand but, later, when he showed slides of the night-gown he had worn on the night in question, there were bursts of laughter and sniggers.

1922   On Easter Day the following year, Dean Inge, who had now begun contributing to the *Evening Standard*, preached a characteristically gloomy sermon in St. Paul's Cathedral. 'The war has not improved the moral tone of our people', he declared, 'in some ways it has made it worse. I cannot doubt that we are threatened with a great outburst of licentiousness such as that which disgraced the country in the reign of Charles II and again during the Regency.'

Three months later, writer G. K. Chesterton was received into the Roman Catholic church, stating that one of his reasons was that he could not bear to be in the same church as the Dean of St. Paul's. Dr. Inge noted in his diary that he hoped the public would 'soon tire of the elephantine capers of an obscene mountebank'.

The same summer, Archbishop Davidson appointed the Rev. Tubby Clayton, whose 'Toc H' movement was now fully established, Rector of the ancient living of All Hallows by-the-Tower, where the remains of Archbishop Laud had temporarily rested three centuries earlier.

1923   The following April, the Chapter of Westminster Abbey objected to the broadcasting of the wedding of the Duke of York and Lady Elizabeth Bowes-Lyon on the grounds that 'the service would be received by a considerable number of persons in an irreverent manner and might even be received by persons in public houses with their hats on'.

A few weeks later, on June 14, John Reith, managing director of the British Broadcasting Company lunched at Simpson's-in-the-Strand with the Rev. Dick Sheppard, Vicar of St. Martin-in-the-Fields. During this meeting, the idea of broadcasting a complete service was first broached.

1924   Six months later, on January 6, 1924, a service was duly broadcast from St. Martin-in-the-Fields. Dich Sheppard reflected afterwards that his sermon on this occasion must have reached more people than John Wesley preached to during his entire life. The event did not please everyone, however. The authorities at St. Paul's and Westminster Abbey treated the service as blasphemy and the Vicar of St. Stephen's, Norbury, declared that it was 'a travesty of Christian worship'.

Three months later, the Bishop of Willesden, Dr. Perrin, criticized the conditions currently prevailing in the West End of London. 'I know of no place today to compare with Piccadilly and Leicester Square for vice and temptation to the youth of England and the Dominions', he declared.

On September 20, the Dean of St. Paul's, Dr. Inge, famous for his pessimistic pronouncements about the future of mankind, was found walking through the streets of London flourishing a fancy, coloured umbrella of the sort carried by stage comedians.

Ten days later, the Bishop of Woolwich, Dr. Hough, denounced the use of birth control at a gathering at Oxford. 'The use of all artificial contrivances is clearly opposed to Christian conduct', he said. 'The sex instinct is a sacramental thing.'

On December 22, a Dangerous Structure notice was served on the Dean and Chapter of St. Paul's by City surveyor Mr. Todd, who ordered that the 230-year-old cathedral must be closed to the public. Dr. Inge regarded this move as 'an act of insolent rudeness' and ignored the order, confident that the Lord Mayor of London, though a Roman Catholic, would support him.

Meanwhile, the Archbishop of York, Dr. Cosmo Gordon Lang, had sat for his portrait by Sir William Orpen. The picture was subsequently presented to the Archbishop by Lord Halifax amidst much comment about the proud and pompous expression which the artist had caught on the sitter's face. 'That is what the devil meant him to be', said Archbishop Söderblom later, 'but, thanks be to God, it is not so'.

1925   On April 11, 1925, the Dean of St. Paul's sailed for America on board the *Mauretania*. On arrival in New York, this famous clergyman was besieged by reporters and asked his opinion of prohibition, 'I am quite willing to stick to it for three weeks', he replied, 'but, since you ask me, I think cold water, with which the Psalmist says wild asses quench their thirst, is a poor beverage to offer a human being.'

Eight months later, on December 21, a grand ceremony marked the in-

Dr. Inge's bedroom at St. Paul's Deanery

stallation of Dr. Foxley-Norris as Dean of Westminster. The abbey clergy
were in crimson and gold copes and the Abbey bells were rung.

The following day, it was announced that the Bishop of Coventry, Dr.
Charles Lisle Carr, was suffering from congestion of the lungs and had to
cancel all his engagements.

1926   On January 15, the following year, the Bishop of London, Dr.
Winnington-Ingram, incensed by a new play by Noël Coward starring
Tallulah Bankhead, petitioned the Prime Minister on behalf of the London
Public Morality Council, urging stricter theatre licensing laws. A few weeks
later he also wrote to the Home Secretary criticizing the 'presentation of un-
desirable plays and the circulation of undesirable publications'.

On May 4, the nation plunged into the General Strike. In the House of
Lords, the following day, the Archbishop of Canterbury, Dr. Davidson,
spoke of its 'unwisdom and mischievousness'. On May 6, the Bishops of
London and Southwark and a group of leading nonconformists met at
Lambeth Palace and issued a call to prayer, adding that they were anxiously
considering how Christian opinion could be harnessed to finding a settlement. Archbishop Davidson also issued an appeal for a reconciliation but
John Reith, Director-General of the B.B.C., refused to allow him to broadcast it.

Meanwhile, the Anglican bishops had been upstaged by the Roman
Catholic leader, Cardinal Bourne, who had announced, 'This strike is a sin
against God. Catholics must support the government.'

A few days later, the Strike was over and Mr. Ben Turner, and Miss Margaret Bondfield and other members of the Trades Union Council called at Lambeth to beg the Primate to use his influence to prevent victimization of workers.

Five months later, on Sunday October 17, an anonymous worshipper put a £1,000 bank note into the collection at Salisbury Cathedral.

Meanwhile, the Rev. Montague Summers had published *Witchcraft and Black Magic* in which he argued that Satanism was still being practised in England.

On January 11, 1927, the Lord Mayor of London threw a fancy dress party at which eleven-year-old Richard Inge, son of the Dean of St. Paul's, appeared dressed as his father, in miniature frock coat and gaiters.

Four months later, Dean Inge himself went to be sculpted by Royal Academician Henry Pegram, who many years earlier had designed two large brass candelabra for the nave of St. Paul's Cathedral.

On Sunday September 25, the controversial Dr. Barnes, who had been given the see of Birmingham three years earlier by Socialist Prime Minister Ramsay MacDonald, preached at Westminster Abbey one of the first of his 'gorilla' sermons, in which he attacked the traditional Christian view of the origin of man.

A few weeks later, on October 16, a service in St. Paul's at which Dr. Barnes was to preach was interrupted by leading Anglo-Catholic Canon Bullock-Webster, who demanded that the bishop should be tried for heresy and then marched out accompanied by several hundred supporters.

Four days later, the public were startled to read an open letter in the press from Bishop Barnes to the Archbishop of Canterbury claiming his right to remodel Christian theology. The Primate replied courteously, begging the Bishop to modify his 'negative and destructive statements'.

Meanwhile, much excitement had been stirred up over the proposed revised Prayer Book, upon which church leaders had been working for some twenty years. On December 12, Archbishop Davidson moved in the House of Lords that the Prayer Book Measure 'be presented to His Majesty for the Royal Assent'. After three days of furious debate, in which Bishop Pollock of Norwich, among others, fiercely opposed the new Prayer Book, the resolution was passed by 241 votes to 88. The following day, however, the measure was thrown out by the House of Commons after a feverish debate in which the M.P. for Paisley had made an ultra-Protestant harangue full of 'no popery' phrases of the past.

On February 20, the following year, seventy-year-old Rev. Francis Bacon, Vicar of All Saints, Mile End, appeared in the dock at the Old Bailey, charged with supplying poisonous drugs to women. 'Your conduct during the past ten years has been despicable and deplorable. You have concealed your illicit trade beneath a cloak of hypocrisy', said the judge, sentencing him to fifteen months' imprisonment.

Five months later, on July 25, affection and admiration were heaped on eighty-year-old Archbishop Davidson following the announcement that he was to resign as Archbishop of Canterbury. 'I don't honestly understand it.' Davidson commented. 'If I was describing myself I should say I was a funny old fellow of quite mediocre, second-rate gifts.'

195

The following day, Prime Minister Stanley Baldwin, between puffs at his pipe, informed Dr. Lang, Archbishop of York, that he proposed to recommend him as new Archbishop of Canterbury. At his first royal audience, the King told Lang that he hoped he would stop the clergy wearing moustaches.

On November 5, the retiring Archbishop left the Old Palace at Canterbury for the last time, making his way to Canterbury East Station on foot, in order to avoid 'any dramatic departure'. Mrs. Davidson followed on a train two hours later.

A month later, on December 4, Archbishop Lang was formally enthroned at Canterbury with much pageantry and the blowing of silver trumpets. Prime Minister Baldwin was unable to attend the ceremony as his services were required at Buckingham Palace, where the King had been struck down with a serious illness.

Following his enthronement, the new Primate moved into Lambeth Palace, accompanied by several of his staff from Bishopthorpe including his chauffeur Walter Wells, his gardener John Budden and his housekeeper Martha Savile. Problems with the soot filled garden at the palace were quickly solved by a gift of 600 tons of earth from his American millionaire friend J. Pierpont Morgan and he was soon delighted by his new home, especially his vast new study. 'When people come to see me in this study', he remarked later, 'they realize that the Church of England is a great institution.'

On December 11, the former Primate, Archbishop Davidson, who was settling into a new home, 10 Cheyne Walk, Chelsea, was a guest of honour at a dinner at the Athenaeum Club, where he had been a member for the past thirty-eight years.

On December 22, Archbishop Lang was suddenly seized by an internal pain while reading Bunyan's *Pilgrim's Progress* at the Old Palace at Canterbury. Eminent surgeon Sir Henry Rigby rushed from the bedside of the King, followed by Lord Dawson of Penn. It was soon decided that Lang was suffering from pleurisy and he was ordered off work for four months.

1929   Meanwhile, the vacant see of York had been filled by the socialist Bishop of Manchester, Dr. William Temple. His enthronement took place on January 10, 1929, with three special trains bringing dignatories from Manchester and Rochdale. A new regime was to begin at Bishopthorpe Palace. The Temples were to employ only female servants and entertain in a very simple style. In his first diocesan letter, Temple also announced that he would not 'attempt to keep up the flower garden in the splendid beauty which has made it so great a delight in recent years'. In due course Mrs. Temple was to disregard a warning from Archbishop Lang, who had prided himself on never setting foot in a local shop, that she would outrage local feeling if she were to travel on the bus between Bishopthorpe and York.

In February, a storm blew up in the Berkshire village of Sutton Courtenay over a proposal to move the grave of the late Lord Oxford fifteen yards to make room for a larger memorial. Villagers feared that their ancestors' graves would be disturbed. 'Why should their bones be dug up to make room for Lord Oxford?' demanded a prominent member of the local community.

At the end of March, Archbishop Lang, who had been convalescing at Bognor in a house next door to that occupied by the King, left for a cruise on board his friend J. Pierpont Morgan's 2,000 ton yacht, *Corsair*, which he boarded at Venice on April 2. The Primate was assigned a cabin the size of an ordinary bedroom with its own bathroom en suite. He said afterwards that this cruise brought him 'more happiness than any other event in my life'.

On June 27, Dr. George Bell, former chaplain to Archbishop Davidson, was enthroned as Bishop of Chichester, where he was to be driven about his diocese by a chauffeur named Monk, covering an average of 1,200 miles a month and continuing to read and write in his car, even at night.

On July 7, a thanksgiving service for the King's return to health was held in Westminster Abbey. Members of the royal family sat on special pink and gold chairs on either side of the presbytery, the silver and gold plate was on display and Archbishop Lang led the procession of clergy. The service ended with the jubilant 'Praise my soul, the King of Heaven', and as the procession passed out of the abbey, 'Jerusalem' was sung.

On Christmas Eve this year the Dean of St. Paul's, Dr. Inge, had his pocket picked in the lift of an Underground station.

1930   Seven weeks later, on February 13, 1930, ex-Archdeacon Wakeford, central figure in a major ecclesiastical scandal nine years earlier, died in Barming Heath Lunatic Asylum. His wife had stood by him throughout his ordeals, maintaining his innocence on charges of immorality to the end.

On May 26, Archbishop Lang was again immobilized by internal pains and the presence of a duodenal ulcer was soon diagnosed by his doctor, Lord Dawson of Penn. The Primate was sent to Bognor again and put on a strict diet.

By Saturday July 7, he had recovered sufficiently to welcome 307 Anglican bishops to the Seventh Lambeth Conference. Proceedings began with a day of devotion at Fulham Palace, at which the 86-year-old former Bishop of Winchester, Dr. Talbot, who was recovering from a broken thigh, gave an address in a fine, clear voice. This year, catering arrangements at Lambeth had been placed in the hands of a firm of race-course caterers, whose waitresses commented later, that they 'preferred bishops to bookies'.

On August 29, the death occurred of Dr. William Spooner, former Warden of New College, and one of the leading clergymen of his day, whose famous lapses of speech had been responsible for the word 'Spoonerism' entering the language.

Four months later on December 12, the Dean of St. Paul's, Dr. Inge, dined at St. James's Palace with the Prince of Wales who, a few weeks earlier, had met Mrs. Ernest Simpson for the first time.

1931   The following March, the death occurred of the ninety-one-year-old Rev. Arthur Tooth, who fifty-four years earlier had been held in Horsemonger Gaol for liturgical irregularities at St. James's church, Hatcham. In more recent years, Mr. Tooth had run an orphanage, a nunnery and a home for drunkards.

The same month, the Labour Prime Minister Ramsay McDonald appointed the theatrical-looking Dr. Hewlett Johnson Dean of Canterbury, where he was to remain for the next thirty-two years embarrassing a succession of archbishops with his communist views.

Meanwhile, Archbishop Lang had been found to be suffering from a malady known as the Fifth Nerve and had been sent to rest at the home of his chaplain Green-Wilkinson in Windsor Forest. Here, he had fallen in his bath, striking his head, and it was proposed that he should continue his convalescence on another cruise. On March 31, he sailed from Monte Carlo via Athens to the Holy Land, where he entered Jerusalem wearing a purple silk cassock, cap and cape and was received by the Anglican bishop, Rennie MacInnes, who wore a scarlet doctor's gown.

Also cruising the Mediterranean at this time were the Dean of St. Paul's and Mrs.Inge, whose fellow passengers included Mr. and Mrs. Bernard Shaw.

On return from his journey, the Archbishop of Canterbury was again struck down, this time by fibrositis, and was despatched to recuperate at Cannes, where Lady Gladstone lent him her villa.

In July 28, the death of ninety-one-year-old Canon John Dalton, who had been appointed tutor to the royal princes as long ago as 1871, deprived the King of one of his oldest friends.

1932   Early the following year, a major scandal engulfed the church when the fifty-six-year-old Rev. Harold Davidson, Rector of Stiffkey on the Norfolk coast, was accused in the press of immoral practices with over a thousand girls. On Sunday February 7, 1932, thousands of sightseers converged on the ancient church of St. John and St. Mary, Stiffkey, to hear the Rector preach, one bus-load coming from as far away as Bournemouth. With his war medals clinking on his surplice, the silver-haired parson received rousing cheers from his flock.

At the end of March, Consistory Court proceedings against the Rector began in the Great Hall of Church House. Amidst immense public interest, the proceedings dragged on until July 8 when Davidson was found guilty on all charges and sentenced to be de-frocked.

On September 21, the consecration of the short and stocky Dr. Geoffrey Fisher as Bishop of Chester took place in York Minster. A special train was laid on to carry dignitaries from Chester to the ceremony. The new Bishop, who had secured a triple first at Oxford and was the father of six sons, was soon to scandalize the diocese by playing a barrel organ in the street to raise money for a local hospital.

On October 18, Dean Inge gave a talk to the younger clergy of the Southwark diocese on practical difficulties connected with sex. Questions afterwards revealed an astonishing ignorance on the part of many of his audience, which led him to reflect that theological colleges 'must be queer places'.

Three days later, cheering crowds outside Norwich Cathedral greeted the Rev. Harold Davidson when he drew up in a small mud-spattered car to be formally de-frocked by the Bishop of Norwich, Dr. Bertram Pollock. During the solemn service that followed, Davidson constantly heckled the Bishop and finally supplanted him in the procession leading to the high altar.

1933   On February 10, 1933, clergyman's wife Mrs. Lucy Burnett, complained to the Church Assembly about the commodiousness of her rectory at Settrington in Yorkshire, which had twenty-one rooms, a thirty foot dining-room and stabling for eleven horses. 'If you played a brass band in my kitchen, I don't think you could hear it in my drawing-room,' she said.

A few weeks later, on May 27, it was announced that the Rev. Frederick Iremonger, Vicar of Vernham Dean in Hampshire and chaplain to the King, was to become director of religious broadcasting.

198

Bishopthorpe Palace, ancient seat of the Archbishops of York

On November 11, the Archbishop of York and Mrs. Temple were found staying at St. Paul's Deanery. During their visit, Dean Inge gave a dinner for them, at which one of the principal guests was the popular German ambassador Leopold von Hoesch, whose country had recently fallen into the hands of the Nazis.

1934   Sixteen months later, at the beginning of September 1934, seventy-four-year-old Dr. Inge, the last Dean of St. Paul's to entertain on a grand scale at his spacious deanery, announced his resignation. 'I would hate to stay here until I became a bore', he explained.

The following month, German ambassador Von Hoesch was summoned to Lambeth Palace, where Archbishop Lang informed him that Christian opinion was outraged by the policies of the Third Reich.

1935   Meanwhile, with many smaller farmers now owning their own land, fresh disturbances had begun over the payment of church tithes. On March 15, 1935, there was a dramatic demonstration at Ashford in Kent when a hundred tithe-payers marched onto the lawn of Ruckinge Rectory and demanded to see the Rector, the Rev. C. P. Newell, while others tolled the church bell and an effigy of Archbishop Lang was publicly burnt.

Three months later, on June 5, Herr Joachim von Ribbentrop, in England as German representative at the Naval Treaty Talks, lunched at Lambeth Palace and was lectured by the Primate.

Later that summer, the former Rector of Stiffkey Harold Davidson and his daughter Pamela entered adjoining 'fasting cabinets' to amuse the crowds on the central beach at Blackpool. On August 10, both were arrested and charged with attempting suicide. On being found not guilty, Davidson sued the Blackpool corporation and was awarded £382 damages.

At the end of August, Archbishop Lang stayed at Balmoral where he had a long and intimate talk with the King about the Prince of Wales's scandalous friendship with Mrs. Ernest Simpson. The King also took this occasion to ban from the castle the Primate's ancient Wolseley touring car, purchased in 1913, on the grounds that it was a public danger. Dr. Lang was soon to replace the offending vehicle with an Armstrong-Siddeley.

The following month, the Dean and Chapter of St. Paul's gave serious consideration to the possibility of breeding ravens to destroy the cathedral's pigeons, but they were discouraged by zoologist Professor Julian Huxley, who informed them that ravens would not prey on pigeons in public.

1936   On January 19, 1936, Archbishop Lang took the train to Sandringham to attend the dying King, to whom he had been a friend for the past thirty-eight years. The following day, as the monarch's life slipped away, Dr. Lang read the Twenty-Third Psalm, followed by prayers and a final benediction.

On the day after the King's funeral, Lang called at Buckingham Palace and made a clumsy attempt to come to terms with the new King, which only served to increase the latter's dislike of him. Later in the year, Lang was not invited to Balmoral but, instead, stayed at nearby Birkhall, as a guest of the Duke and Duchess of York.

Meanwhile, parliament had passed a bill for the final extinction of church tithes, in spite of the opposition of staunch churchman, Lord Hugh Cecil, who denounced this legislation as a robbery of tithe-owners.

On December 1, the storm at last broke over the King's relationship with Mrs. Simpson following comments by the Bishop of Bradford, Dr. Blunt, on the King's lack of church-going in an address to his Diocesan Conference.

On December 4, Archbishop Lang appealed to his clergy to refrain from speaking directly on 'the King's matter' but asking them to pray instead for the King and his Ministers. In spite of this caution, many people believed that the Primate had organized a conspiracy to chase the King from his throne and, two days later, he got a hostile reception from the crowds outside 10 Downing Street, when he went to visit Prime Minister Stanley Baldwin.

On December 10, the King's abdication message was read to both Houses of Parliament and was followed by a brief speech by the Archbishop of Canterbury.

Three days later, Lang caused much offence by making an uncharitable broadcast in which he criticized the ex-King's 'craving for private happiness', exclaimed 'Oh, the pity of it' and attacked his social circle. One member of this circle, Lord Brownlow, expressed his indignation in person, visiting the Archbishop and demanding an apology, and even the Archbishop's chaplain, Dr. Don, declared that his master had been 'a little unfair on the poor King'.*

---

* Dr. Lang received the following verse through the post at this time:
My Lord Archbishop, what a scold you are!
And when your man is down how bold you are!
Of Christian charity how scant you are!
And, auld Lang swine, how full of cant you are!

On December 21, Dr. Lang visited the new King and Queen at their house in Piccadilly to discuss arrangements for the forthcoming coronation.

1937   On March 29, 1937, following the outbreak of the Spanish Civil War the previous year, the Dean of Canterbury Dr. Hewlett Johnson flew to the Basque country in a private plane, without the approval or permission of either the Archbishop of Canterbury or the Foreign Secretary.

Six weeks later, on May 12, accompanied by a police superintendent on horseback, Dr. Lang made his way from Lambeth Palace to Westminster Abbey where, dressed in a white cope adorned with gold bullion, he conducted the coronation of King George VI. Sitting in the south transept throughout the ceremony was the Primate's doctor, Lord Dawson of Penn, who was ready with a hypodermic syringe to give his patient a revitalizing injection should this prove necessary. From a small hut hidden behind the high altar Dr. Iremonger, Dean of Lichfield, broadcast a commentary on the proceedings to the world, though he could not in fact see much of what was going on.

Less than a month later, on June 3, the marriage of the Duke of Windsor and Mrs. Simpson took place in France, conducted by the Rev. R. A. Jardine of Darlington, who had volunteered for this task, incurring the anger of both the Bishop of Durham, Dr. Hensley Henson, and the Bishop of Fulham, Dr. Basil Batty, whose field of jurisdiction included France. 'I don't mind if it means I have to leave the church', commented Mr. Jardine 'I'm getting on now in any case.' The rosy-cheeked Vicar and his wife later left for a publicity tour of America where they opened a church called the 'Windsor Cathedral' and were finally arrested for over-staying their permit.

On July 28, the notorious de-frocked Rector of Stiffkey, Harold Davidson, was savaged by a lion in Skegness Amusement Park. He had been addressing holiday-makers from inside a lion's cage when a beast named Freddie pounced on him, causing severe lacerations to the face and neck. He was rushed to Skegness Cottage Hospital, where two days later he died.

On October 31, the Rev. Dick Sheppard also died in unhappy circumstances, deserted by his wife and alone in a canon's house near St. Paul's Cathedral. His body later lay in state at St. Martin-in-the-Fields, which had become the most famous parish in England under Sheppard's rule. Over 100,000 people paid their last respects, tramps and prostitutes among them.

1938   Ten months later, in September 1938, the country trembled on the brink of war and Archbishop Lang transmitted a telegram to the Pope, via Cardinal Hinsley, begging him to ask Hitler to hold his hand. A few weeks later, the crisis had passed and, on November 24, a meeting took place at the Athenaeum Club in Pall Mall between Lang and Hinsley at which the two leaders discussed how to safeguard Christian missions in the German colonies.

Meanwhile, work had begun on the new Church House in Dean's Yard, Westminster, featuring a wood-panelled chapel and large circular assembly hall.

1939   On February 27, 1939, a fire destroyed the notorious Borley Rectory in Essex, which had been described by ghost-hunter Harry Price as 'the most haunted house in England'.

Two months later, after consulting Prime Minister Neville Chamberlain, the Archbishop of Canterbury left for another cruise on board J. Pierpont Morgan's sumptuous yacht, *Corsair*. The party sailed as far as Istanbul, but turned back earlier than expected after receiving menacing international news.

In June, the Bishop of Chester, Dr. Geoffrey Fisher, was appointed to succeed the eighty-year-old Dr. Winnington-Ingram who had served as Bishop of London since 1901 and had recently begun to lose his grip. Showing Fisher around the garden at Fulham Palace, the retiring Bishop declared that the diocese was 'just one gloriously happy family'.

On July 25 it was announced that the famous cricketing parson Frank Gillingham, who had played for Essex for twenty-five years, had been appointed a chaplain to the King.

Six days later, a chorister at St. Paul's Cathedral, Mr. Charles Mayhew, celebrated his hundredth birthday. It was stated that Mr. Mayhew had first sung in the choir at St. Paul's on the occasion of the Duke of Wellington's funeral in 1852.

On August 24, Archbishop Lang announced from Lambeth Palace that there should be a special and united act of prayer that the crime and horror of war might be averted. The following Sunday, the King, the Duke of Kent and the Duke of Gloucester, all in morning dress, duly attended a special service in Westminster Abbey, which was supported by services in churches across the country.

Meanwhile, stained glass was being removed from the great window in the south-west transept of Canterbury Cathedral as a precautionary measure.

On Sunday September 3, it was announced that the country was at war. In York Minster, worshippers learnt of this grave news from Dr. Temple himself.

THE SECOND WORLD WAR

1939–1945

During the next six years, hundreds of historic churches were destroyed and many humbling experiences were inflicted on the leaders of the church. Bishops' palaces were filled with evacuees, their chaplains and chauffeurs joined the forces, the Archbishop of Canterbury got stuck in the gun-turret on board a battleship and the Bishop of Exeter was refused an extra petrol allowance on the grounds that he was 'not involved in work of national importance'. Meanwhile, ninety-six chaplains were killed on active service.

1939 On the afternoon of September 3, the Archbishop of Canterbury, Dr. Lang, drove from Lambeth Palace to the House of Lords, where he conducted prayers.

On September 12, it was announced that the Bishop of Lichfield, Dr. Woods, had forbidden clergy in his diocese to join the army as combatants. Among those to disregard this order was the twenty-three-year-old Rev. Kenneth Stephens, curate of Chell, near Stoke-on-Trent, who joined up quoting the 37th Article 'It is lawful for Christian men at the commandment of the magistrate to wear weapons and serve in wars'.

Meanwhile, two teachers and seven children from Southampton had been billeted on the Bishop of Winchester at historic Wolvesey Palace. On September 23, the palace was invaded by the children's parents. 'They treated the house as their own', noted the Bishop, Dr. Cyril Garbett. 'They sat in the drawing-room, went up to the bedrooms, filled the passages and came in without ringing.'

On October 14, it was announced that the Lambeth Conference, scheduled to take place the following year, had been postponed.

A few days later, the Rev. James Cree, chaplain on board the *Royal Oak*, was among those who died when the ship was torpedoed and sunk as she lay at anchor near Scapa Flow.

On November 3, the Lord Mayor of London gave a luncheon at the Mansion House in honour of the new Bishop of London, Dr. Fisher. Among those present were the Dean of St. Paul's, Dr. Matthews, the Lord Mayor's chaplain, the Rev. W. E. S. Holland, and Sheriff Denys Lowson.

1940 In January 1940, the Bishop of Winchester, Dr. Garbett, was nearly knocked down by a lorry when he emerged from a bishops' meeting at Lambeth Palace into the black-out.

Four months later, on May 10, Dr. Garbett was staying with the Governor of Guernsey, when he was woken by the butler with the news that the German invasion of Belgium and Holland had begun.

At the end of the month, the Dunkirk evacuation began. The chaplain at the Dover base, the Rev. Francis Leonard, welcomed arrivals with prayers and encouragement. Among those captured during the operation was ex-chorister the Rev. J. F. O. Brown who was to enliven his spell in prison camp by arranging services and hymn-singings.

Early in June, a bomb fell on the garden of the Bishop of Peterborough, sixty-six-year-old Dr. Blagden, smashing the windows of his study and blowing in the door of his chauffeur's house.

On July 15, the Rev. Robert Graham, Rector of Bolingbroke-cum-Hareby in Lincolnshire, was sentenced to four weeks' imprisonment for ringing his church bell, contrary to the new Defence Regulations which ruled that bells were only to be rung for military purposes, such as warning that parachutists had landed in the area. Mr. Graham subsequently appealed successfully against the conviction on the grounds that he was ignorant of the order.

Meanwhile the Bishop of Winchester's chauffeur, Mr. Payne, had gone to work in an aircraft factory and the sixty-five-year-old Dr. Garbett had laid off his big Vauxhall and begun driving lessons in his sister's small car. 'If the peacetime system of motoring tests had been in operation', his biographer wrote later, 'it is inconceivable that he would ever have received a licence.'

On August 26, the Archbishop of Canterbury, Dr. Lang, lunched at 10 Downing Street with the new Prime Minister Winston Churchill.*

The following month, the bombing of London began in earnest. At 2.50 a.m. on September 15, a bomb fell on Wren's famous church of St. Mary-le-Bow in Cheapside causing its celebrated bells to crash to the ground. Four days later, another bomb burst through the great oriel window into the drawing-room of Lambeth Palace, damaging many of the surrounding rooms but to his great relief, leaving the Primate's bathroom untouched. Seventy-five-year-old Dr. Lang had already decided to close down most of the palace and was in future to confine himself to a solitary existence in the old housekeeper's sitting-room in the basement, taking most of his meals out, often at the Athenaeum Club. The Archbishop's butler, McDade, stayed on to rule over the ruins of the palace and to act as chief warden of the air-raid shelter set up in the crypt.

Meanwhile, at Fulham Palace, Dr. Fisher had abandoned the great rooms and moved into the Tudor wing, once occupied by Bishop Laud. Here, most of the household slept in an underground shelter beneath the Porteus Library, with the notable exception of the bishop's chaplain, the Rev. F. C. Synge, who chose to sleep on a camp bed on the lawn, saying that he preferred to be hit by shrapnel than be buried alive beneath Fulham Palace.

On October 10, a bomb fell on St. Paul's Cathedral, making a gaping hole above the high altar but leaving the rest of the building unscathed. Sleeping in a camp bed in the crypt at the time was the elderly Canon Sidney Alexander, who hurried up the stone steps of the sanctuary in his pyjamas to inspect the damage. 'The binding of the masonry put in by Wren must have been marvellous', he remarked.

* Churchill never showed much interest in the internal workings of the Church of England but declared that he was a staunch supporter of the institution from the outside – 'like a buttress'.

A few days later, Canterbury was attacked by a formation of Messerschmidts while the Dean, Dr. Hewlett Johnson, was having lunch. Dr. Hewlett Johnson and his household staff took shelter in the old vaulted pantry of the deanery while bombs crashed around them.

The following month, the famous Bishop of Birmingham, Dr. Barnes, accused the Cement Makers Federation of monopolism and deliberately holding up the supply of cement. An action for slander followed and the companies concerned were awarded £1,600 in damages, though the controversial Bishop did not himself appear in court.

On December 30, incendiary bombs destroyed eight famous Wren churches including St. Bride's, Fleet Street, St. Lawrence Jewry and St. Andrews-by-the-Wardrobe. The Rector of the last named church, the Rev. J. R. Sankey, rushed into the flaming building to rescue parish registers dating back to 1566.

1941 The following March, the Bishop of London, Dr. Fisher, drove through the ruined capital to have a simple lunch of beer and sandwiches with the Lord Mayor. He was driven by his chauffeur, John Binley, whose father had worked as a coachman to Fisher's predecessor, Dr. Winnington-Ingram.

Two months later, on May 10, four more bombs fell on Lambeth Palace, damaging the roof of the Great Library, built by Archbishop Juxon, and gutting both the chapel and Lollard's Tower. In his diocesan notes published later in the month, Dr. Lang wrote, 'I was there myself on that fateful night. The experience of crashing bombs and crackling flames was a trying ordeal.'

The same night, the medieval Westminster Deanery had been destroyed and the Old Harrovian Dean, Dr. de Labilliere, had lost all his possessions, including his clothes.

1942 Eight months later, on January 21, 1942, the resignation of seventy-seven-year-old Archbishop Lang was announced. 'I deem it my duty', he said, 'to hand over my charge to someone younger in years, more vigorous in mind and spirit, who will be better able to prepare us for the post-war years.' Dr. Lang now had to manage on a tenth of his £15,000 a salary and for a while feared he would have to move into 'a villa in the outer suburbs'. Fortunately, the King came to his rescue with the offer of a large grace and favour residence at Kew, known as the King's Cottage, into which he moved on April 13, accompanied by his cook, Gertrude Castle, and his butler McDade. Dr. Lang had already parted with his Armstrong-Siddeley motor-car and was to become again 'a bus bishop'.

Eleven days later, on April 24, Dr. William Temple was enthroned as the new Archbishop of Canterbury with much pomp and ceremony. 'This is not the moment to say much about the war', he told his vast congregation, which included forty-five bishops. The new primate, who neither drank nor smoked, was to tour his new diocese in a small car belonging to a chaplain.

Meanwhile, Dr. Cyril Garbett had been appointed Archbishop of York. Early in April, he had visited his enormous new home, Bishopthorpe Palace, to interview gardeners and arrange for a new carpet for the parlour.

On May 31, Archbishop and Mrs. Temple were staying at the Old Palace at Canterbury when the town was again bombarded. The palace and cathedral survived the attack and Dr. Temple remained unruffled, supplying rescue workers with cups of tea.

On June 3, the new Archbishop of York visited the Royal Academy Summer Exhibition with his chaplain, former rowing Blue Gerald Ellison, who had been serving as chaplain on board the cruiser *Orion*. That evening the Archbishop was to be found in the audience of a popular farce *The Man who came to Dinner* at the Savoy Theatre, starring Robert Morley and Coral Browne.

In August, bishop's son General Montgomery selected as senior chaplain for the Eighth Army the Rev. Frederick Llewellyn Hughes. A short, thickset man, Hughes was described by a fellow padre as 'a ball of fire'.

In September, the portly Archbishop Temple paid a memorable visit to the home fleet at Scapa Flow, during which he raised lower-deck morale by getting stuck in a gun-turret on board the battleship *King George V*.

1943 Five months later, on February 26, 1943, Temple spoke at a conference on venereal disease at Friends House, Euston Road. Criticizing the government for ignoring the moral aspect of the problem, he declared, 'There is a great menace and a great evil to be met. What is quite deadly is to give the impression that misconduct should be accepted as normal.'

The following month, on March 26, General Carpenter of the Salvation Army and his wife surprised Dr. Garbett, Archbishop of York, by arriving an hour and a half late for dinner at Bishopthorpe Palace. Before the end of the evening, this discourtesy was forgotten and the Carpenters departed the following day leaving 'an odour of holiness'.

A few weeks later, Dr. Garbett announced that he would be giving up half his £9,000 salary. A conservative M.P. Sir Herbert Williams, promptly suggested that this was an attempt on the Archbishop's part to avoid income tax. 'That was not the case', retorted Garbett. 'The measure was fully discussed with the Inland Revenue and the Treasury. There has been no kind of evasion.'

In September, Garbett flew to Moscow where he was given a suite in the National Hotel overlooking the Kremlin. During his visit to Russia he was offered vodka, but found it tasted 'rather like methylated spirits'.

1944 On February 9, 1944, the Bishop of Chichester, Dr. Bell, who had never fully supported the war effort, made a long speech in the House of Lords in which he criticized the bombing of civilians by the R.A.F. 'Do the government understand the full force of what our aerial bombardment is doing?' he asked.

At the end of the month, the Italian Campaign began. Among chaplains to distinguish themselves were the Rev. Ronald Edwards, chaplain to the 2/4 Hampshires, who raised a Red Cross flag in the midst of heavy machine gun fire, and Canon A. V. Hurley, a former Oxford soccer blue whose nickname was 'Pope'. In due course, the area was visited by the Bishop of Portsmouth, Dr. Anderson, and the tennis-playing Bishop of Lichfield, Dr. Woods, and other church leaders.

Meanwhile, plans were being made for the Normandy landings, which duly took place on June 6 with eighteen naval chaplains taking part. Among them was the Rev. David Walters, whose chapel on board the cruiser *Hawkins* was cleared to make room for stretcher cases.

The Bishop of Mombasa, the Rt. Rev. R. P. Crabbe, surrounded by chaplains of several denominations in the East Africa command

The Archbishop of York, Dr. Garbett, the Bishop of London, Dr. Fisher, and the Archbishop of Canterbury, Dr. Temple, photographed outside the Old Palace at Canterbury during the dark days of World War Two

The following month, Lambeth Palace was assailed by flying bombs, breaking practically every window left in the place. Archbishop Temple tried to sleep through the raids on a sofa in a ground floor passage.

At the end of the summer, Dr. Temple was struck down by an attack of gout from which he had suffered intermittently most of his adult life. On October 3, he was taken by ambulance to a hotel at Westgate-on-Sea, where it was hoped, the change of air would save him. His death on October 26, caused widespread grief: President Roosevelt sent a telegram to the King expressing his sympathy, while back-stage at the New Theatre Dame Sybil Thorndike's dresser remarked, 'The poor man has lost a friend.'

Five days later, Archbishop Garbett travelled south for the funeral in the guard's van of a crowded train, sitting on a bundle of sailors' hammocks. At the service at Canterbury, young clergyman Joseph McCulloch was moved to reflect, 'We are burying the hopes of the Church of England.'

1945   On January 2, 1945, the appointment of Dr. Geoffrey Fisher as new Archbishop of Canterbury was announced. The Fishers were to move into the ruined Lambeth Palace accompanied by two maids from Fulham Palace. Among the staff they inherited was Mr. Clements, an elderly stenographer, who had started life as boot-boy at Winchester under Bishop Davidson at the end of the last century.

Three months later, at the beginning of April, Archbishop Garbett flew to Naples, where he stayed at the luxurious Villa Emma, the setting for Lord Nelson's first meeting with Lady Hamilton, before setting off on a strenuous tour of Italy, during which he was given the status of a Field Marshal, a special plate being made for his car bearing six stars, and accompanied by two motor-cyclists. *

Back in England on April 19, Dr. Fisher's enthronement as 99th Archbishop of Canterbury, was interrupted by an elderly woman, who cried out 'In the name of Jesus, I stop this ceremony! The Ecclesiastical Commissioners have six million pounds while children are starving!', but continued without further incident and as the Archbishop, in a mitre of cream embroidered with gold, moved to the high altar of Canterbury Cathedral the choir sang the Forty-sixth Psalm 'God is our hope and strength'.

Nineteen days later, on May 8, the bishops gathered in the House of Lords to hear the final victory announcement.

* In fact, an Archbishop takes precedence over a Field Marshal.

MODERN TIMES

1945–1980

Within weeks of the ending of hostilities, the church began to put its house in order. The restoration and modernization of Lambeth Palace was soon authorized and the repair of many of the historic churches damaged by enemy action was quickly underway. The combining of the resources of the Ecclesiastical Commissioners and the Queen Anne's Bounty in 1948 woke up the church to the possibilities of property development and industrial investment and at last enabled it to pay its parsons a decent wage. Between 1945 and 1963, £17 million was spent on new church buildings and further major restoration programmes were launched. Slowly, the church adapted itself to the nuclear age. Public relations officers were recruited, management consultants were called in and at the coronation of Elizabeth II television cameras were at last permitted into Westminster Abbey. In due course, many bishops moved into a corner of their historic homes and Dr. Ramsey replaced his official Daimler with a Ford and then later with a chauffeur driven Morris Minor. In the years that followed, a new modernized liturgy was introduced, homosexual clergy were officially accepted and, under the primacy of Dr. Coggan, the ordination of women began to look more feasible. Ironically, these developments were accompanied by an unmistakable decline in the church's spiritual life. From 1945 onwards, Christianity came under relentless attack and many of its essential beliefs were questioned, not least by the bishops themselves. Year by year, church attendance figures slumped and by 1980 it was estimated that only 2½ per cent of the population – one and a quarter million people – attended an Anglican church on an average Sunday. The numbers of those presenting themselves for ordination also plummeted with the result that many famous theological colleges were closed. Rectories and parsonages fell into the hands of wealthy laymen, churches were blown up by dynamite, demolished to make way for supermarkets, converted into homes or preyed on by vandals. The populace found their spiritual stimulation elsewhere. During the last decade of this period, while some 800 churches were being made redundant, Jesus Christ Superstar *was playing to packed houses. The period ends on an optimistic note, however, with the enthronement of war hero Robert Runcie as 102nd Archbishop of Canterbury, who on the day his appointment was announced expressed his dread of becoming 'a platitude machine'.*

1945   On May 13, 1945, the King and Queen, Queen Mary and the young Princesses drove in open, horse-drawn carriages to a great service of thanksgiving in St. Paul's Cathedral. They were greeted by Archbishop Fisher, in cope and mitre, who in his sermon declared, 'This is such a national thanksgiving as never was before'.

Three months later, following the bombing of Hiroshima and Nagasaki and the surrender of Japan, a row broke out at St. Albans when the Dean, the

Very Rev. Cuthbert Thicknesse, forbade the use of his abbey for another thanksgiving service. 'I cannot honestly give thanks to God for an event brought about by an act of wholesale, indiscriminate massacre,' he declared.

At the same time, the Bishop of Chichester, Dr. Bell, who had also criticized the recent bombing, was banned from preaching in his own cathedral by the Dean.

On November 9, Archbishop Fisher brought an informal touch to a luncheon given by the Lord Mayor in honour of Prime Minister Attlee when he brought out his old briar pipe.

On December 4, the former Archbishop of Canterbury, Lord Lang, was hurrying to Kew Gardens Underground Station on his way to the House of Lords, when he collapsed in the roadway. Lady Cynthia Slessor, who was queueing outside a fish shop, rushed to his assistance and summoned an ambulance but the ex-Primate was dead before he reached Richmond Hospital.

1946 Eight months later, on July 11, 1946, the King and Queen and Princess Elizabeth visited Canterbury where they were shown round the cathedral by Dr. Hewlett Johnson and lunched afterwards at the Old Palace with the Fishers. Asked if he would like to watch a local cricket match, the King replied, 'Ah, no, I am all religious today.'

A few weeks later, on August 19, Dr. Fisher left for America on board the *Mauretania*. On the same ship was Field Marshal Montgomery, who accosted the Primate during the voyage and said, 'Archbishop, I want to hear how you run the Church of England. Will you come with Mrs. Fisher one day to my cabin?' After their conversation, Monty told Fisher, 'You need more discipline.'

On August 25, the sixty-eight-year-old Ven. Horace Lambart, Archdeacon Emeritus of Salop, inherited the Earldom of Cavan. The title made little difference to his life style and he continued to live at Plex House, Hadnall, Salop.

On November 12, the Church Assembly approved plans for the restoration of Lambeth Palace. The ancient palace was to be restructured internally to include a hostel of fifteen bedrooms for the use of bishops and lay visitors from Britain and overseas, and a new self-contained lodging for the Primate. The work was placed in the hands of Messrs. Seely and Paget and was to take nearly a decade to complete.

1947 On March 4, 1947, the surplice worn by the Rev. C. A. Wheeler, Rural Dean of Bletchley, caught fire during a service in Leighton Buzzard church. The Vicar, the Rev. S. J. Forrester, stopped the service, rushed to his assistance and beat out the flames with his hands.

Later that spring, the elderly Bishop of Birmingham, Dr. Barnes, unleashed another storm by publishing his *Rise of Christianity* in which he argued that miracles do not happen and queried the idea of the Virgin Birth and the Resurrection. Among those outraged by this book was the Archbishop of York, Dr. Garbett, who wrote to Archbishop Fisher on June 9 saying, 'I do not think that in the whole course of my ministry anything has happened more likely to injure the work and influence of the church than this miserable book. Something ought to be done about it.' Letters poured into Lambeth Palace demanding Dr. Barnes's resignation and the Dean of

Winchester, Dr. Selwyn, demanded that he should be brought before an ecclesiastical court. In spite of this pressure, Dr. Fisher refused to sponsor such a trial but was to deliver a hard-hitting attack on the book in the Convocation and also encourage Bishop Blunt of Bradford to write a series of articles condemning the book in the *Sunday Pictorial*.

At the beginning of August, work began on the restoration of St. James's, Piccadilly, which had been wrecked by enemy bombs during the war. The new light fittings which were to be attached to the pews were to annoy architectural historian Dr. Pevsner, who wrote later, 'They are in the spirit of neither Wren nor the Twentieth Century'.

On November 20, the marriage of Princess Elizabeth and Lieutenant Philip Mountbatten took place in Westminster Abbey, presided over by Archbishop Fisher of Canterbury in a white and gold mitre. In his address to the congregation, Dr. Fisher stated that the rite was 'in all essentials exactly the same as it would be for any cottager who might be married this afternoon in some small country church in a remote village in the dales'. The B.B.C. had its cameras outside the abbey but were not permitted to film the ceremony itself.

On December 16, utterances by the Dean of Canterbury, Dr. Hewlett Johnson, during a recent tour of Eastern Europe prompted the Primate to issue a statement that he had 'neither responsibility for what the Dean may say or do, nor power to control it'.

The same month, the Bishop of Chichester, Dr. Bell, was lunching at the Athenaeum Club when he learnt that a number of valuable books from the library of Chichester Cathedral had been put up for sale at Sotheby's by the Dean and Chapter. He rushed to the auction rooms and managed to retrieve ten of the most valuable volumes before the sale took place.

1948   In April 1948 the Ecclesiastical Commissioners were united with Queen Anne's Bounty and renamed the Church Commissioners, their total assets now assessed at over £200 million. The new body was to take over the archiepiscopal estate, pay the archbishop a fixed income and invest the church's assets more boldly than before, adding industrial and commercial investments to the traditional holdings of government bonds and land. This development was soon to provide more cash for needy parish clergy.

Three months later, the Eighth Lambeth Conference opened. Among the 329 bishops present was Bishop Yasiro of Japan who brought with him a heavily embroidered cope as a peace offering to the Primate. For some days this costly garment got held up at the docks but after some confusion the £200 import fee had been generously waived by the Chancellor of the Exchequer so that Dr. Fisher could wear the outfit at the conference's opening service in St. Paul's Cathedral.

On December 29, the death occurred of the eighty-three-year-old Rev. Henry Copinger Hill, Rector of Buxhall in Suffolk. It was claimed that Mr. Hill's ancestors had been rectors of Buxhall in an unbroken line for the last 400 years.

The same month, a home for aged clergy and their wives, or widows, was opened at Worthing.

1949   On February 25, 1949, the curtains and altar furnishing at the Hawksmoor church of St. George-in-the-East in Stepney were vandalized.

Police were simultaneously investigating a case of sacrilege at the church of St. James the Great in Bethnal Green, where pages had been torn from a bible and a crucifix removed from the altar.

Later that spring, a pair of robins was found nesting in a lectern at All Saints Church at Ringsfield in Suffolk and were soon to hatch a family of six. The Rector, the Rev. H. S. Vervells, described this event as 'a trivial but charming incident'.

On Sunday June 19, the 400th anniversary of the authorization of the first Book of Common Prayer was celebrated with services of thanksgiving in churches throughout the country.

On July 19, the Rev. W. H. H. Cooper, Rector of Tockenham in Wiltshire since 1892, celebrated his ninety-ninth birthday. 'I am as good as ever, I have not even considered retiring' said this ancient parson, who could still read without spectacles and remembered hearing Disraeli speak.

The end of the year saw the appointment as Bishop of Exeter of the hockey-playing Dr. Robert Mortimer. He was later described as 'a prince bishop and autocrat of the old school' and unlike his famous predecessor, Dr. Phillpotts, was to defend fox-hunting to the end.

1950   On February 3, 1950, Archbishop Fisher was interrupted while giving evidence before the Royal Commission on Capital Punishment. 'You dare to call yourself a Christian after what you have said?' shouted famous abolitionist Mrs. Van der Elst, 'You are a wicked man!'

Three months later, on May 5, the Dean of Canterbury left for a tour of Canada, during which he was to be assailed with eggs and tomatoes by his political opponents.

On June 1, an appeal was launched on behalf of York Minster, where medieval timbers had been ravaged by the death-watch beetle and the pinnacles of the famous tower were now supported by iron stays. It was noted that the lead-work at this famous church had last been renewed in 1744 and anxiety was expressed about the shortage of skilled stone-masons.

On October 13, the York Convocation briefly discussed the televising of the service of Holy Communion and what steps should be taken to regulate it.

On Christmas Day, the famous historic Stone of Scone was found to be missing from Westminster Abbey where it had lain beneath the Coronation chair for the last 600 years. A gigantic police operation was immediately mounted and for the first time for several centuries the border between England and Scotland was closed. 'This senseless crime has clearly been carefully planned and carried out', said the Dean of Westminster, Dr. Don, in a special broadcast two days later. 'You can imagine my feelings when, early on Christmas morning, the Clerk of the Works rushed into my bedroom and told me the Coronation Stone was missing.' Some three

1951   months later on April 11, 1951, the sacred slab of granite was found on the altar of the ruined abbey of Arbroath in Scotland. 'I am very much relieved. More than that would be improper for me to say', commented the gaunt Dr. Don.

Two months later, on Sunday June 17, the Queen and Princess Margaret attended a service of thanksgiving in St. Paul's Cathedral to celebrate the 250th anniversary of the founding of the Society for the Propagation of the

Gospel. A sermon was preached on this occasion by the Archbishop of Rupert's Land.

On October 4, Prime Minister Attlee and the Leader of the Opposition Winston Churchill interrupted their electioneering to attend a special service at St. Paul's at which Archbishop Fisher urged that the nation's affairs 'should be governed by the true application of the principles of justice and mercy'.

Meanwhile, the seventy-six-year-old Archbishop of York, Dr. Garbett, had left for a four-month visit to Australia and the Pacific.

1952 On February 6, the following year, King George VI, Supreme Governor of the Church of England, died suddenly at Sandringham. Five days later, his coffin was carried from Sandringham Church to strains of 'The King of love my shepherd is' and 'Abide with me' and at the funeral service held later at St. George's Chapel Windsor the hymns included 'The strife is o'er'.

In the weeks that followed, Cardinal Heenan, Roman Catholic Archbishop of Westminster, chided the nation for wrapping itself in 'organized gloom'.

A few months later, another storm erupted over the unpatriotic activities of the Dean of Canterbury, Dr. Hewlett Johnson, who had recently appeared in the Kremlin in the full rig of an Anglican dignitary. On July 14, Conservative M.P. Irene Ward asked the Attorney General if 'this wicked and irresponsible old man' would be prosecuted for treason. In the exchange that followed Labour M.P. Emrys Hughes asked, 'In the event of this witch hunt being successful, will the dean be hung at Tynemouth or Canterbury?'

The following month, Archbishop Fisher visited America again. Stepping from his ship on arrival in New York on August 17, he shouted, 'I am *not* the Red Dean! I repeat, I am *not* the Red Dean!'

1953 Ten months later, on June 2, 1953, the coronation of Queen Elizabeth II in Westminster Abbey was televised from start to finish, providing the B.B.C. with its greatest technical triumph to date. Archbishop Fisher presided over the ceremony, remaining completely at ease throughout but allowing himself one dramatic gesture when he lifted King Edward's crown high into the air before actually crowning the twenty-seven-year-old Queen.

Also participating in this great event was the Archbishop of York, Dr. Garbett, who was still in full command of his faculties at the age of seventy-eight, and was to make a strenuous tour of the West Indies at the end of the year. That Christmas, he was to be found pausing at Government House in Barbados, where he bathed twice in the sea, wearing a pair of pale blue bathing trunks.

1954 On February 17, 1954, the Church Assembly bemoaned the shortage of candidates for ordination. The Bishop of Southwell, Dr. Barry, blamed the shortage on unawareness of the need for new priests and misconceptions about the nature of the ministerial life. The Bishop of Bath and Wells estimated that the church was now losing some 500 men a year, by death or retirement.

Nine days later, the celebrated Dr. Inge, former Dean of St. Paul's, died aged ninety-three at his Berkshire home. 'If I could live my life again I don't think I would be a clergyman', he had declared in a recent interview, 'I know

Archbishop Fisher lifts King Edward's crown high into the air before crowning Queen Elizabeth II

as much about the after-life as you do. I don't even know if there is one – in the sense the Church teaches.'

On June 4, the menace of the death-watch beetle was tackled at a meeting of the Historic Churches Trust in London. The use of gamma radiation was proposed by one speaker, and another, Mr. McKenny Hughes, chief scientific officer of the British Museum urged vicars to clear out 'glory holes' in corners of their crypts and vestries, which encouraged infestation.

Four days later, the Central Council of Bell Ringers passed a unanimous resolution deprecating the installation of recordings of bells in churches. They described this innovation as 'synthetic' and 'unworthy of use in the service of God'.

On December 16, forty-nine Kentish farmers, tenants of the Church Commissioners, met for a high-spirited dinner at a hotel in Canterbury. Toasts to the Commissioners, the biggest agricultural landowners in England, were proposed and Archbishop Fisher described the dinner as 'a family affair'.

1955 On February 6, 1955, Dr. Garbett celebrated his eightieth birthday. The indoor and outdoor staffs at Bishopthorpe Palace combined their resources to present the Archbishop with a luncheon basket.

Meanwhile, the call for new priests had been answered by forty-year-old Antony Bridge, a former professional painter, major in the Buffs and atheist, who was ordained a deacon on June 5, and by twenty-six-year-old

215

David Sheppard, a former England cricket captain, who was ordained a deacon on September 29.

At the end of September the death occurred of eighty-five-year-old Canon Douglas, a former chairman of the House of Clergy at the Church Assembly, whose natty line in white spats had been much admired.

A month later, the romance between Princess Margaret and Group Captain Peter Townsend, the innocent party in a recent divorce case, excited intense speculation and controversy. On October 27, the twenty-five-year-old Princess visited Archbishop Fisher at Lambeth Palace, where she is said to have declared on entering the room, 'Archbishop, you may put your books away.' In answer to Press enquiries, Dr. Fisher's chaplain said afterwards, 'No statement will be made. No information will be given out.'

On October 31, the Princess issued a formal statement that she would not be going ahead with her marriage to the Group Captain. 'Mindful of the church's teaching that Christian marriage is indissoluble and conscious of my duty to the Commonwealth, I have decided to put these considerations before any other', she announced. For the next few days, a hail of vitriolic letters was to descend on Archbishop Fisher, whom many people felt had destroyed the royal romance. For a while there were hostile headlines in the popular press such as 'The Archbishop Must Go' and 'The Archbishop has gone too far'.

On November 2, Fisher made things worse by saying during a television interview with Richard Dimbleby, that he did not care 'two hoots' what people might be saying and any how it probably only represented 'a popular wave of stupid emotionalism'.

The same month, the Church Commissioners did a deal with property tycoon Max Rayne over the development of part of the Paddington estate which the Church had owned since before the Reformation. This enterprise was to produce profits of over £5 million within a few years.

Meanwhile, St. Nicholas's Church, Colchester, had been demolished to make way for a supermarket.

1956 On December 31, the Archbishop of York died suddenly at Bishopthorpe Palace. A few weeks later, it was announced that he would be succeeded by the medieval-looking Dr. Michael Ramsey, Bishop of Durham, and the appointment was duly confirmed on March 16, 1956, in spite of objections from Mr. Kensit, leader of the Protestant Truth Society who claimed that Ramsey had failed to take decisive action in the case of 'illegal practices of a Romish character' at St. Mary's Church, Tyne Dock, South Shields.

On April 6, Dr. Fisher plunged into another controversy when he criticized the proposed introduction of Premium Bonds. In a House of Lords debate he denounced Premium Bonds as 'a second-rate expedient which may attract savings but which adds nothing to the spiritual capital of the nation'.

The following month, the Red Dean of Canterbury attended a reception at Claridge's Hotel in honour of Russian leaders Bulganin and Khruschev, at which he was found engaging in conversation with Mr. Charlie Chaplin.

That autumn, church leaders were split over the Suez Crisis. Bishops Mortimer of Exeter and Harland of Durham supported the Government while Archbishop Fisher took the opposite view and, on November 1, submitted the Lord Chancellor, Lord Kilmuir, to a savage five-minute interrogation in the House of Lords about the government's intervention.

1957   On July 9, 1957, an appeal was launched for the enrichment of the library at Lambeth Palace, originally established on the death of Archbishop Bancroft in 1610 and now housing such curiosities as Mr. Gladstone's private diaries.

Later that summer, the fifty-six-year-old Bishop of Worcester, Dr. Charles-Edwards, set off in flowing purple cassock to tour the villages of his diocese on foot.

In October, the Archbishops of Canterbury and York both responded in their diocesan letters to the publication of the Wolfenden report on Prostitution and Homosexuality. 'In a civilized society', wrote Dr. Fisher, 'all crimes are likely to be sins also but most sins are not, and ought not, to be treated as crimes.' 'Christianity abhors the indulgence of lust, whether by fornication, adultery or homosexuality', declared Dr. Ramsey, 'but morality is not best promoted by giving criminal status to every kind of grievous sin.'

On December 19, St. Bride's Church, Fleet Street, which had now been magnificently restored after being wrecked in the war, was formally re-opened and re-dedicated in the presence of the Queen and Prince Philip.

1958   A few weeks later, on January 29, 1958, Princess Margaret was found lunching with the Rev. Simon Phipps, Chaplain of Trinity College Cambridge. It was revealed that the couple ate tournedos steaks, cauliflower Béarnaise and creamed potatoes accompanied by a bottle of Calon-Ségur, 1949.

Less than a fortnight later, on February 11, a mystery fire broke out at Cuddesdon Palace, historic seat of the Bishops of Oxford built before the Civil War. Some three dozen firemen fought the blaze and water was pumped from the swimming pool of the nearby theological college.

On May 21, the revelation that Archbishop Makarios had been invited to this year's Lambeth Conference was greeted with a storm of protest. An Exeter vicar was quoted as saying that the invitation was 'an outrage on our Christian consciences' and Major-General Sir Edward Spears offered to lend his support to anyone willing to prosecute the Archbishop for murder. A more liberal note was struck by the Bishop of Worcester, Dr. Charles-Edwards, who said that Makarios's presence at the conference would not deter him from attending. 'After all,' he explained, 'if I spent all my time living among the righteous, I would not be doing my job.' In the event, the Cypriot leader announced his inability to attend the gathering and when, in due course, the bishops met, they were able to give their undivided attention to the principles of family planning, the danger of nuclear weapons and other pressing problems.

On October 3, the Bishop of Chichester, Dr. Bell, died leaving vast quantities of papers, files, notebooks, diocesan records and even menu cards of dinners he had attended.

1959   The following March, a row blew up in the Somerset village of Chedzoy over the Vicar's practice of bringing his fourteen-year-old terrier, named Pet, into church. 'I regard all animals as God's creatures and I would never turn any animal out of a church', declared the Rev. Mervyn Bazell. A member of the Parochial Church Council objected and consulted the rural dean and finally the Bishop of Bath and Wells, Dr. Bradfield, who stated later, 'I am advised that there is no ground upon which a parishioner can be restrained from bringing his dog into church.'

Three months later, on June 3, the Rt. Rev. Robert Nelson, suffragan Bishop of Middleton, was found dead in a gas-filled room in a hotel in Craven Street, London W.C.2. 'Why was it', Dr. Greer, Bishop of Manchester, asked later at the crowded memorial service, 'that a man of his goodness and deep devotion was driven to this extremity? We shall never fully understand but I want you to know that he did not do so because of any family or domestic trouble or because of any friction or difficulties over anything connected with his work. He took his own life because of an un-disclosed personal anxiety.'

On October 24, the flamboyant Bishop of Southwark, Dr. Mervyn Stockwood, appealed from his pulpit in Southwark Cathedral for 'young men with sufficient guts' to choose to be vicars in areas like Bermondsey and Camberwell rather than in places like Bournemouth and Cheltenham.

Meanwhile, Archbishop Fisher had appealed for more convenient vicarages. 'We want to ease from the backs of the vicar and his wife the burden of that large but inefficient kitchen, those freezing passages and those awful cellars.'

1960   The following March, following the destruction by fire of the large and ancient home of the Bishops of Oxford, plans for a new bishop's house on the same spot were announced.

On April 17, the Rev. John Collins, Canon of St. Paul's Cathedral, took part in the Ban-the-Bomb march from Aldermaston and addressed a meeting of 60,000 in Trafalgar Square. Also speaking at this gathering was the Bishop of Southwark, Dr. Stockwood, who stated that Canon Collins would 'go down in history as one of the true priests of the church at this time'.

Three months later, on July 16, Archbishop Fisher explained the significance of gaiters to the Canterbury Diocesan Conference. 'One ex-planation is that they are for the restriction of the blood circulation to the legs and I have heard it said that that is why gaitered people suffer from swollen heads. In fact, gaiters are a sign of bondage and nothing else. I myself find them a very comfortable form of bondage. They are not a sign of pride or privilege or pomp or property or anything else.'

At the end of October, the Bishop of Woolwich, Dr. John Robinson, gave evidence in favour of the publication of *Lady Chatterley's Lover*, 'I think neither in intention nor in the effect is the book depraving', he said at the Old Bailey obscenity trial. He was followed into the witness box by the Rev. A. S. Hopkinson, Vicar of St. Katharine Cree, who declared that the book was studded with compassion and human tenderness. 'I would like my children to read it and I like to think they would discuss it with me and with their mother.'

On November 5, the Archbishop of Canterbury said that he thought Dr. Robinson was mistaken in giving evidence in this case. 'The Christian fact is that adultery, whether in fact or in lustful longing, is always a sin and presents a very prominent, even all pervasive sin', he said.

A few days later, on November 22, Dr. Fisher left for the Holy Land. On his return journey, he paused in Rome and made history by visiting the Pope: the first visit by an Archbishop of Canterbury to the Vatican since before the Reformation. 'The whole interview was as friendly and natural and sympathetic as possible', said Fisher afterwards.

Meanwhile, the organ at Westminster Abbey had been repainted in garish red, blue and gilt to the design of the building's Surveyor of Fabric, S. E. Dykes-Bower.

1961 On January 17, 1961, Dr. Fisher, now seventy-three-years-old, tendered his resignation as Archbishop of Canterbury. He was to exchange the Primacy for the post of assistant curate in the small Dorsetshire village of Trent.

A few days later, the venerable-looking Dr. Michael Ramsey, Archbishop of York, was appointed to succeed him. Dr. Ramsey's enthronement took place on June 27 witnessed by 4,000 people in Canterbury Cathedral and several million television viewers. Attired in a cope and mitre of cloth of gold bordered with deep rose pink damask, Dr. Ramsey was welcomed to the cathedral by the eighty-six-year-old 'Red' Dean, Dr. Hewlett Johnson, and later in the service concluded his address with the words, 'Help one another, serve one another, for the times are urgent and the days are evil.'

Two months later the new Primate – whose salary was now £7,500 a year – was found staying with his wife at an inn in Devon. 'We enjoy the quiet, homely atmosphere', he explained, 'I like the food. It's good plain stuff. It suits me. And I like a drop of cider with it. It rounds off the meal.'

The new Archbishop of Canterbury, Dr. Ramsey, with the retiring Archbishop Fisher and the new Archbishop of York, Dr. Coggan

1962   On May 25, 1962, the new Coventry Cathedral which had taken seven years to build and featured disguised under-floor central heating, was consecrated by the Old Etonian Bishop of Coventry, Dr. Cuthbert Bardsley, in the presence of the Queen, Princess Margaret and her husband Lord Snowdon. The occasion was marked by the fainting of the Lord Mayor of Coventry, weighed down by his heavy official robes which contained no pocket in which smelling salts could be hidden.

Five months later, on October 24, the new Archbishop of York, Dr. Donald Coggan, told a meeting of the Mothers Union in London that he hoped parents would revive the practice of saying grace at meals.

The following month, the Rev. Thomas Watson described his rectory at Quarnford in the Peak District as the coldest house in England. 'It is impossible to keep warm', he complained. 'When the wind blows, the floor covering billows up. When I sit at my desk, my hands are too cold to write. The Church Dilapidations Board carried out some repairs but they have not been effective.' Mr. Watson declared his intention of moving to a council house thrity miles away. 'I have no comment to make on this', said the Bishop of Stafford, Dr. Clitheroe.

1963   The following spring, a storm broke over the publication of *Honest to God* by the Bishop of Woolwich, Dr. John Robinson, which questioned many of the foundations of traditional Christianity, including the idea of a personal God. On Sunday March 31, Archbishop Ramsey went onto television to attack the book. 'It is utterly wrong and misleading to denounce the imagery of God held by Christian men and women', he declared. A few weeks later, on May 7, preaching in St. Margaret's Westminster at the opening of the Canterbury Convocation, he repeated that the book had done 'much damage'.

On May 15, Archbishop and Mrs. Ramsey were among guests at a state banquet at Buckingham Palace in honour of the King and Queen of the Belgians.

At the end of that month, the retirement of the 'Red' Dean of Canterbury was announced. Eighty-nine-year-old Dr. Hewlett Johnson was to move out of the historic deanery where he had lived for the last thirty-two years into a new home in the town, which he was to re-name 'The Red House'. He was succeeded as Dean by the Ven. Ian White-Thomson whose recreations included walking and golf.

A few days later, the country was rocked by the Profumo scandal. Among churchmen who felt moved to comment on this affair was the Bishop of Carlisle, Dr. Bloomer, who issued a statement on June 14, in which he declared that the scandal was 'but a symptom of the general moral deterioration in this country in which we all share'.

Two days earlier, the Bishop of Ely, Dr. Hudson, had called for better bishops at his Diocesan Conference and accused the laity of 'still living in the Victorian era'.

On October 30, a man appeared at Stafford Assizes accused of falsely pretending to be in Holy Orders and conducting a wedding at Oldberrow Church in Warwickshire according to the rites of the Church of England and dressed in a cassock and clerical collar hired from a theatrical costumiers. He was found guilty of the offence but fined only £50 with 25 guineas costs.

A week later, on November 6, three workmen were inadvertently locked inside the thirteenth-century Lincoln Cathedral. In order to draw attention to their plight they rang the cathedral's five and a half ton Big Tom bell, usually used only to announce the death of prominent persons. The cathedral's surveyor, Mr. Higgins, rushed to the building to release them.

1964   Early in the New Year, Archbishop Ramsey denounced hare-coursing as cruel and offered to support the League against Cruel Sports in their campaign to get the practice made illegal.

A few days later, on January 17, a 75,000 word report written by sociologist Leslie Paul was published calling for sweeping changes in the church. In addition to attacking the ancient system of patronage, the report urged that there should be a restriction on the length of time bishops and vicars should hold office.

On May 11, the cleaning of St. Paul's Cathedral began. It was stated that this immense operation would be done by pure 'elbow grease' and the cleaning of the drum of the dome alone would cost £40,000.

The same day, ninety-year-old ex-Dean of Canterbury, Dr. Hewlett Johnson and his wife, Nowell, flew to China where they were welcomed at Peking airport by Premier Chou-en-lai. During their visit, they were to visit silk factories and medicinal baths and have talks with Bishop K. H. Ting, head of the Holy Catholic Church of China.

Meanwhile, back in England, a new fashion for top-less dresses was being flaunted and, on June 30, Archbishop Ramsey was asked for his comments on this development. 'We must just accept that young people express themselves in new methods of dress that may seem queer to the older of us', he replied. 'We must accept the fact and get alongside them and understand them.'

A month later, on July 31, the Church Vestments Bill which made permissible a wide variety of vestments already in common use, received the Royal Assent. Archbishop Ramsey dismissed suggestions that the Church of England was trying to assimilate the Church of Rome as 'scandalous or silly'.

On August 7, it was announced that Canon Collins was to serve on a committee pressing for the reduction of the thirty year gaol sentences recently passed on the Great Train Robbers.

1965   On January 30, 1965, Archbishop Ramsey officiated at the State Funeral of Sir Winston Churchill in St. Paul's Cathedral dressed in a white linen mitre and black wool cope, with velvet on the front and hood. His domestic chaplain, the Rev. J. Andrew, carried the gold cross of Canterbury originally presented to Archbishop Benson in 1889, and the Bishop of London, Dr. Stopford, wore a black damask cope trimmed with silver.

Five months later, a row erupted at St. Augustine's Church, Guildford over the Rev. John Growns' refusal to baptize a child whose parents and god-parents were not practising Christians. 'If they do not worship regularly, it is effrontery', he declared.

A week later, on June 19, the Archbishop of York, Dr. Coggan, told the Liverpool Diocesan Conference that he was becoming 'a little tired of the washing of Anglican dirty linen in public.'

In October, the Archbishop of Canterbury, Dr. Ramsey, caused offence when he spoke of the Rhodesia crisis at a meeting of the British Council of

Churches. 'If the British government thought it practical to use force for the protection of the rights of the Rhodesian people then I think, as Christians, we have to say that it would be right to use force to that end.' This statement drew hostile comments from the Press and there was talk of a motion of censure in the House of Commons.

Meanwhile, church leaders had been working on an alternative set of services in modern English and on December 15 the House of Lords agreed that the Prayer Book Measure sanctioning their use in churches should be presented for the Royal Assent.

On December 28, the Queen and twelve members of the royal family attended a service to celebrate the 900th anniversary of the consecration of Westminster Abbey by Edward the Confessor. In his address on this occasion, the Dean of Westminster, Dr. Eric Abbott, urged that 'the enmities and animosities of the 900 years' should lie buried and that there should be 'a resurrection of the divided Christians in the one body of the undivided Lord'.

1966 On February 25, 1966, it was revealed that the Rev. John Hencher, bachelor Vicar of Amblecote near Stourbridge, had appealed in the *Worcester Diocesan Messenger* for a wife to share his fifteen-room vicarage. 'I would like a nice cosy wife', he wrote. 'If anyone would like to take me on, I'd be glad to hear from them. She must adore Shakespeare and be prepared to sleep in a four poster bed.' Immediately inundated with callers, the Vicar fled to a secret address and later admitted that he had behaved foolishly and did not wish to obtain a wife in this manner.

Four months later, on June 16, Archbishop Ramsey spoke in the House of Lords in favour of Lord Arran's bill to ease penalties for homosexuals and lamented the long delays in the bill's passage.

On September 9, the Rector of Manton in Rutland, the Rev. A. Gracie, warned teenagers against 'cuddling' in his church which conduct he described as 'deplorable'.

On September 23, work began on the building of an underground church at Heathrow Airport, for the use of Anglican, Roman Catholic and Free Churches.

The same month, the Church Missionary Society was moving from its

The silver teapot used in the eighteenth century by the members of **The Eclectic** Society. It is now the property of the Church Missionary Society

premises in Salisbury Square, which it had occupied for the past 100 years, to new quarters near the Old Vic. Among the 40,000 objects and souvenirs being transported was the silver tea-pot used by the early members of the Eclectic Society at the end of the eighteenth century.

On November 3, the General Manager of the Ecclesiastical Insurance Office revealed that some ten churches a week were being looted.

Meanwhile, the Commission on Women and Holy Orders had been sitting, presided over by the Bishop of Chester, Dr. Ellison. On December 15, its report was published, giving no clear cut line on the matter though Dr. Ellison stated that admitting women to Holy Orders at this time would be 'divisive'. Among those dismayed by the Commission's caution was the Rev. Joseph McCulloch, Rector of St. Mary-le-Bow, who wrote a letter to *The*
1967 *Times*, published on January 2, 1967, in which he stated 'Alas, Elizabeth I, not Elizabeth II, is the dominant influence over the minds of English ecclesiastics'. Some three weeks later, on January 22, the Bishop of Southwark, Dr. Mervyn Stockwood, declared that the issue was a lost cause. 'To fight a long battle to get women admitted to the priesthood and then to find that only an infinitesimally small number of them want to be ordained would be bad in these days when there are so many causes that one can fight for, causes that have a chance of being victorious.'

On April 22, Archbishop Ramsey gave a banquet at Lambeth Palace to celebrate the golden wedding of Lord and Lady Fisher.

On June 21, the elderly Field Marshal Montgomery read the lesson at a memorial service in the Guards Chapel for the late Dean of Ripon, the Ven. F. L. Hughes, who had served as senior chaplain to the Eighth Army during the last war.

On July 26, four days after Lord Arran's bill permitting homosexual acts between consenting adults had passed through the House of Lords, Canon Hugh Montefiore caused an uproar by suggesting at a conference at Oxford that Christ might have been homosexual. The suggestion drew an immediate rebuke from Archbishop Ramsey, 'There is no evidence whatsoever to support Canon Montefiore's reported ideas', he declared, 'Christians believe that Christ's dealings with both men and women were those of a perfect man.'

1968 Six months later, in January there was a storm of protest over the opening of a licensed bar in the crypt of St. Mary's Church, Woolwich. On January 24, 1968, Sir Cyril Black, leader of the Temperance group of M.P.s, announced that he would complain to the Archbishop of Canterbury over the undesirability of granting a drink licence to consecrated premises.

The same month, the Rev. Patrick Tracey, Vicar of Edlesborough near Dunstable, spoke of the damage done to unique and priceless monuments by brass-rubbers. Mr. Tracey complained that these enthusiasts often used graphite pencils and other abrasive materials, smoked cigarettes and listened to pop music while pursuing their hobby.

On February 8, the Bishop of Exeter, Dr. Mortimer, urged the House of Lords to withdraw the new Street Offences Bill, which would impose fresh penalties for loitering for an immoral purpose. 'From such observations as I have been able to make I am inclined to think this nuisance is greatly exaggerated', he said.

On March 20, it was announced that the over-worked Archbishop of York, Dr. Coggan, had cancelled all his engagements and retired to bed at Bishopthorpe Palace. 'He is not ill', said a spokesman, 'it is more a case of being one degree under.'

On April 20, Conservative M.P. Enoch Powell delivered a strongly worded speech on immigration, which caused a public outcry. The following day, Mr. Powell attended a service of Holy Communion at St. Peter's Church, Wolverhampton.

Three months later, on July 25, the Tenth Lambeth Conference opened in the midst of a controversy over a glossy brochure issued to bishops, which included a list of places for them to eat in London. 'This was a major public relations brick. An absolute clanger,' declared Dr. Trevor Huddleston, who had recently been driven out of South Africa after displeasing the authorities with his remarks on apartheid.

A few days later the 460 bishops attending the Conference won back some good will by going without their lunch and contributing the money they would have spent to War on Want.

On November 16, the Vicar of Emmanuel Church, West Hampstead, the Rev. J. Dover-Wellman, chased an intruder out of the vicarage with a sword and effected his arrest. 'I cannot think what Merrie England is coming to', said his wife.

1969   On January 22, 1969, there were dramatic scenes at St. Paul's Cathedral when the Archbishop of Canterbury Dr. Ramsey welcomed Roman Catholic leader Cardinal Heenan to a special unity service. The ceremony was interrupted by jeers and catcalls and when the Cardinal ascended the pulpit a man shouted 'You are the representative of the Anti-christ!' Some fifty people were ejected from the building while, outside, eggs and tomatoes were hurled at extreme protestant leader the Rev. Ian Paisley, who had flown in from Northern Ireland with a band of supporters.

Earlier that day, Dr. Ramsey had given a sedate luncheon for members of the press at Lambeth Palace.

Four months later, on May 21, hecklers broke up a meeting in Church House when Dr. Trevor Huddleston, Bishop of Stepney, spoke on racialism as a major obstacle to world community.

The same day, Dr. Ramsey clashed with the leader of the British Black Power Party, Mr. Roy Sawh, at a meeting in Notting Hill. After being stopped speaking by the Archbishop, Mr. Sawh walked out. Dr. Ramsey apologized afterwards for his handling of 'this little episode'.

On June 6, it was announced that the church's recruitment officer, the Rev. Colin Semper, was to attempt to attract more candidates for ordination by using a mobile van, which would tour county shows, diocesan conferences, career conventions, universities and schools.

On October 22, the Archbishop of York, Dr. Coggan, attacked the recent Sunday paper serialization of Miss Christine Keeler's memoirs and urged the country to return to the values of Christ.

Meanwhile, the Archbishop of Canterbury, Dr. Ramsey, had begun sitting for his portrait by artist Guy Roddon. He was to drive to and from the artist's Chelsea studio in a chauffeur-driven Morris Minor, with which he had replaced his predecessor's Daimler.

On January 25, 1970, it was announced that Dr. Coggan had appointed a management consultant, the dynamic thirty-six-year-old John Adair, to look into the workings of his see. 'I think everybody is thrilled that at long last this has happened', commented the Bishop of Whitby, Dr. Snow.

A few weeks later, on February 4, the Rev. Robert Runcie, a former Guards officer who had been awarded the M.C. for an act of bravery in the last war, was consecrated Bishop of St. Albans in a ceremony in Westminster Abbey.

On Maundy Thursday, the Bishop of Southwark, Dr. Mervyn Stockwood washed the feet of a coloured man in his diocese. The experience caused him to reflect later on B.B.C. radio that Christ was 'probably coloured'.

On June 26, it was announced that the Church Commissioners had sold the freehold of the Adelphi building, on the site of the former palace of the Bishops of Durham, between the Strand and the River Thames, for an estimated £8 million.

On July 13, much publicity attended the sacking of the Primate's press secretary, Mr. Michael De-la-Noy, who had annoyed the authorities by writing articles on sex in *Forum* and *New Society*. 'It was my decision to dismiss him not the Archbishop's', said the church's chief information officer Major-General Adam Block.

Four days later, the Marquess of Anglesey, president of the Friends of Friendless Churches Society, spoke of the new fashion for turning redundant churches into homes. 'Baths in the belfries may be very well but kitchens in the choir and nurseries in the nave are less acceptable', he declared.

On November 9, it was announced that the Rev. Ronald Stephens, fifty-seven-year-old vicar of Stanstead Abbots in Hertfordshire, had agreed to appear in a TV commercial for Blue Band margarine. 'I expect a lot of people will criticize me', said Mr. Stephens, explaining that he had only agreed to promote the margarine concerned if he was allowed to write his own script and incorporate in the forty-five second commercial a short plug for God. 'Never before has a clergyman appeared in a TV commercial', said a spokesman for the advertising agency involved. 'We believe it could be a very good thing.' 'Of course I would not have agreed to the commercial if I did not believe completely in the product', added the Vicar.*

On December 26, the death of the elderly Dr. Montgomery Campbell, a former Bishop of London, was attributed to the power crisis which had recently hit the country.

Six days later, on January 1, 1971, Archbishop Ramsey stated that England was in a mess. He referred specifically to the state of crime, violence, broken marriages, industrial disruption, blasphemy and obscenity, and explained,' 'The heart of our trouble is that a nation which ignores God loses sight of him, and to lose sight of him is to be in a fog.'

Meanwhile, the Rev. Cyril Carter, Vicar of Hounslow, had been making a film on Adam and Eve in which two teenagers were to appear nude. 'We have been very careful with what shots we show', he said on January 8, 'and what is out of focus'.

* In November 1919, Jesuit priest Father Bernard Vaughan had appeared in a press advertisement for Sanatogen tonic wine. 'It promises when you are run down to pick you up. It does so.'

Four months later, on Sunday May 16, 2,500 people watched the Rt. Rev. Kenneth Sansbury, assistant bishop in the diocese of London, eat a symbolic meal of grass in Trafalgar Square. This curious event marked the beginning of Christian Aid Week and was designed to draw attention to the needs of a hungry world.

On July 28, the Archbishop of Canterbury and Mrs. Ramsey were taken by an admiral's barge from Lambeth to dine at the Royal Naval College at Greenwich.

October 1 saw the official closure of Tyndale Hall, Bristol, and three other theological colleges, which were no longer required owing to the shortage of men entering the ministry.

Eleven days later, Archbishop Coggan spoke at the York Convocation on the 'torturing' problem of the remarrying of divorced people in church. 'When a parish priest asks me if he can marry a divorced person I am often tempted to say "go ahead" and make an exception. But in fact I have never done this and always say "no" because I want to bear witness to the church's belief in the life-long existence of marriages.'

1972   The following February, details were released of the new 'cassock alb' dreamed up by the church's working party on vestments. This all purpose garment, costing £15, combined cassock, alb and surplice and dispensed with the need for amice and girdle. It was to be made of cream-coloured, crease-resistant rayon twist weave and was lined in satin with a detachable, washable linen neck-liner.

On Tuesday May 30, the four and a half ton state bell of St. Paul's Cathedral was tolled in honour of the Duke of Windsor, who had died two days earlier in Paris.

On June 5, the funeral of the ex-King took place in St. George's Chapel, Windsor, conducted by the Dean of Windsor, Dr. Launcelot Fleming. Archbishop Ramsey pronounced a blessing and the service ended with the great nineteenth-century hymn 'Lead us, heavenly father, lead us'.

Early the following month, the Bishop of Southwark, Dr. Mervyn Stockwood attacked the synodical government of the Church of England in his diocesan letter. 'I regard it as a disaster, a playground for bureaucrats or bores', he wrote. 'Worse still is the time wasted on endless chatter and the money wasted on cascades of memoranda and minutes, stamps, envelopes and secretarial expenses. The older I get the less I find myself interested in ecclesiastical affairs.'

A few days later, Dr. Stockwood, appeared at a Church of England experimental weekend session wearing a floral tie and coloured shirt.

On August 9, the musical *Jesus Christ Superstar* opened at the Palace Theatre in Shaftesbury Avenue, amidst protests from a group of nuns from the Evangelical Sisterhood of Mary.

On September 1, Bishop Trevor Huddleston opened an exhibition of paintings by former Communist shop steward Jack Dash in a church in South London. The show included a portrait of Christ entitled *The First Socialist*.

1973   On January 4, 1973, fourteen younger clergy, who had resolved to sample life as down-and-outs, were turned out on the streets of London with only fifty pence each on which to survive for the next forty hours.

On March 2, Archbishop Ramsey welcomed the 'Jesus Freaks' as a genuine religious movement of the young. 'The established church has something to learn about their enthusiasm for Jesus', he said.

On April 17, Archbishop Coggan stated on B.B.C. radio that many Anglican clergymen were homosexual. 'They put up a tremendous fight against being practising homosexuals', he added. 'When they give in we must treat them with great sympathy and understanding, remembering of course that they are in a position of great responsibility having under their care a lot of youngsters'.

A fortnight later, on May 1, Dr. John Habgood, one of a new breed of Old Etonian churchmen, was consecrated Bishop of Durham. He was to move into the historic Auckland Castle in County Durham where some fifty-seven Bishops of Durham had lived before him. This house was situated on the edge of an 800-acre park and possessed a huge kitchen garden in which Dr. Habgood's gardener was soon to produce forty-four different kinds of vegetable.

On May 15, Dr. Gerald Ellison, Bishop of Chester and former rowing Blue, was elevated to the vacant see of London, amidst protests from leading churchmen in the diocese that they had not been consulted about the appointment.

Meanwhile, a massive repair and renewal programme, for which several million pounds had been raised, was in full swing at St. Paul's Cathedral. In September, architectural sculptor Kenneth Gardner was found working on a cherub's face for the south portico of the building, which had become badly decayed, affected by both weather and industrial pollution.

On October 3, Dr. Coggan criticized the abortion system at a meeting of the Shaftesbury Society. He said that abortion led to 'an appalling trivialization of the act of procreation'.

On November 14, following the marriage of Princess Anne and Captain Mark Phillips, at which the bride had promised to 'obey' her husband, Archbishop Ramsey and the Dean of Westminster, Dr. Eric Abbott, were among the select few who were invited to a wedding breakfast at Buckingham Palace, where the menu included partridges 'set about with mushrooms'.

Meanwhile, the church of St. Mary's, Paddington Green, had been sumptuously restored at the cost of £100,000. This tiny church now featured marble flooring, new box pews, and fine Georgian-style fixtures and fittings. This Christmas, the Vicar, the Rev. Thomas Foster, justified the expenditure by quoting from St. Matthew's gospel, 'Man does not live by bread alone'.

1974   On February 27, the following year, the row over the sale of church treasures was accelerated when the Duke of Devonshire bought back two lots of church plate at Christie's which an eighteenth-century ancestor of his had originally presented to St. Mary's Church, Oxted in Surrey.

A few weeks later, on April 7, Holy Trinity Church at Bingley in Yorkshire, designed by Norman Shaw in the 1860s, was blown up with dynamite following the discovery that its foundations were unsound.

On May 14, it was announced that Dr. Donald Coggan, who had a Double First in oriental languages, would replace the retiring Dr. Ramsey as

Archbishop of Canterbury. It was revealed later that Dr. Coggan had spent four days thinking over the matter, and had also undergone a complete medical check-up, before accepting Prime Minister Harold Wilson's offer. 'The Prime Minister wanted the answer earlier but I wanted time to say my prayers and talk to my wife,' he said.

The day after his appointment to this high office was announced, Dr. Coggan stated on the 'World at One' radio programme, 'There is a lot to be said for the Ten Commandments.'

Archbishop Ramsey struggles out of the well-kept Morris Minor, with which he replaced the official limousines used by his predecessors

In November this year, Archbishop Ramsey's furniture and personal effects were sold for £10,000, half of which sum he was to give to Christian Aid. 'We are delighted with this very characteristic gesture', said the charity's director. 'Many would have regarded the proceeds of such a sale as a means to ease the burdens of retirement.'

1975   On January 24, 1975, Mrs. Coggan had her handbag searched as she entered Canterbury Cathedral for her husband's enthronement as new Primate. This great ceremony was also attended by the Prince of Wales, Princess Margaret and the Duchess of Kent, who arrived in an aircraft of the Queen's Flight, and by the gardeners and household staff of Dr. Coggan's previous residence, Bishopthorpe Palace, who arrived on board a special train from Victoria. In his address to the congregation, Dr. Coggan, who wore a gold mitre, gold and red cope and his distinctive heavy-lensed, frameless spectacles, spoke highly of the modern priesthood. 'There is no finer life than that of a parish priest. Covet this calling. Train for it. Pour your best into it. Count yourself thrice-blessed if you hear God calling you to it.'

Ten days later, Dr. Coggan's call for a renewal of patriotism in his address to the General Synod of the Church of England was bitterly attacked by Enoch Powell, M.P., who spoke of the new Primate's 'economic errors' and described parts of the address as 'dangerous nonsense'.

On March 29, the Rev. Joseph McCulloch, Rector of St. Mary-le-Bow in Cheapside, contributed an article to *The Times* entitled 'Is the day of the parish priest drawing to a close?' in which he argued that the church must rediscover the missionary zeal of the Early Christians.

On May 14, a group of sixty-five academics including the Bishop of St. Albans, Dr. Runcie, wrote an open letter to the Archbishops of Canterbury and York, begging them to disown exorcism, which they argued was a step back to the Middle Ages. 'It is very dangerous', they wrote, 'to give encouragement to the belief that there are occult evil powers which may possess men and deprive them of their normal moral responsibilities.'

Five months later, on October 15, Dr. Coggan launched his Call to the Nation to renew its sense of moral purpose, at a crowded press conference at Lambeth Palace. 'Guzzling does not satisfy. Grabbing and getting is a poor creed. Envy is a cancer', he declared. The press conference was followed by seven radio and television appearances.

Within a week, some 10,000 letters of support had reached Lambeth Palace though leading churchmen were by no means unanimous in approving of the Call. Dr. Stockwood, Bishop of Southwark, attacked the Primate in an article in the *Morning Star* while a group of Anglo-Catholic clergy issued a statement that Dr. Coggan had shown 'a most appalling failure' to understand the position of families under economic stress at a time of high unemployment.

Meanwhile, Dr. Ellison, the first Bishop of London not to reside at Fulham Palace for over 900 years, had complained that the house provided for him in Cowley Street, Westminster, was too small. Early in November, the General Synod agreed that the Bishop should move to larger quarters in nearby Barton Street.

On November 15, Archbishop Coggan's first class flight to Nairobi, where he was to attend the assembly of the World Council of Churches, drew critical comments from the press but was defended by Kenneth Slack, British Director of Christian Aid, who stated, 'The Archbishop is no longer a young man. There are laid on him immense responsibilities and an appalling workload. Any business which did not care for the comfort of one of whom it had asked so much would rightly be condemned. Is it not decent for the Christian church to see that a hard-worked leader travels comfortably?'

A few days later, Dr. Coggan's car got stuck in a dried-up river bed in the Ngorongoro game park and natives were enlisted to help rescue it.

1976   On January 11, 1976, the Dean of Manchester, the Ven. Alfred Jowett, said that the church should throw out some of its hymns, mostly nineteenth-century ones, because they were 'misleading, dangerous and bad for today'.

Two months later, on March 6, the Cod War broke out. In the weeks that followed naval chaplain, the Rev. William Ernest Weldon, was to conduct twenty-one religious services in Icelandic waters, travelling from ship to ship by helicopter, motor dinghy and jackstay.

Meanwhile the marriage between Princess Margaret and Lord Snowdon had foundered. On March 16, the Queen telephoned Archbishop Coggan, currently on a tour of the West Indies, about a possible separation. The official announcement followed three days later and Dr. Coggan, who was said to have heard the news with 'great regret' put out a statement via his press secretary in London that he hoped 'every understanding would be shown to the royal family at this time of distress'.

The following month, the Rev. Peter Elers, Vicar of Thaxted in Essex, was elected president of the newly formed Gay Christian Movement. The Bishop of Chelmsford, the Rt. Rev. John Trillo, who received many vindictive letters concerning Mr. Elers' acceptance of this position, gave him public support.

In July, it was announced that Dr. Vernon Nicholls, Bishop of Sodor and Man and a staunch supporter of birching on the island, had sold his ancient and rambling official residence, Bishop's Court, to the Manx government because it was too large to live in.

On September 2, Mrs. Coggan gave a tea party to launch her biography by Anne Arnott. On this occasion, canvas-seated, stackable steel chairs were brought into the Lambeth Palace sitting-room to supplement the usual chairs and sofas and journalists were offered short-cake, lemon iced sponge cake and dainty watercress sandwiches. 'I don't actually do the catering', said Mrs. Coggan, 'but I do discuss things pretty closely with the cook.'

A few weeks later, the controversial Rev. Peter Elers conducted a service of blessing for two lesbian couples at his church in Essex. The Bishops of Chelmsford and Colchester subsequently issued a joint statement condemning this event. 'We entirely dissociate ourselves from this action', they said, 'Mr. Elers has given us a solemn undertaking not to conduct such a service in the future.'

On December 22, the Bishop of Durham, Dr. Habgood, spoke in the House of Lords on the nuclear energy programme, urging that great caution should be used in its development.

1977   On January 31, 1977, Dr. Coggan revealed that the number of men presenting themselves for ordination the previous year was the lowest on record. 'If these low figures continue', he said, 'the church will face a manpower shortage of considerable magnitude.'

The following month, *Vogue* revealed that the larder of the Bishop of Woolwich, forty-year-old Michael Marshall, was stocked with Cadbury's instant dried skimmed milk, Bird's custard powder, tinned salmon and other convenience foods.

On June 7, the Queen's Silver Jubilee was celebrated with a great service of thanksgiving in St. Paul's Cathedral. As the monarch was escorted up the central aisle, the congregation sang 'All people that on earth do dwell' and, later in the service, Archbishop Coggan gave an address in which he compared the monarchy to a house built on firm foundations. 'It is something at the heart of our national life of incalculable value – a spirit of devotion to duty and of service to others which has found its focus in a family and in a person.'

Two days later, the Queen took tea at Lambeth Palace with Archbishop and Mrs. Coggan.

The same month, Northumbrian Vicar, the Rev. Peter Haywood, suggested that the church could help itself out of its current financial difficulties by selling unwanted gravestones to the Americans.

Four months later, on October 15, the Rev. Terry Spong, assistant Anglican chaplain at Brixton Prison, announced that he was a member of the extreme right wing National Front party. 'I am appalled at what has happened to the country of my birth', he declared, adding, 'There is no clash between my Christian views and those of the National Front.' In the uproar that followed, Mr. Spong resigned his job at the prison and the National Front's chairman John Tyndall accused Britain's clergy of 'joining the ranks of race-traitors and professional do-gooders'.

This Christmas, Dr. Coggan spoke in his sermon in Canterbury Cathedral of the 'almost sadistic flaunting' of declining church attendance figures. 'I sometimes wonder whether I can detect a death wish in the way these figures are being used.'

1978   On March 13, 1978, it was announced that the young Bishop of Woolwich, Michael Marshall was to leave his smart official residence in the suburbs and live in a commune in Lewisham High Street. 'There has got to be more to this job than a comfortable life drinking tea and eating cucumber sandwiches,' he explained.

A few weeks later, the Bishop of Truro, Dr. Graham Leonard, caused offence by making certain remarks about Princess Margaret and her friend Roddy Llewellyn. On April 3, the Bishop felt obliged to issue a statement calling for 'compassion and understanding' for the Queen's sister.

On Sunday July 23, some 400 bishops gathered in London for the eleventh Lambeth Conference. In his sermon at the opening ceremony in Canterbury Cathedral, Dr. Coggan stated that some bishops had 'almost stopped believing God still speaks to the church'. Later, he tried to define his own role as Primate. 'It is not of the genius of Anglicanism to have someone at its head who is papal or patriarchal,' he explained.

The bishops' wives were later separated from their husbands, lodging in a teachers' training college near Canterbury under the care of Mrs. Coggan.

Four months later, on November 8, the General Synod again rejected a motion in favour of the ordination of women. When the result of the voting was announced, women in the gallery at Church House shouted, 'We asked for bread and you gave us a stone'. The leader of the demonstration, Dr. Una Kroll, afterwards accused the church of, 'listening to the fears and prejudices of a vociferous minority'.

On November 27, Archbishop Coggan launched an anti-litter campaign at Canterbury by pushing a dust-cart through the streets.

1979   The following February, a Court of Inquiry was established to look into an alleged breakdown in the relationship between the Rev. Kenneth Flenley, Vicar of Bathford, and his flock. It was stated that the Rev. Kenneth Flenley's relationship with the widow of an R.A.F. pilot had upset certain parishioners. The inquiry dragged on until the end of April and, in spite of evidence in Mr. Flenley's favour by many of his parishioners, ended with his dismissal after twenty-eight years as vicar.

On Sunday, April 28, the Bishop of Bath and Wells, Dr. Bickersteth, visited the troubled parish and conducted a communion service. 'I am sure you will all pull together and help the church go forward', he said.

On June 5, the sixty-nine-year-old Dr. Coggan announced his resignation as Archbishop of Canterbury at a crowded press conference at Church House. Following his surprise statement, he drove back to Lambeth Palace in his official blue Morris Minor motor-car.

On July 1, a special service was held in the eleventh-century church at Bratton Fleming in Devonshire to celebrate the acquittal of former Liberal leader Jeremy Thorpe on a charge of incitement to murder. 'The darkness is now past and the true light shines', said the portly Rev. John Hornby in his address to the congregation. 'This is the day which the Lord hath made.' The Bishop of Exeter, Dover Grammar School educated Eric Mercer, was said to be unhappy about the publicity surrounding the service.

The following month, the former Bishop of Peterborough, eighty-two-year-old Dr. Cyril Eastaugh, confessed in a woman's magazine that one of his most agreeable fanatasies was 'to imagine that some kind benefactor had left me the contents of his, or her, wine cellar'. He went on to enthuse about the Premier Grand Crus, good white burgundies and the ports of 1955, 1960 and 1963.

On August 7, a storm broke out in the Lincolnshire village of Brant Broughton over a decision by the Rector, the Rev. Robin Clark, to kill a sparrow which had got into his church disturbing a guitar recital. 'I am not the devil incarnate as people are trying to suggest', said Mr. Clark, 'I am a man of God and I love animals:' The Bishop of Lincoln, the Rt. Rev. Simon Phipps, was on holiday at the time but stated later that Mr. Clark had his 'complete confidence and support'.

On September 7, it was announced that the fifty-seven-year-old Dr. Robert Runcie, Bishop of St. Albans, pig-breeder and former war hero, was to be next Archbishop of Canterbury. 'I was genuinely astonished when I was told of the choice', he said. 'The Church of England is a lovable and in-furiating body.I hope I shall not be buried by memos and papers. One of my chief fears is of being a platitude machine.' Later Mrs. Runcie spoke of her apprehension about moving into Lambeth Palace. 'Do you realize that our bedroom there is the size of most people's council house?'

A few days after the announcement, the clergy working party of the Association of Scientific, Technical and Managerial Staffs, wrote to the archbishop-designate asking him to look into the existence of the 'Green List', a top secret file of scandalous clergymen barred from holding office or ministering in the Church of England.

On Sunday September 16, members of the Hunt Saboteurs Association disrupted a service at Preston in Lancashire where the Rector, Canon Roland Meredith, was said to be a keen follower of the local Bleasdale Hounds. 'I think this kind of interruption of divine service is deplorable', he said.

The following night, the retiring Primate Dr. Coggan gave a dinner at Lambeth Palace in honour of the Lord Mayor of London.

On September 25, half an acre of church land at Lymington in Hampshire was sold to developers for £210,000. The local Vicar, Canon E. J. C.

Dr. Robert Runcie proceeds down the nave of Canterbury Cathedral following his enthronement as 102nd Archbishop of Canterbury

Haselden, described the transaction as 'most satisfactory' and stated that some of the money would be used to build a new church hall.

Six weeks later, on November 6, a massive petition defending Cranmer's Book of Common Prayer against the new modernized liturgy first introduced in 1965, was presented to the Church's General Synod. Signatories included twenty-eight Privy Councillors, six Knights of the Garter and the masters of music in many English cathedrals. 'The liturgy is a national possession', stated the organizer Professor David Martin. 'It belongs to the people in the same way as Salisbury Cathedral.'

1980   On January 11, 1980, the Rev. Peter Sutton, Vicar of Bradworthy in North Devon, advertised in the *Church Times* for a parson's hard hat or 'Traveller', size seven and five-eighths.

Two days later, in a television interview, Lord Chancellor Hailsham criticized clergy who tried to meddle in politics. 'Parsons who try to tell you what the Prime Minister should or should not do are talking about something they don't begin to understand', he said.

At the end of the following month, the deep-rooted patronage system of appointing clergy was once again discussed by the General Synod. Miss Christian Howard stated that the present system 'looks very much like jobs for the boys. I'm sorry, but it does!'

A few weeks later, on March 25, Dr. Robert Runcie was enthroned as Archbishop of Canterbury. Dressed in a cope and mitre of vivid yellow silk adorned with amethyst bugle beads and jap gold, he told the 2,000 people present in Canterbury Cathedral, 'The Church must live now as Jesus Christ would live now. Like Isaiah of old, we must begin by admitting that we have fallen short of the vision which is given to us.'

SELECTED BIBLIOGRAPHY

Addison, W., *Worthy Doctor Fuller*, 1951

Andrews, W., *Old Church Life*, 1899

Arnott, A., *Wife to the Archbishop: the life story of Jean Coggan*, 1976

Ashwell, A. R. and Wilberforce, R. eds., *The Life of the Rt. Rev. Samuel Wilber-force*, 1880–3

Baring-Gould, S., *The Vicar of Morwenstow*, 1876

Baskerville, G., *English Monks and the Suppression of the Monasteries*, 1937

Bax, B. A., *The English Parsonage*, 1964

Begbie, H., *Painted Windows*, 1922

Bell, G., *Randall Davidson, Archbishop of Canterbury*, 1935

Bentley, J., *Ritualism and Politics in Victorian Britain*, 1978

Benson, E. F., *As We Were*, 1932

Beresford, J., *Gossip of the 17th and 18th Centuries*, 1923

Binney, M. and Burman, P., *Change and Decay: The Future of our Church*, 1977

Blunt, W., *The Use and Abuse of Church Bells*, 1846

Bouch, C. M. L., *Prelates and People of the Lake Counties*, 1948

Carpenter, E., *Cantuar: The Archbishops in Office*, 1971

Chadwick, O., *Victorian Miniature*, 1960

Chesney, K., *The Victorian Underworld*, 1970

Church Times

Colloms, B., *Victorian Country Parsons*, 1977

Cooper, J. E., *Bellringers and Bell Ringing*, 1950

Cripps, H. W., *The Law Relating to the Church and Clergy*, 1937

Crockford's Clerical Directories

Cunningham, P., *Handbook of London*, 1850

Davidson, R. and Benham, W., *Life of Archibald Campbell Tait*, 1891

Davies, G. C. B., *Henry Phillpotts, Bishop of Exeter*, 1954

Davies, H., *Varieties of English Preaching 1900–1960*, 1963

Dearmer, P., *Songs of Praise Discussed*, 1933

De-la-Noy, M., *A Day in the Life of God*, 1971

Dickens, A. G., *The English Reformation*, 1964

The Dictionary of National Biography

Ditchfield, P. H., *The Old Time Parson*, 1908

Downey, J., *The 18th Century Pulpit*, 1969

Edwards, D. L., *Leaders of the Church of England 1828–1978*, 1978

Ferriday, P., *Lord Grimthorpe*, 1957

Fitzgerald, P., *The Life of Laurence Sterne*, 1906

Godolphin Osborne, S., *Life and Letters*, 1891

Grubb, Sir Kenneth, *The Crypts of Power*, 1971

Hair, P., *Before the Baudy Court: Selection from Church Court and other records*, 1972

Head, R. E., *Royal Supremacy and the Trials of the Bishops 1558–1725*, 1962

Hennell, M. M., *John Venn and the Clapham Sect*, 1958

Hill, C., *Antichrist in 17th Century England*, 1971

Hopkins, H., *Charles Simeon of Cambridge*, 1977

Inge, W. R., *Diary of a Dean*, 1949

Johnson, H., *Searching for Light*, 1968

Laver, J., *Wesley*, 1932

Lockhart, J. G., *Cosmo Gordon Lang*, 1949

Long, K. R., *The Music of the English Church*, 1972

Macalister, R. A. S., *Ecclesiastical Vestments: their Development and History*, 1896

MacLure, M., *The Paul's Cross Sermons 1534–1642*, 1958

Massingham, B., *Turn on the Fountain: A Life of Dean Hole*, 1974

Menzies, Mrs., *Sportsmen Parsons in Peace and War*, 1919

Mitchell, W. F., *English Pulpit Oratory*, 1932

Ollard, S. L. et al., *A Dictionary of English Church History*, 1919

Pevsner, N., *The Cities of London and Westminster*, 1973

—— *North East Norfolk and Norwich*, 1962

Plumb, J. H., ed., *Studies in Social History*, 1955

Pullar, P., *Consuming Passions*, 1970

Purcell, W., *Fisher of Lambeth*, 1969

Ridley, J., *Thomas Cranmer*, 1962

Roscoe, E. S., *The Bishop of Lincoln's Case*, 1889

Smyth, C., *Cyril Forster Garbett, Archbishop of York*, 1959

Smyth, Brig. Sir John, *In This Sign Conquer*, 1968

Stephenson, A. M. G., *The First Lambeth Conference*, 1967

Strachey, L., *Eminent Victorians*, 1920

Sutherland, J., ed., *The Oxford Book of English Talk*, 1953

Taylor, G., *The Sea Chaplains*, 1978

The Times

Thompson, K., *Bureaucracy and Church Reform*, 1970

Tindal Hart, A., *Country Clergy in Elizabethan and Stuart Times*, 1958

—— *John Sharp, Archbishop of York*, 1949

Trevelyan, G. M., *English Social History*, 1942

Wade, J., *The Black Book or Corruption Unmasked*, 1820

Walker, E. C., *William Dell, Master Puritan*, 1970

Walker, Rev. J., *The Sufferings of the Clergy during the Great Rebellion*, 1862

Welsby, P. A., *George Abbot: The Unwanted Archbishop*, 1962

Woodforde, J., *Diary of a Country Parson*, 1924–31

White, T. H., *The Age of Scandal*, 1950

Wright, T., *Caricature History of the Georges*, 1876

SOURCES OF ILLUSTRATIONS

page

2   *Country Life*

5   Mansell Collection, London

7   Mansell Collection, London

12   Portrait by G. Flicke, National Portrait Gallery, London

16   Contemporary engraving, author's collection

18   Contemporary engraving, author's collection

26   Artist unknown, National Portrait Gallery, London

27   Reproduced by kind permission of the Archbishop of Canterbury and the Church Commissioners for England, copyright reserved to the Church Commissioners and the Courtauld Institute of Art

35   Greater London Council (Print Collection). Photograph Godfrey New

37   Reproduced by kind permission of the Archbishop of Canterbury and the Church Commissioners for England, copyright reserved to the Church Commissioners and the Courtauld Institute of Art

40   Artist unknown, National Portrait Gallery, London

42   Contemporary engraving, author's collection

43   After A. Van Dyck, National Portrait Gallery, London

46   Contemporary woodcut, B.B.C. Hulton Picture Library, London

53   Artist unknown. By courtesy of the Warden and Fellows of Wadham College, Oxford

57   Contemporary engraving, author's collection

63   Artist unknown. By courtesy of the Master and Fellows of Trinity College, Cambridge

66   Studio of Lely, National Portrait Gallery, London

71   Engraving by R. White, National Portrait Gallery, London

74   Mansell Collection, London

76   Engraving from *Engelands Godsdienst ...*, Amsterdam, 1689. Mansell Collection, London

81   Artist unknown, B.B.C. Hulton Picture Library, London

85   Greater London Council (Print Collection). Photograph Godfrey New

89   Mansell Collection, London

91   Engraving by G. Vertue after I. Seeman, Mansell Collection, London

92   Engraving by William Hogarth. By courtesy of Andrew Edmunds

93   Greater London Council (Print Collection). Photograph Godfrey New

95   Engraving by William Hogarth. By courtesy of Andrew Edmunds

100   By J. Woolaston, National Portrait Gallery, London

102   Contemporary engraving. Mansell Collection, London

103   Reproduced by kind permission of the Archbishop of Canterbury and the Church Commissioners for England, copyright reserved to the Church Commissioners and the Courtauld Institute of Art. Photograph Simon Barrow

104   From *The Old Time Parson* by P. H. Ditchfield, Methuen, 1908

107   Artist unknown. National Portrait Gallery, London

109   By Thomas Patch. By courtesy of the Master and Fellows of Jesus College, Cambridge

110   Coloured etching by Matthew or Mary Darly. By courtesy of Andrew Edmunds

114   By H. W. Pickersgill, National Portrait Gallery, London

115   Silhouettes by Edouart. Church Pastoral Aid Society

117   Coloured etching by William Heath. By courtesy of Andrew Edmunds

118   Coloured etching by John Boyne. By courtesy of Andrew Edmunds

120   Etching. Anon after George Moutard Woodward. By courtesy of Andrew Edmunds

122 Etching with aquatint by R. Newton. By courtesy of Andrew Edmunds

123 Etching by R. Newton. By courtesy of Andrew Edmunds

125 National Gallery of Scotland

129 Coloured etching by Robert Dighton. Courtesy of Andrew Edmunds

133 By George Dawe. By courtesy of the Master and Fellows of St. John's College, Cambridge

139 By H. P. Briggs, National Portrait Gallery, London

145 By kind permission of H.M. the Queen

149 By W. Owen, National Portrait Gallery, London

151 Detail from picture by Colam. B.B.C. Hulton Picture Library

155 By 'Cecioni'. National Portrait Gallery, London

157 National Portrait Gallery, London

158 Frontispiece from *Sportsmen Parsons in Peace and War* by Mrs. Stuart Menzies, Hutchinson, 1919.

159 Spy cartoon. Author's collection

162 B.B.C. Hulton Picture Library

167 Spy cartoon. Author's collection

172 Frontispiece to *The Life and Work of Bishop Thorold* by C. H. Sim

177 From *Cosmo Gordon Lang* by J. G. Lockhart, Hodder & Stoughton, 1949

179 Photograph by Tino Zervudachi

181 From *Conrad Noel and the Thaxted Movement* by Reg Groves, Merlin Press, 1967

186 *Sunday Pictorial*, 4 June 1916

189 From *Diary of a Dean* by W. R. Inge, Hutchinson, 1949

191 By kind permission of David & Charles Ltd

194 From *Diary of a Dean* by W. R. Inge, Hutchinson, 1949

199 *Country Life*

207 From *The Sea Chaplains* by Gordon Taylor, Oxford Illustrated Press, 1978

208 From *Cyril Forster Garbett* by Charles Smyth, Hodder & Stoughton, 1959

215 Popperfoto

219 Keystone Press Agency

222 Church Missionary Society

228 Popperfoto

233 Popperfoto

INDEX

Abbot, George, Archbishop of Canterbury, 33, 36, 37, 37, 38, 39, 41, 42, 45; his hunting accident, 33, 39, 45
Abbott, Eric, Dean of Westminster, 222, 227
Abdication crisis, 200
Abel, Rev. Thomas, 9
'Abide with me!', 148, 214
Adair, John, management consultant, 225
Adams, Rev. J. W., V.C., 165, 176
Addington Palace, near Croydon, 127, 149, 155, 166, 171, 173, 174
Advowsons, sale of, 175
Alabaster, Rev. William, 31, 43
Albemarle, Earl of, 106
Albert, Prince, 144, 145, 154–5
Aldrich, Dr., Dean of Christ Church, 84
Alexander, Canon Sydney, 204
Alexandra, Queen, 156, 163, 183
All Hallows-by-the-Tower, 55, 67
All Saints, Margaret Street, 150
'All things bright and beautiful', 149
Allen, Rev. Mr., 115
Anderson, Dr., Bishop of Portsmouth, 206
Andrew, Rev. J., 221
Andrewes, Lancelot, Bishop of Winchester, 38, 40, 41, 42, 171
Anglesey, Marquess of, 225
Anne, Princess, 227
Anne, Queen, 76, 82, 83, 84, 86; see also Queen Anne's Bounty
Anne, Queen, wife of James I, 38, 39
Anne of Cleves, 8
Antichrist, the, 4, 34, 49, 52, 224
'Apostle of the North'; see Gilpin, Rev. Bernard
Apsley, Lady, 111
Arbuthnot, Dr. John, 84
'Archbishop of Society'; see Thomson, William
Argyll, Dukes of, 169, 176, 187
Army chaplains, 82, 122, 128, 130, 165, 176, 184, 185, 186, 187, 188, 203, 206, 223
Arnold, Matthew, 141
Arnold, Dr. Thomas, 136, 138, 146
Arran, Earl of, 222, 223
Ascham, Rev. Roger, 23
Askew, Anne, 10
Athenaeum Club, 144, 170, 183, 196, 201, 204, 212
Atherton, John, Bishop of Waterford and Lismore, 48–9

Atkin, Rev. Joseph, murder of, 161
Atterbury, Francis, Bishop of Rochester, 84, 87, 88, 90
Attlee, Clement, 214
Auckland Castle, 4, 110, 172, 227
Augustine, Saint, 144
'Awake my soul and with the sun', 80

Babington Plot, 28
Bacon, Rev. Francis, 195
Bacon-Phillips, Rev. James, 175
Bagot, Dr., Bishop of Norwich, luncheon at his palace, 116
Bagshawe, Dr., 62
Bailey, Rev. William, deportation of, 146
Baker, Rev. Sir H. W., Bart., 154
Baldwin, Stanley, 196, 200
Bale, John, 8, 13
Balfour, A. J., 176
Bampfylde, Rev. C. F., 'The Worst Man in the West of England', 138
Ban-the-Bomb march, 218
Bancroft, John, Bishop of Oxford, 45
Bancroft, Richard, Archbishop of Canterbury, 34, 34–6; his library, 36, 217
Bankhead, Tallulah, 194
Bardsley, Cuthbert, Bishop of Coventry, 220
Bardsley, John, Bishop of Carlisle, 178
Barge, Primate's, 34, 42, 45, 54, 73, 78, 87, 94; sinking of, 45
Bargrave, Dr. Isaac, Dean of Canterbury, 51, 92
Barham, Rev. R. H., 129
Baring-Gould, Rev. Sabine, 156–7, 191
Barnardo, Dr. Thomas, 160
Barnes, Ernest, Bishop of Birmingham, 195, 205, 211–12
Barnes, Robert, 8
Barnes, Rev. William, 156
Barrington, Dr. Shute, Bishop of Durham, 112–13, 122, 123
Barrow, Henry, 28, 30; execution of, 30
Barrow, Dr. Isaac, 63, 70
Barry, Dr., Bishop of Southwell, 214
Barton, Elizabeth, 2
Barwick, Rev. John, 50, 59, 62
Bastille, fall of, 119
Bastwick, John, 47
Bate, Rev. Henry, journalist-parson, 115, 123
Bath, city of, 86, 96, 101, 108, 111, 143
Bath Abbey, 36

Bath, Dowager Marchioness of, 150
Bathurst, Dr., Bishop of Norwich, 143
Batty, Dr. Basil, Bishop of Fulham, 201
Baxter, Rev. Richard, 55, 163
Bazell, Rev. Mervyn, 217–18
Beale, Dr., 50, 52, 60
Beaton, Cardinal, murder of, 10
Beauchamp, Earl, 187
Beauclerk, Rev. Lord Frederick, 136
Bedford, Duke of, 127, 134
Bedford, Duchess of, 131
Bedford, Earl of, 6, 16
Bee-keeping, 36
Bell, George, Bishop of Chichester, 184, 197, 206, 211, 212, 217
Bell, Rev. William, robbed of his watch, 111
Bell-ringer, death of, 168
Belloc, Hilaire, 11
Belvoir Castle, 116, 119, 129
Benison, Rev. Ernest, 187
Bennett, Rev. W. J. E., 150
Benson, Dr., Bishop of Gloucester, 101
Benson, Edward White, Archbishop of Canterbury, 153, 164, 167, 168–9, 169, 169–70, 171, 173, 174, 221; death of, 173; horror of socialism, 167, 169
Benson, Mrs. E. W., 183, 185
Bentley, Dr., Master of Trinity, 86
Beresford, Lord John, Archbishop of Armagh, 147
Berkeley, Bishop, 93, 97, 98; see also Tar water
Berridge, Rev. John, 104, 104
Berry, Godfrey, Sir Edmund, 71
Bessborough, Countess of, 131
Bible, the, 6, 7, 8, 20, 36, 58, 64
'Bible moths', 93
Bickersteth, John, Bishop of Bath and Wells, 232
Bigge, Sir Arthur, 174
Bill, Rev. William, 20
Binley, John, chauffeur to Dr. Fisher, 205
Birch, Rev. Thomas, 106
Bird, John, Bishop of Chester, 15
Birds in church, 213, 232
Birkbie, Rev. John, 23
'Bishop of Hammersmith'; see Hacket, John
'Bishop of Hell'; see Gainham, Dr.
Bishop's Court, Isle of Man, 46, 103, 230
Bishops' effigies burnt, 138, 190, 199
Bishops Exclusion Act, 50
Bishops Resignation Act, 160
Bishopthorpe Palace, 38, 65, 73, 97–8, 105, 148, 180, 196, 199, 205, 206, 215, 216, 224, 228; garden at, 196
Black Book, the, 132
Black, Sir Cyril, 223
Black Power, 224
Blackburne, Lancelot, Archbishop of York, 88, 90–1, 91, 97–8, 101
Blagden, Bishop, 204

Blandford, Walter, Bishop of Worcester, 69
Blasphemy, 131, 135, 138, 153
Blenheim, Battle of, 83
Block, Maj.-Gen. Adam, 225
Blomfield, Charles, Bishop of London, 136, 137–8
Blood of Hailes, the, 6
Bloomer, Dr., Bishop of Carlisle, 220
Blore, Canon, 170
Blunt, Dr., Bishop of Bradford, 200, 212
Boat Race, the, 137
Bocher, Joan, 12
Body stealing, 108, 112
Bogus priests, 92, 92, 131, 220
Boleyn, Anne, 4
Boniface, 25, 52
Bonner, Edmund, Bishop of London, 10, 12, 14, 15, 17, 18, 21, 119
Booth, General, 166
Borlaise, Rev. William, 98
Borley Rectory, 'the most haunted house in England', 201–2
Boswell, James, 114
Boughton Castle, 56
Bourne, Cardinal, 194
Bourne, Dr. Gilbert, dagger thrown at, 14
Bousfield, Rev. C. H., death of, 174
Bradfield, Dr., Bishop of Bath and Wells, 218
Bradlaugh, Charles, M.P., 165
Bramhall, John, Archbishop of Armagh, 54
Brass-rubbing, 223
Brawls, 22, 25, 27, 30, 39, 65
Bray, Dr. Thomas, 81
Bridge, Rev. Antony, 215
Bridgeman, John, Bishop of Chester, 56
'Brightest and best of the sons of the morning', 128
Brighton Pavilion, 131
Bristol, Earl of; see Hervey, Frederick
Bristol, episcopal palace at, stripped of its roof, 55; burnt down, 138
British and Foreign Bible Society, 126
British and Foreign Temperance Society, 134
Broadcasting, 193, 194, 198–9, 201, 210, 212, 213, 214, 216, 219, 220, 225, 226, 228, 232
Brompton, Richard, painter, 112
Brontë, Rev. Patrick, 128, 132, 134; his family, 132
Brookes, Rev. Joshua, 119
Brown, Rev. J. F. O., 204
Browne, Coral, 206
Browne, Dr., Bishop of Cork, 108
Browne, Edward, Bishop of Winchester, health of, 167
Brownjohn, Rev. S. J., 174
Brownlow, Lord, 200
Bruherne, Rev. Richard, 22
Buchan, Earl of, Methodist convert, 99, 108
Buckden Palace, 30, 39
Buckingham, Duchess of, 97

Buckner, Dr., Bishop of Chichester, 131
Budden, J. Archbishop Lang's gardener, 196
Bulganin and Khruschev, 216
Bull, George, Bishop of St. David's, 83
Bullock-Webster, Canon, 183, 195
Bunyan, John, 70, 196
Burden, Rev. R., dinner for workmen, 154
Burdett-Coutts, Baroness, 141, 150, 180
'Burglar Bill'; see Williams, Henry Herbert
Burgoyne, Sir Montague, 130
Burial Act, the, 165
Burnably, Rev. Evelyn, 172
Burnet, Gilbert, Bishop of Salisbury, 72, 76, 77, 82, 84
Burroughs, Rev. Jeremiah, 50
Burt, Rev. Robert, 117
Burton, Edward, death of, 19
Busby, Dr. Richard, headmaster of Westminster School, 62, 80
Butler, Rev. Billy, 124
Butler, Rev. Charles, 36
Butler, Joseph, Bishop of Bristol and Durham, 89, 96, 101, 108, 111, 143
Butler, Mrs. Josephine, 160
Butler, Dr. Samuel, 143
Buxton, Sir Thomas Fowell, 135
Byron, Rev. H., 128

Caddick, Dr. Richard, 121
Cadley, Jacob, 141
Cairncross, Alexander, Archbishop of Glasgow, 75
Calumy, Dr. Edmund, 60, 67
Cambridge, Duke of, 132
Campbell, Rev. Thomas, 54
Campbell-Douglas, Rev. Leopold, 182
Campion, Edmund, 27
Canaries, Dr. James, 75
Canterbury, Archbishop's palace at, 8, 23, 24; new building, 174, 184, 205–6, 208, 211
Canterbury Cathedral, 1, 51, 80, 164, 184, 190, 202, 205, 209, 219, 228, 231, 233, 234
Cardmaker, Rev. John, burnt at the stake, 17
Carlisle Cathedral, 98
Caroline, Queen, wife of George II, 94
Caroline, Queen, wife of George IV, 122, 132–4; death of, 134
Carpenter, General and Mrs., 206
Carr, Lisle, Bishop of Coventry, 194
Carter, Rev. Cyril, 225
Cartwright, Rev. Edmund, 116–17, 127
Castle, Gertrude, Archbishop Lang's cook, 205
Cat, in Exeter Cathedral, 31
Catherine of Aragon, 2, 9
Celibacy, priestly, 8, 11, 14, 14–15, 15, 20, 21, 154
Chaderton, William, Bishop of Lincoln, 30
Chalmers, Rev. James, eaten by savages, 175
Chandler, Edward, Bishop of Durham, 93

Chandler, Dr. Samuel, 106
Chandos, Duke of, 89
Chaplin, Charlie, 216
Charles, Prince of Wales, 228
Charles I, King, 33, 39, 41, 42, 43, 45, 46, 47, 48, 49, 50, 51, 52, 54, 56, 57, 58, 59
Charles II, King, 44, 51, 59, 60, 62, 63, 64, 66, 68, 69, 70, 72, 73, 128, 192
Charles-Edwards, Dr., Bishop of Worcester, 217
Chase, Frederick, Bishop of Ely, 179, 183
Cheltenham, 130, 218
Chesterfield, Lady, Methodist convert, 99
Chesterfield, Lord, 112
Chesterton, G. K., 192
Chestlin, Rev. Robert, 51
Chillingworth, Rev. William, pestered to death, 54
Cholera, 134, 138, 152, 154
Christian Socialism, 141, 155, 181
Church, Richard, Dean of St. Paul's, 160, 170
Church Commissioners, 210, 212, 215, 225
Church Discipline Act, 146
Church Missionary Society, 223
Churchill, Rev. Charles, 104, 106; his cider cellar, 104
Churchill, Sir Winston, 204, 214; funeral of, 221
Clandestine Marriages Bill, 102, 103
Clapham, the Holy Village of, 103, 120, 121, 128
Claridge's Hotel, 188, 216
Clark, Rev. Robin, 232
Clarke, Jeremiah, 83
Clayton, Rev. Tubby, 186, 192–3
Clements, Bishop Davidson's boot-boy, 209
Clergy Discipline Act, 172
Clergy Incapacitation Act, 124
Clergy Residence Act, 121
Clitheroe, Dr., Bishop of Stafford, 220
Cock-fighting, 23, 122
'Cod fish'; see Thomson, William
Coffee houses, 71, 78, 83, 84, 87, 90, 93, 96, 128
Coggan, Donald, Archbishop of York and Canterbury, 210, 219, 220, 221, 224, 225, 226, 227–8, 228–9, 230, 231, 233; his call to the nation, 229
Coggan, Mrs. Jean, 228, 230, 231, 232
'Coldest house in England', 220
Colenso, John, Bishop of Natal, 151–2, 156, 157
Collier, Rev. Jeremy, 81
Collins, Canon John, 218, 221
Common Prayer, Book of, 1, 11, 12, 13, 34, 48, 55, 56, 57, 64, 65, 66, 132, 195, 213, 222, 234
Compton, Lord Alwyne, Bishop of Ely, 179
Compton, Henry, Bishop of London, 70, 72, 73, 76, 77, 78, 86

'Conservative Party at Prayer', 141
Conyngham, Lord and Lady, 135, 143
Cooper, Lady Diana, 192
Cooper, Rev. W. H. H., 99th birthday, 213
Cope, Sir John, 98
Coppock, Rev. Thomas, would-be Bishop of Carlisle, 98, 99
Corbett, Richard, Bishop of Norwich, 39, 45
Cornwallis, Frederick, Archbishop of Canterbury, 108, 111, 113, 115, 116
Cornwallis, Mrs., 113–14, 115
Cosin, John, Bishop of Durham, 43, 54, 69
Costobadie, Rev. Hugh, 144
Courtenay, Rev. Francis, attacked by mob, 147
Coventry Cathedral, 220
Coverdale, Miles, 10
Coward, Noël, 194
Cowherd, Rev. William, 130
Cowper, William, 113
Cox, Rev. James Bell, imprisonment of, 169
Cox, Richard, Bishop of Ely, 25, 26
Crabbe, George, parson-poet, 116, 119, 130–1
Crabbe, Rt. Rev. R. P., Bishop of Mombasa, 207
Cranmer, Mrs., 3, 8, 19; carried in tub or trunk, 3
Cranmer, Thomas, Archbishop of Canterbury, 1, 2, 3, 4, 6, 7, 8, 9, 10, 11, *12*, 13, 15, *16*, 17, 234; degradation of, 18; death of, 18–19
Crawley, Rev. A. S., 182
Creighton, Mandell, Bishop of London, 163, 173, 174
Creighton, Rev. Oswin, 188
Creighton, Robert, Bishop of Bath and Wells, 69
Cricket, 99, 136, 142, 143, 155, 161, 178–9, 202, 211, 216
Crimean War, 152
Croft, Herbert, Bishop of Hereford, 56, 69
Cromwell, Mrs., funeral of, 61
Cromwell, Oliver, 56, 59, 60, 61, 62, 62–3, 67, 79; corpse attacked, 64, 65
Cromwell, Richard, 63
Cromwell, Thomas, vicar general, 1, 3, 5, 7, 8
Crone, Dr. Edward, 10
Croydon, Primate's palace at, 10, 13, 45, 103, 113–14, 127
Cuddesdon Palace, 45, 46, 217, 218
Cuddesdon Theological College, 147, 153, 217
Culloden, Battle of, 98
Curll, Walter, Bishop of Winchester, 56
Curzon, Lord, 186
Cussons, Rev. John, death of, 164

Daffy's Elixir, 68–9
Dalton, Canon John, 198

Dampier, Thomas, Bishop of Ely, 128
Daniel, Rev. William, 124
Darby, Rev. John, 135
Darby, John, Dean of Chester, 173
Darrel, Rev. John, 31
Dartmouth, Lady, Methodist convert, 99
Darwin, Charles, 154, 165, 166
Dashwood, Sir Francis, 99, 106, 126; his church at West Wycombe, 106
Davenant, John, Bishop of Salisbury, 44
Davidson, Rev. Harold, Rector of Stiffkey, 198, 200, 201
Davidson, Randall, Archbishop of Canterbury, 167, 167–8, 170, 174, 175, 176, 180, 181, 182, 183, 184, 184–5, 185, 186, 187, 188, 189, 190, 194, 195; his lumbago, 189, 192
Dawes, William, Archbishop of York, 90
Dawson of Penn, Lord, 196, 197, 201
Day, William, Bishop of Winchester, 22, 30
Day, Rev. William, suspension of, 147–8
Dead cats, 15, 97, 130, 138
Death watch beetle, 213, 215
Dee, Dr. John, astrologer, 24–5
Defrockings; *see* Deprivations and degradations
de Labilliere, Dr., Dean of Westminster, 205
De-la-Noy, Michael, 225
Dell, William, 61
Demolition of churches, 216, 227
Denison, Archdeacon George, 138–40, 151, 152–3, 161
Deprivations and degradations, 12, 18, 29, 48, 52, 72, 73, 73–5, 77–8, 82, 134, 137, 146, 192, 198
Derby, Lord, 159
Devonshire, Duke of, 227
Dickens, Charles, 150
Diggle, John, Bishop of Carlisle, 183
Dimbleby, Richard, 216
Disraeli, Benjamin, 158–9, 213
Ditcher, Rev. Mr., 151
Divine Right of Kings, 10, 39
Divine Right of the Episcopacy, 48
Dobey, Rev. Mr., 112
Dodd, Dr. William, debts of, 111; execution of, 111–12
Dodington, Bubb, 101, 105
Dogs in church, 20, 31, 38, 217–18
Dolben, John, Archbishop of York, 68, 72, 73
Dolling, Rev. Robert, 168
Don, Dr., Dean of Westminster, 200, 213
Donne, John, Dean of St. Paul's, 35, 37, 39, 40, *40*, 41, 44
Dove, Rev. Henry, 70
Dover-Wellman, Rev. J., 224
Dowsing, William, church desecrator, 54
Drummond, Robert Hay, Archbishop of York, 105
Drunkenness, 23, 31, 38, 45, 52, 62, 72, 87, 99,

Drunkenness—*cont.*
103, 114, 122, 137, 143, 147–8, 148, 161, 162, 165, 168, 172, 172–3; *see also* Teetotallers
Dublin Horse Show, 172
Duppa, Brian, Bishop of Winchester, 59, 66
Durham Cathedral, 23, 33, 45, 49
Durham House in the Strand, 15, 38, 42, 55, 63, 225
Durham Miners Strike, 172
Durrell, Dr., Dean of Windsor, 71
Dykes-Bower, S. E., 219

Ear cropping, 45, 46, 47
Earle, John, Dean of Westminster, 60, 66, 67, 68; his dinner party, 67
Eastaugh, Cyril, Bishop of Peterborough, 233
Easter offerings, *117*
Eccleshall Castle, 53, 54
Ecclesiastical Commissioners, 142, 149, 210, 212
Eclectic Society, 116, 222
Edgehill, Battle of, 51
Edmeston, James, 128
Edward the Confessor, 19, 222
Edward VI, King, 1, 6, 10, 11, 13
Edward VII, King, 156, 157, 161, 162–3, 168, 171, 173, 175, 176; typhoid attack, 161
Edward VIII, King, 197, 200, 201; funeral of, 226
Edwards, Rev. Ronald, 206
Egerton, Rev. Francis, eccentric Earl of Bridgwater, 136
Egerton, John, Bishop of Durham, 110, 112; his dinner party, 112
Elegy Written in a Country Churchyard, 101
Elers, Rev. Peter, 230
Elizabeth I, Queen, 2, 19, 20, 21, 22, 23, 24, 25, 26, 29, 32, 223; excommunication of, 23; death of, 32
Elizabeth II, Queen, 210, 211, 217, 220, 222; coronation of, 210, 214, *215*; Silver Jubilee, 230–1
Elizabeth the Queen Mother, Queen, 193, 210, 211, 213
Ellacombe, Rev. H. T., 150
Ellerton, Rev. John, 161
Ellicott, Charles, Bishop of Gloucester, foolish voice and manner of, 159
Ellison, Gerald, Bishop of Chester and London, 206, 223, 227, 229
Ellman, Rev. Edward Boys, 179
Ely House, Dover Street, 110, 128, 179, *179*
Ely House, Holborn, 25, 26, 47, 52, 70, 86, 110
'England's Oldest Rector', 185
Enraght, Rev. R. W., imprisonment of, 165
Epstein, Jacob, controversial statues by, 177
Eric, or Little by Little, 164

Essex, Countess of, 37
Essex, Earl of, 32
Eton, 9, 18, 108, 138, 178–9
Evans, Lewis, harpist, death of, 68
Evelyn, John, 61, 67, 73
Evening Standard, 190, 192
Execution of clergymen, 2, 3, 4, 5, 8, 30, 49, 55, 82, 88, 99, 112, 113
Exeter, bishop's palace at, 105–6, 131, 160
Exorcism, 31, 118, 229

Faithful, Miss Amy, 184
Farnham Castle, 24, 66, 70, 171, 172; entertaining at, 66, 172
Farrar, Archdeacon, 164, 166
Farrer, Robert, Bishop of St. David's, execution of, *16*, 17
Fawkes, Guy, 34
Feake, Rev. Christopher, 61
Featley, Dr. Daniel, attack upon, 52
Feckenham, John, Dean of St. Paul's, 19
Fell, John, Bishop of Oxford, 65, 67
Fell, Dr. Samuel, 57
Ferne, Rev. Henry, 57, 63
Fifth Monarchy Men, 62
'Fight the good fight', 163
Fillingham, Rev. Robert, 175
Fish, Stuyvesant, 188
Fisher, Geoffrey, Archbishop of Canterbury, 198, 202, 203, 204, 205, *208*, 209, 210, 211, 212, 213, 214, *215*, 215, 216, 216–17, 218, *219*, 219
Fisher, John, Bishop of Rochester, 2, 3
Fitzherbert, Mrs., 117, 122
Fitzmaurice, Rev. Maurice, 176
Fleet marriages, 87, 98, 102, *102*, 103
Fleet Prison, 14, 17, 28, 29, 42, 47, 51, *89*, 102, *102*
Fleetwood, Dr. James, Bishop of Worcester, 51
Flenley, Rev. Kenneth, 231
Fletcher, Richard, Bishop of London, 29, 30, 31
Forgery by parsons, 92, 131, 146
'For he's a jolly good fellow', 180
Forrest, Friar, execution of, 6
Forrester, Rev. S. J., 211
Foster, Rev. Thomas, 227
Fotherby, Martin, Archdeacon of Canterbury, 36
Fowler, Rev. Henry, 52
Foxe, Rev. John, 22
Foxe's Book of Martyrs, 22
Frederick, Prince of Wales, 93, 94, 96, 97, 112
Free, Dr. Edward Drax, scandalous Rector of Sutton, 137
Freeman, Archdeacon, 163
Frewen, Accepted, Archbishop of York, 65
'From Greenland's icy mountains', 134

Froude, Rev. Hurrel, 140
Froude, Rev. John, 'guilty of every crime in the calendar', 138
Fulham Palace, 23, 34, 42, 50, 73, 78, 86, 119, 124, 197, 204, 229; gardens of, 86, 202, 204
Fuller, Dr. Thomas, 52, 54, 56, 66

Gainham, Dr., 'Bishop of Hell', 93–4, 102
Gaiters, Archbishop Fisher explains significance of, 218
Gamble, Rev. John, chaplain general, 122, 123
Garbett, Cyril, Archbishop of York, 191, 203, 204, 205, 206, 208, 209, 211, 214, 215
Gardiner, Stephen, Bishop of Winchester, 8, 9, 10, 11, 14, 15, 16, 18, 171; dies of gout, 17
Gardner, Kenneth, 227
Garrick, David, 105, 112
Gay Christian Movement, 230
Geddes, Jenny, 47
General Strike, 190, 194
'Gentle Jesus, meek and mild', 106
George I, King, 87, 88, 90, 91
George II, King, 88, 91, 94, 105
George III, King, 96, 105, 108, 117–18, 118, 126; his proclamations, 105, 118; insanity, 118, 128, 129, 132
George IV, King, 117, 122, 124, 127, 129, 131, 132, 134, 135, 137
George V, King, 173, 182, 183, 185
George VI, King, 193, 200, 201, 202, 205, 209, 210, 211, 214
Gibbon, Edward, 112, 114, 115
Gibbons, Grinling, 75, 80, 183
Gibbons, Orlando, 31, 34, 38, 39, 41
Gibson, Edmund, Bishop of London, 90, 91, 99
Gilbert, Ashurst, Bishop of Chichester, 159
Gilbert, John, Archbishop of York, 106
Gillingham, Rev. Frank, 202
Gilpin, Rev. Bernard, 21, 24, 27–8
Gin, keg found in vestry, 129
Girdlestone, Rev. Edward, 161, 168
Gladstone, Lady, 198
Gladstone, Rev. Stephen, 174
Gladstone, William Ewart, 141, 142, 150, 160, 167, 168, 173, 174; death and funeral, 174; his private diaries, 217
'Glorious things of thee are spoken', 113
'Glory to thee, my God, this night', 80
Gloucester, Duke of, 202
'God is English', 25
'God moves in a mysterious way', 113
Godolphin Osborne, Rev. Sydney, 147, 148, 152
Gordon, Lord George, 113, 114
Gordon, Rev. Lockhart, 126
Gordon riots, 113

Gore, Charles, Bishop of Worcester and Oxford, 171, 173, 176, 188
Gorham, Rev. George, 148, 150–1
'Gorilla' sermons, 195
Gostling, Rev. John, singer, 71, 77
Gout, clergymen afflicted by, 17, 99, 209
Gracie, Rev. A., 222
Graham, Rev. Robert, 204
Grantham, Rev. G., death of, 144–6
Grave diggers, 112
Gray, Robert, Bishop of Bristol, 138
Gray, Robert, Bishop of Capetown, 156
Great Storm, the, 82–3
Great Train Robbers, 221
Green, Rev. S. F., imprisonment of, 166
Green-Wilkinson, Rev. Mr., 198
Gregory, Robert, Dean of St. Paul's, 174, 182
Grey, Lady Jane, 13
Grier, Rev. R. M., 161–2
Grierson, Rev. John, deportation of, 103
Grimshaw, Rev. William, 'the mad parson of the Yorkshire moors', 97, 99, 132
Grimthorpe, Lord, 172
Grindal, Edmund, Archbishop of Canterbury, 21, 22, 23, 25, 28; suspension of, 25; death, 28
Growns, Rev. John, 221
Guinness Brewery, 169
Gull, Sir William, 166
Gunning, Rev. Peter, 62, 63
Gwynn, Nell, 72, 75
Gwynne, Bishop, deputy chaplain general, 186

Habgood, John, Bishop of Durham, 4, 227, 230
Hacket, John, Bishop of Down and Connor, 79
Hackman, Rev. James, murderer, 113
Haig, Sir Douglas, 186
Hailsham, Lord, 234
Halifax, Lord, 193
Hall, George, Bishop of Chester, accidental death of, 68
Hall, Joseph, Bishop of Exeter and Norwich, 48, 52, 62
Hallam, Henry, 142
Halloran, Laurence, deportation of, 131
Hammond, Dr. Henry, 57
Hampden, Renn Dickson, Bishop of Hereford, 148
Hampton Court Conference, 34
Handel, George Frederick, 89, 92, 97
Hannaford, Rev. Jack, 138
Hannington, Bishop, murder of, 168
'Happy, happy, happy, happy, happy, shalt thou be', 122
Harding, Dean, 68
Hardy, Dr. Nathaniel, 62
Hardy, Rev. Theodore, V.C., 188

'Hark! the herald angels sing', 97
Harland, Dr., Bishop of Durham, 216
Harris, Rev. Alfred, 172–3
Harris, Renatus, 75
Harrison, Rev. Joseph, arrest of, 131
Harrow School, 143, 148, 151
Harsnett, Samuel, Archbishop of York, 44
Hart, Dr., 60
Hartlebury Castle, 88, 104, 111, 114–15, 118, 154, 171, 176
Haselden, Canon, E. J. C., 232–4
Hastings, Lady Margaret, 97
Hatton, Sir Christopher, 25
Hawker, Rev. Stephen, 142
Hawksmoor, Nicholas, 103, 116
Hayter, Thomas, Bishop of Norwich, 101
Haywood, Rev. Peter, 231
Headlam, Rev. Stuart, 'the outsider's friend', 173
Healey, Dr., 131
Heath, Nicholas, Archbishop of York, 9, 17, 21
Heathrow Airport, church at, 222
Heber, Reginald, Bishop of Calcutta, 128, 134
Heenan, Cardinal, 214, 224
Helena, Princess, 184–5
Hell Fire Club, 89–90
Hencher, Rev. John, 222
Henchman, Humfrey, Bishop of London, 63, 68
Henley, John, 92, 92
Henrietta Maria, Queen, 54, 60
Henry, Prince of Wales, 36
Henry VIII, King, 1, 2, 3, 4, 5, 6, 7, 8, 9, 14, 15; excommunication of, 6
Henson, Hensley, Bishop of Hereford, 188, 201
Herbert, Rev. George, 41, 43, 57
Hereward the Wake, 88
Herrick, Nicholas, 30
Herrick, Rev. Robert, 43
Herring, Thomas, Archbishop of Canterbury, 96, 98, 99, 103
Hervey, Frederick, Earl of Bristol and Bishop of Derry, 108, 113, 116
Hervey, Rev. James, 98
Hewett, Dr., 62
Hewlett Johnson, Dean of Canterbury, 197, 201, 205, 211, 212, 213, 214, 216, 219, 220, 221
Hickeringill, Rev. Edmund, 72, 83
Hicks, Edward Lee, teetotal Bishop of Lincoln, 181
Higgins, Archdeacon William, 51
Hill, Rev. Adam, 30
Hill, Rev. James Coppinger, 212
Hilsey, John, Bishop of Rochester, 6
Hinchliffe, John, Bishop of Peterborough, 112

Hinds, Samuel, Bishop of Norwich, 152
Hinsley, Cardinal, 201
Hiroshima and Nagasaki, 210–11
Hitler, Adolf, 201
Hoadley, Benjamin, Bishop of Winchester, 83, 88, 105
Hoare, Joseph, Bishop of Hong Kong, 180
Hogarth, *caricatures by, 92, 95*
Holbeach, Robert, Bishop of Worcester, 11
Hole, Samuel, Dean of Rochester, 152, 164, 169, 171, 172
Holgate, Robert, wealthy Archbishop of York, 9, 11, 12, 13, 14, 15, 16
Holland, Lady, 126
Holland House, 126, 131
Homosexuality, 14, 22, 48–9, 134, 153–4, 217, 222, 223, 227, 230; *see also* Immorality
Hone, William, bookseller, 131
Honest to God, 220
Hood, Alexander, 123
Hood, Rev. Ivo, 188
Hook, Rev. Walter, Vicar of Leeds, 144, 153
Hooker, Rev. Richard, 28, 30, 31
Hooper, John, Bishop of Gloucester, 11, 14, *16*, 17, 89; execution of, 17
Hopkinson, Rev. A. S., 218
Hornby, Rev. John, 232
Horne, John, Bishop of Winchester, 24, 26
Horne Tooke, Rev. John, 112, 121, 124
Horsley, Samuel, Dean of Westminster, 122
Hough, John, Bishop of Worcester, 97
'How sweet the name of Jesus sounds', 113
Howard, Catherine, 8, 9
Howard, Christian, 234
Howell, Thomas, Bishop of Bristol, 55
Howley, William, Archbishop of Canterbury, 131, 132, 134, 136, 137, 138, 143, 144, *145, 149*; his funeral procession, 149; his coach and four, 149
Huddleston, Father, 60, 73
Huddleston, Trevor, Bishop of Stepney, 224, 226
Hudson, Dr., Bishop of Ely, 220
Hudson, Dr. Michael, royal chaplain, 56, 57
Hughes, Emrys, M.P., 214
Hughes, Frederick, Dean of Ripon, 206, 223
Humphrey, Miss Frances, 149
Hunter, John, surgeon, 112
Hunter, Rev. Thomas, murderer, 82
Hunting parsons, 27, 33, 39, 59, 87, 99, 123, 124, 125–6, 135, 138, 141, 144, 154, 157, 163, 172, 178, 182, 213, 232; accidents, 33, 39, 45, 171, 178, 182; Hunt Saboteurs Association, 232
Huntingdon, Selina Countess of, 96–7, 97, 99, 106, 107, 108, 110
Hurd, Richard, Bishop of Worcester, 114–15, 116, 118
Hurley, Canon A. V., 206
Hustler, Rev. George, 154, 178

Hutton, Matthew, Archbishop of Canterbury, 104
Huxley, Sir Julian, 200
Huxley, Professor Thomas, 154
Hymns Ancient and Modern, 141, 154
Hymns for Little Children, 149

Ickworth, Suffolk, 113
Imber, Rev. Luke, 111
Immorality, 3, 23, 24, 25, 73, 79, 87, 99, 137, 178, 181, 190, 192, 198, 218; *see also* Homosexuality
Imprisonment for debt, 83, 88, 121
Indian Mutiny, 152, 163
Inflammation of the bowels, 90
Inge, W. R., Dean of St. Paul's, 182, 183, 187, 190, 191–2, 192, 193, 195, 197, 198, 199; his pocket picked, 197; his bedroom, *194*; his dinner parties, 199
Ingham, Rev. Benjamin, 97
Inglis, Rev. Rupert, 187
Intoxicating Liquor Bill, 161
Inventors; *see* Cartwright, Rev. Edmund; Ellacombe, Rev. H. T.; Moule, Rev. Henry; Watson, Richard, Bishop of Llandaff; Wilkins, John, Bishop of Chester
Ireland, John, Dean of Westminster, 142
Iremonger, Frederick, Dean of Lichfield, 198–9, 201

Jackson, Rev. John, 98
James I, King, 33, 34, 36, 37, 38, 39, 40
James II, King, 66, 69, 70, 71, 73, 75, 76, 77, 78, 79, 97
Jardine, Rev. R. A., 201
Jayne, Francis, Bishop of Chester, 173
Jeffreys, Judge, 73
Jellicoe, Admiral, 185
Jenner, Dr., Bishop of Dunedin, 163
Jersey, Lady, 124
Jesus Christ Superstar, 210, 226
Jesus Freaks, 227
Jocelyn, Percy, Bishop of Clogher, 134, 147
Johnson, Miss Esther, 83
Johnson, Rev. Robert, 36
Johnson, Dr. Samuel, parson, 73–4, 77–8
Johnson, Dr. Samuel, writer, 106, 112, 114
Jones, Edward, scandalous Bishop of St. Asaph, 80, 82
Jones, Inigo, 40, 47, 56
Josselin, Rev. Ralph, 60
Jowett, Alfred, Dean of Manchester, 229
Jutland, battle of, 186
Juxon, William, Archbishop of Canterbury, 45, 50, 58, 59, 65, 136, 205

Kaiser, the, 175, 184
Keate, Rev. John, headmaster of Eton, 138
Keble, Rev. John, 135, 140, 141, 143

Keeler, Christine, memoirs of, 224
Keith, Rev. Alexander, 102
Keith, Rev. George, 82
Kelly, Rev. George, 90, 94
Kem, Rev. Samuel, 52–3, 56
Ken, Thomas, Bishop of Bath and Wells, 72, 73, 75, 78, 80, 166
Keppel, Alice, 192
Keppel, Frederick, Bishop of Exeter, 105–6, 106, 111
Kersley, James, Archbishop Tait's manservant, 166
Kidder, Richard, Bishop of Bath and Wells, death of, 83
Kilmuir, Lord, 217
King, Dr., Dean of Tuam, 59
King, Edward, Bishop of Lincoln, 168, 169, 181; trial of, 169–70
King, John, Bishop of London, 38, 39
King, Rev. John, racehorse owner, 163
King's Bench Prison, 112, 115, 121
Kingsley, Rev. Charles, 141, 147, 150, 155, *155*, 156
Kingsley, Rev. William, 154, 185
Kingswood School, alarming scenes at, 110
Kinnersley, Rev. Thomas, forger, 92
Kroll, Dr. Una, 231

Lady Chatterley's Lover, 218
Lambart, Ven. Horace, Earl of Cavan, 211
Lambart, Rev. John, 6
Lambeth Conferences, 141, 157–8, 164, 169, 174, 180, 197, 203, 212, 217, 224, 231
Lambeth Palace, 2, 4, 8, 9, 14, 21, 23, 24, 28, 31, 34, 45, 52, 65, 67, 68, 70, 78, 78–9, 82, 87, 88, *93*, 94, 96, 102, 108, 116, 123, 124, 129, 134, 136, 149, 157–8, 160, 164, 170, 176, 181, 183, 184, 188, 194, 195, 196, 197, 199, 201, 202, 203, 204, 205, 210, 211, 216, 217, 227, 229, 232; entertaining at, 21, 28, 36, 36–7, 67, 69, 73, 80, 87, 104, 108, 111, 113, 164, 169, 180, 183, 197, 223, 224, 230, 231, 232; bombing of, 204, 205, 209; refurbishing of, 67, 136, 210, 211; chapel made into dance-hall, 65; burglary at, 134; gardens of, 2, 102, 196
Lambton Castle, Co. Durham, 132
Lamplugh, Thomas, Bishop of Exeter, 76
Lancing School Chapel, 159
Landor, Rev. Robert, 132
Lanfranc, 10, 103
Lang, Cosmo Gordon, Archbishop of Canterbury, 174, 176, *177*, 180, 182–3, 184, 185, 187–8, 188, 189, 190, 193, 196, 196–7, 197, 197–8, 199, 200, 202, 203, 204, 205, 211; his Mediterranean cruises, 197, 198, 202; his motor-cars, 176, 200, 205
Latimer, Hugh, 11, 13, 14, 15, *16*; death of, 17

Laud, William, Archbishop of Canterbury, 33, 38, 39, 41, 42, *43*, 45, 46, *46*, 47, 48, 49, 50, 52, 54–5, 102, 204; death of, 55; re-burial, 67; his tortoise, 45, 102, *103*
Lavatories, 105, 154, 160, 128, 153
Lavington, George, Bishop of Exeter, 101
Law, George, Bishop of Bath and Wells, 144
Law, Rev. William, 92
Lawes, William, composer, 56
Lawson, Wilfred, teetotaller, 161
Layton, Richard, Dean of York, 3, 9
'Lead kindly light', 140, 170, 180
'Lead us, heavenly father, lead us', 128, 226
League Against Cruel Sports, 221
Lee, Edward, Archbishop of York, 4, 5
Lee-Warner, Rev. Mr., assault charge, 166
Lees, Dr. Frederick, teetotaller, 163
Legard, Rev. Cecil, *172*
Legh, Dr. Thomas, 3
Leighton, Rev. Alexander, savage punishment of, 44, 52
Leng, John, Bishop of Norwich, smallpox victim, 92
Leonard, Rev. Francis, 204
Le Patourel, Rev. W. M., *186*
'Let us with a gladsome mind', 40
Lewes, Dr., Bishop of Ontario, 158
Life and Liberty Movement, 187, 188, 191
Lincoln Cathedral, 44, 168, 220
Lincoln, Old Palace at, 168, 181
Lindsay, Hon. Colin, 154
Llewellyn, Roddy, 231
Lloyd, William, Bishop of Worcester, 79, 84–6, 88
Lloyd George, David, 189
Londesborough, Lord, 161
London, Dr. John, 9
London Public Morality Council, 194
Longleat, 78, 150
Longley, Charles, Archbishop of Canterbury, 143, 155, 156, 158
Love, Rev. Christopher, execution of, 60
Love's Plot, 60
Lovibond, Rev. Frederick, 181
Lowder, Rev. Charles, 153
Lowes, Rev. John, accused of witchcraft, 55
Lowson, Sheriff Denys, 203
Lucan, Lady, 115
Lucy, Rev. John, fox-hunting parson, 163
Lucy, William, Bishop of St. David's, 67–8, 70
Luddite Riots, 128
Ludham Palace, wine cellar at, 45
Lyttelton, Rev. Edward, headmaster of Eton, 178–9

Macaroni parsons, 23, 44, 106, *110*, 111, 116, 121
McCulloch, Rev. Joseph, 209, 223, 229
McDade, Archbishop Lang's butler, 204, 205

MacDonald, Ramsay, ecclesiastical appointments by, 195, 197
MacInnes, Rennie, Bishop in Jerusalem, 198
Mackarness, Archdeacon, 185
Mackensie, Charles, Bishop of Central Africa, 155
Maclagan, William, Archbishop of York, 171–2, 174, 180
Macmillan, John, Bishop of Guildford, 186
Maddox, Isaac, Bishop of Worcester, 97, 104
Magee, William, Bishop of Peterborough, 161–2, *162*, 165
Mainwaring, Rev. Roger, 41–2
Makarios, Archbishop, 217
Maltby, Edward, Bishop of Durham, 144
Malthus, Rev. Thomas, 124
Man, John, Dean of Gloucester, 23
Manners Sutton, Charles, Archbishop of Canterbury, 126, 127, 128, 129, 131, 132, 134, 136
Manning, Cardinal, 142, 143, 150, 172; cricketing activities, 143
Margaret, Princess, 210, 213, 216, 217, 220, 228, 230
Markham, William, Archbishop of York, 111, 113, 127; attacked by mob, 113
Marlborough, Duke and Duchess of, 82, 83, 97
Marprelate Tracts, 29, 30
Marsh, Narcissus, Archbishop of Armagh, 81
Marshall, Michael, Bishop of Woolwich, 230, 231
Marshall, Stephen, 50, 52, 66
Marston Moor, battle of, 54
Martin, Prof. David, 234
Mary I, Queen, 2, 9, 12, 13, 14, 15, 16, 17, 19; funeral of, 20
Mary II, Queen, 70, 77, 78, 79, 80
Mary, Queen of Scots, 24, 28, 28–9, 30
Mary, Queen, wife of George V, 173, 182, 190
Mason, Rev. John, 79
Matthew, Toby, Archbishop of York, 33, 38, 42
Maxey, Anthony, Dean of Windsor, tobacco-hater, 38
May, William, Archbishop of York, 21
Mayhew, Charles, centenarian chorister, 202
Meditations among the Tombs, 98
Mellish, Rev. Edward Noel, V.C., *186*
Melville, Andrew, 34
Mental illness, 4, 67, 70, 84–6, 88, 98, 144, 153, 168, 180, 197
Merbecke, John, 9
Mercer, Eric, Bishop of Exeter, 232
Meredith, Canon Roland, hunting parson, 232
Methodism, 87, 96–7, 97, 98, 99, 101, 104, 106
Methodist bashing, 97, 99
Mickleburgh, Rev. Mr., 103

Middleton, Sir Charles, 117
Middleton, Marmaduke, Bishop of St. David's, 26, 29
Middleton, Thomas, first Bishop of Calcutta, 129, 134
Miller, Rev. James, playwright, 93
Milman, Henry Hart, 150
Milner, Rev. Isaac, 116
Milton, John, 40, 42
Mitford, Rev. John, 128, 153
Missionaries, 81, 82, 93, 94, 124; eaten by cannibals, 175
Mob violence, 5, 33, 50, 51, 97, 99, 113, 119–20, 130, 131, 138, 141, 144, 147, 183, 199
Monasteries, dissolution of, 1, 3, 4, 5, 6, 8, 14
Monck, General, 60, 66
Monck, Nicholas, Bishop of Hereford, 66
Monk, Bishop Bell's chauffeur, 197
Monmouth, Duke of, 73
Mons, retreat from, 184
Monsell, Rev. J., 163
Montagu, James, Bishop of Bath and Wells, 36
Montagu, Rev. Richard, 40
Montefiore, Hugh, Bishop of Birmingham, 223
Montgomery, Field Marshal, 206, 211, 223
Moore, Rev. George, 178
Moore, John, Archbishop of Canterbury, 116, 118, 119, 122, 124, 126
Moore, John, Bishop of Ely, 86
Mordaunt, Rev. Osbert, 164
More, Hannah, 114, *114*, 119
More, Sir Thomas, 2, 3
Morley, George, Bishop of Winchester, 66, *66*, 67, 68, 71
Moreton, Rev. William, 122–3
Morley, Robert, 206
Morris, William, 160
Mortimer, Robert, Bishop of Exeter, 213, 216, 223
Morton, Thomas, Bishop of Durham, 50, 55, 63
Moss, Rev. Henry, headmaster of Shrewsbury, 163
Motoring and motor-cars, 171, 176, 187, 200, 204, 210, 228, 232; accidents, 176, 190, 229
Moule, Rev. Henry, lavatory-inventor, 154
Mountain, George, Bishop of Durham, 42
Moustaches, clerical, 154, 172, 196
Muggleton, Lodowicke, 60
Murray, George, Bishop of Rochester, 154
Murray, Rev. Lord George, 123, 126
Muscular Christianity, 141

Naseby, battle of, 55
Nash, Beau, 96
National Front, 231

National Mission for Repentance and Hope, 185, 186–7
Natural History of Selborne, 118–19
Neile, Richard, Bishop of Durham, 38
Nelson, Lord, 127, 209
Nelson, Robert, Bishop of Middleton, 218
Nepotism, 114, 128
Newcastle, Duke of, 99, 104, 105
Newcomen, Rev. Thomas, attack on, 51
Newell, Rev. C. P., 199
Newgate prison, 44, 63, 67, 92, 96
Newman, Cardinal, 131, 136, 140, 141–2, 146, 146–7, 147, 170
Newton, Rev. John, former slave trafficker, 106, 113, 116, 127
Nicholas II, Czar, 173
Nicholls, Vernon, Bishop of Sodor and Man, 230
Nicholson, William, Bishop of Gloucester, 67–8
Nightingale, Florence, 152, 160
Noah's Flood, predicted repetition of, 62
'No Popery!', 50, 72, 113, 147, 150, 195
Noel, Rev. Conrad, 181
North, Brownlow, Bishop of Winchester, 110, 114, 132
Northern Rebellion, 23
Northumberland, Duke of, 72
Nowell, Alexander, Dean of St. Paul's, 22, 29, 32

Oates, Rev. Samuel, 61
Oates, Rev. Titus, 64, 70, *71*, 71, 72, 73
Ogden, Rev. Samuel, 101
Oglethorpe, Owen, Bishop of Carlisle, 19, 20
Olney Hymns, 113
'Onward, Christian soldiers', 157, 191
Opera House, London, 123, 148
Opium-addiction, 119, 142, 176–7
Original sin, 100
Osbaldeston, Rev. Lambert, headmaster of Westminster School, 47–8
Owen, Archdeacon John, chaplain general, 128
Oxford and Asquith, Lord, 184, 191, 196
Oxford Movement, 130, 141, 141–2, 144
Ozinda's Chocolate House, 84

Page, Rev. Thomas, 148
Paget, Henry Luke, Bishop of Chester, 191
Paisley, Rev. Ian, 224
Parker, John, porter at Lambeth Palace, 184
Parker, Matthew, Archbishop of Canterbury, 21, 22, 22–3, 23, 24, 25; his walking stick, 25
Parker, Mrs., 21, 22–3, 24, 79
Parkhurst prison, 161
Parr, Catharine, 9

Parr, Richard, Bishop of Sodor and Man, 46
Parr, Dr. Samuel, 117, 124, 132, *133*, 134
Parry, Sir Hubert, composer, 176
Parsonages: Benhall, 128; Borley, 202;
    Combe Florey, 137; Foston-le-Clay, 129;
    Frome, 182; Gotham, 98; Hammersmith,
    83; Much Marcle, 82; Quarnford, 220; Set-
    trington, 198; Shirley, 165; Winterbourne
    Came, 156
Patteson, John, Bishop of Melanesia, murder
    of, 161
Paul, Rev. William, execution of, 88
Paul's Cross, 1, 4, 5, 6, 8, 10, 11, 13, 14, 15, 16,
    20, 23, 26, 28, 29, 30, 32, 33, *35*, 36, 38, 39,
    39–40, 44; violence at, 14, 15; insanitary
    condition of, 13
Pearson, Rev. John, 61
Peel, Rev. and Hon. Maurice, 185–7
Peel, Sir Robert, 136, 144
Pegram, Henry, 195
Pelham, George, Bishop of Exeter, 127, 131;
    haughtiness of his wife, 131
Pelham, John, Bishop of Norwich, 152
Penruddock, Colonel, 61
Penry, John, 30
Peploe, Samuel, Bishop of Chester, 96
Pepys, Henry, Bishop of Worcester, 163
Percy, Hugh, Bishop of Carlisle, 135; his
    coach and four, 135
Perrin, Dr., Bishop of Willesden, 193
Peters, Hugh, 57, *57*, 59
Pews, disputes over, 20, 44–5, 169
Philip, Prince, 212, 217
Phillips, Captain Mark, 227
Phillpotts, Henry, Bishop of Exeter, 137, 138,
    147, 148, 157–8, 160; disputes with fox-
    hunting parsons, 138
Philpot, Archdeacon John, 17
Phipps, Simon, Bishop of Lincoln, 217, 233
Pickard-Cambridge, Rev. Octavius, expert on
    spiders, 156, 165, 187
Pierpont Morgan, J., 196, 197, 202
Pig-breeding, 232
Pilgrim Fathers, 39
Pilgrimage of Grace, 4, 5
Pilgrim's Progress, 70, 196
Pillory, parsons in, 24, 44, 48, 75, 92
Pipe-smoking parsons, 31, 83, 84, 117, 132,
    133, 211
Pitt, William, 118, 126, 127
Plague, the, 24, 31, 33, 38, 41, 96, 134; the
    Great Plague, 68
Plumptre, Dr. Edward, 166
Plumptre, Dr. Robert, 105
Plymouth Brethren, 135
Pole, Cardinal, Archbishop of Canterbury, 6,
    9, 16, 17, 173
Polehampton, Rev. Henry, 152
Pooley, Thomas, madman, 153
Popish Plot, 71

Portal, Abbé Fernand, 173
Porter, Rev. Mr., drunken vicar of East
    Hoathly, 103
Porteus, Beilby, Bishop of London, 114, 117,
    118, 119, 123, 124, 127
Potter, John, Archbishop of Canterbury, 91,
    94, 96, 99; his son Thomas, 99, 101, 113
Powell, Enoch, M.P., 224, 229
Practical jokes, 39
'Praise my soul the king of heaven', 148, 197
'Praise to the holiest in the height', 174
Premium Bonds, Archbishop Fisher's attack
    on, 216
Pretyman Tomline, George, Bishop of
    Lincoln, 117, 126, 127
Price, Rev. Daniel, 36
Price, Harry, ghost-hunter, 202
Price, Rev. Richard, 119
Prideaux, John, Bishop of Worcester, 119
Priestly, Rev. Joseph, desecration of his
    library, 119–20
Profumo affair, 220
Property development, 151, 210, 216
Prostitutes, 132, 160, 201, 223
Protestant Truth Society, 216
Prynne, William, 45, 47, 48
Pulmonary tuberculosis, 99
Purcell, Henry, 73
Purchas, Rev. John, 160
Purey-Cust, Dean of York, 185
Pusey, Rev. Edward Bouverie, 136, 144, 146,
    150, 162, 166, *167*; death of Mrs. Pusey,
    144

Quakers, 64
Queckett, Rev. William, 150
Queen Anne's Bounty, 83, 210, 212
Queen's Chapel, St. James's Palace, 40

Racing, 163
Radford, Rev. John, 138
Raikes, Robert, 113
Railways, 141, 146, 163, 175, 196, 200,
    209, 211; accidents, 163, 163–4, 173
Rainbow, Edward, Bishop of Carlisle, 67
Ralegh, Sir Walter, 33
Raleigh, Walter, Dean of Wells, 56
Ramsey, Michael, Archbishop of Canterbury,
    216, 217, 219, *219*, 220, 221, 221–2, 223,
    224, 225, 226, 227, *228*
Randolph, John, Bishop of London, 127
Rayne, Max, 216
Reeve, John, 60
Reform Bill, 138
Reith, Lord, 193, 194
Religious Tract Society, 124
Reynolds, Sir Joshua, 112, 114
Reynolds, Father Richard, 3
Rham, Rev. Lewis, 127
Rich, Mr., feast given by, 68

Richmond, Duke of, 72
Richmond, Richard, Bishop of Sodor and
  Man, 111
'Ride on, ride on in majesty', 150
Ridley, Nicholas, Bishop of London, 12, 13,
  14, 15, *16*; death of, 17
Rigby, Sir Henry, 196
Riley, Athelstan, 187
Riot Act, 88
Ritualistic disputes, 158, 160, 163, 164, 165,
  166, 169, 169–70; passing of the Public
  Worship Regulation Act, 163, 164; im-
  prisonment, 164, 165, 166, 169
Roberts, Lord, 176
Robins, John, fanatic, 60
Robinson, Armitage, Dean of Wells, 183, 184
Robinson, Henry, Bishop of Carlisle, 38
Robinson, John, Bishop of Woolwich, 218,
  220
'Rock of Ages', 105, 111, 174, 182
Roddon, Guy, 224
Rogers, John, 13, 14
Rogers, Samuel, 131
Rolle, Lady, 164
Romaine, Rev. William, 101
Roman Catholic emancipation, 112, 119,
  136, 136–7
'Rood of Grace', the, 6
Rose Castle, seat of the Bishop of Carlisle, 31,
  38, 67, 135, 178, 183; gardens at, 135, 183
Roses, cultivation of: *see* Hole, Very Rev.
  Samuel
Rotten eggs, 97, 147, 153, 213
Rous, Rev. Francis, provost of Eton, 60
Royal Academy Summer Exhibition, 206
Rugby School, 136, 160
Rugg, William, Bishop of Norwich, 4
Runcie, Robert, Archbishop of Canterbury,
  225, 229, 232, *233*, 234; Mrs. Runcie, 232
Russell, Rev. Jack, M.F.H., 135, 138, 152, 157,
  158, 163, 167
Rust, George, Bishop of Dromore, 69
Rutland, Duke of, 116
Ryder, Henry, Bishop of Gloucester, 130
Ryle, John, Bishop of Liverpool, 165, 169
Ryle, Herbert, Dean of Westminster, 182, 189

Sacheverell, Dr. Henry, 84, 86, 90; death of,
  91; coffin stolen, 99
St. Albans, Duke of, 72
St. Andrew-by-the-Wardrobe, 205
St. Barnabas, Pimlico, 150
St. Bartholomew's Day massacre, 24
St. Bride's, Fleet Street, 70, 79, 205, 217
St. George's, Bloomsbury, 112
St. George's, Hanover Square, 90, 101, 111,
  112
St. George's Chapel, Windsor, 6, 58, 137, 155,
  156, 175, 226
St. Giles Cathedral, Edinburgh, 47

St. James's, Piccadilly, 70, 72, 79, 93, 94, 123,
  185, 212
St James's Square, Bishop of London's house
  in, 132; Bishop of Winchester's house in,
  135, 160
St. John's College, Oxford, feast at, 46
St. Lawrence Jewry, 205
St. Leger, the, 163
St. Margaret's, Westminster, 11, 17, 57, 220
St. Martin-in-the-Fields, 71, 73, 75, 91, 124,
  183, 184, 187, 188, 193, 201
St. Mary-le-Bow, 96, 204, 223, 229; bells of,
  96, 204
St. Mary's, Paddington Green, 227
St. Pancras Church, 137
St. Paul's, Covent Garden, 47
St. Paul's Cathedral, 1, 6, 8, 10, 22, 24, 34, 35,
  37, 44, 45, 60, 67; burnt down, 68; new
  building, 70, 75, 80–81, 83, 84, *85*, 90, 119,
  127, 132, 138, 143–4, 147, 154–5, 160, 161,
  168, 174, 175, 182, 183, 188, 192, 193, 195,
  210, 213–14, 221, 224, 226, 227, 230;
  'God's railway station', 160; pigeons at,
  200
St. Paul's Deanery, 39, 52, 68, 69, 182, 183,
  187, 199
St. Stephen's, Rochester Row, 150
St. Stephen's Wallbrook, 69
Salisbury Cathedral, 22, 75, 195, 233
Salvation Army, 206
Sampson, Richard, Bishop of Chichester, 6
Sampson, Thomas, Dean of Christ Church,
  23
Sanatogen Tonic Wine, 225
Sancroft, William, Archbishop of Canter-
  bury, 68, 70–1, 71, 73, 75, 76, 77, 78;
  ejection from Lambeth Palace, 78
Sandwich, Earl of, 113
Sandys, Edwin, Archbishop of York, 21, 23,
  24, 25, 27, 28
Sanitary reform, 137, 141, 154, 160, 161
Sankey, Rev. J. R., 205
Sansbury, Bishop Kenneth, 226
Sargent, John, 182
Savile, Sir George, 112
Savile, Martha, Archbishop Lang's
  housekeeper, 196
Savoy Conference, 65
Scandalum Magnatum, 47, 72
Scarsdale, Rev. Lord, 152, 186
Schmidt, Father Bernard, organ-builder, 80
Scott Holland, Henry, 168
Scott, Dr. Alexander, 127
Scott of the Antarctic, 127
Scott, Canon and Mrs. J. J., their dinner
  parties, 192
Scott, Thomas, execution of, 65
Sea bathing, 108
Sea chaplains, 25, 29, 31, 32, 39, 60, 68, 88,
  121, 123, 131, 184, 186, 187, 203, 206, 229

Second Coming of Christ, 79
Secker, Thomas, Archbishop of Canterbury, 93, 94, 96, 98, 104, 105, 108
Sedgwick, Rev. Adam, 154
Sedgwick, Rev. John, 51
Sedgwick, Rev. Joseph, 60, 61
Sedgwick, Rev. Obadiah, 48
Selwyn, George, Bishop of New Zealand, 146
Seven Bishops, the, 75–6, 76
Seymour, Jane, 5, 6
Shaftesbury, Earl of, bishop-maker, 141, 160
Sharp, James, Archbishop of St. Andrews, murder of, 71–2
Sharp, John, Archbishop of York, 73, 77, 82, 86
Sharp, Rev. Lionel, 37
Shaw, Mr. and Mrs. Bernard, 198
Shaw, Rev. Timothy, 105
Sheldon, Gilbert, Archbishop of Canterbury, 57, 64, 67, 68, 69, 70
Sheppard, David, Bishop of Liverpool, 215–6
Sheppard, Rev. Dick, 183, 184, 187, 188, 193, 201
Sherlock, William, Dean of St. Paul's, 78, 79, 81, 99, 101
Shipley, Jonathan, Bishop of St. Asaph, his dinner parties, 112, 114
Shrewsbury School, 143, 163
Sibthorpe, Rev. Robert, 41, 56
Sick in church, 41
Simeon, Rev. Charles, 115, 115, 122, 124, 130, 135, 143
Simpson, Mrs. Ernest, 197, 200, 201
Simpson's-in-the-Strand, 193
'Sixteen String Jack', 111
Skating, 125
Skinner, Robert, Bishop of Oxford, 59
Slack, Kenneth, 229
Slave trade, 91, 106, 113, 116, 117, 124, 127
Slessor, Lady Cynthia, 211
Slingsby, Rev. Charles, death in the hunting-field, 182
Smallpox, 73, 80, 92, 134, 156
Smart, Rev. Peter, 42–3, 49
Smelling salts, 105, 220
Smith, Rev. Sydney, 121, 124, 126, 127–8, 129, 132, 134–5, 135–6, 137, 138, 139, 142, 143, 144, 146, 147
Smoking in church, 79, 117, 223
Snow, Dr., Bishop of Whitby, 225
'Soapy Sam': see Wilberforce, Samuel
Society for Promoting Christian Knowledge, 81
Society for the Propagation of the Gospel, 82, 93, 101, 152, 213–14
Society for the Suppression of Vice, 126
Söderblom, Archbishop, 193
Sodomy: see Homosexuality
Somerset, Duke of, 10, 12
Sotheby's auction rooms, 153, 212

Soup kitchen, 122
South Sea Company, collapse of, 89
South, Dr. Robert, 64, 73
Spanish Armada, defeat of, 29
Sparke, Edward, Bishop of Ely, 128
Spears, Maj.-Gen. Sir Edward, 217
Speed, Rev. Samuel, ex-pirate, 68
Spencer, Lord and Lady, 114
'Spiritual influenza', 104
Spong, Rev. Terry, 231
Spooner, Dr. William, 197
Spottiswood, Archbishop, 47
Sprat, Thomas, Bishop of Rochester, 72, 75, 79, 86
Spurgeon, Charles, 169
Stafford, Lord, trial of, 79
Stanley, Arthur, Dean of Westminster, 156, 161
Stanley, Edward, Bishop of Norwich, 146, 149–50
Stephens, Rev. Kenneth, 203
Stephens, Rev. Ronald, 225
Sterne, Rev. Laurence, 96, 99, 105, 108, 109
Sterne, Richard, Archbishop of York, 50, 52, 67
Stiffkey, Rector of: see Davidson, Rev. Harold
Stillingfleet, Edward, Bishop of Worcester, 81
Stocks, the, 162
Stockwood, Mervyn, Bishop of Southwark, 218, 225, 226, 229
Stokes, Rev. Edward, blind hunting parson, 99
Stokesley, John, Bishop of London, 6
Street Offences Bill, 223
Stuart, Charles, the Young Pretender, 98
Stuart, James, the Old Pretender, 86, 90
Stubbs, William, Bishop of Oxford, 70, 173
Studdert-Kennedy, Rev. G., 185
Suez Crisis, 216
Suffragettes, 171, 183
Suicide, 30, 83, 105, 218
Sullivan, Sir Arthur, 161
Summers, Rev. Montague, 195
Sumner, Charles, Bishop of Winchester, 135, 160
Sumner, John Bird, Archbishop of Canterbury, 149, 152, 155
Sunday school, first to open, 113
Surplice fires, 191, 211
Surplice riots, 147
Sutcliffe, Matthew, Dean of Exeter, 39
Sutton, Rev. Peter, 234
Swearing, 31, 38, 72, 80, 178
Sweet, Rev. J. B., 153
Swift, Jonathan, Dean of St. Patrick's, 80, 82, 83, 84, 86, 89, 98
Swift, Rev. Thomas, 55
Swinton, Rev. John, 102, 106
Synge, Rev. F. C., sleeps in garden of Fulham Palace, 203

Tait, Archibald, Archbishop of Canterbury, 152, 159, 160, 161, 163, 164, 165, 166
Talbot, Edward, Bishop of Winchester, 197
Talleyrand, Prince, 135
Tallis, Thomas, 8
Tany, Thomas, eccentric, 61
Tar water, Bishop Berkeley's, 97, 98, 105
Tate, Nahum, 88
Taylor, Rev. Robert, 131, 135, 138
Taylor, Dr. Rowland, execution of, 17
Teetotallers and the temperance movement, 130, 134, 137, 141, 146, 148, 150, 161, 161–2, 165, 169, 172, 173, 175, 180, 181, 223
Temple, Frederick, Archbishop of Canterbury, 160, 161, 168, 170, 171, 173–4, 174, 175, 176, 185; intervenes in London Dockers Strike, 170
Temple, William, Archbishop of Canterbury, 185, 187, 191, 192, 196, 199, 202, 203, 205, 205–6, 208, 209
Tenison, Thomas, Archbishop of Canterbury, 72, 73, 75, 80, 82, 87, 88
Tennis, 183, 206
Tennyson, Rev. Charles, 142
The Art of Happiness, 60
'The Beauty of Holiness': *see* Stillingfleet, Edward
'The day thou gavest, Lord, has ended', 161
The Dean and the Drink, 172
'The king of love my shepherd is', 154, 214
The Man who Came to Dinner, 206
The Origin of Species, 154
Thicknesse, Very Rev. Cuthbert, 201–11
Thirlby, Thomas, Bishop of Ely, 18
Thom, John, 144
Thomas, John, Bishop of Salisbury, 106–8
Thomson, William, Archbishop of York, 155–6, 158, 159, *159*, 169
Thompson, Rev. J. M., 183
Thorndike, Dame Sybil, 209
Thorold, Anthony, Bishop of Winchester, 165, 171, *172*
Thorpe, Jeremy, 232
Thrisco, Dr., 63
Thurlow, Thomas, Bishop of Lincoln, 113
'Thy hand, O God, has guided', 166
Thynne, Rev. Lord John, 142, 165–6
Tillotson, John, Archbishop of Canterbury, 67, 78, 78–9, 80
Ting, Bishop, 221
Titanic, disaster, 182
Tithes, 40, *118*, 143, 171, 199; tithe dinners, 120, 124, 137
Tolpuddle Martyrs, 142
Tomkins, Rev. O. C., eaten by savages, 175
Tomline, Marmaduke, 124
Tomlinson, Dr., Bishop of Gibraltar, 152
Tonge, Dr. Israel, 71
Tooth, Rev. Arthur, 164, 197

Toplady, Rev. Augustus, 105, 111, 112
Topless dresses, 221
Tower of London, 2, 3, 4, 5, 8, 9, 10, 14, 15, 21, 31, 33, 36, 37, 46, 47, 49, 50, 51, 53, 54, 57, 59, 75, 90, 94, 121, 169
Tracey, Rev. Patrick, 223
Trafalgar, battle of, 127, 131
Tranby Croft scandal, 171
Trapp, Dr. Joseph, 96
Tricycles, 151, 174
Trillo, John, Bishop of Chelmsford, 230
Tristram Shandy, 105
Trumpet Voluntary, 83
Truro Cathedral, 164, 165
Trusler, Rev. John, 108
Tunstall, Cuthbert, Bishop of Durham, 2, 4, 15, 21
Turner, Francis, Bishop of Ely, 73, 78, 80, 81
Tyndale, William, execution of, 4

Udal, Rev. Ephraim, attack upon, 52
Udal, John, 29
Udal, Rev. Nicholas, headmaster of Eton, 9
Uganda, King of, 168
Umbrellas, clerical, 118, 149, *157*, 174, 193
'Unnatural crime', 9, 49
Ussher, James, Archbishop of Armagh, 41, 49, 59, 61–2

Vandalism and looting, 54, 212–13, 223
Van der Elst, Mrs., 213
Vanhomrigh, Esther, 84
Van Mildert, William, Bishop of Llandaff, 132
Vaughan, Father Bernard, 225
Vaughan, Rev. Charles, headmaster of Harrow, 148, 153–4
V.C.s, 165, 184, 186, 188, 192
Venereal disease, 188, 206
Venn, Rev. Henry, 99
Venn, Rev. John, 120, 124, 128
Vervells, Rev. H. S., 213
Viall, Rev. Thomas, act of violence by, 134
Victoria, Queen, 131, 141, 143, 144, *145*, 150, 152, 154, 156, 159, 163, 166, 167, 168, 169, 171, 174, 175, 184; clerical blunders at her coronation, 144; clerical blunders at her wedding, 144; threatens to abdicate, 163
Villiers, George, Duke of Buckingham, 37, 39
von Hoesch, Leopold, 199
von Ribbentrop, Joachim, 199

Wade, Dr. Arthur, 142
Wagner, Rev. A. D., assaulted in street, 157
Wake, William, Archbishop of Canterbury, 88, 89, 90, 91
Wake, Rev. Mr., 55
Wakeford, Archdeacon John, 192, 197
Walker, Dr. Samuel, land speculator, 151
Walters, Rev. David, 206

War On Want, 224
Warburton, William, Bishop of Gloucester, 105, 113, 114
Ward, Irene, M.P., 214
Warmestry, Dr. Thomas, 62
Warner, John, Bishop of Rochester, 68
Water Babies, 156
Waterloo, battle of, 129
Waterloo Station, 163
Watson, Rev. John Selby, 161
Watson, Richard, Bishop of Llandaff, 116, 130
Watson, Rev. Thomas, 220
Watson, Rev. William, 33
Weightman, Rev. William, cholera victim, 134
Wellesley, Very Rev. Hon. Gerald, Dean of Windsor, 152, 163
Wellington College, 153
Wellington, Duke of, 128, 132, 137, 142, 151, 202; his funeral carriage, *151*
Wells, bishop's palace at, *2*, 83
Wells, Walter, Archbishop Lang's chauffeur, 196
Welton, Rev. Richard, 86
Wentworth, Thomas, Earl of Strafford, 45, 48, 49
Wesley, Rev. Charles, 87, 93, 94, 96, 97, 106, 110
Wesley, Rev. John, 84, 87, 88, 91, 92, 93, 94, 96, 97, 98, 99, 106, 110, 112, 119, 193; his disastrous marriage, 101
Wesley, Rev. Samuel, 79, 83, 84, 88, 93
Wesley, Samuel, son of Charles, 116
Wesley, Samuel Sebastian, 138
West Wycombe, scandalous brotherhood at, 99, 106
Westcott, Brooke, Bishop of Durham, 151, 172
Westley, Rev. Mr., 60
Westminster Abbey, 8, 14, 19, 20, 20–1, 21, 33, 40–1, 50, 59, 62, 63, 65, 66, 73, 77, 81, 82, 87, 91, 103, 105, 122, 132, 142, 164, 166, 169, 170, 180, 183, 189, 190, 190–1, 193, 193–4, 197, 201, 202, 212, 213, 218, 222
Westminster Deanery, bombing of, 205
Westminster Hall, 65, 75–6, 84, 134, 182
Westminster School, 47–8, 62, 80
Weston, Hugh, scandalous Dean of Westminster, 14, 19
Wharton, Duke of, 90
Whateley, Richard, Archbishop of Dublin, 142
Wheatlie, Rev. William, 36
Wheeler, Rev. C. A., 211
'When I survey the wondrous cross', 83
'While shepherds watched their flocks', 88
Whippings, 44, 62, 73, 75, 112, 134, 138
White, Francis, Bishop of Ely, 47

White, Rev. George, belligerent curate of Colne, 99
White, Rev. Gilbert, 103, 118–19
White, Jeremiah, 62
White, John, Bishop of Winchester, 20
White, Kennett, Bishop of Peterborough, 86, 90
White, Thomas, Bishop of Peterborough, 75, 81
White-Thomson, Ian, Dean of Canterbury, 220
Whitechapel Bell Foundry, 25, 96
Whitechapel murders, 170
Whitefield, Rev. George, 96, 97, 99, *100*, 103, 108, 108–10; 'Whitefield's Soul Trap', 103
Whitgift, John, Archbishop of Canterbury, 27, 28, 29, 31–2, 32, 33, 34; loses his temper, 28
Wigram, Joseph, Bishop of Rochester, 154
Wigs, 78, 101, 111, 127, 137, 149, 154, 188
Wilberforce, Samuel, Bishop of Oxford, 137, 146, 147, 153, 154, 155, 156, 160; 'translated to a higher see', 162
Wilberforce, William, M.P., 116, 117, 118, 122, 132, 142
Wild, Dr. George, 59, 61, 62, 63
Wilde, Oscar, 173
Wilkins, John, Bishop of Chester, 69
Wilkinson, Rev. Henry, 54
Wilkinson, Rev. Horace, 187
Wilkinson, Dr., deportation of, 103
Wilks, Rev. William, 165
William the Conqueror, 6, 10, 103
William III, King, 70, 76, 77, 82
William IV, King, 137, 143
Williams, Henry Herbert, Bishop of Carlisle, 192
Williams, Sir Herbert, 206
Williams, John, Archbishop of York, 39, 41, 46, 47, 50; attacked by mob, 50
Wilson, Harold, 228
Wilson, Thomas, Bishop of Sodor and Man, 81, *81*, 90, 94, 103
Winchester, bishop's palace at, 15, 66, 203
Winchester House, Chelsea, 66, 105, 114, 128, 132
Winchester House, Southwark, 9, 20, 26, 30, 41, 52
Winnington-Ingram, Arthur, Bishop of London, 180, 183, 186, 190, 192, 194, 202, 205
Wise, Michael, master chorister, 75
Wiseman, Cardinal, 150
Witchcraft, 55, 89, 195
Witches of Worboys, 30
Woburn Abbey, 6, 16, 127
'Woe to Drunkards', 106
Women, ordination of, 186, 210, 223, 231
Women, preaching by, 106

'Woodbine Willie': *see* Studdert-Kennedy, Rev. G.

Woodforde, Parson, 111, 114, 117, 118, 119, 120, 121, 124, 126; toothache, 111; earache, 117

Woods, Edward, Bishop of Lichfield, 203

Woolley, Rev. Geoffrey, V.C., 192

Wordsworth, Christopher, Bishop of Lincoln, 143, 159, 162, 163, 164, 168

Wordsworth, William, 143

Wren, Sir Christopher, 64, 66, 68, 69, 70, 84, 90, 204, 212

Wren, Matthew, Bishop of Ely, 47, 51

Wright, Robert, Bishop of Lichfield and Coventry, 45, 47, 53, 54

Wroughton, Rev. William, 106

Yasiro, Bishop of Japan, 212

Yelverton, Sir Christopher, 63

York House in the Strand, 17, 66

York Minster, 9, 33, 45, 185, 198, 202, 213

Zeppelin raids, 185